Business Calculations

Made Simple

The Made Simple series
has been created
especially for self-education
but can equally well
be used as
an aid to group study.
However complex the subject,
the reader is taken
step by step,
clearly and methodically,
through the course. Each volume
has been prepared by experts,
taking account of
modern educational requirements,
to ensure the most
effective way of
acquiring knowledge.

In the same series

Business Calculations

Made Simple

Ken Hoyle, BSc (Econ)

**MADE SIMPLE
BOOKS**

Heinemann Professional Publishing

Made Simple Books
An imprint of Heinemann Professional Publishing Ltd
Halley Court, Jordan Hill, Oxford OX2 8EJ

OXFORD LONDON MELBOURNE AUCKLAND

First published 1983
Second edition 1988

British Library Cataloguing in Publication Data
Hoyle, Ken
   Business calculations made simple.—(Made simple
   books) ISSN 0265–0541
   1. Management—Mathematics—Problems, exercises, etc.
   I. Title
   510'24658   HD30.25

ISBN 0 434 98587 2

Made and printed in Great Britain by
Richard Clay Ltd, Bungay, Suffolk

Foreword

This book covers the elementary examination requirements in business calculations for all the major examining bodies. In particular it covers the Business Calculations requirements for the Business and Technician Education Council's General Examination; the Examinations of the Royal Society of Arts and the London Chamber of Commerce and Industry; and the Basic Arithmetic and Proficiency in Arithmetic courses of such GCSE bodies as the Associated Examining Board.

To assist students of the Chartered Institute of Bankers a number of chapters have been added to meet the requirements of their syllabus. These will also be of general interest as they deal with business accounts, computerisation and the difficult 'interest' aspect of consumer credit—annual percentage rates.

In preparing this book I have been greatly assisted by a number of organisations who have permitted the use of illustrations, etc. Their courtesy is acknowledged overleaf. I must also thank Robert Postema for encouragement and advice on the project.

Ken Hoyle

Acknowledgements

The assistance of the following institutions and organisations is gratefully acknowledged for the use of illustrations, statistics, etc.:

Economic Progress Report
Finance and Development
Kalamazoo PLC, Northfield, Birmingham, B31 2RW
Sharp Electronics (UK) Ltd, Sharp House, Thorp Rd, Newton Heath, Manchester, M10 9BE
Which? Magazine and the Consumers' Association
The Comptroller General: Her Majesty's Stationery Office

Contents

1
An Introduction
to Business Calculations

1.1 The Need for Business Calculations

Although mathematics is more widely taught these days than at
any time in history, modern mathematics syllabuses tend to divert
attention in the schools from basic arithmetic processes which are
fundamental to the routine activities of everyday life. People are
inevitably required to labour on an economic treadmill to some
extent: we go to work to get the cash, to buy the food, to get the
strength, to go to work, etc. For many of these everyday activities
a sound knowledge of basic number work is all that is required.
The control engineer may have need of mathematics or games
theory, but the ordinary employer is looking for young people who
can use an adding–listing machine or an electronic calculator, or
can add and subtract without errors.

A wide range of jobs is therefore available for those who have
mastered the basic processes of arithmetic in business calculations
and elementary book-keeping. These are very simple matters, which
the vast majority of school leavers can master without difficulty,
providing a reasonable amount of time is given to the studies and
some degree of perseverance is shown. School pupils in their last
two years at school, college entrants and young people starting
commercial employment will therefore find Business Calculations a
useful and worthwhile study.

1.2 Electronic Calculators and Business Calculations

In the last 15 years a wide range of electronic calculators has
appeared on the market, rendering mechanical calculators and
comptometers obsolete. Branches of calculations which were
formerly performed rather laboriously by logarithms are now performed in fractions of a second. A multiplication sum involving 10

digits in both the multiplier and the multiplicand, for example:

$$2\ 786\ 495\ 236 \times 1\ 598\ 721\ 686$$

is performed quickly and accurately. The answers are shown in a display panel of lighted figures, and in the more expensive 'printing calculators' the machine prints out a record of the calculation and the result on a roll of paper like an ordinary adding–listing machine. The reader may feel as a result that there is no need to do business calculations at all. Unfortunately, it still remains true that one can use such machines well only if one is reasonably familiar with general processes in arithmetic. Since errors in putting numbers into the machine are quite common, and electronic miscircuits are not unknown, it is important to have a rough idea what the answer is likely to be so that an obviously incorrect answer is detected. Almost everyone uses calculators today, and the student who is quite good at business arithmetic, but not used to using calculators, might like to use the exercises in the chapters which follow for familiarising himself with the machine of his choice.

Before purchasing a calculator it is advisable to seek the help of a *qualified* shop assistant in this field. Many assistants have no idea what the machines they sell are supposed to do. All calculators will add up, subtract, multiply and divide. Most will perform almost all the routine calculations required in business, but some are much

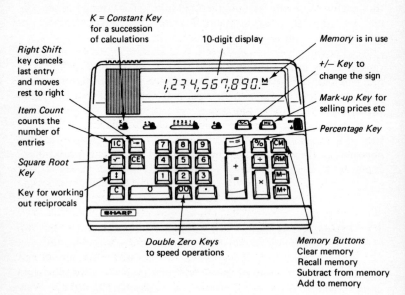

K = Constant Key for a succession of calculations

10-digit display

Memory is in use

Right Shift key cancels last entry and moves rest to right

+/– Key to change the sign

Mark-up Key for selling prices etc

Item Count counts the number of entries

Percentage Key

Square Root Key

Key for working out reciprocals

Double Zero Keys to speed operations

Memory Buttons Clear memory Recall memory Subtract from memory Add to memory

Fig. 1.1   A desk-top calculator.

(Courtesy of Sharp Electronics (UK) Ltd)

more useful than others. For example, a 'clear last entry' facility is very useful if an entry is miskeyed. It removes the last entry made without cancelling out any earlier work in the machine. Some calculators cannot be cleared in this way, and a mis-key means the whole calculation must be reworked. Some machines will work out percentages, mark-ups, mark-downs and discounts at the touch of a button. In statistical work, where it is frequently necessary to do the same type of calculation on a whole column of different figures, a 'constant factor' facility is a great help. Many of the more expensive calculators will provide intricate scientific and statistical data instantaneously, but they may be more expensive and sophisticated than most students need. Readers of this book should opt for a commercial machine of medium price, with a display panel of 8–10 digits, for personal use. For class use a machine of the type illustrated in Fig. 1.1 would be appropriate.

1.3 Business Calculations and the Microprocessor

Most people have heard of the 'silicon chip', and know that it is a form of high technology which is likely to make a significant difference to both manufacturing and service industries. The silicon chip is a silicon 'integrated circuit', manufactured by taking as a base a thin wafer of silicon (about the size of a child's small fingernail) and building up a series of circuits and desired interconnections upon it. The circuitry and interconnections are constructed using photographic masks and electron beams. A single chip can have thousands of separate circuit components upon it. The chip is in fact an extension of the miniaturisation process in electronics which received such a boost with the transistor. Compared to the transistor the circuits on a silicon chip are microscopic.

The importance of silicon chips is their very low cost. Relative to their output silicon chips are not expensive. Their small size also means that miniature versions of familiar items can be built inexpensively. The multimillion-pound mainframe computer was not only expensive in itself—its bulk meant that special buildings were often required, usually equipped with air-conditioning and dust-filtration plants. A computer built around silicon chips (and known as a microprocessor because it is so small that it sits on a desk top!) can perform most of the tasks of a mainframe computer, and at a tiny fraction of the cost (tens of thousands, rather than millions of pounds). The micro-circuit thus makes available computer facilities on a much wider basis. In addition, it opens up the possibility of automatic, electronic control in countless situations where previously either price or bulk, or both, have militated against this.

Such an advance in technology is bound to affect business calculations, which are easily performed by the micro-chip as the electronic calculator has shown. The microprocessor carries the use of technology forward into more complex fields. Even so, it is unlikely that we shall cease to need workers who can perform basic calculations. The work of feeding information into the microprocessor will still have to be done, statistics will have to be collected even if the processing of these statistics is done by the machine. It is therefore highly desirable that as many students as possible should master business calculations, which are inseparable from economic activity of every sort.

2
The Four Basic Rules of Arithmetic

2.1 Introduction

There are four basic rules of arithmetic: **addition**, **subtraction**, **multiplication** and **division**. These four rules can be applied not only to whole numbers (integers)—as in this chapter—but also to both common and decimal fractions (see Chapters 3 and 4). As a number can represent units of money, length, weight, capacity and time the four rules can be used in a wide variety of situations.

In this chapter we consider these four rules of number. Much of this elementary work is learned in the junior school and it is not proposed to do more than define the terms used and give examples of the various types of calculation that are met in everyday life. The exercises provided may be used for practice by those who are weak at basic arithmetic. Others are recommended to practise their use of the electronic calculator and the adding–listing calculator instead. Working such simple examples gives excellent practice in rough estimates, to check that the calculator is giving a sensible answer to the sum being keyed into it.

2.2 Addition

Addition is the process of putting two or more numbers together: the result of the addition is called the **sum**. Clearly the sum of two positive numbers is always larger than either of the original numbers. The sign for addition is +.

Errors in addition often result from incorrect layout. Each digit in a number has a place value. Thus in the number 999 the first 9 is nine hundreds (900), the second 9 is 9 tens (90) and the third 9 is nine units (9). If we are to add two numbers 4927 + 385 we must set them down with units under units, tens under tens, etc., as shown below:

Example 2.1

Th	H	T	U
4	9	2	7
	3	8	5

5	3	1	2
I	I	I	

The figures below the double line are carrying figures, which may be put in if desired.

Mental arithmetic is arithmetic performed mentally without setting down the working in a set format. The more work we can do in our heads the better, of course. The sum above could have been written down as follows:

$$4927 + 385 =$$

The answer could then be written out as the calculations are performed in the head, starting with the units. $7 + 5 = 12$, put down the 2 and carry one 10. Now adding the tens we have $2 + 8 = 10$, $+ 1$ we are carrying in our heads $= 11$ tens, etc.

$$4927 + 385 = 5312$$

2.3   Exercises: Addition of Numbers

The following should be set down in a proper manner and added to find the sum. (*Alternatively students who are thoroughly familiar with basic arithmetic may use these sums as practice exercises to develop facility with an electronic calculator.*) *Do not write the answers in this book unless it is your own property.*

1. $723 + 416 + 852$

2. $294 + 1246 + 3875$

3. $4905 + 2716 + 4983$

4. $7216 + 8164 + 9236 + 4785$

5. $27\ 296 + 1874 + 326\ 578 + 49\ 204$

6. $78\ 365 + 295\ 726 + 42\ 854 + 47\ 162$

7. 27 526
   34 894
   27 851

8. 491 326
   275 859
   763 259

Use subtotals in adding the following columns of figures:

9.	1247	10.	5874
	3856		3256
	7259		4384
	4560		7721
	3281		9636
	....		....
	4851		7254
	2368		3987
	3721		7236
	4395		2581
	7864		3265
	....		....

2.4   Subtraction of Numbers

Subtraction is the process of taking one number from another. The result of subtracting one number from another is called the **difference**, and clearly this result will always be smaller than the number started with.

Once again layout is important, subtraction sums being written down with proper attention to place value, with units under units, tens under tens, etc. An example is given below.

Example 2.2

$$\begin{array}{r} \text{Th} \quad \text{H} \quad \text{T} \quad \text{U} \\ 5 \quad 7 \quad 2 \quad 6 \\ - \quad 3 \quad 8 \quad 5 \quad 4 \\ \hline 1 \quad 8 \quad 7 \quad 2 \end{array}$$

Subtraction can be taught in different ways, and it is unwise for students to try to undo habits learned in childhood. For example, in subtracting the units figures shown above, there is little difficulty. Since 4 is smaller than 6 we can take 4 from 6 quite easily—the difference is 2. So $6 - 4 = 2$ gives us the answer to the units column. In the tens column we have to take 5 tens from 2 tens, which clearly is not possible. We have to take one of the hundreds to help us. As 100 is ten tens, with two tens in the top row already we have 12 tens $-$ 5 tens $=$ 7 tens. This gives us the figure 7 in the tens column in the answer row.

When we turn to the hundreds row we have to remember that we have already broken into the 'hundreds' to solve the 'tens' difficulty.

Some people now say '6 hundreds − 8 hundreds'. Others pay the ten back to the bottom row, and ask themselves '7 hundreds − 9 hundreds'. You can't do either of these subtractions, so we have to borrow a thousand to help over the difficulty. As one thousand is the same as 10 hundreds we can now put this with the top row and either say '16 hundreds − 8 hundreds' or '17 hundreds − 9 hundreds'. Whichever way you learned this at school the answer comes to 8 hundreds.

Moving on into the thousands column we can now say either '4 thousands − 3 thousands = 1 thousand', or if we use the 'pay back to the bottom row' method we have '5 thousands − 4 thousands = 1 thousand'. Either way the full answer is 1872. Use the method you normally use to do the following subtraction sums.

2.5   Exercises: Subtraction of Numbers

1. 475 − 234	**2.** 385 − 277
3. 5812 − 3275	**4.** 6875 − 2939
5. 7284 − 5816	**6.** 8125 − 3989
7. 175 264 − 29 578	**8.** 283 725 − 149 395
9. 518 642 − 387 495	**10.** 1 786 574 − 1 297 388

2.6   Exercises: Subtraction of Numbers

1. 1384 − 856	**2.** 2753 − 1487
3. 8765 − 3824	**4.** 7256 − 3854
5. 19 256 − 13 872	**6.** 27 356 − 14 859
7. 168 726 − 32 574	**8.** 276 354 − 158 965
9. 4 273 726 − 1 385 898	**10.** 13 726 585 − 4 256 875

2.7   Multiplication

Multiplication is a process of repeated addition. It always includes the word times, so that 3 times 4 means 3 taken 4 times—that is, 3 + 3 + 3 + 3 = 12, i.e. $3 \times 4 = 12$. The sign for multiplication is ×. The number to be multiplied is called the **multiplicand** and the quantity by which it is to be multiplied is called the **multiplier**. The answer to a multiplication calculation is called the **product**.

Multiplication Tables

In order to make it easy to calculate quickly we need to know the links between all the small numbers, as far as multiplication is concerned. Thus 5 × 7 = 35 is a multiplication '**bond**', a link between these two numbers. We could equally say that 7 × 5 = 35 is another, and very similar, bond. A more difficult bond is 13 × 20 = 260, and a very difficult one is 27 × 195 = 5265. Clearly it is very sensible to learn all the simple bonds, and we do this at school when we learn multiplication tables. It would not be worth while learning the 195 times table, for we are not likely to need it often enough to make it worth while. Unfortunately, many junior schools these days believe that it is not worth while learning the multiplication tables—since what we really need to know is the multiplication 'bonds', i.e. the little parts that make up the table. If you are weak at calculations and don't know your multiplication tables there may be some connection between these two facts—you may be one of those people who needs the formal knowledge of the tables to improve your general grasp of number work.

To assist you to learn the tables they appear in their usual form on pages 10 and 11. One table that does not appear is a table that often gives a great deal of trouble, the 0 times table. For example consider the calculation

$$205 \times 7$$

When set down as a multiplication sum we have

```
H   T   U
2   0   5
    ×   7
_____

_____
```

The answer to this calculation is obtained as follows:

(i) 7 × 5 units = 35. Place the 5 in the units column and carry the 3 tens into the tens column. We can either carry the 3 tens in our heads, or actually write them down in the tens column below the line, as shown below.

(ii) 7 × 0 = 0. If you have nothing seven times you still have nothing. It is a common mistake to say 7 × 0 = 7, but of course 7 × 1 = 7. So our 0 times table is really as shown on page 10. In the meantime, 7 × 0 tens = 0 tens, and 3 tens to carry from (i) above makes 3 tens altogether.

(iii) Moving on to the hundreds column, 7 × 2 hundreds = 14 hundreds, and as this is the end of the calculation we can write 4 of these hundreds in the hundreds column and the other 10 hundreds make one thousand, which we put in the thousands column. The full calculation therefore is as follows.

$$
\begin{array}{cccc}
\text{Th} & \text{H} & \text{T} & \text{U} \\
 & 2 & 0 & 5 \\
 & & \times & 7 \\
\hline
1 & 4 & 3 & 5 \\
\hline\hline
 & & & 3 \\
\end{array}
$$

The 0 times table and the 1 times table are as follows:

$1 \times 0 = 0$	$1 \times 1 = 1$
$2 \times 0 = 0$	$2 \times 1 = 2$
$3 \times 0 = 0$	$3 \times 1 = 3$
$4 \times 0 = 0$	$4 \times 1 = 4$
$5 \times 0 = 0$	$5 \times 1 = 5$
$6 \times 0 = 0$	$6 \times 1 = 6$
$7 \times 0 = 0$	$7 \times 1 = 7$
$8 \times 0 = 0$	$8 \times 1 = 8$
$9 \times 0 = 0$	$9 \times 1 = 9$
$10 \times 0 = 0$	$10 \times 1 = 10$
$11 \times 0 = 0$	$11 \times 1 = 11$
$12 \times 0 = 0$	$12 \times 1 = 12$

Clearly this could continue indefinitely

$431 \times 0 = 0$	$5278 \times 1 = 5278$
$432 \times 0 = 0$	$5279 \times 1 = 5279$

These are very important tables, although rarely taught in schools, where 'tables' often begin with the '2 times' table. The tables which are usually learned at the junior school are given on pages 10 to 11.

$1 \times 2 = 2$	$1 \times 3 = 3$	$1 \times 4 = 4$
$2 \times 2 = 4$	$2 \times 3 = 6$	$2 \times 4 = 8$
$3 \times 2 = 6$	$3 \times 3 = 9$	$3 \times 4 = 12$
$4 \times 2 = 8$	$4 \times 3 = 12$	$4 \times 4 = 16$
$5 \times 2 = 10$	$5 \times 3 = 15$	$5 \times 4 = 20$
$6 \times 2 = 12$	$6 \times 3 = 18$	$6 \times 4 = 24$
$7 \times 2 = 14$	$7 \times 3 = 21$	$7 \times 4 = 28$
$8 \times 2 = 16$	$8 \times 3 = 24$	$8 \times 4 = 32$
$9 \times 2 = 18$	$9 \times 3 = 27$	$9 \times 4 = 36$
$10 \times 2 = 20$	$10 \times 3 = 30$	$10 \times 4 = 40$
$11 \times 2 = 22$	$11 \times 3 = 33$	$11 \times 4 = 44$
$12 \times 2 = 24$	$12 \times 3 = 36$	$12 \times 4 = 48$

1 × 5 = 5	1 × 6 = 6	1 × 7 = 7
2 × 5 = 10	2 × 6 = 12	2 × 7 = 14
3 × 5 = 15	3 × 6 = 18	3 × 7 = 21
4 × 5 = 20	4 × 6 = 24	4 × 7 = 28
5 × 5 = 25	5 × 6 = 30	5 × 7 = 35
6 × 5 = 30	6 × 6 = 36	6 × 7 = 42
7 × 5 = 35	7 × 6 = 42	7 × 7 = 49
8 × 5 = 40	8 × 6 = 48	8 × 7 = 56
9 × 5 = 45	9 × 6 = 54	9 × 7 = 63
10 × 5 = 50	10 × 6 = 60	10 × 7 = 70
11 × 5 = 55	11 × 6 = 66	11 × 7 = 77
12 × 5 = 60	12 × 6 = 72	12 × 7 = 84

1 × 8 = 8	1 × 9 = 9	1 × 10 = 10
2 × 8 = 16	2 × 9 = 18	2 × 10 = 20
3 × 8 = 24	3 × 9 = 27	3 × 10 = 30
4 × 8 = 32	4 × 9 = 36	4 × 10 = 40
5 × 8 = 40	5 × 9 = 45	5 × 10 = 50
6 × 8 = 48	6 × 9 = 54	6 × 10 = 60
7 × 8 = 56	7 × 9 = 63	7 × 10 = 70
8 × 8 = 64	8 × 9 = 72	8 × 10 = 80
9 × 8 = 72	9 × 9 = 81	9 × 10 = 90
10 × 8 = 80	10 × 9 = 90	10 × 10 = 100
11 × 8 = 88	11 × 9 = 99	11 × 10 = 110
12 × 8 = 96	12 × 9 = 108	12 × 10 = 120

1 × 11 = 11	1 × 12 = 12
2 × 11 = 22	2 × 12 = 24
3 × 11 = 33	3 × 12 = 36
4 × 11 = 44	4 × 12 = 48
5 × 11 = 55	5 × 12 = 60
6 × 11 = 66	6 × 12 = 72
7 × 11 = 77	7 × 12 = 84
8 × 11 = 88	8 × 12 = 96
9 × 11 = 99	9 × 12 = 108
10 × 11 = 110	10 × 12 = 120
11 × 11 = 121	11 × 12 = 132
12 × 11 = 132	12 × 12 = 144

Although it is usual to stop at the 12 times table we could make up tables for every number. Here, for example, is the 13 times table.

1 × 13 = 13	5 × 13 = 65	9 × 13 = 117
2 × 13 = 26	6 × 13 = 78	10 × 13 = 130
3 × 13 = 39	7 × 13 = 91	11 × 13 = 143
4 × 13 = 52	8 × 13 = 104	12 × 13 = 156

More Difficult Multiplication Sums

A simple multiplication sum is set down as shown on page 10. As long as the multiplier is not larger than 12 we can do such multiplication sums in our head—now that we know the multiplication tables (or, rather, the little bonds that make up the tables). If the multiplier is greater than 12 we cannot use the tables, but must multiply by each part of the multiplier separately. This is called **long multiplication**. It is shown in the example below, and explained in the notes below it.

Example 2.3

$$7352 \times 238$$

7352	(Multiplicand)
238	(Multiplier)
58 816	(7352 × 8)
220 560	(7352 × 30)
1 470 400	(7352 × 200)
1 749 776	(Product)

Notes

(i) In the example we multiplied by 8 first, then by the 30 and finally by the 200. It would have been just as correct to start with the 200, and then multiply by 30 and then by 8.

(ii) When we multiply by 30 it is like multiplying by ten and then by 3. When multiplying by 10 there will be no units, so we put a 0 in the units column and after that it is just like multiplying by 3, using the '3 times table'.

(iii) When we multiply by 200 it is like multiplying by 100 and then by 2. Multiplying by 100 there will be no units and no tens, so we can just put a 0 in each of these columns and after that it is just like multiplying by 2, using the '2 times table'.

(iv) When we have completed the three separate lines of multiplication we add up the three partial answers to get the final 'product'. Notice that in a multiplication sum the number to be multiplied is called the *multiplicand*, the number you are multiplying by is the *multiplier* and the final answer is the *product*.

2.8   Exercises: Short Multiplication

1. 258 × 7   **2.** 362 × 9

3. 4176 × 5   **4.** 3278 × 6

5. 7125 × 8   **6.** 8723 × 12

7. 4976 × 4   **8.** 2356 × 11

9. 17 281 × 5   **10.** 29 324 × 7

2.9 Exercises: Long Multiplication

1. 327 × 29   **2.** 426 × 83

3. 5149 × 37   **4.** 6238 × 56

5. 1279 × 89   **6.** 3854 × 75

7. 21 765 × 123   **8.** 31 864 × 289

9. 72 656 × 279   **10.** 85 637 × 1285

2.10 Division

Division is the mathematical process we use when we share out things. It is really a continued process of subtraction. Thus if we share 10 apples between two boys, we can first of all give them one apple each (this will use up $1 \times 2 = 2$). Of the eight apples left we can now give them a further one each, which will use up a second group of 2 ($2 \times 2 = 4$), etc. Continuing this process we finish up with each boy getting 5 ($2 \times 5 = 10$). Since we know our table bonds after studying pages 10 to 11 we can simply use them the other way round. The simplest form of writing such a table is given below, in what is called 'short division' form. The table is read as follows: two into two goes once; two into four goes twice; two into six goes three times, etc.

$$2\overline{)2} = 1$$
$$2\overline{)4} = 2$$
$$2\overline{)6} = 3$$
$$2\overline{)8} = 4$$
$$2\overline{)10} = 5$$
$$2\overline{)12} = 6$$
$$2\overline{)14} = 7$$
$$2\overline{)16} = 8$$
$$2\overline{)18} = 9$$
$$2\overline{)20} = 10$$
$$2\overline{)22} = 11$$
$$2\overline{)22} = 12$$

When dividing numbers which do not come within the ordinary tables that we have learned by heart, the process is as shown in the examples below.

Examples 2.4

(*a*)   268 ÷ 2

$$= 2 \overline{)\, 268}^{\,134}$$

Notes

(i) First we say 2 into 2 hundreds goes 1 hundred, and we put the answer, 1 hundred over the top of the 2 hundreds, so that it is still in the hundreds column.

(ii) Next we say 2 into 6 tens goes 3 tens and place this answer 3 over the 6 in the tens column.

(iii) Next we say 2 into 8 units goes 4 units so that the final answer is 134. If 268 items are shared up between two people they will receive 134 each.

(*b*)   278 ÷ 2

$$= 2 \overline{)\, 278}^{\,139}$$

Notes

(i) The only difference between this division calculation and the one above is that one of the numbers—the 7 tens—does not share up equally. We say 2 into 7 tens goes 3 tens and 1 ten left over. This ten is carried into the units column where it changes the 8 units to 18 units.

(ii) 2 into 18 units goes 9 times, so we have an answer of 139 altogether.

(*c*)   4275 ÷ 9

$$= 9 \overline{)\, 4275}^{\,475}$$

Notes

(i) 9 into 4 thousands will not go. We must treat the 4 thousand as 40 hundreds, making 42 hundreds in all.

(ii) 9 into 42 hundreds goes 4 (4 × 9 = 36) and 6 hundreds over. These must be carried into the tens row, as 60 tens.

(iii) 9 into 67 tens = 7 (7 × 9 = 63) and 4 tens over. These are carried into the units row, as 40 units.

(iv) 9 into 45 goes 5 exactly, so the final answer is 475.

(*d*) $\qquad\qquad\qquad\qquad$ $4278 \div 9$

$$= 9\overline{)42^67^49}\ \begin{array}{l}4\ 7\ 5\quad\text{remainder 4}\\ \end{array}$$

Notes

(i) The only difference between this sum and (3) above is that there is a final remainder of 4 units. We can either leave this as a remainder, undivided, or the better thing is to show it mathematically as a fraction. This means we continue to share it up. It is then written as $\frac{4}{9}$ (4 cut up in 9 equal parts) and the final answer would be

$$= 475\tfrac{4}{9}$$

In division calculations the number by which we are dividing is called the **divisor** and the number we are dividing into is the **dividend**. The result of a division calculation is called the **quotient**. As explained above it sometimes happens that a divisor will not divide into a dividend an exact number of times. The amount left over is called the **remainder**: $12 \div 4 = 3$, but $13 \div 4 = 3$ remainder 1 and $14 \div 4 = 3$ remainder 2. As mentioned above, we can write the remainder as a fraction, in which case we have $13 \div 4 = 3\tfrac{1}{4}$ and $14 \div 4 = 3\tfrac{2}{4}$ which, we shall see later, reduces down to $3\tfrac{1}{2}$.

2.11   Exercises: Short Division

1. $236 \div 2$	**2.** $425 \div 3$
3. $192 \div 3$	**4.** $626 \div 6$
5. $478 \div 6$	**6.** $834 \div 8$
7. $2346 \div 9$	**8.** $1729 \div 4$
9. $5124 \div 5$	**10.** $6928 \div 9$
11. $17\,389 \div 8$	**12.** $15\,845 \div 5$
13. $42\,965 \div 9$	**14.** $16\,726 \div 12$
15. $82\,725 \div 12$	**16.** $78\,248 \div 11$
17. $63\,656 \div 9$	**18.** $24\,729 \div 10$
19. $72\,959 \div 7$	**20.** $136\,295 \div 9$

2.12   Long Division

Long division sums present quite serious difficulties to many students, and in these days of electronic calculators they would seem to be a technique we no longer need to master. On the other hand, one group of medical advisers recently suggested that failure to exercise the brain was as bad as failing to exercise any other part of the body, and recommended the abandonment of electronic calculators.

The difficulty about 'long division' is that we do not know the tables for numbers greater than 12, and consequently cannot do the calculations in our heads, as we do in 'short division'. For example, when dividing by 19, since we do not learn the '19 × table' we have to work out the bonds on a piece of scrap paper, or in the margin of the page we are using for our calculation. Having found the correct bond, we have to do a small subtraction sum to find any remainder, and the small chain of subtraction sums gives us a style of calculation called 'long division', as illustrated below.

Example 2.5

$$132\,792 \div 19$$

<pre>
          6 989 1/19
    19) 132 792   5 × 19 = 95
          114   6 × 19 = 114
          ___   7 × 19 = 133
          187
          171   9 × 19 = 171
          ___   10 × 19 = 190
          169   8 × 19 = 152
          152
          ___
          172
          171
          ___
          . . 1
</pre>

Notes

(i) We start by asking ourselves '19 into 1 (hundred thousand)—will it go?' The answer is of course 'No'. Carrying the 1 (hundred thousand) into the 'ten thousands' column, we can now enquire '19 into 13 (ten thousands)—will it go?' The answer is 'No' again. We now ask 19 into 132 (thousands). Clearly this will go, but how many times. To find out we set down a few little calculations, in the margin, and discover that $6 \times 19 = 114$ and $7 \times 19 = 133$, which is too large. The answer is therefore that when we share up 132 thousands between 19 people they can each have 6 thousands. We put 6 in the answer and set down 114 below the 132 to subtract it and find the remainder. This remainder must be carried into the hundreds row and become 180 hundreds, but as we have 7 hundreds already we bring the 7 hundreds down next to the 18 and we have 187 hundreds to divide up.

(ii) A few more bond calculations in the margin soon tell us that $187 \div 19$ will go 9 times ($9 \times 19 = 171$). Put 9 in the answer and take 171 from 187 to find the remaining hundreds. There are 16 hundreds left over.

(iii) The 16 hundreds must now become 160 tens, but as we have 9 tens already we add these to 160 to give us 169 tens. $169 \div 19$? Another little bond calculation tells us that $8 \times 19 = 152$. Another little subtraction sum tells us that 152 from 169 leaves us 17 tens.

(iv) 17 tens becomes 170 units, but as we have 2 units already these are added to the 170 to give 172. We can see from the bonds already calculated that 19 into 172 goes 9 times ($9 \times 19 = 171$) and there is one left over. This remainder, when shared up gives us $6989\frac{1}{19}$ as the final answer.

Those who have always found difficulty with long division, or who wish to exercise their brains, should perform the calculations in 2.13 below. Others might at least like to use them to perfect their skills with the electronic calculator.

2.13   Exercises: Long Division

1. $2795 \div 13$	**2.** $3812 \div 15$
3. $4976 \div 17$	**4.** $5845 \div 16$
5. $21\,735 \div 19$	**6.** $32\,649 \div 14$
7. $27\,235 \div 23$	**8.** $36\,954 \div 29$
9. $72\,686 \div 28$	**10.** $42\,795 \div 33$
11. $85\,698 \div 72$	**12.** $76\,256 \div 86$
13. $38\,721 \div 95$	**14.** $49\,526 \div 137$
15. $86\,234 \div 128$	**16.** $72\,562 \div 279$
17. $816\,325 \div 256$	**18.** $725\,294 \div 228$
19. $848\,176 \div 449$	**20.** $385\,296 \div 295$

3
Decimals

3.1 The Decimal System

The decimal system is a system where each class of numbers is ten times bigger than the class immediately below it. The name comes from the Latin *decem* = 10. The ordinary number system of hundreds, tens and units is a decimal system, since 10 units = 1 ten, 10 tens = 1 hundred, 10 hundreds = 1 thousand, etc. Since it is a very simple system it is logical that we should use the same system for **fractions**.

A fraction is a part of a whole number. There are certain fractions we call **common fractions** which are not part of the decimal system. For example, a very common fraction is one half, which is written $\frac{1}{2}$. Young children are often taught to say 'cut into' for the line that separates the top half of a common fraction from the bottom half. So $\frac{1}{2}$ becomes 'one cut into two equal parts', which is exactly what $\frac{1}{2}$ is. Similarly, $\frac{1}{4}$ is 'one cut into four equal parts' and is called 'one quarter', and 'one third' is 'one cut into three equal parts' and is written $\frac{1}{3}$. All common fractions have this line separating the top half of the fraction from the bottom half of the fraction. So the common fraction 'one tenth' would be written $\frac{1}{10}$, and the common fraction 'one hundredth' would be written $\frac{1}{100}$.

When we decide to use the ordinary decimal system for fractions we continue the decimal system down below whole numbers. To separate the whole numbers from the fractions we use a decimal point. By international agreement this is now printed on the line. A typical decimal number might therefore look like this

$$139.765$$

The whole numbers are 139 and the fractions are 7 tenths, 6 hundredths and 5 thousandths. The letters 'th' at the end of these names indicate that we are dealing with a fraction, i.e. a number smaller than 1. Seven tenths is smaller than 1, and so is the fraction 6 hundredths and the fraction 5 thousandths.

In using decimal fractions in business it is essential to be really familiar with the four processes of addition, subtraction, multiplication and division.

3.2　The Addition and Subtraction of Decimals

When adding and subtracting decimals it is important to keep units under units, tens under tens, tenths under tenths, hundredths under hundredths, etc. This is easily done if the decimal points are aligned, because all the different place values will then fall into line.

Example 3.1. Add up 27.65, 325.78 and 4.317.
　Aligning the decimal points we have:

$$
\begin{array}{r}
27.65 \\
325.78 \\
4.317 \\
\hline
357.747 \quad \text{Answer} \\
\hline
\end{array}
$$

(*Note:* When the decimal points are aligned, the various place values automatically fall correctly underneath one another, units under units, tens under tens, tenths under tenths, hundredths under hundredths, etc.)

The beauty of this system of fractions is, of course, that there is nothing new to learn. We have already mastered the addition of whole numbers, and there is no difference when it comes to dealing with the fractions. Ten hundredths makes one tenth, and will be carried into the tenths column, and ten tenths makes one whole unit and will be carried past the decimal point—which separates the decimal fractions from the whole numbers—and into the units column.

Example 3.2. Subtract 17.45 from 236.5.
　Again we align the decimal points when we set the calculation down.

$$
\begin{array}{r}
236.5 \\
17.45 \\
\hline
219.05 \quad \text{Answer} \\
\hline
\end{array}
$$

Again there is no real difficulty. We cannot take 5 hundredths from the hundredths in the top row because there are none. We must go to the tenths column and borrow one of the tenths, turning it into 10 hundredths. Now 5 hundredths from 10 hundredths leaves 5 hundredths to put in the answer column.

(*Check:* To check a subtraction sum always add the answer back to the number subtracted: this should come back to the number from which we started, i.e. 17.45 + 219.05 = 236.5)

3.3 Exercises: Addition and Subtraction of Decimals

1. (a) 2.57 + 3.65 + 17.29 + 16.416
   (b) 14.953 + 2.75 + 38.06 + 297.256
   (c) 48.65 + 27.23 + 183.7 + 2.9576
   (d) 72.65 + 7.7863 + 294.6 + 4273.5
   (e) 84.75 + 4.617 + 295.6 + 4.1178
   (f) 9.732 + 3.864 + 274.95 + 276.1
   (g) 527.859 + 32.647 + 14.9 + 247.5086
   (h) 3656.71 + 272.8156 + 47.2956 + 427.563 85
   (i) 27.59 + 385.6 + 427.6358 + 47.815 68
   (j) 4197.65 + 23 856.5 + 475.629 + 27.465 68

2. (a) 27.654 − 14.723
   (b) 497.6 − 256.85
   (c) 38.565 − 4.716
   (d) 2798.69 − 585.95
   (e) 426.95 − 236.873 65
   (f) 8.0875 − 4.798
   (g) 375.62 − 49.756
   (h) 7856.95 − 328.569
   (i) 29.816 − 11.7785
   (j) 385.8 − 289.956

3.4 Multiplication and Division of Decimals—Simple Cases

Multiplication and division of decimals are very similar to multiplication and division of ordinary numbers, but it is necessary to learn some simple tricks which remove the difficulties created by the decimal points. It helps to understand these tricks if we first learn how to multiply and divide by 10, 100, 1000, etc.

Since the system is a decimal system, any multiplication sum involving 10 simply results in every digit moving up one place in the number system. For instance

$$5 \times 10 = 50$$
$$27 \times 10 = 270$$
$$3.1 \times 10 = 31$$
$$3.1726 \times 10 = 31.726$$

This is often explained by saying 'move the decimal point one place to the right'. This is not a good explanation, because what is really happening is that the decimal point remains stationary, and the number moves one place to the left, so that every figure is now in the next highest column. Thus the 3 units has become 3 tens and the 1 tenth has become 1 unit. It is therefore better to say 'push the number through the decimal point one place to the left'.

To multiply by 100 we need to push the number through the decimal point two places, and to multiply by 1000 we need to push the number through the decimal point three places.

Example 3.3
$$2.75 \times 10 = 27.5$$
$$38.725 \times 100 = 3872.5$$
$$3.95 \times 1000 = 3950.$$

Here we can leave out the decimal point because 3950 is a whole number and there are no decimal fractions. So

$$3.95 \times 1000 = 3950$$

In a rather similar way, when dividing by 10, 100 or 1000 the number simply moves through the decimal point in the opposite direction.

Example 3.4
$$52.6 \div 10 = 5.26$$
$$589.5 \div 100 = 5.895$$
$$27.63 \div 1000 = .02763$$

In this example we have to insert the 0 in the tenths row because the figure 2 is now only 2 hundredths, and there are no tenths.

3.5 Exercises: Simple Multiplication and Division of Decimals

1. (a) 4.275×10 (b) 38.75×10
   (c) 52.585×100 (d) 6.385×100
   (e) 72.5×1000 (f) 83.5695×1000
   (g) 2.4×100 (h) $7.83 \times 10\,000$
   (i) 86.95×100 (j) $2.1 \times 10\,000$

2. (a) $27.6 \div 10$ (b) $328.5 \div 10$
   (c) $127.25 \div 100$ (d) $1.86 \div 100$
   (e) $4256.5 \div 1000$ (f) $72.56 \div 1000$
   (g) $2186.5 \div 100$ (h) $2.7985 \div 100$
   (i) $8.757 \div 1000$ (j) $96.956 \div 10\,000$

3.6 Multiplication of Decimals

There is more than one way of multiplying decimals but the simplest is to disregard the decimal point when doing the actual calculation and only insert it in the answer. For example, the multiplication sum 21.6 × 1.8 can be performed as 216 × 18 by ordinary arithmetic and the decimal point inserted after the answer has been found.

Example 3.5

$$21.6 \times 1.8$$

Ignoring the decimal points, we have

$$
\begin{array}{r}
216 \\
18 \\
\hline
1728 \\
2160 \\
\hline
3888 \\
\hline
\end{array}
$$

To insert the decimal point, count up the figures after the decimal point in both the multiplier and the multiplicand. There will be the same number of figures after the decimal point in the answer.

Thus 21.6 has one figure after the decimal point, and 1.8 also has one figure after the decimal point. There will therefore be two figures after the decimal point in the answer. Therefore we have

$$21.6 \times 1.8 = 38.88 \quad \text{Answer}$$

The explanation of this method is that in doing the multiplication as if it was 216 × 18 we have effectively multiplied both figures by ten, because we have pushed both numbers through the decimal point one place. This means that the answer is 10 × 10 = 100 times too big. To arrive at the correct answer we must therefore move the answer 3888 through the decimal point two places to the right, i.e. divide the answer by 100, and this gives us the true answer of 38.88.

To take a further example, the multiplication sum

$$2.16 \times .18$$

would still be worked out as 216 × 18. In this case the numbers have both been moved two places through the decimal point, making four places in all. The answer will therefore need to be moved back four places, and it will therefore be .3888. Sometimes it is useful to check your answer by a rough estimate, and this is absolutely essential when using an electronic calculator. A rough estimate of 2.16 × .18 is that the answer will be a little larger than

$2 \times .18 = .36$. Have we arrived at an answer a little larger than .36? Yes we have: .3888 is a little larger than .36. Had we worked out the position of our decimal point incorrectly, to give an answer of say 3.888 or 38.88 or even .038 88, we should have seen at once that they were wrong, for they are not a little larger than .36.

Note: In order to make it clear that there are no whole numbers involved when a figure like .18 is under consideration, it is usual to write 0.18.

3.7 Exercises: Multiplication of Decimals

1. 4.635×2.8 **2.** 7.659×1.7

3. 23.85×1.45 **4.** 49.72×27.6

5. 38.165×4.35 **6.** 7165.2×2.95

7. 35.65×1.35 **8.** 279.615×3.81

9. 4256.17×2.203 **10.** 38.795×47.05

3.8 Division of Decimals

When dividing decimals the trick is to make the divisor a whole number. Thus in the calculation $276.95 \div 1.5$ we make the divisor a whole number 15. It is easy to divide by 15, since we know how to do long division. To make 1.5 into 15 we need to move the number one place to the left through the decimal point—in other words, we multiply the divisor by 10. Of course if we do that we shall get the wrong answer, unless we compensate by also making the dividend ten times bigger. So the rule is:

(a) Make the divisor a whole number.

(b) What you did to the divisor you must now do to the dividend.

As we multiplied the divisor by 10, we must multiply the dividend by 10. So

$$276.95 \div 1.5$$
$$= 2769.5 \div 15$$

Similarly

$$27.255 \div 0.25$$
$$= 2725.5 \div 25$$

Here we made the divisor 25 (by multiplying it by 100), so we have to multiply the dividend by 100. We can now proceed

$$
\begin{array}{r}
109.02 \\
25\overline{)\ 2725.5} \\
25 \\
\hline
225 \\
225 \\
\hline
50
\end{array}
$$

Division sums which do not work out exactly. Since the decimal system is a system of fractions as well as of whole numbers, a division sum must continue down into the fractions part of the sum if it does not work out exactly. Thus

$$12 \div 0.3 = 120 \div 3 = 40$$

By contrast

$$13 \div 0.3 = 130 \div 3 = 43.333\ 33, \text{ etc.}$$

It never will come to an end. This is called a **recurring number** and it is usually shortened to 43.3̇. The dot over the 3̇ indicates that the number recurs endlessly.

Similarly

$$50 \div 0.7 = 500 \div 7 = 71.428\ 571\ 4 \text{ etc.}$$

Here the numbers 428 571 are going to repeat endlessly, and this is written 71.428 57̇1̇ with a dot over the first and the last numbers in the chain that is going to recur.

Answers correct to an agreed number of decimal places. Whether a particular division sum actually works out exactly may take some time to discover (unless of course, one is using a calculator) but in any case at each calculation a figure moves down one place in the fraction scale. The degree of accuracy required in an answer varies—for some engineering work we might need to work to very fine limits. In most statistical calculations, answers correct to one decimal place, or at most two decimal places, are accurate enough.

When asked to give an answer correct to one decimal place it is necessary to work to two decimal places and then consider what answer is most correct to one decimal place. For example, consider the division sum

$$
\begin{aligned}
385 &\div 1.7 \\
= 3850 &\div 17 \\
= 226.47 &\text{ to two decimal places}
\end{aligned}
$$

To give this answer correct to one decimal place we must round the answer up to 226.5. This is in error by 0.03. To give the answer rounded down to 226.4 would be in error by 0.07. Clearly 226.5 is more correct than 226.4.

An answer of 189.23 would be rounded down to 189.2. When the last figure comes to a '5' a little difficulty arises. For example, an answer of 27.35—if the division sum continued further—might go on 27.351 64, etc. Clearly any continuation beyond 27.35 makes the fraction of hundredths bigger than half, and the answer correct to one decimal place is 27.4.

If the answer works out exactly to 27.35, what should be done about rounding up or down? The answer is that we round to make the final answer an even number. Thus

27.35 rounds up to 27.4
27.25 rounds down to 27.2

This evens out the rounded figures in any set of statistics.

3.9   Exercises: Division of Decimals

1. 27.56 ÷ 2.5

2. 32.35 ÷ 4.7 (correct to one decimal place)

3. 386.5 ÷ 1.95 (correct to two decimal places)

4. 427.95 ÷ 1.25

5. 25.62 ÷ 1.65 (correct to one decimal place)

6. 31.75 ÷ 2.73 (correct to two decimal places)

7. 495.61 ÷ 3.8 (correct to one decimal place)

8. 7.65 ÷ 2.7 (correct to two decimal places)

9. 475.6 ÷ 0.85 (correct to three decimal places)

10. 2.73 ÷ 1.17 (correct to three decimal places)

4
Fractions

4.1 The Nature of Common Fractions

Common fractions, or vulgar fractions, are used to describe quantities smaller than a whole unit. Unlike decimal fractions, which are linked to tenths, hundreds, etc., vulgar fractions are very versatile. The parts into which a whole unit can be divided are exceedingly numerous. We have halves, thirds, quarters, fifths, sixths, etc.—not just tenths, hundredths, thousandths, etc.

Every vulgar fraction is expressed in two parts: a **denominator** which tells us the name of the fraction we are using, and a **numerator** which tells us the number of parts we have. Thus the fractions $\frac{1}{7}$, $\frac{2}{7}$, $\frac{3}{7}$, $\frac{4}{7}$, $\frac{5}{7}$, $\frac{6}{7}$ all have the same denominator (from Latin *nomen* = name), 7, so it is sevenths that they all deal with. How many sevenths is told us in the numerator; one seventh, two sevenths, three sevenths, etc.

$$\frac{\text{Numerator}}{\text{Denominator}} \quad \frac{1}{7}, \frac{2}{7}, \frac{3}{7}, \frac{4}{7}, \frac{5}{7}, \frac{6}{7}, \frac{7}{7}, \frac{8}{7}$$

Mixed Numbers

Once the numerator becomes as large as the denominator, $\frac{7}{7}$, we have a whole unit, for seven sevenths makes one whole one. So $\frac{7}{7}$ can be written as 1, and $\frac{8}{7} = 1\frac{1}{7}$. This is called a **mixed number**. Similarly, $\frac{9}{7} = 1\frac{2}{7}$ and $\frac{15}{7} = 2\frac{1}{7}$.

A number with a numerator larger than its denominator is called an **improper fraction**, or a **top-heavy fraction**, and should be changed to a mixed number. We divide the denominator into the numerator to find how many whole numbers:

So
$$\frac{15}{4} = 3\frac{3}{4}$$

$$\frac{17}{5} = 3\frac{2}{5}$$

$$\frac{19}{10} = 1\frac{9}{10}$$

Note

(i) In the first example above we have $\frac{15}{4}$. Since $\frac{4}{4} = 1$ we must have several whole numbers. How many fours in 15? The answer is $3 \times 4 = 12$ and 3 remainder. So when we divide a top-heavy (improper) fraction by its denominator we find how many whole numbers and how many fractions left over (in this case $3\frac{3}{4}$). The reader will notice that once again we use our tables to do this sort of calculation.

(ii) $\frac{17}{5}$: dividing by 5 we have 5 into 17 goes 3 times ($3 \times 5 = 15$) and $\frac{2}{5}$ remain.

(iii) $\frac{19}{10}$: 10 into 19 goes once ($1 \times 10 = 10$) and $\frac{9}{10}$ remain.

Cancelling Fractions Down to Lower terms

One further point is that where a fraction can be reduced to simpler terms it should be. Thus two quarters ($\frac{2}{4}$) is more easily written as one half ($\frac{1}{2}$) and three ninths ($\frac{3}{9}$) is more easily written as one third ($\frac{1}{3}$). This is called **cancelling down**.

Before discussing cancelling we must first learn two further arithmetical terms, **factors** and **multiples**.

Factors. A factor is a number which will divide into another number an exact number of times. Thus 2 is a factor of 6, and 7 is a factor of 14. Some numbers have many factors. For example, the numbers 2, 3, 4, 6, 8, 12, 24 and 48 are all factors of 96. Other numbers have only two factors, themselves and 1. Thus 7 has only two factors, 7 and 1, and 19 has only two factors, 19 and 1. Such numbers are called **prime numbers**.

Where two numbers can both be divided by the same factor it is said to be a **common factor**. Thus 22 and 20 have a common factor 2, and 25 and 35 have a common factor 5.

Multiples. Multiples are large numbers into which other numbers will divide exactly. Thus 100 is a multiple of 10, and 20 is a multiple of 5. There are an infinitely large number of multiples of any number. For example, the multiples of 6 include 12, 18, 24, 30 and so on, in an infinite series.

It is usual to reduce a fraction to its lowest terms by cancellation. When cancelling a fraction down we need to divide both the numerator and the denominator by a common factor, or several common factors until we have *reduced the fraction to its lowest terms*. This is explained in Example 4.1 below.

Example 4.1. Reduce down the following fractions to their lowest terms:

$$\frac{2}{4}, \frac{6}{9}, \frac{10}{15}, \frac{24}{48}, \frac{24}{60}$$

To cancel down we must divide both the numerator and the denominator by a common factor. Sometimes they have several common factors which will cancel into the top and bottom lines, as shown below.

$\frac{2}{4}$ Cancelling by 2 we have $\frac{\cancel{2}^{1}}{\cancel{4}_{2}} = \frac{1}{2}$

$\frac{6}{9}$ Cancelling by 3 we have $\frac{\cancel{6}^{2}}{\cancel{9}_{3}} = \frac{2}{3}$

$\frac{10}{15}$ Cancelling by 5 we have $\frac{\cancel{10}^{2}}{\cancel{15}_{3}} = \frac{2}{3}$

$\frac{24}{48}$ Cancelling by 2, 2, 2 and 3 we have $\frac{\cancel{24}\,\cancel{12}\,\cancel{6}\,\cancel{3}\,1}{\cancel{48}\,\cancel{24}\,\cancel{12}\,\cancel{6}\,2} = \frac{1}{2}$

$\frac{24}{60}$ Cancelling by 2, 2 and 3 we have $\frac{\cancel{24}\,\cancel{12}\,\cancel{6}\,2}{\cancel{60}\,\cancel{30}\,\cancel{15}\,5} = \frac{2}{5}$

4.2   Exercises: Cancelling Fractions

In each of the following groups of fractions you are required to cancel them down to their lowest terms:

1. $\frac{2}{4}$; $\frac{4}{8}$; $\frac{10}{15}$ 2. $\frac{3}{6}$; $\frac{4}{6}$; $\frac{8}{12}$

3. $\frac{2}{8}$; $\frac{4}{8}$; $\frac{6}{8}$ 4. $\frac{3}{9}$; $\frac{6}{9}$; $\frac{9}{18}$

5. $\frac{5}{10}$; $\frac{10}{15}$; $\frac{25}{30}$ 6. $\frac{2}{12}$; $\frac{8}{12}$; $\frac{10}{12}$

7. $\frac{6}{24}$; $\frac{12}{24}$; $\frac{20}{24}$ 8. $\frac{3}{27}$; $\frac{9}{27}$; $\frac{21}{27}$

9. $\frac{18}{36}$; $\frac{24}{36}$; $\frac{30}{36}$ 10. $\frac{5}{60}$; $\frac{15}{60}$; $\frac{25}{60}$

4.3   Exercises: Mixed Numbers

In each of the following groups of improper (top-heavy) fractions you are required to change the improper fraction to a mixed number. If the remaining fractional part can be reduced, express it in its lowest terms.

1. $\frac{3}{2}$; $\frac{5}{4}$; $\frac{6}{4}$ 2. $\frac{7}{2}$; $\frac{14}{3}$; $\frac{18}{4}$

3. $\frac{18}{5}$; $\frac{20}{6}$; $\frac{26}{8}$ 4. $\frac{30}{4}$; $\frac{19}{9}$; $\frac{26}{4}$

5. $\frac{38}{8}$; $\frac{86}{12}$ 6. $\frac{42}{5}$; $\frac{80}{15}$

7. $\frac{28}{8}, \frac{87}{12}$ **8.** $\frac{93}{10}, \frac{75}{20}$

9. $\frac{84}{16}, \frac{72}{10}$ **10.** $\frac{124}{48}, \frac{160}{24}$

4.4 The Addition of Fractions

In adding fractions we face a difficulty, in that fractions with different denominators are quite different things, and cannot be added together directly. Thus we can add

$$\frac{1}{3} + \frac{1}{3} = \frac{2}{3}$$

but we cannot add $\frac{1}{2} + \frac{1}{3}$ without first changing them into some common form. Fortunately we can always find a **common denominator**, which is another name for a **common multiple**.

A common denominator is therefore a number into which the other denominators will both divide. This can be seen at once to be 6 in the case of 2 and 3. They will both go into 6 an exact number of times. It is not quite so obvious with $\frac{1}{2} + \frac{3}{5} + \frac{2}{3}$. What is the common denominator now?

To find a common denominator we go through the following procedure:

(*a*) Look at the largest denominator, in this case 5.

(*b*) Will the other denominators divide into it? No!

(*c*) Double 5 = 10. Will they divide into it now? 2 will, but 3 will not.

(*d*) Since we are seeking a common multiple, we must simply carry on taking multiples of 5. It is obvious that odd numbers are no use, since 2 will not divide into them, so we must try the even multiples of 5, i.e. $4 \times 5 = 20$? $6 \times 5 = 30$? Three will divide into 30, so 30 is the common denominator, since 2, 3 and 5 will all divide into it. Let us now proceed to add the fractions $\frac{1}{2} + \frac{3}{5} + \frac{2}{3}$.

Example 4.2

$$\frac{1}{2} + \frac{3}{5} + \frac{2}{3}$$

First, we know that the common denominator is 30. We can therefore add these fractions together if we turn them all to thirtieths. What is $\frac{1}{2}$ when turned to thirtieths. The answer is $\frac{15}{30}$. To find the numerator we divide the original denominator into the common denominator, and then multiply the answer by the original numerator. So

$$\frac{1}{2} = \frac{15}{30} \ (30 \div 2 = 15; \ 15 \times 1 = 15)$$

$$\frac{3}{5} = \frac{18}{30} \ (30 \div 5 = 6; \ 6 \times 3 = 18)$$

$$\frac{2}{3} = \frac{20}{30} \ (30 \div 3 = 10; \ 10 \times 2 = 20)$$

To save time we usually write

$$\frac{1}{2} + \frac{3}{5} + \frac{2}{3}$$

$$= \frac{15 + 18 + 20}{30}$$

$$= \frac{53}{30}$$

$$= 1\frac{23}{30}$$

(*Note:* $\frac{53}{30}$ is an improper fraction and, of course, must be turned into a mixed number.)

Example 4.3

$$1\frac{1}{2} + 2\frac{2}{3} + 3\frac{3}{4}$$

Here we have three mixed numbers to add together. We can add the whole numbers at once: $1 + 2 + 3 = 6$. We now have:

$$1\frac{1}{2} + 2\frac{2}{3} + 3\frac{3}{4}$$

$$= 6\frac{6 + 8 + 9}{12} \qquad \text{(12 is the common denominator)}$$

$$= 6\frac{23}{12}$$

$$= 7\frac{11}{12}$$

4.5   Exercises: The Addition of Fractions

1. $\frac{1}{2} + \frac{3}{5} + \frac{7}{15}$ 2. $\frac{2}{3} + \frac{3}{4} + \frac{5}{8}$

3. $1\frac{1}{2} + 2\frac{2}{5} + 3\frac{7}{10}$ 4. $5\frac{1}{4} + 2\frac{3}{8} + 1\frac{7}{12}$

5. $4\frac{1}{4} + 3\frac{2}{3} + 2\frac{1}{2}$ 6. $5\frac{7}{8} + 3\frac{2}{3} + 1\frac{11}{12}$

7. $6\frac{3}{5} + 2\frac{1}{2} + 4\frac{5}{6}$ 8. $3\frac{1}{4} + 2\frac{4}{5} + 3\frac{1}{3}$

9. $4\frac{7}{10} + 3\frac{2}{5} + 5\frac{1}{4}$ 10. $3\frac{5}{12} + 2\frac{3}{7} + 4\frac{2}{3}$

4.6   Subtraction of Fractions

Subtraction of fractions is very similar to addition of fractions. Fractions which are not alike must be turned into similar fractions by finding a common denominator. Thus

$$\frac{2}{3} - \frac{1}{6} = \frac{4 - 1}{6} = \frac{3}{6} = \frac{1}{2}$$

Turning the two fractions to a common fraction, sixths, enables the subtraction process to be carried out, and the final result is always cancelled down to give the answer in its lowest terms.

Clearly we can never take a large fraction from a small one, any more than we can take a large number from a small one. We do often have to subtract mixed numbers, however, where the fractional part is larger. Consider Example 4.4.

Example 4.4

$$3\frac{1}{2} - 2\frac{7}{12}$$

(Subtract the whole numbers first, and find a common denominator.)

$$= 1\frac{6 - 7}{12}$$

Clearly $\frac{7}{12}$ is larger than $\frac{6}{12}$ so we cannot subtract it. We do have one whole unit, which we can turn into $\frac{12}{12}$. The result is that we can subtract the $\frac{7}{12}$ from the whole number $\frac{12}{12}$ which leaves $\frac{5}{12}$. This $\frac{5}{12}$ with $\frac{6}{12}$ already available makes $\frac{11}{12}$ for the final result. So the calculation continues:

$$= 1\frac{6 - 7}{12}$$

(turn 1 to $\frac{12}{12}$ and subtract $\frac{7}{12}$ from it)

(add the $\frac{5}{12}$ left to the $\frac{6}{12}$, making $\frac{11}{12}$ in all)

$$= \frac{11}{12}$$

Example 4.5

$$3\frac{3}{4} - 1\frac{7}{8}$$

$$= 2\frac{6 - 7}{8}$$

$$= 1\frac{7}{8}$$

4.7 Exercises: Subtraction of Fractions

1. $\frac{3}{4} - \frac{2}{3}$ 2. $\frac{3}{8} - \frac{1}{4}$

3. $\frac{9}{10} - \frac{3}{4}$ 4. $\frac{4}{5} - \frac{7}{10}$

5. $\frac{5}{9} - \frac{3}{8}$ 6. $\frac{11}{12} - \frac{2}{3}$

7. $\frac{8}{9} - \frac{5}{8}$ 8. $\frac{13}{15} - \frac{4}{5}$

9. $\frac{29}{30} - \frac{7}{10}$ 10. $\frac{7}{8} - \frac{2}{3}$

11. $1\frac{1}{2} - 1\frac{1}{2}$ 12. $2\frac{3}{4} - 1\frac{9}{10}$

13. $7\frac{2}{3} - 3\frac{3}{4}$ 14. $5\frac{5}{8} - 3\frac{11}{12}$

15. $6\frac{2}{3} - 1\frac{11}{15}$ 16. $7\frac{1}{2} - 3\frac{15}{16}$

17. $9\frac{2}{3} - 4\frac{7}{10}$ 18. $5\frac{5}{8} - 3\frac{3}{4}$

19. $17\frac{1}{4} - 15\frac{2}{3}$ 20. $27\frac{1}{3} - 16\frac{15}{16}$

4.8 Multiplication of Fractions

Whenever numbers are multiplied together we expect the answer to be bigger. Thus $4 \times 4 = 16$ and $7 \times 29 = 203$. In the first example we have four of the 4's, and in the second we have seven of the 29's. When we multiply fractions, the answer becomes smaller. For example, if we have half of $\frac{1}{2}$ it will be $\frac{1}{4}$ and one third of $\frac{1}{3}$ will be $\frac{1}{9}$.

$$\frac{1}{2} \times \frac{1}{2} = \frac{1}{4}$$

$$\frac{1}{3} \times \frac{1}{3} = \frac{1}{9}$$

In fact, to multiply fractions we multiply the numerators and multiply the denominators. Thus

$$\frac{2}{3} \times \frac{5}{9} = \frac{10}{27}$$

Sometimes we can simplify the work by cancelling first. For example

$$\frac{3}{\underset{2}{8}} \times \frac{4^{1}}{5} = \frac{3}{10} \text{ (the 4 and the 8 cancel by 4)}$$

The rules for multiplying fractions are therefore:

(a) Cancel if you can.
(b) Multiply the numerators that are left after cancelling.
(c) Multiply the denominators that are left after cancelling.

If we have to multiply mixed numbers a further difficulty arises.

We must make the mixed numbers into improper fractions before we can proceed. This is illustrated in Example 4.6.

Example 4.6

$$1\frac{3}{4} \times 7\frac{1}{3} \qquad \text{(i)}$$

$$= \frac{7}{4_2} \times \frac{22^{11}}{3} \qquad \text{(ii)}$$

$$= \frac{77}{6} \qquad \text{(iii)}$$

$$= 12\frac{5}{6} \qquad \text{(iv)}$$

Notes

(i) Make the mixed numbers into improper fractions. Thus $1\frac{3}{4}$ becomes $\frac{7}{4}$ and $7\frac{1}{3}$ becomes $\frac{22}{3}$.

(ii) Cancel if you can. The 22 and the 4 have a common factor 2. We cancel these down to 11 and 2.

(iii) Multiply the numerators and multiply the denominators.

(iv) Convert the improper fraction $\frac{77}{6}$ back to a mixed number $12\frac{5}{6}$.

4.9 Exercises: Multiplication of Fractions

1. $\frac{2}{3} \times \frac{3}{4}$ 2. $\frac{3}{8} \times \frac{5}{6}$

3. $\frac{4}{5} \times \frac{7}{16}$ 4. $\frac{5}{8} \times \frac{4}{15}$

5. $\frac{3}{8} \times \frac{5}{6} \times \frac{2}{3}$ 6. $\frac{3}{4} \times \frac{2}{5} \times \frac{7}{9}$

7. $\frac{1}{6} \times \frac{3}{4} \times \frac{5}{8}$ 8. $\frac{2}{5} \times \frac{15}{16} \times \frac{7}{9}$

9. $\frac{4}{5} \times \frac{3}{4} \times \frac{10}{11}$ 10. $\frac{22}{25} \times \frac{5}{8} \times \frac{6}{7}$

11. $1\frac{1}{12} \times 2\frac{2}{13} \times 3\frac{1}{4}$ 12. $1\frac{2}{5} \times 2\frac{1}{2} \times 3\frac{3}{4}$

13. $5\frac{1}{2} \times 1\frac{3}{22} \times 1\frac{2}{5}$ 14. $8\frac{1}{2} \times 1\frac{2}{8} \times 1\frac{1}{17}$

15. $5\frac{1}{3} \times 2\frac{1}{4} \times 1\frac{7}{8}$ 16. $2\frac{1}{3} \times 1\frac{1}{11} \times 3\frac{1}{7}$

17. $4\frac{1}{2} \times 2\frac{2}{3} \times 1\frac{5}{16}$ 18. $4\frac{1}{2} \times 1\frac{1}{3} \times \frac{7}{16}$

19. $7\frac{1}{2} \times 2\frac{2}{3} \times 1\frac{1}{5}$ 20. $2\frac{5}{8} \times 1\frac{3}{7} \times 2\frac{2}{3}$

4.10 Division by Fractions

If we divide 10 by 5 the answer is 2, because 5 goes into 10 two times exactly; $10 \div 5 = 2$. Suppose we now ask how many times

$\frac{1}{5}$ goes into 10. The answer is 50, because $\frac{1}{5}$ will go into one whole number 5 times, so it must go into 10 whole numbers 50 times. So $10 \div \frac{1}{5} = 50$. When we divide by proper fractions the answer is always a larger number.

Consider the following cases:

$$\frac{1}{5} \div \frac{1}{5} = 1 \quad \text{(because } \frac{1}{5} \text{ goes into } \frac{1}{5} \text{ once)}$$

$$\frac{1}{\cancel{5}_1} \times \frac{\cancel{5}^1}{1} = 1 \quad \text{(the same answer as above)}$$

$$\frac{3}{4} \div \frac{3}{4} = 1 \quad \text{(because } \frac{3}{4} \text{ goes into } \frac{3}{4} \text{ once)}$$

$$\frac{\cancel{3}^1}{\cancel{4}_1} \times \frac{\cancel{4}^1}{\cancel{3}_1} = 1 \quad \text{(the same answer as above)}$$

$$10 \div \frac{1}{2} = 20 \quad \text{(because } \frac{1}{2} \text{ goes into 10}$$
$$\text{whole ones twenty times)}$$

$$10 \times \frac{2}{1} = 20 \quad \text{(the same answer as above)}$$

We can see that a very simple way to divide by a fraction is to change the divisor upside down and multiply instead.

Thus

$$\frac{3}{4} \div \frac{1}{2} = \frac{3}{\cancel{4}_2} \times \frac{\cancel{2}^1}{1} = \frac{3}{2} = 1\frac{1}{2}$$

And

$$\frac{2}{5} \div \frac{1}{3} = \frac{2}{5} \times \frac{3}{1} = \frac{6}{5} = 1\frac{1}{5}$$

When we divide by mixed numbers (for example, $1\frac{1}{2} \div 2\frac{1}{2}$) we must convert the mixed number to an improper fraction before we can change the divisor upside down.

Example 4.7

$$1\frac{1}{2} \div 2\frac{1}{2}$$

$$= \frac{3}{2} \div \frac{5}{2}$$

$$= \frac{3}{\cancel{2}_1} \times \frac{\cancel{2}^1}{5}$$

$$= \frac{3}{5}$$

$$=$$

We can now summarise the rules for division by fractions. They are:

(*a*) Change any mixed numbers to improper (top-heavy) fractions. (To do this we multiply the number of whole numbers by the denominator, and add on any other fractions in the numerator—e.g. $2\frac{1}{2} = \frac{5}{2}$, two whole ones multiplied by the denominator 2 gives 4 halves and one half in the numerator gives us $\frac{5}{2}$.)

(*b*) Turn the divisor upside down and change the sign to multiply.

(*c*) Cancel if you can.

(*d*) Multiply the numerators, and multiply the denominators. Finally, if the answer to (*d*) is a top-heavy fraction—

(*e*) Change the top-heavy fraction back to a mixed number.

4.11 Exercises: Division by Fractions

1. $\frac{2}{3} \div \frac{5}{9}$ 2. $\frac{4}{5} \div \frac{7}{10}$

3. $\frac{3}{8} \div \frac{9}{14}$ 4. $\frac{5}{6} \div \frac{2}{3}$

5. $\frac{5}{9} \div \frac{2}{3}$ 6. $\frac{17}{20} \div \frac{3}{5}$

7. $\frac{23}{24} \div \frac{5}{8}$ 8. $\frac{35}{36} \div \frac{5}{12}$

9. $\frac{17}{30} \div 1\frac{1}{16}$ 10. $1\frac{1}{2} \div 1\frac{3}{4}$

11. $1\frac{2}{3} \div 1\frac{1}{4}$ 12. $2\frac{2}{3} \div 1\frac{2}{5}$

13. $2\frac{1}{2} \div 3\frac{1}{8}$ 14. $4\frac{1}{4} \div 2\frac{5}{6}$

15. $3\frac{1}{2} \div 2\frac{5}{8}$ 16. $5\frac{1}{2} \div 8\frac{1}{4}$

17. $4\frac{1}{2} \div 3\frac{3}{10}$ 18. $4\frac{1}{3} \div 1\frac{1}{12}$

19. $7\frac{1}{2} \div 2\frac{1}{7}$ 20. $11\frac{1}{2} \div 1\frac{3}{8}$

4.12 Difficult Fraction Sums

If a fraction calculation involves more than one process (for example, multiplication and addition in the same calculation) different results will be reached if the calculation is done in different ways:

Example 4.8

$$\frac{2}{3} + \frac{4}{5} \times \frac{3}{8}$$

Method 1. Doing the addition first, we have

$$\frac{2}{3} + \frac{4}{5} \times \frac{3}{8}$$

$$= \frac{10 + 12}{15} \times \frac{3}{8}$$

$$= \frac{\cancel{22}^{11}}{\cancel{15}_5} \times \frac{\cancel{3}^1}{\cancel{8}_4}$$

$$= \frac{11}{20}$$

Method 2. Doing the multiplication first, we have

$$\frac{2}{3} + \frac{\cancel{4}^1}{5} \times \frac{3}{\cancel{8}_2}$$

$$= \frac{2}{3} + \frac{3}{10}$$

$$= \frac{20 + 9}{30}$$

$$= \frac{29}{30}$$

Clearly we must know which part of the calculation to do first. The usual rule, attributed to Mr E. J. Hopkins, is the Bodmas rule which says that complex fractions must be done in order as follows:

(*a*) **B**rackets first
(*b*) **'Of'** next—the word 'of' acting as a bracket
(*c*) **D**ivision
(*d*) **M**ultiplication
(*e*) **A**ddition
(*f*) **S**ubtraction last

If the Bodmas rule is followed the correct answer to Example 4.8 is therefore found by Method 2 and is $\frac{29}{30}$.

Example 4.9

$$\left(\frac{2}{3} + \frac{5}{8}\right) \div \left(\frac{3}{4} \times \frac{2}{3}\right)$$

$$\left(\frac{16 + 15}{24}\right) \div \left(\frac{\cancel{3}^1}{\cancel{4}_2} \times \frac{\cancel{2}^1}{\cancel{3}_1}\right) \qquad \text{(Brackets first)}$$

$$= \frac{31}{24} \div \frac{1}{2} \qquad \text{(Now the division)}$$

$$= \frac{31}{\overset{}{24}_{12}} \times \frac{\overset{1}{2}}{1} \qquad \text{(Change the divisor upside down and multiply)}$$

$$= \frac{31}{12}$$

$$= 2\frac{7}{12}$$

4.13 Exercises: Difficult Fraction Sums

1. $\frac{1}{2} + \frac{2}{3} \times \frac{3}{4}$
2. $\frac{3}{5} \div \frac{7}{10} - \frac{5}{14}$
3. $14\frac{1}{4} - 2\frac{2}{3} \div \frac{3}{8}$
4. $3\frac{1}{2} \times 1\frac{5}{14} + \frac{2}{3}$
5. $(\frac{1}{2} + \frac{3}{4}) \div 2\frac{1}{2}$
6. $(3\frac{7}{10} + 2\frac{4}{5}) \times \frac{8}{9}$
7. $(2\frac{1}{2} + 1\frac{3}{8}) \div (2\frac{1}{5} + \frac{9}{10})$
8. $1\frac{1}{3} \times (\frac{1}{2} + \frac{3}{4}) \times 1\frac{1}{5}$
9. $1\frac{1}{2} \times (\frac{3}{5} + \frac{2}{3})$
10. $(12\frac{1}{2} - \frac{5}{8}) \times 3\frac{1}{5}$
11. $(5\frac{1}{2} + 3\frac{1}{4}) \div 2\frac{1}{7}$
12. $(1\frac{3}{8} - \frac{2}{3}) \times \frac{8}{17}$

4.14 Changing Fractions to Decimals

It is frequently necessary to change common fractions to decimal fractions, and vice versa. These are quite simple processes which are best illustrated by a few examples.

Example 4.10. Change $\frac{1}{4}$ to a decimal fraction.

Rule for changing fractions to decimals: Write down the numerator and follow it by a decimal point. Then divide by the denominator. (As many 0's may be added after the decimal point as necessary.)

$$\frac{1}{4} = 4 \overline{)\ 1.00}^{\ 0.25}$$

Example 4.11. Change $\frac{11}{25}$ to a decimal fraction.

$$
\begin{array}{r}
0.44 \\
25\overline{)11.00} \\
10\ 0 \\
\hline
1\ 00 \\
1\ 00 \\
\hline
\end{array}
$$

Example 4.12. Change $\frac{3}{40}$ to a decimal fraction.

$$
\begin{array}{r}
0.075 \\
40\overline{)3.000} \\
2\ 80 \\
\hline
200 \\
\end{array}
$$

Example 4.13. Change $\frac{5}{9}$ to a decimal fraction.

$$
\begin{array}{r}
0.555 \\
9\overline{)5.000} \\
\end{array}
$$

This is clearly a recurring decimal and the answer is therefore $0.\dot{5}$.

Example 4.14. Change 0.95 to a proper fraction.

Rule for changing decimals to fractions: Write down the decimal fraction without its decimal point—in this case 95—as the numerator of the fraction. Draw a short line under it and then put as a denominator a number 1 followed by as many noughts as there are figures in the decimal fraction. As 95 has two figures it is of course 95 hundredths and we need two noughts in the denominator. Now cancel if possible.

$$0.95 = \frac{95}{100} = \frac{19}{20} \qquad \text{(cancelling by 5)}$$

Example 4.15. Change 0.495 to a proper fraction.

$$0.495 = \frac{495}{1000} = \frac{99}{200} \qquad \text{(cancelling by 5)}$$

Example 4.16. Change 0.072 to a proper fraction.

$$0.072 = \frac{72}{1000} = \frac{9}{125} \qquad \text{(cancelling by 8)}$$

4.15 Exercises: Changing Fractions to Decimals

Change each of the fractions below to a decimal fraction. Where appropriate give the answer correct to three decimal places.

1. $\frac{3}{8}$ 2. $\frac{4}{5}$ 3. $\frac{7}{10}$

4. $\frac{8}{15}$ 5. $\frac{7}{9}$ 6. $\frac{6}{7}$

7. $\frac{5}{12}$ 8. $\frac{11}{12}$ 9. $\frac{3}{11}$

10. $\frac{15}{16}$ 11. $\frac{19}{20}$ 12. $\frac{23}{40}$

13. $\frac{17}{80}$ 14. $\frac{4}{13}$ 15. $\frac{39}{40}$

4.16 Exercises: Changing Decimals to Fractions

Change each of the following decimal fractions to proper fractions:

1. 0.4   2. 0.9   3. 0.36

4. 0.54   5. 0.88   6. 0.625

7. 0.495   8. 0.885   9. 0.722

10. 0.348   11. 0.804   12. 0.6275

13. 0.3864   14. 0.7248   15. 0.9265

5
Mental Arithmetic

5.1 An Active Mind in a Healthy Body

Scientists have repeatedly drawn attention in the last few years to the need to exercise the mind as well as the body. One researcher particularly denigrated the electronic calculator as a device which was encouraging laziness so that even the simplest calculations are performed on it. These could, and should, be performed mentally by most people. A television series which specialises in observing the oddities of human life today, made a collection of ridiculous till receipts from mechanical and electronic tills. The prize was awarded to a till receipt which stretched across several rooms in the television studios. A purchase of several hundred 4p bags of crisps had been recorded one at a time and added up, as if multiplication had never been invented. So much for progress!

It is essential to study business calculations to such effect that most of the ordinary calculations of business life can be performed in the head, and short cuts and simple methods should be practised until they are perfect. Since the range of possible questions that could be asked is very great, and increases with every chapter of this book, it has been decided to add at the end of all subsequent chapters a small section on mental arithmetic which may be nothing to do with the chapter itself, though at times it will follow directly from the material in the chapter. This section on mental arithmetic will then be followed by a mental arithmetic test which reviews not only the aspect of mental arithmetic that has just been studied, but all the aspects studied to date. In this chapter, which is the first to introduce mental arithmetic, we begin with two aspects: Roman numbers and simple addition sums.

It may be argued that there is not much mental calculation involved in knowing Roman numbers. This is true, but it is usual to examine students' knowledge of Roman numbers in the 'mental arithmetic' part of any examination paper. When we stand in front of a memorial stone, or a classical building, trying to discover the year engraved on the stonework, we do usually convert the Roman figures mentally, to Arabic numerals, so this explains why it is regarded as 'mental arithmetic'.

5.2   Roman Numbers

Today, with our decimal system, we can easily represent very large numbers. Our **Arabic numerals** use the zero sign, 0 (sometimes called 'cipher' from the Arabic). Generally supposed to have been invented by the Arabs, but perhaps only introduced into Europe by them, the zero and the use of a 'place value' enables us to represent very large numbers easily. The Romans did not have the 0 sign and instead made use of the letters used for writing to signify numbers, and a system of **Roman numerals** was developed. Today it is chiefly used for the chapter headings of books (though not in the Made Simple series), for the hours on clock faces, and for the years.

The system from 1 to 5 is as follows:

1	2	3	4	5
I	II	III	IV	V

Note that 4 is 'one before five'. On some clock faces 4 is given as IIII but the more usual sign is IV. The Roman system tends to be a system based on 'five' rather than a decimal system based on 10. Continuing the series we have

6	7	8	9	10
VI	VII	VIII	IX	X

Six is 'one after five', seven is 'two after five', eight is 'three after five', but nine is 'one before 10'. Continuing the series we have:

11	12	13	14	15
XI	XII	XIII	XIV	XV

16	17	18	19	20
XVI	XVII	XVIII	XIX	XX

Counting in tens we have

10	20	30	40	50
X	XX	XXX	XL	L

Again a new symbol has to be adopted at five tens to prevent having a long row of X signs: 50 = L, and 40 is 10 before 50, XL.

60	70	80	90	100
LX	LXX	LXXX	XC	C

A further sign is needed for 100, and it is C for *centum* (from which our word 'century' is derived): 90 is 10 before 100, XC.

Counting in hundreds we have

100	200	300	400	500
C	CC	CCC	CD	D

600	700	800	900	1000
DC	DCC	DCCC	CM	M

Here the new signs are D for 500 and M for 1000.

The First World War lasted from 1914 to 1918. These years often appear on monuments as

MCMXIV – MCMXVIII

The Second World War, from 1939 to 1945, would appear as

MCMXXXIX – MCMXLV

Note: As a matter of interest we may note that the Romans found it impossible to do any sort of multiplication or division. Consider the sum

$$51 \times 29 =$$

In Roman numbers this would be

LI
times   XXIX
————

There is just no way of multiplying these numbers together to get any meaningful answer.

5.3   Exercises: Roman Numbers

1. Write down the following numbers in Roman figures:

(a) 27   (b) 34
(c) 49 (careful)   (d) 53
(e) 72   (f) 85
(g) 125   (h) 365
(i) 1720   (j) 1895

2. Write down these Roman numbers in Arabic numbers:

(a) XVII   (b) XXXIX
(c) LXI   (d) LXXVIII
(e) XCV   (f) CV
(g) CCCLXII   (h) MCMLXXXIV
(i) MCMLXVI   (j) MM

5.4   Adding up Mentally

If we know our 'addition bonds' like 1 + 1 = 2 and 3 + 7 = 10, we can do even the hardest addition sums in our heads, so long as we have a pencil to jot down the answer as we go along.

Thus $7 + 6 = 13$

This is a simple addition bond; we ought to know it and be able to write the answer down straight away.

Now consider $27 + 36 = ?$

Clearly, the units part of this addition sum is the same as the sum above, $7 + 6 = 13$. Therefore we can write down the first part of the answer at once. The units figure of the answer is going to be a 3. Carrying the 10 from the 13 in our heads we must now say '1 ten to carry, plus 2 tens (from 27) makes 3 tens, and 3 more (from 36) = 6 tens'. So the full answer is 63.

$$27 + 36 = 63$$

Taking a more difficult example

$$27 + 49 + 256 + 385 + 1275 = ?$$

Adding up the units first, we say $7 + 9 = 16 + 6 = 22 + 5 = 27 + 5 = 32$. So the units figure of the answer is **2** and we have 3 tens to carry.

Now adding the tens we have 3 tens to carry + 2 tens = 5 tens + 4 tens = 9 tens + 5 tens = 14 tens + 8 tens = 22 tens + 7 tens = 29 tens. So the tens figure of the answer is a **9**.

The 20 tens become 2 hundreds and have to be carried as 2 hundreds into the addition of the hundreds. The hundreds are then added up as 2 hundreds to carry, plus 2 more (from 256) = 4 hundreds and 3 more from 385 makes 7 hundreds and 2 more from 1275 makes 9 hundreds altogether. The hundreds figure in the answer is therefore a **9**:

992

There is only one thousand, so the final answer is

1992

Although this section is about addition of numbers, clearly the same sort of calculations can be carried out mentally for subtraction, multiplication and division. The same principles also apply to calculations involving decimals fractions and vulgar fractions.

5.5   Exercises: Mental Addition Sums

Add the sums shown below in your head, and write down *the answers only* in your exercise book. Do *not* write in this text book, unless it is your own property.

1. (a) $7 + 5 + 9 + 8 + 4 =$
   (b) $12 + 19 + 17 + 27 + 35 =$
   (c) $64 + 72 + 18 + 9 + 195 =$
   (d) $275 + 324 + 176 + 95 =$
   (e) $686 + 285 + 421 + 623 =$

2. (a) $1275 + 2384 + 3261 =$
   (b) $5719 + 2493 + 6218 =$
   (c) $7256 + 4936 + 8878 =$
   (d) $12\ 975 + 24\ 321 + 49\ 465$
   $\qquad\qquad\qquad + 72\ 631 =$
   (e) $182\ 656 + 482\ 721$
   $\qquad\qquad\qquad + 381\ 699 =$

5.6   Mental Arithmetic Test

Take a sheet of paper or your exercise book and write the numbers 1–15 down the edge of a page. Now write *the answers only* to these 15 questions. Do not copy out the questions themselves.

1. Add up $24 + 72$
2. Add up $2 + 5 + 8 + 17 + 36$
3. $136 + 149 + 225 =$
4. $8 \times 8 =$
5. $127 \times 8 =$
6. $464 \div 4 =$
7. $3825 \div 5 =$
8. $4.3 + 2.5 + 1.6 =$
9. Take 17.5 from 32.8
10. Write down 27 in Roman numbers
11. What is LXIV in Arabic numerals?
12. $\frac{2}{5} + \frac{1}{3} =$
13. $\frac{3}{8} - \frac{1}{4} =$
14. $\frac{1}{2} \times \frac{2}{3} =$
15. $\frac{7}{8} \times \frac{2}{3} =$

6
Money

6.1 Decimal Currency

In 1971 the United Kingdom turned from its traditional currency
in pounds, shillings and pence to a decimal currency where the
pound sterling is divided into one hundred new pence. The word
'new' is already obsolete, and we simply say 100 pence = one
pound sterling.

The symbol for pence is p and the symbol for pound is £, so

$$100p = £1$$

There are coins for £2, £1, 50p, 20p, 10p, 5p, 2p and 1p. Notes are
issued for £5, £10, £20 and £50. Such coins and notes are in wide
circulation as **legal tender**.

In recent years inflation has had a serious effect on the value of
both coins and notes and the farthing and halfpenny have ceased to
be used. The £1 note has been replaced by a £1 coin, to save heavy
printing and distribution costs. The size and usefulness of some coins,
notably the 50p coin and the 10p coin are under discussion at present.

The term 'legal tender' referred to above when applied to currency means that the citizens of the country concerned must accept
the notes and coins as payment for any debt. Notes are legal tender
for any amount, but it would be unfair to pay debts with huge bags
of coins so that decimal bronze coins are legal tender only up to 20
pence, and cupro-nickel coins (often mistakenly called silver) are
legal tender only up to £5, except for the 20p, 50p and the new £1
coins, which are legal tender up to £10.

Money is not only a means of payment, but also the unit of
account in which all business records are kept, so that business
calculations are largely concerned with money. It is essential to be
completely competent in the addition, subtraction, multiplication
and division of money. These processes are now very simple indeed
since the decimal system was introduced and the phasing out of the
halfpenny means that the system is now completely decimalised
and the last remnant of the old coinage has disappeared.

Honesty and money. Asked by a student what he regarded as the most vital attribute of any future employee, a visiting businessman replied unhesitatingly 'Honesty'. Young readers are reminded that employment in any business premises is a position of trust which requires the employee to be honest and trustworthy at all times. An employer may still dismiss an employee without notice if dishonesty can be proved, and it is very difficult to re-establish one's character once dishonesty has been admitted or proved.

How to write money

A sum of money which is greater than £1 is always written with the £ sign preceding the number of pounds. Thus £5, £65 and £127 are all correctly written down as shown. Where the sum of money has pence as well, the decimal point is used to separate the whole pounds from the fractional part of the £1. Thus £167.85, £233.95 and £45.28 are all correctly written down as shown.

Where the sum of money to be written down is in pence only there are two ways of writing it. We may continue the method used above, but putting a 0 in the £ column. Thus £0.58 or £0.72 would be correct. The other method is to write down the number of pence without a decimal point, but followed by the abbreviation for pence, which is p without any abbreviation point. Thus 72p is correct and so is 38p, but 38p. is incorrect, and so is £0.38p. We do not use both the £ sign and the p sign.

When writing a cheque the amount of the cheque has to be written in both words and numbers, but because of the limited space on the cheque it is permitted to use numbers for the pence part of the

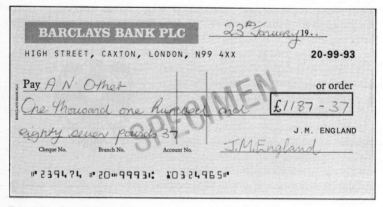

Fig. 6.1. A correctly written cheque.
(Courtesy of Barclays Bank PLC)

payment in both parts of the cheque. This is illustrated in the cheque shown in Fig. 6.1. The abbreviation p is omitted when the sum of money is written out in words. A common error in writing cheques is to omit the word 'pounds' on the line where the money is written out fully in words: 'one thousand one hundred and eighty-seven 37' would *not* be correct.

6.2 Addition of Money

The addition of decimal money is exactly the same as the addition of decimal fractions, now that the use of halfpennies has been discontinued. The rule that is always used for adding decimal fractions is *'keep the decimal points under one another, so that the various place values are all aligned, units under units, tens under tens, tenths under tenths, etc.'*. With money this brings the pence underneath one another, in the tenths and hundredths column only. The addition is then straightforward, the figures being added as shown in Example 6.1 below.

Example 6.1
£13.26 + £17.50 + £19.62 + £54.73 + £256.74 + £295.68 + £495.75.

$$
\begin{array}{r}
£ \\
13.26 \\
17.50 \\
19.62 \\
54.73 \\
256.74 \\
295.68 \\
495.75 \\
\hline
£1153.28 \\
\hline
344\ 2
\end{array}
$$

Notes
 (i) What we have, in effect, is an ordinary decimal sum, but we cannot have figures smaller than the hundredths column, because the smallest fraction of £1 is now one hundredth of a pound, i.e. one penny.
 (ii) When added the pence column comes to 28 pence. The 8 is written in the answer and the 20 pence becomes 2 tenpenny pieces and is carried into the next column. This in turn totals 42 tenpenny pieces and must therefore give us 2 tenpenny pieces in the answer, while the 40 tenpenny pieces become four pounds to be carried into the pounds column. The pounds are then added in the same way.

6.3 Subtraction of Money

In business life the subtraction of money is a calculation that must constantly be performed. Not only do we frequently deduct **discounts** from the price of goods, but in **double-entry book-keeping**, which is the basis of all accounting, one side of an account must be deducted from the other to give the **balance** on the account. The rule is the same as the rule for addition of money, *keep the decimal points under one another*.

Example 6.2. In a clearance sale a shopkeeper marks down his usual prices. An item selling normally for £62.50 is reduced by £8.35. What will be the sale price?

Subtracting £8.35 from £62.50, we have

$$\begin{array}{r} £ \\ 62.50 \\ -\ 8.35 \\ \hline £54.15 \end{array}$$

Notes

(i) First the five pence must be deducted from no pence. Since this is impossible we must use one of the five tenpenny pieces. Five pence from ten pence leaves five pence in the answer.

(ii) 3 tenpenny pieces are now taken from 4 tenpenny pieces, leaving one in the answer. The subtraction then continues in the normal way, since the money system is a simple decimal system.

6.4 Exercises: Addition and Subtraction of Money

1. Add up the following amounts of money:

(a) £	(b) £	(c) £	(d) £
32.54	42.65	38.17	71.65
76.30	37.35	29.16	92.72
+ 25.42	+ 29.62	+ 42.85	+ 185.36

(e) £3.26, £4.72, £3.84, £4.76
(f) £17.25, £13.85, £27.65, £72.95
(g) £29.50, £282.75, £92.77, £18.66
(h) £63.85, £136.75, £148.35, £27.55
(i) £1237.65, £2385.60, £4386.27
(j) £2954.70, £4725.95, £2935.20

2. The sales of two models of vacuum cleaner are as follows in the four quarters of the current year. What were the total sales of each model for the year?

	Junior Model	DeLuxe Model
	£	£
Spring	127 254.60	118 264.65
Summer	38 326.75	25 381.24
Autumn	64 285.50	45 816.72
Winter	56 350.75	62 735.80

3. Find the total sales for each quarter and the total annual sales for each department and for the whole firm from this table of departmental results.

	Dept. A	Dept. B	Dept. C	Dept. D
Spring	13 726.55	11 712.50	54 236.24	27 365.72
Summer	14 812.62	23 625.25	48 726.35	29 256.36
Autumn	15 385.27	17 365.25	68 362.72	31 756.27
Winter	14 726.32	14 295.75	47 256.36	33 856.34

4. (a) Subtract £27.56 from £185.60
(b) Subtract £13.28 from £195
(c) Subtract £14.29 from £205.60
(d) Subtract £136.75 from £2387.50
(e) Subtract £278.75 from £3500

5. In the examples below we have the normal price of an article in a shop, and the discount allowed in a sale. What was the sale price in each case?

	Normal price	Discount allowed
(a)	£2.50	31p
(b)	£17.50	£2.18
(c)	£85.95	£10.74
(d)	£136.75	£30.77
(e)	£254.35	£57.22

6. The gross wages of eight employees are given below, with the deductions for pension contributions, income tax and national insurance to be made before payment. What will each of the employees receive in his/her pay packet?

Name	£ Gross wages	£ Pension contribution	£ Income tax	£ National Insurance
(a) Mr S	126.50	8.50	—	9.14
(b) Mrs T	84.75	4.32	7.24	6.23
(c) Miss U	48.25	2.27	2.65	3.56
(d) Mr V	64.70	3.65	1.50	4.73

(e)	Miss W	138.50	9.42	12.25	10.00
(f)	Miss X	126.25	8.50	8.40	9.12
(g)	Mr Y	88.72	4.50	—	6.53
(h)	Mr Z	46.50	2.13	—	3.44

6.5   Multiplication of Money

Multiplication of money is a simple multiplication of decimals, now that inflation has caused the cancellation of halfpennies. The usual rules for multiplication of decimals apply. In Chapter 3 we multiplied decimals by disregarding the decimal points in both the multiplier and the multiplicand, and putting the decimal point in the answer only. With the multiplication of money this will still be a satisfactory method, but since the decimal point is always going to be placed at the point where it separates the pounds from the pence, we could use the second method of multiplying decimals. The rules are:

(a) Set down the multiplicand (the sum of money to be multiplied).

(b) Set down the multiplier, *with the units figure of the multiplier under the last figure of the multiplicand.*

(c) The decimal point will then come at the same point in the answer as it is in the multiplier.

Two examples will illustrate the method.

$$(i) \quad £27.36 \times 5$$
$$(ii) \ £136.54 \times 17$$

Example 6.3. £27.36 × 5

£	
27.36	(set down the multiplicand)
× 5	(put the units figure of the
———	multiplier under the last figure
£136.80	of the multiplicand)
═══	
1 3	

Example 6.4. £136.54 × 17

£	
136.54	
× 17	
———	
955.78	(£136.54 × 7)
1365.40	(£136.54 × 10)
———	
£2321.18	(£136.54 × 17)
═══	

In each case the decimal point in the answer comes in the same place as the decimal point in the multiplicand above it.

6.6   Exercises: Multiplication of Money

1. Each of the following items appears on a separate invoice of a certain publishing house. What was the value of the invoices concerned?

(a) 20 copies of *Journey to the Moon* at £8.65 each
(b) 24 copies of *A Space Observatory* at £17.25 each
(c) 350 copies of *Tales of Mystery and Suspense* at £3.65 each
(d) 7 copies of *Astronomical Atlas* at £38.72 each
(e) 3 copies of *Medieval Presentations* at £12.75 each

2. A firm sells three grades of metal: low-grade is £25.50 per tonne, high-grade is £85.90 per tonne and 'pure' is £195.50 per tonne. Orders for five customers are as follows:

		Low-grade (tonnes)	High-grade (tonnes)	Pure (tonnes)
(a)	A and Co.	25	15	3
(b)	B Plc	15	12	5
(c)	C Plc	50	42	12
(d)	D and Co.	12	7	4
(e)	E Plc	8	5	3

Work out the invoice value in each case.

3. A school orders 35 desks for a typing pool at £37.95 each, and 35 typist's chairs at £23.35 each. What is the total invoice value?

4. What is the cost of 136 word-processing typewriters at £985.50 each?

5. A firm employs 14 technicians at £85.50 per week, 12 operators at £73.50 per week, 7 designers at £95.85 per week and 114 labourers at £88.75. What is its total weekly wage bill?

6. What is the total cost of the following:

60 copies *Economics Made Simple* at £3.95 each
50 copies *Book-keeping Made Simple* at £4.95 each
36 copies *Business Law Made Simple* at £5.95 each
45 copies *Business Calculations Made Simple* at £4.50 each

7. Roadworks costing £129.50 per metre are measured as being 385 metres long. What will be the total cost?

8. A port authority orders 12 fork lift trucks at £1795.65 each, and 4 straddle carriers at £17 285.60 each. What will be the total value of the invoice?

9. A market gardener supplies a supermarket with produce as follows:

46 baskets of blackcurrants at £5.50 per basket
35 baskets of redcurrants at £6.25 per basket
42 sacks of carrots at £2.30 per sack
60 sacks of runner beans at £4.20 per sack

What is the total bill?

10. The International Chamber of Commerce supplies a college with publications as follows:

20 copies of the *Uniform Rules on Clean Collections* at £4.50 per copy
36 copies of the *Guide to Incoterms* at £7.75 per copy
24 copies of the *Carriage by Air and Road Act* at £4.75 per copy

What is the total cost?

6.7   Division of Money

The division of money is again a simple matter of division by decimals. We may have a 'short division' calculation if the divisor is a number of which we know the multiplication tables. If it is a number greater than 12 we must do a 'long division' calculation.

Although halfpennies have been discontinued it would often be necessary to work to three places of decimals, to get answers correct to the nearest penny.

Example 6.6. Twelve laboratory scientists decide to share the cost of a presentation to a colleague who is retiring. What must each pay if the gift costs £65.95?

$$
\begin{array}{r}
£ \\
12\,\overline{)\,65.95} \\
\hline
5.49 \text{ remainder } 7p
\end{array}
$$

The cost to each is £5.49 but seven of them must pay an extra penny towards the gift i.e. £5.50.

Example 6.7. Under the agreed wages scheme of a stevedoring company gangs of 16 workers are paid a group bonus for 'dirty work' which is shared equally among them. The total group bonus for clearing a particular cargo is £575. By general consent the money is divided only as far as pounds are concerned, any balance left over is paid to Dr Barnardo's Homes. What will each receive, and what balance is paid to the charity?

$$
\begin{array}{r}
£ \\
35 \\
16 \overline{)\,575} \\
48 \\
\overline{} \\
95 \\
80 \\
\overline{} \\
15
\end{array}
$$

Each employee receives £35 bonus, and £15 is paid to Dr Barnardo's Homes.

6.8 Exercises: Division of Money

1. (a) Divide £15.50 by 9   (b) Divide £38.60 by 6
   (c) Divide £27.85 by 7   (d) Divide £72.86 by 8
   (e) Divide £36.50 by 6   (f) Divide £85.75 by 5
   (g) Divide £95.80 by 12   (h) Divide £92.15 by 7
   (i) Divide £84.75 by 8   (j) Divide £84.65 by 12

2. (a) Divide £325.65 by 15   (b) Divide £726.60 by 16
   (c) Divide £2584.95 by 18   (d) Divide £3276.48 by 14
   (e) Divide £4725.65 by 48   (f) Divide £4295.65 by 18

3. The total value of a consignment of 36 photo copiers is £11 484. What does each one cost?

4. A bulk shipment of 250 clock radios is invoiced at £5812.50. What is the cost of one?

5. At an auction 28 similar typewriters sold as one lot realised £825. What was the cost of one? (Answer to the nearest penny.)

6.9 Quick Calculations with Money

Many money calculations can be performed mentally if the amount is closely linked to a whole number of pounds. Thus items at £7.99 are almost £8 each and can be multiplied mentally if treated as £8 less 1 penny. Thus

$$
\begin{aligned}
£7.99 \times 8 &= (£8 - 1\text{p}) \times 8 \\
&= £64 - 8\text{p} \\
&= £63.92
\end{aligned}
$$

Similarly, £9.95 × 12 is best treated as (£10 − 5 pence) × 12 = £120 − 60 pence = £119.40

6.10   Exercises on Quick Calculations

Now try these calculations mentally:

1. (a) 99p × 24 =   (d) £4.95 × 36 =
   (b) £1.98 × 50 =   (e) £9.95 × 18 =
   (c) £3.99 × 27 =

6.11   Mental Arithmetic Test

Write the numbers 1–15 on a piece of paper or your exercise book. Then write *the answers only* to these questions:

1. 24 + 38 + 147 =

2. 365 + 127 + 294 =

3. 25 × 7 =

4. 38 × 6 =

5. £2.95 × 6 =

6. £13.99 × 5 =

7. £2.36 + £4.29 + £15.75 =

8. 0.11 × 0.5 =

9. 2.6 × 0.03 =

10. $\frac{2}{3} + \frac{3}{8}$ =

11. $1\frac{1}{2} \times 1\frac{1}{2}$ =

12. $\frac{5}{8} \times \frac{3}{5} \times \frac{4}{7}$ =

13. $\frac{2}{3} \div \frac{2}{3}$ =

14. What year was MCMLXXII?

15. Give the Roman numbers for 49

7
Metric Weights and Measures

7.1 Symbols in SI Units

The metric system is a system of international units of weights and measures, which was developed shortly after the French Revolution, in 1790. It began as an attempt to choose more scientific units of length, weight and capacity than the units in use at that time. For example, in the United Kingdom the units used for length, which were miles, yards, feet and inches, had no sensible scientific base. Gradually the countries of the world have adopted metric units, at first for scientific work but more recently for general use. In the United Kingdom these changes are still being made, and a lack of clear direction from Government sources is partly to blame for some confusion, but with more than 150 nations now using the metric system it is inevitable that the United Kingdom will complete the change to a metric system in the near future.

The whole system takes its name from the French words *Système International d'Unités* and is called the SI System. Note that any symbol used in a mathematical system is not an abbreviation, so that it is incorrect to write kg., for example, meaning kilograms. The various units in the SI system make use of symbols, not abbreviations, and symbols do not have a plural form. The units are as follows:

The unit of length is the **metre**, for which the symbol is m: so 1 m means 1 metre; 5 m means 5 metres; and 25 m means 25 metres.

The unit of weight is the **gram**, and the symbol is g: 1 g means 1 gram, 5 g means 5 grams, etc.

The unit of capacity (liquid measure) is the **litre**: 1 l means 1 litre, 5 l means 5 litres, etc. (*Note:* Because of the confusion between 1 and l it is officially recommended that 'litres' is written in full where the symbol would cause confusion.)

The tables of length, weight and capacity are as follows:

Table of Length

10 millimetres	=	1 centimetre
10 centimetres	=	1 decimetre
10 decimetres	=	1 **metre**
10 metres	=	1 decametre
10 decametres	=	1 hectometre
10 hectometres	=	1 kilometre

Written in symbol form we add the prefixes m, c and d to the symbol for metre—to give us mm (millimetres), cm (centimetres) and dm (decimetres). For decametres, to prevent confusion with decimetres, the prefix is da so that dam is the symbol for decametres. The other prefixes are hm (hectometre) and km (kilometre). Notice that all these symbols have small letters, not capital letters. We thus have:

Table of Length in Symbol Form

10 mm	=	1 cm
10 cm	=	1 dm
10 dm	=	1 m
10 m	=	1 dam
10 dam	=	1 hm
10 hm	=	1 km

The metre is the most important unit of length, but the millimetre is also very important in practical subjects like metalwork and woodwork, while the kilometre is very important for distances. *Eight kilometres are approximately the same as five English miles.*

Table of Weight

10 milligrams	=	1 centigram	10 mg	=	1 cg
10 centigrams	=	1 decigram	10 cg	=	1 dg
10 decigrams	=	1 **gram**	10 dg	=	1 g
10 grams	=	1 decagram	10 g	=	1 dag
10 decagrams	=	1 hectogram	10 dag	=	1 hg
10 hectograms	=	1 kilogram	10 hg	=	1 kg
1000 kilograms	=	1 metric tonne	1000 kg	=	1 tonne

Since a gram is a very small unit of weight, it is of most interest in scientific work. The commonest weight for everyday use is the kilogram, which is about 2.2 pounds in the old Imperial units of weight; 1 tonne is approximately the same as 1 British ton.

Table of Capacity

10 millilitres	=	1 centilitre	10 ml	=	1 cl
10 centilitres	=	1 decilitre	10 cl	=	1 dl
10 decilitres	=	1 **litre**	10 dl	=	1 l
10 litres	=	1 decalitre	10 l	=	1 dal
10 decalitres	=	1 hectolitre	10 dal	=	1 hl
10 hectolitres	=	1 kilolitre	10 hl	=	1 kl

The litre is the most important unit of capacity, and is equivalent to 1.76 pints in the old Imperial units of capacity. Millilitres are important in medicine, where doses are very small. Most plastic measuring spoons used for giving medicines to children are marked '5 ml dose'.

The Full Range of Metric Symbols

Because the metric system is a scientific system it must be able to express the full range of measurements—for instance, from the microscopic measurements inside the atom to the ultimate limits of outer space. We have seen that the unit is centrally placed in the system with prefixes which show multiples of the unit (decametres, hectometres and kilometres) and fractions of the unit (decimetres, centimetres and millimetres). The full range of symbols is shown in Table 7.1.

Table 7.1. The full range of metric prefixes.

Prefix	symbol	Factor by which the unit (*e.g. metres*) is multiplied	
exa	E	1 000 000 000 000 000 000	$= 10^{18}$
peta	P	1 000 000 000 000 000	$= 10^{15}$
tera	T	1 000 000 000 000	$= 10^{12}$
giga	G	1 000 000 000	$= 10^{9}$
mega	M	1 000 000	$= 10^{6}$
kilo	k	1 000	$= 10^{3}$
hecto	h	100	$= 10^{2}$
deca	da	10	$= 10^{1}$
		1 metre	
deci	d	0.1	$= 10^{-1}$
centi	c	0.01	$= 10^{-2}$
milli	m	0.001	$= 10^{-3}$
micro	μ	0.000 001	$= 10^{-6}$
nano	n	0.000 000 001	$= 10^{-9}$
pico	p	0.000 000 000 001	$= 10^{-12}$
femto	f	0.000 000 000 000 001	$= 10^{-15}$
atto	a	0.000 000 000 000 000 001	$= 10^{-18}$

Note: The prefixes exa (E), peta (P), tera (T), giga (G) and mega (M) have capital letters as symbols; the remainder have small letters. The symbol for micro is the Greek letter μ (mu).

7.2 Manipulation of Metric Units

It is essential for the student to become thoroughly familiar with metric units and able to convert one unit to another unit in the same table. Thus metres, kilometres, centimetres and millimetres are inter-related and can be converted from one to another at will if the pattern of the system is fully understood. This pattern has the unit itself centrally placed, with multiples of the unit on the left-hand side and fractions of the unit on the right-hand side. Consider the distance

1725.634 metres

The 5 metres are centrally placed. The fractions of the metres are on the right-hand side, following the decimal point: 6 decimetres, 3 centimetres and 4 millimetres. The multiples of the metres are on the left-hand side: 2 decametres, 7 hectometres and 1 kilometre.

The pattern of the metric system is therefore as follows:

Thousands	*Hundreds*	*Tens*	*Units*	*Tenths*	*Hundredths*	*Thousandths*
km	hm	dam	metre	dm	cm	mm
1	7	2	5 .	6	3	4

To convert metres into decimetres we can simply move the number through the decimal point one place, because there are 10 decimetres in one metre. Thus

	1725.634	metres
becomes	17256.34	decimetres or
	172563.4	centimetres or
	1725634.	millimetres

Similarly we can change metres to decametres, hectometres and kilometres by moving the number through the decimal point in the opposite direction, for we shall have fewer of these bigger units. Thus

	1725.634	metres
becomes	172.5634	decametres or
	17.25634	hectametres or
	1.725634	kilometres

Example 7.1. Change 45 grams to (a) milligrams (b) decigrams.

(a) 45 grams can be written 45.000 000 (as many 0's as we like). There are 1000 mg in a gram, so we shall need to move the number three places to the left through the decimal point. This gives us 45 000.000 mg.

Ans. = 45 000 mg

(b) 45 grams can be written 45.000 000, etc. There are 10 dg in 1 g, so we need to move the number one place to the left through the decimal point. This gives us 450 dg.

Ans. = 450 dg

Example 7.2. Change 27.56 metres to (a) km and (b) dam.

(a) Kilometres are 1000 times larger than metres so 27.56 metres will not even be 1 kilometre—it must be a fraction of a kilometre. We need to move the number through the decimal point three places to the right. Any spaces which result must be filled by zeros. So

$$27.56 \text{ m} = 0.027\ 56 \text{ km}$$

Note: There are no whole kilometres, no tenths of kilometres (hectometres), 2 hundredths of a kilometre (decametres), etc.

$$\text{Ans.} = 0.027\ 56 \text{ km}$$

(b) A decametre is 10 times as big as a metre so we shall need to move the number through the decimal point one place to the right. There will be fewer decametres than metres, so

$$27.56 \text{ m} = 2.756 \text{ dam}$$

7.3   Exercises: Manipulation of Metric Units

1. Change each of the following metric measurements to (i) metres and (ii) millimetres:

(a) 27.5 km	(b) 312.2 km
(c) 1.465 km	(d) 2.735 km
(e) 4.6 dam	(f) 3.857 dam
(g) 7.2 cm	(h) 8.5 cm
(i) 4.956 hm	(j) 38.725 hm

2. Change each of the following weights in kilograms to (i) grams and (ii) milligrams:

(a) 7.5 kg	(b) 8.6 kg
(c) 27.545 kg	(d) 326.55 kg
(e) 425.5 kg	(f) 872.55 kg

Change the following measurements in metric tonnes to (i) kilograms (ii) grams. (*Note:* Since tonne and ton are written differently the metric measure is not likely to be confused with the old Imperial ton—see Chapter 8. When speaking it is necessary to use the term 'metric tonne' to distinguish the two measures.)

(g) 7.5 tonnes	(h) 18.4 tonnes
(i) 250 tonnes	(j) 149.25 tonnes

3. Change each of the following measures of capacity to (i) litres (ii) millilitres:

(a) 5.7 kilolitres	(b) 4.3 kilolitres
(c) 7.8 hectolitres	(d) 4.9 hectolitres
(e) 275 centilitres	(f) 3856 centilitres
(g) 42.5 decalitres	(h) 175.5 decalitres
(i) 1250 kilolitres	(j) 875 kilolitres

7.4   Metric Units in Business Calculations

The change to the metric system has been made because metric calculations are so much easier than calculations using the old Imperial units. For example the Imperial table of weight makes use of 16 ounces to one pound, 14 pounds to one stone, two stones to one quarter, four quarters to one hundredweight and 20 hundredweights to one ton. How much simpler it is to use the metric system which is a decimal system: compare the metric tables in this chapter with the tables in Imperial units in Chapter 8.

Some examples of calculations using metric units are given below. Problems in business calculations are usually fairly simple, but as in real life we can only sort out a problem if we consider the facts presented to us, think carefully and then decide what to do.

Example 7.3. A continental representative travels around his sales area in a particular month and records the following distances, in kilometres:

Week	Distance
1–7	742
8–14	856
15–21	1232
22–28	1175
29–30	237

His travel allowance is 14.5 pence per kilometre. What will he charge his firm for the month's travelling?

$$
\begin{array}{rr}
 & 742 \\
 & 856 \\
 & 1232 \\
 & 1175 \\
+ & 237 \\
\hline
\end{array}
$$

Total distance   4242 km

$$
\begin{array}{r}
4\,242 \\
\times\ 145 \\
\hline
21\,210 \\
169\,680 \\
424\,200 \\
\hline
615\,09.0 \text{ pence} \\
\hline
\end{array}
$$

$$= £615.09$$

Total charge for travelling $= £615.09$

Example 7.4. Currants, sultanas, raisins and dried peel are pur-chased in sacks each of which holds 50 kg. They are mixed to form 'mixed fruit', with three sacks of currants and two of sultanas to one sack of each of the others. The resulting mixture is made up into packets. Small packets contain 125 grams, large packets 250 grams. If there are 800 large packets, how many small packets are made up?

$$
\begin{aligned}
\text{Total mixture} &= 7 \times 50 \text{ kg} \\
&= 350 \text{ kg} \\
800 \text{ large packets} &= 800 \times 250 \text{ g} \\
&= 200\,000 \text{ g} \\
&= 200 \text{ kg (used to make the large packets)}
\end{aligned}
$$

Weight of fruit still available

$$
\begin{aligned}
&350 \text{ kg} \\
-\ &200 \text{ kg} \\
\hline
&150 \text{ kg}
\end{aligned}
$$

$$
\begin{aligned}
\text{Number of small packets made up} &= 150 \text{ kg} \div 125 \text{ g} \\
\text{Turning both to grams} &= 150\,000 \div 125 \\
&= 1200 \text{ small packets}
\end{aligned}
$$

7.5 Exercises: Problems Involving Metric Weights and Measures

1. An aircraft flies the following journeys in a particular week: 7 return trips to Athens, 3 return trips to Majorca and 3 return trips to Madeira. If its home airport is 2420 kilometres from Athens, 2200 kilometres from Madeira and 1350 kilometres from Majorca, what will its fuel bill be for the week, at 13.5 pence per kilometre?

2. A garage sells petrol in litres. Its stocks on a particular day start at 12 800 litres and a tanker delivers 25 000 litres at 11 am and a further 18 000 litres at 3 pm. During the day supplies are purchased as follows: 84 drivers take 5 litres each, 276 drivers take 10 litres each, 584 drivers take 15 litres each and 362 take 20 litres each. How much petrol was still avail-able at the end of the day and what were the total petrol takings for the day at 31 pence per litre?

3. $2\frac{1}{2}$ tonnes of sugar are made up into three types of packets containing 1 kg, $\frac{1}{2}$ kg and 250 g respectively. There are 5000 of the smallest packets and 800 packets containing 1 kg. How many are there of the middle-sized packets?

4. How many packets of tea can be made up from a blend of three varieties if each packet is to contain 125 g? The quantities in the mixture are 1.5 tonnes of variety A, 1.2 tonnes of variety B and 350 kg of variety C.

5. A supermarket retails potatoes in polythene bags holding either 2½ kg or 5 kg. A farmer delivers a truckload holding 38 tonnes. Staff bag up 5000 of the small bags and the rest are put in 5 kg bags. How many of these were there?

6. 25.5 litres of an antibiotic preparation are used to make up ampoules containing 5 ml each. How many of these doses will be prepared?

7. A wine vat holds 8000 litres; 800 bottles each holding 2½ litres are filled from the vat, and the rest is bottled in half-litre bottles, except for the last 75 litres which is cloudy and is discarded as lees. How many half-litre bottles are filled?

8. A famine relief organisation sends flour to four towns as follows: Town A 220 sacks; Town B 335 sacks; Town C 125 sacks; Town D 280 sacks. A further 860 sacks are held in reserve for a later distribution. If all sacks hold 50 kg what weight of supplies in tonnes was received from Head Office?

9. A biscuit factory receives sugar in bulk deliveries by road tanker. Each load is of 35 tonnes and in a particular month five deliveries are received. The factory also agrees to take a part-load of 20 tonnes sent COD to a factory in the area and refused by them. The charge is based on a flat rate of £18.50 per 100 kg. What is the total cost for the month?

10. Butter is sold by a leading chain store in packets of 500 g and 250 g. Sales in a particular week total 1284 of the larger packs and 4726 of the smaller packs. What is the total weight of butter used?

7.6   Aids to Mental Arithmetic

Multiplication by 25, 125 and 250. It is often necessary to manipulate the numbers 25, 125 and 250, especially now that the metric system is part of our everyday lives. Let us deal with each in turn.

Multiplying by 25
  The point here is that $4 \times 25 = 100$ so that every 4 twenty-fives that we have makes 100. Thus

$$4 \times 25 = 100$$
$$5 \times 25 = 125$$

What would 17×25 amount to?
  There are 4 fours in 17 ($4 \times 4 = 16$ and 1 over), so

$$17 \times 25 = 400 \text{ and 1 more } 25$$
$$= 425$$

Another way to arrive at the same answer is to multiply the number by 100 and divide by four:

Thus:
$$17 \times 25 = 17 \times \frac{100}{4} = 1700 \div 4$$
$$= 425$$

This is a very easy way to do even a difficult calculation:

$$2736 \times 25$$
$$= 273\ 600 \div 4 \qquad \text{(Multiply by 100 and}$$
$$= 68\ 400 \qquad\qquad\qquad \text{divide by 4)}$$

Note that the quick way to multiply by 100 is to add two 0's to the number:

$$4763 \times 25$$
$$= 476\ 300 \div 4 \qquad \text{(Add two 0's and divide}$$
$$= 119\ 075 \qquad\qquad\qquad \text{by 4)}$$

Multiplying by 125

The point here is that $8 \times 125 = 1000$. Therefore to multiply by 125 we can multiply by 1000 and divide by 8. Multiplying by 1000 means we must add three 0's:

$$2784 \times 125$$
$$= 2\ 784\ 000 \div 8 \qquad \text{(Add three 0's and}$$
$$= 348\ 000 \qquad\qquad\qquad \text{divide by 8)}$$

$$4795 \times 125$$
$$= 4\ 795\ 000 \div 8$$
$$= 599\ 375$$

Multiplying by 250

The reader will see at once that this is very similar to multiplying by 25, but this time we must say $4 \times 250 = 1000$. To multiply by 250 multiply by 1000 (add three 0's) and divide by 4:

$$427 \times 250$$
$$= 427\ 000 \div 4$$
$$= 106\ 750$$

7.7   Exercises: Mental Arithmetic

1. Multiply each of these numbers by 25:

   (a) 36   (b) 45
   (c) 98   (d) 126
   (e) 142   (f) 780

2. Multiply each of these numbers by 125:

   (a) 27   (b) 56
   (c) 149   (d) 185
   (e) 278   (f) 384

3. Multiply each of these numbers by 250:

   (a) 17   (b) 25
   (c) 385   (d) 492
   (e) 861   (f) 7384

7.8   Mental Arithmetic Test

Write down *the answers only* to these questions:

1. $127 \times 9 =$

2. Write 31 in Roman figures

3. Divide 399 by 19

4. Add up 2.5 kg 3.6 kg and 250 g and give your answer in kilograms.

5. Divide 5.5 by 0.22

6. $\frac{1}{3} + \frac{3}{5} + \frac{7}{15} =$

7. $\frac{3}{4} \times \frac{4}{5} =$

8. What must I pay for 7 articles at 23 pence each?

9. $\frac{3}{4} \div \frac{1}{2} =$

10. How many grams in a kilogram?

11. $36 \times 25 =$

12. How many millimetres in a kilometre?

13. How many 250 g packets of tea can be made up from 25 kg?

14. $48 \times 125 =$

15. What year is written MCMXXXIX in Roman numbers?

8
Imperial Weights and Measures

8.1 The Change to Metric Units

The system of weights and measures called 'Imperial Weights and Measures' grew up in the Middle Ages when international trade was concerned chiefly with luxury items and it was not necessary to have international standard units. Today the situation is very different and almost all countries have adopted metric units, the SI units described in Chapter 7. The tables of Imperial Weights and Measures given below are hardly worth learning by heart today, despite some conservative use of the old units by a few trades. These vestiges of an outmoded era are likely to be swept away in the 1980s, and certainly before the turn of the century.

There is little point today in converting Imperial measures into metric measures—the only sensible thing is to think metric all the time. There are certain major links between the units which enable us to convert one unit into another—for example, yards into metres—but it is an activity which should become less and less necessary in the years ahead.

8.2 The Imperial Table of Length

12 inches	= 1 foot
3 feet	= 1 yard
22 yards	= 1 chain
10 chains	= 1 furlong
8 furlongs	= 1 mile
3 miles	= 1 league

Useful links to the metric system

1 metre	= 39.37 inches
8 kilometres	= 5 miles (approximately)

8.3   The Imperial Table of Weight

16 ounces	= 1 pound (lb)
14 pounds	= 1 stone
2 stones	= 1 quarter
4 quarters	= 1 hundredweight (cwt)
20 cwts	= 1 ton

Useful link to the metric system

1 kg   = 2.2 pounds (actually 2.205 pounds)

8.4   The Imperial Table of Capacity

4 gills	= 1 pint
2 pints	= 1 quart
4 quarts	= 1 gallon
2 gallons	= 1 peck
4 pecks	= 1 bushel
8 bushels	= 1 quarter

Useful link to the metric system

1 litre   = 1.76 pints

8.5   The Table of Time

The only group of measures common to the two systems is the table of time and the calendar. These tables are of course astronomical in nature, and related to the rotation of the earth and the passage of the earth around the sun. Clearly even the French Revolution could not have much impact on the movements of the heavenly bodies.

60 seconds	= 1 minute
60 minutes	= 1 hour
24 hours	= 1 day
7 days	= 1 week
4 weeks	= 1 month (Approximately)
365 days	= 1 year
366 days	= 1 leap year

To tell if a year is a leap year divide the last two numbers by 4. If it divides exactly it will be a leap year. Thus 1984: 84 divides by 4 and is therefore a leap year.

The last year in a century, like 1900, is not a leap year unless the number of hundreds divides by 4. So the year A.D. 2000 will be a leap year, because 20 divides by 4.

These rules come from the Gregorian Calendar (named after Pope Gregory XIII, who revised the Julian Calendar, introduced by Julius Caesar).

8.6   The Calendar: The Table of Months

> 30 days hath September,
> April, June and November,
> All the rest have 31,
> Excepting February all alone,
> Which has but 28 days clear,
> And 29 in each leap year.

8.7   Exercises: Inclusive Days

When we calculate the number of days between two dates it is possible to arrive at different answers according to whether the days at either end of the period are to be included or not. Thus if a businessman arrives at an hotel on Wednesday and leaves on Friday, has he spent three days at the hotel or only two? Most hotels work on the basis that rooms are available from 12 noon on the day of arrival until 12 noon on the day of departure. Thus a traveller arriving at 5 pm on Wednesday to stay two nights will occupy the room on Wednesday night and Thursday night but would leave on the morning of Friday.

The term **'inclusive'** implies that both days at the start and the end of the period are to be counted so that a visiting executive who 'will be available from 7th to the 10th July inclusive' implies that he/she will be available on the 7th, 8th, 9th and 10th July. This is four days not three. The calculation is

$$(10 - 7) + 1 = 3 + 1 = 4 \text{ days}$$

Example 8.1. How many days from 4th July to 27th July inclusive?

$$(27 - 4) + 1 = 24 \text{ days}$$

Example 8.2. How many days from 21st September to 4th November inclusive?

$$
\begin{aligned}
\text{Days in November} &= \ \ 4 \\
\text{Days in October} &= 31 \\
\text{Days in September} & \\
= (30 - 21) + 1 &= 10 \\
\hline
45 \text{ days} &
\end{aligned}
$$

8.8   Mental Arithmetic Test

1. How many days from 24th June to 6th July inclusive?
2. $36 + 47 + 235 + 89 =$
3. How many days from 4th November to 20th December inclusive?
4. $1\frac{1}{2} \times 2\frac{1}{2} =$
5. $0.75 \times 0.2 =$
6. How many days from 23rd March to 5th June inclusive?
7. Was 1973 a leap year?
8. Was 1976 a leap year?
9. Add up 2.14 m + 3.825 m =
10. $2173 \times 12 =$
11. Was the year 1900 a leap year?
12. Write 19 in Roman figures
13. Will the year A.D. 2000 be a leap year?
14. $2\frac{2}{3} \div \frac{3}{5} =$
15. How many seconds in one hour?

9
Simple Ratios

9.1 What is a Ratio?

A ratio is a relationship between two quantities which helps us to compare them. We are all familiar in everyday life with such terms as 2:1 (as two is to one) or 3:1 (as three is to one) or 4:1 (as four is to one) used to describe such relationships. Thus the sales of 'Junior' models and 'Senior' models of an appliance might be in the ratio of 2:1, meaning that for every two 'Junior' models sold one 'Senior' model is sold. Similarly, we compare speeds of vehicles in this way. If two cars are travelling at speeds of 80 km per hour and 40 km per hour their speeds are in the ratio of 80:40. This is an inconvenient ratio, because it is not as simple as it could be, and it is usual to express ratios (rather like fractions) in their lowest terms. Thus

$$
\begin{array}{ll}
80:40 & \\
8:4 & \text{(dividing both sides by 10)} \\
2:1 & \text{(dividing both sides by 4)}
\end{array}
$$

is the same as
and

The cars' speeds, when expressed in their lowest terms, are therefore in the ratio of 2:1.

Example 9.1. Two buses are travelling at average speeds of 30 km per hour and 75 km per hour respectively. What is the ratio of the speeds? A ratio has to do with numbers, but before the numbers can be used they must refer to the same units. In this case they both refer to kilometres, so the ratio is

$$
\begin{array}{ll}
30:75 & \\
= \ 6:15 & \text{(cancelling by 5)} \\
= \ 2:5 & \text{(cancelling by 3)}
\end{array}
$$

Note that the units used (in this case kilometres) also cancel out from the ratio, since they appear on both sides, and leave us with an answer in numerical terms only.

It is sufficient in many cases to come down to some simple ratio of whole numbers since such a ratio is easily understood. For greater precision we can continue to divide out until one side of the ratio is 1, with the result that the other side will include a fractional part.

Continuing Example 9.1 to this point, we have

$$2:5$$
$$= 1:2.5 \qquad \text{(dividing both sides by 2)}$$

For every kilometre the first bus travels the second bus travels 2.5 km.

If a ratio does not work out exactly it is necessary to do the calculation correct to a certain number of decimal places. Usually one decimal place will be sufficient, because the comparison between the two sets of facts is generally not improved very much by further decimal places.

Example 9.2. Two aircraft fly at speeds of 600 kilometres per hour and 700 kilometres per hour. What is the ratio of their speeds?

$$600 \text{ km}:700 \text{ km}$$
$$= 600:700$$
$$= \quad 6:7$$
$$= \quad 1:1.166\ 66$$
$$= \quad 1:1.2 \quad \text{(Correct to one decimal place)}$$

Example 9.3. What is the ratio between 25 metres and 5 kilometres?

Here we must note that a ratio cannot be cancelled down unless both parts of the ratio are in the same terms. Thus we require the ratio between 25 metres and 5000 metres.

$$25 \text{ m}:5 \text{ km}$$
$$= 25 \text{ m}:5\ 000 \text{ m} \qquad \text{(changing the km to m)}$$
$$= \quad 1:200 \qquad \text{(dividing both sides by 25)}$$

9.2   Exercises: Simple Ratios

1. Express the following ratios as simply as possible:
   (a) £25 to £100   (b) £16 to £64
   (c) 300 m to 6 m   (d) 72 m to 3.6 m
   (e) 25 km/h to 80 km/h   (f) 100 km/h to $12\frac{1}{2}$ km/h

(g) 20 seconds to 45 seconds   (h) 550 kg to 800 kg
(i) £720 to £2160   (j) £6 000 000 to £45 000 000

2. Express the following ratios in as simple a form as possible. Remember that before items can be compared they must both be in the same units. If necessary give the answers correct to two decimal places.

(a) 45 seconds to 1 minute 30 seconds   (b) 6 hours to 3 days
(c) 50 pence to £100   (d) 500 m to 7 km
(e) 24 kilograms to 84 tonnes   (f) 19 metres to 27 decametres
(g) 5 millilitres to 2½ litres   (h) 30 minutes to 2 days
(i) 500 grams to 1 tonne   (j) 24 mm to 25 m

3. In the following questions give the answer correct to two decimal places where necessary.

(a) A railway charges £27 first-class fare from A to B. The corresponding second-class fare is £22.50. What is the ratio between the fares?

(b) A salesman's basic wage is £45 and he also receives commission of £32.50. What is the ratio of his basic wage to his total earnings?

(c) An electronic calculator is priced at £17.50 and an electronic printing calculator at £37.50. What is the ratio of their prices?

(d) A typist earns £64 per week, but must pay £10.50 tax and £2.30 national insurance. What is the ratio between her total deductions and her total earnings?

(e) Two telescopes are priced at £10.50 and £36.75. What is the ratio of their prices?

4. In the following questions give the answer correct to two decimal places where necessary:

(a) Two new cars are priced at £6750 and £3500 respectively. One year later they are valued at £4500 and £2750 respectively. What is the ratio of their prices (i) when new (ii) one year after manufacture?

(b) Two artists each sell a picture. One charges £150, the other £250. Fifty years later the first picture is auctioned for £28 000, the second for £14 500. What is the ratio of the prices of the pictures (i) when both are new (ii) when both are 50 years old?

(c) (i) What is the ratio between the length of the River Congo (4600 km) and the length of the River Nile (6600 km)? (ii) What is the ratio between the height of Mount Everest (8850 m) and the height of Mount Popocatapetl (5450 m)?

(d) A child sleeps 10½ hours per day. What is the ratio between the time spent sleeping and the time the child is awake?

9.3 Proportional Parts

In some business situations arrangements are made to share things out in some agreed simple proportions, such as ½ and ½, or ⅔ and ⅓, or ¾ and ¼. Thus profits might be shared among three partners in the ratio 3:2:1. The youngest partner perhaps is to receive one share of the profits, the next partner two shares and the oldest and most experienced partner will receive three shares. Thus there will be six shares in all. One partner will take $\frac{1}{6}$ of the profits, the next $\frac{2}{6} = \frac{1}{3}$ of the profits and the third partner $\frac{3}{6} = \frac{1}{2}$ of the profits.

Suppose an inheritance of £24 000 is to be shared between three sons in the ratio 2:2:1. The son entitled to one share died the previous year and the will says that in the event of the prior death of one of the sons, his share shall be divided equally among any of his children, of either sex. The son in question had three children, two boys and a girl.

Now there were originally 5 shares (2 + 2 + 1)

$$£24 000 \div 5 = £4800$$

Therefore the money is shared £9600:£9600:£4800.

The third son's share £4800 is to be divided equally among the three grandchildren:

$$£4800 \div 3$$
$$= £1600 \text{ each}$$

Example 9.4. Share the sum of £2400 in the proportions 3:2.
  3:2 means there will be 5 shares

$$\text{Each share} = £2400 \div 5$$
$$= £480$$

The two amounts are therefore £1440 and £960.

Example 9.5. Profits are shared between three partners A, B and C in the following way: the youngest partner A is paid a salary of £1500 and then takes 1 share of the profits; the next partner B takes 3 shares; and the third partner 4 shares. What will each partner receive out of profits of £30 500?

$$\text{Sum to be shared after payment of salary} = £30 500 - £1500$$
$$= £29 000$$

Shared 1:3:4: there are 8 shares:

$$\text{Each share} = £29 000 \div 8$$
$$= £3625$$
$$\text{A's share} = £3625 + £1500$$
$$= £5125$$

$$\text{B's share} = £3625 \times 3$$
$$= £10 875$$

$$\begin{aligned} \text{C's share} &= £3625 \times 4 \\ &= £14\,500 \end{aligned}$$

(Check: £5125 + £10 875 + £14 500 = £30 500)

Example 9.5. An inheritance of £24 500 is shared among three daughters so that Janet has twice as much as Jill who has twice as much as Jean. How much does each receive?

Give the person receiving least 1 share

Jean has 1 share
Jill has 2 shares (twice as much as Jean)
Janet has 4 shares (twice as much as Jill)

There are 7 shares in all:

$$\begin{aligned} \text{Each share} &= £24\,500 \div 7 \\ &= £3500 \end{aligned}$$

Jean has   £3500

Jill has   £7000

Janet has £14 000

(Check: Total = £24 500)

9.4 Exercises: Sharing in Proportional Parts

1. Share the following sums of money in the proportions given below:

   (a) £1400 in the proportions 3:1
   (b) £2825 in the proportions 3:2
   (c) £7350 in the proportions 5:3:2
   (d) £28 280 in the proportions 4:2:1
   (e) £75 000 in the proportions 4:3:1

2. Share the following profits in the proportions shown:

   (a) A, B and C share £27 500 in the proportions 4:4:3
   (b) X, Y and Z share £36 600 in the proportions 3:3:2
   (c) R, S, T and U share £24 615 in the proportions 3:3:2:1
   (d) G, H and J share £24 600 in the proportions 5:4:3
   (e) M, N, O, P and Q share £40 784 in the proportions 4:4:3:3:2

3. A chemical is to be used in two preparations. For every four parts going into mixture A three will go into mixture B. There are 20 barrels of the chemical each holding 245 litres. How much will go into mixture A?

4. A collection of £2740 is shared between three charities in such a way that Charity A receives twice as much as Charity B which receives three times as much as Charity C. How much does each receive?

5. A consignment of gold bars is packed into three boxes in the proportions 6:5:4. If the total weight of gold is 1.05 tonnes how much is packed in each box?

6. A legacy of £15 000 is shared so that Tom has three times as much as George and half as much again as Robert. How much does each receive?

7. Five porters are given loads on a Himalayan expedition, in the proportions 6:6:5:5:4. If the weakest man carries 20 kilograms how much does each carry and what was the total load?

8. The fuel consumption of two vehicles is in the ratio 5:3. The more expensive vehicle uses 65 litres of petrol on a journey. How much does the petrol for the other car cost on the same journey at 32 pence per litre?

9.5   Simple Unitary Method

Many business calculations are concerned with simple proportion sums, and involve a direct variation in the quantities concerned. For example, if three standards of timber cost £540 what will eight standards cost? If the price is to be at the same rate per standard it is clear that eight standards will cost more than three standards, in **direct proportion** or **direct variation**. A useful rule here is to work all such calculations as a three-line sum, with the second line devoted to the cost of one unit. This gives the method its name, unitary method.

Line 1: State what you know with the quantity to be found (cost) at the end.

Line 2: State how to find the cost of one unit.

Line 3: Now state how to find the required result. The calculation is not done until line 3 has been completed.

Example 9.6. In the example mentioned above we have

Line 1: 3 standards cost £540

Line 2: 1 standard costs $\dfrac{£540}{3}$

Line 3: 8 standards cost $\dfrac{£540}{3} \times 8$

$$= £180 \times 8$$
$$= £1440$$

Example 9.7. A hotel charges £88 for a visitor who stays five days. What will it charge at the same rate for a 9 day visit?

$$5 \text{ days cost } £88$$

$$1 \text{ day costs } \frac{£88}{5}$$

$$9 \text{ days cost } \frac{£88}{5} \times 9$$

$$= \frac{£792}{5}$$

$$= £158.40$$

Our 'unit' need not actually be one item, as is shown in Examples 9.8 and 9.9 below:

Example 9.8. 200 cigarettes cost £6.50. What will 500 cost?

$$200 \text{ cigarettes cost } £6.50$$

$$100 \text{ cigarettes cost } \frac{£6.50}{2}$$

$$500 \text{ cigarettes cost } \frac{£6.50}{2} \times 5$$

$$= £16.25$$

The 'unit' chosen for the calculation was 100 cigarettes.

Example 9.9. A hotel charges £185 for a 10-day stay. What will it charge, at the same rate, for 15 days?
  Here the most sensible unit is not 1 day but 5 days.

$$10 \text{ days cost } £185$$

$$5 \text{ days cost } \frac{£185}{1}$$

$$15 \text{ days cost } \frac{£185}{2} \times 3$$

$$= \frac{£555}{2}$$

$$= £277.50$$

Note: The reason why 5 is the most sensible unit is that 5 will divide into both 10 and 15. There is therefore no need to go down to 1 day, we can go down to 5 days and then up to 15 days.

9.6   Exercises: Unitary Method Calculations

1. Write down the answers to these simple proportion sums. They can be worked out mentally without setting down on paper.

(a) 5 buns cost 10p. What will 7 buns cost?
(b) 2 cost 6p. How much for 3?
(c) 8 cost £1.20. How much for 5?
(d) 4 cost £20. How much for 7?
(e) 6 cost £36. How much for 5?

2. Write down, without any written calculation, the answers to these simple proportion sums:

(a) 15 cost £30. How much for 20?
(b) 8 cost £6. How much for 12?
(c) 9 cost £15. How much for 15?
(d) 6 cost £16. How much for 9?
(e) 8 cost £20. How much for 10?

3. Here are ten calculations which can be solved using the unitary method. Set each of them down as a three-line calculation.

(a) A railway journey of 75 km costs £9.00. What will a journey of 108 km cost at the same rate?

(b) A flight to Gibraltar (1800 km) costs £68.10. What will a flight to Athens (2400 km) at the same rate cost?

(c) 5 typewriters cost £3280. What will 27 cost at the same rate?

(d) A college budget officer is offered 25 typist's chairs for £650. What will he pay at the same rate for 80 chairs, if a major expansion of secretarial schemes is proposed in an alternative budget?

(e) 25 motor vehicles cost £71 250 altogether. What will a fleet of 33 similar vehicles cost, at the same rate?

(f) A telephone answering machine has a rental charge of £182 per year. At the same rate what will it cost to hire one for a nine-week period? (Take a year as 52 weeks.)

(g) A ship is charged £27 505.50 for an 11-day stay in a major port. What will it be charged for 17 days at the same rate?

(h) A firm orders three automatic binding machines for £27 564. What will it cost to equip a new works with eight such machines at the same rate?

(i) A group plays 8 tunes in a 37-minute spot on local radio. How long at the same rate would a programme of 14 tunes last?

(j) A vehicle covers 160 km on 30 litres of fuel. How far would it go on 42 litres at the same rate of fuel consumption?

9.7   Inverse Variation

Some calculations involve the opposite of direct proportion, the variation that occurs being an inverse one. Thus suppose three men can do a certain job in 12 days, it is clear that one man on his own would take longer, not less time. Eight men would take less time, not more. We therefore have calculations which are very similar to the 'direct proportion' sums of the unitary method described above, but where 'inverse variation' occurs.

Setting down the example given above, we have to find the answer to the question 'How long would eight men take?'.

Example 9.10

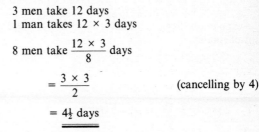

3 men take 12 days

1 man takes 12 × 3 days

8 men take $\dfrac{12 \times 3}{8}$ days

$= \dfrac{3 \times 3}{2}$ (cancelling by 4)

$= 4\frac{1}{2}$ days

Example 9.11. A grower packs 30 boxes with peaches at 18 to the box. How many boxes would be needed if only 12 were packed to the box?

With 18 in a box 30 boxes are required

With 1 in a box 30 × 18 boxes are required

With 12 in a box $\dfrac{30 \times 18}{12}$ are required

$= 15 \times 3$ (cancelling by 2 and by 6)

$= 45$ boxes

9.8 Exercises on Inverse Variation

1. Write down the answers only to the following questions. Assume that the rates are uniform in each case.

(a) 4 men can dig a trench in 3 days. How long will it take 6 men?

(b) 7 painters can paint a college in 6 weeks. How long will it take 12 painters?

(c) A hopper of animal feed will last 42 cows for 5 days. How long will it last 30 cows?

(d) A holidaymaker has enough money to last 7 days at £15 per day. How long will it last at £21 per day?

(e) If 6 cakes are packed in a carton 10 cartons are required. How many cartons will be needed if 4 cakes are packed in each?

2. Set down a calculation for each of the following sums. Assume that the rates are uniform in each case.

(a) 8 men can repair a road in 42 days. How long will 14 men take?

(b) A florist makes up 102 bunches of flowers with 10 flowers to a bunch. How many bunches would have been made if there had been 12 flowers in a bunch?

(c) At an open-cast mine 6 excavators extract 258 000 tonnes in a 10-week period. How long would 8 excavators have taken for the same tonnage?

(d) Six hoses empty a static water tank in a fire hazard zone in 36 minutes. How long would it have taken 4 hoses to empty it?

(e) An expedition plans to spend £18 a day for the 126 days' duration of the expedition. In fact, the costs come to £21 per day. When will they run out of funds?

9.9   Exercises: Posts and Fences

When fences are erected the panels today are usually 2 metres wide, and the posts to which the panels are fixed are 1 decimetre square. It is necessary in a straight line of fencing to have one more post than panel, as illustrated below:

post PANEL post PANEL post PANEL post

Thus three panels require four posts.

This is not the case when an area of land is completely enclosed because the last panel comes back onto the first post. Thus a square enclosed with three panels on each side would need 12 panels, and only 12 posts. (Students who find this difficult to follow should draw a diagram and prove to themselves that it is correct.)

Now try the following mental questions. You may use scrap paper for remembering part answers.

1. (a) A fence along one side of a garden needs 5 panels at £4 each. The posts are £2 each and labour costs £8. What is the total cost?

(b) A fence along one side of an orchard needs 40 panels of fencing. The panels are £3 and the posts are £2 each. What is the total cost, if labour charges are £25?

(c) A school yard has a fence erected across the front of the school in a straight line. There are 12 panels at £5 each and posts are £3. A suggestion by the contractor that one panel should be replaced by a gate costing £15 is accepted. Labour costs are £20. What is the total cost?

(d) A pig pen is 8 metres square. It is completely enclosed by two-metre concrete panels at £10 each, except for one panel which is replaced by a gate at £20. Posts are £5 each, and labour costs £50. Ignore the thickness of the posts. What is the total cost?

(e) A playground is 40 m square. What will it cost to fence it in with 2 m panels at £5 each and posts at £2 each? Labour is £100, the gateway which replaces one of the panels costs £10.

9.10   Mental Arithmetic Test

Write down *the answers only* to these questions:

 1. 25 + 79 + 123 + 495 =

 2. £385.65 + £72.56 + £195.80 =

 3. £4500 × 600 =

 4. £1725 ÷ 5 =

 5. How many centimetres in 25.5 metres?

 6. $\frac{1}{2} + \frac{1}{3} + 1\frac{1}{2} =$

 7. How many days are there in 21 weeks?

 8. Share £100 between Mary and John so that Mary has three times as much as John

 9. A telephone call costs 4 pence for 10 seconds. What will it cost for 3 minutes?

10. 5 buns cost 35 pence. What will 12 cost?

11. 6 men take 3 days to dig a trench. How long will 4 men take at the same rate?

12. How many days from July 4th to August 14th inclusive?

13. Change $4\frac{1}{2}$ hours to minutes

14. Write 75 in Roman figures

15. A straight fence has 6 panels each costing £5 and posts which cost £2 each. What is the total cost if the labour charge was £10?

10
Percentages

10.1 Introduction

The word 'percentage' means 'out of 100'. A percentage is a convenient way to represent many figures. For example, to say that there are $1\frac{1}{2}$ million unemployed is a rather fearsome statistic. To say that this figure is 5.9 per cent of the working population makes it at the same time both less appalling and easier to understand—though this is small consolation to the $1\frac{1}{2}$ million people involved.

The sign for a percentage is % (read as 'per cent'), so 40% = 40 per cent = 40 out of 100; 60% = 60 per cent = 60 out of every 100, etc.

There is a close link between percentages and the fractions and decimals we have already studied. Before considering the uses made of percentages in business life let us examine the links between percentages, fractions and decimals.

10.2 Converting Percentages to Fractions

Since a percentage is a special type of fraction (the denominator being 100 in every case) it is easy to write down a percentage as a fraction. For example, $45\% = \frac{45}{100}$, $10\% = \frac{10}{100}$, etc.

We usually do not consider a fraction to be as well expressed as possible until we have reduced it to its lowest terms. Both the examples given above will cancel down, so really we should continue the process of turning these percentages into fractions by cancelling them, as shown below:

$$45\% = \frac{45}{100} = \frac{9}{20} \qquad \text{(cancelling by 5)}$$

$$10\% = \frac{10}{100} = \frac{1}{10} \qquad \text{(cancelling by 10)}$$

Rule for writing a percentage as a fraction

(a) Write down the percentage as the numerator of the fraction.
(b) Draw a short line under it.
(c) Put 100 as the denominator of the fraction.
(d) Cancel it if you can.

Example 10.1. Change 95% to a fraction.

$$95\% = \frac{95}{100} = \frac{19}{20} \qquad \text{(cancelling by 5)}$$

Example 10.2. Change $6\frac{1}{4}\%$ to a fraction. Here it will be necessary to use our fraction rules to eliminate the quarter:

$$6\frac{1}{4}\% = \frac{6\frac{1}{4}}{100} = \frac{25}{100 \times 4} = \frac{25}{400} = \frac{1}{16} \text{ (cancelling by 25)}$$

Certain percentages are so commonly used that we should be aware of their values as fractions. The most important groups are:

$25\% = \frac{1}{4}$	$16\frac{2}{3}\% = \frac{1}{6}$	$20\% = \frac{1}{5}$
$50\% = \frac{1}{2}$	$33\frac{1}{3}\% = \frac{1}{3}$	$40\% = \frac{2}{5}$
$75\% = \frac{3}{4}$	$66\frac{2}{3}\% = \frac{2}{3}$	$60\% = \frac{3}{5}$
		$80\% = \frac{4}{5}$
$10\% = \frac{1}{10}$	$12\frac{1}{2}\% = \frac{1}{8}$	$5\% = \frac{1}{20}$
$30\% = \frac{3}{10}$	$37\frac{1}{2}\% = \frac{3}{8}$	$2\frac{1}{2}\% = \frac{1}{40}$
$70\% = \frac{7}{10}$	$62\frac{1}{2}\% = \frac{5}{8}$	$1\frac{1}{4}\% = \frac{1}{80}$
$90\% = \frac{9}{10}$	$87\frac{1}{2}\% = \frac{7}{8}$	

10.3 Converting Fractions to Percentages

Just as it is sometimes convenient to change percentages to fractions, it is also useful at times to turn fractions into percentages. For example, it is not easy to compare $\frac{3}{8}$ with $\frac{2}{5}$, but we can see from the tables of common percentages given above, as follows:

$$\frac{3}{8} = 37\frac{1}{2}\% \qquad \frac{2}{5} = 40\%$$

We can see at once that $\frac{2}{5}$ is slightly larger than $\frac{3}{8}$.

Rule for changing a fraction to a percentage

(a) Write down the fraction.
(b) Multiply it by $\frac{100}{1}$ and call it per cent.

(c) Cancel if you can.
(d) Complete the multiplication.

Example 10.3. Change $\frac{5}{8}$ to a percentage.

$$\frac{5}{8} = \frac{5}{\cancel{8}2} \times \frac{\cancel{100}^{25}}{1}\% \qquad \text{(cancelling by 4)}$$

$$= \frac{125}{2}$$

$$= 62\frac{1}{2}\%$$

10.4   Exercises: Percentages and Fractions

1. Write down the following fractions as percentages:

(a) $\frac{1}{2}$ (b) $\frac{1}{4}$ (c) $\frac{2}{3}$ (d) $\frac{7}{10}$ (e) $\frac{4}{5}$

2. Change the following fractions to percentages:

(a) $\frac{3}{8}$ (b) $\frac{7}{8}$ (c) $\frac{5}{16}$ (d) $\frac{3}{25}$ (e) $\frac{7}{12}$

3. Change the following percentages to fractions:

(a) 75%   (b) 35%   (c) 15%   (d) 42%   (e) 64%

4. Change the following percentages to fractions:

(a) $37\frac{1}{2}\%$ (b) $18\frac{3}{4}\%$ (c) $83\frac{1}{3}\%$ (d) $93\frac{3}{4}\%$ (e) $52\frac{1}{2}\%$

10.5   Converting Percentages to Decimals

Since 1% is $\frac{1}{100}$, or one hundredth, clearly in decimals it is 0.01. Similarly, 2% = 0.02 and 3% = 0.03, 27% is 0.27 and 49% is 0.49.

Clearly the rules for changing a percentage to a decimal are very simple. They are:

(i) Write down the percentage without the per cent sign.
(ii) If it is less than 10% put a 0 in front of it (since there are no tenths).
(iii) Put a decimal point in front of the percentage, or in front of the 0 if (ii) above applies.

Example 10.4. Change 7%, 14% and 98% to decimals.

(i) 7%: Write down the percentage without the sign   7
     If it is less than 10, put a 0 in front of it   07
     Put a decimal point in front of that   0.07

$$7\% = 0.07$$

(ii) 14%

$$14$$
$$14$$
$$14\% = 0.14$$

(iii) 98%

$$98$$
$$98$$
$$98\% = 0.98$$

Example 10.5. Change $27\frac{1}{2}\%$ to decimals. With a percentage that includes a fraction the fractional part must be changed to decimals. In this case $\frac{1}{2}$ of 1% is clearly 5 thousandths.

$$27\tfrac{1}{2}\% = 0.27\tfrac{1}{2} = 0.275$$

We could have looked at this another way and changed the $\frac{1}{2}$ to decimals first. Thus

$$27\tfrac{1}{2}\% = 27.5\%$$

Since 27.5% = 27.5 hundredths, it is 0.275 units; in other words, we must push the number through the decimal point two places in the usual way.

$$27.5\% = 0.275$$

Similarly $33\tfrac{1}{3}\% = 33.333\% = 0.33333$

$$= 0.\dot{3}$$

Example 10.6. If the percentage is greater than 100% (for example 150%, 230%, etc.) then the decimal point must be inserted to separate off the units from the decimal fraction: 100% = 1 whole unit, so the examples given above change to decimals as follows:

$$150\% = 1.50$$
$$230\% = 2.30$$

10.6 Converting Decimals to Percentages

The reverse of the process described above is equally easy. The decimal 0.25 is one quarter, which is 25%. Since a percentage tells us how many hundredths we have, all we need to do to change a decimal number to percentages is to read it off in hundredths. Thus

$$0.17 = 17\% \text{ (There are 17 hundredths)}$$
$$0.95 = 95\% \text{ (There are 95 hundredths)}$$

If the decimal number is larger than one it makes no difference. Thus a firm whose sales increase 1.5 times has experienced a 150% increase. Similarly

$$2.3 = 230\%$$
$$1.75 = 175\%$$
and $$1.555 = 155\tfrac{1}{2}\%$$

10.7   Exercises: Percentages and Decimals

1. Write down the following percentages as decimals:
   (a) 36%   (b) 42%   (c) 38½%   (d) 55½%   (e) 66⅔%
2. Change the following percentages to decimals:
   (a) 11½%   (b) 17¾%   (c) 87½%   (d) 33⅓%   (e) 180%
3. Change the following decimals to percentages:
   (a) 0.24   (b) 0.36   (c) 0.04   (d) 0.09   (e) 0.375
4. Change the following decimals to percentages:
   (a) 1.75   (b) 1.32   (c) 2.30   (d) 0.3025   (e) 0.4575

10.8   Calculating Percentages of Given Quantities

One of the commonest calculations in business life is the calculation of percentages of given quantities. Such routine calculations as 'What is 30% of 800 tons?' or 'What is 55% of £27 300?' are easily solved.

Rule for calculating a percentage of a given quantity

   (a) Write down the required percentage as a fraction, with 100 as the denominator.
   (b) Multiply this fraction by the full quantity given.
   (c) Cancel if you can.
   (d) Finally, multiply out.

Example 10.7. What is 30% of 800 tons?

$$30\% \text{ of } 800 \text{ tons}$$

$$= \frac{30}{1\cancel{0}\cancel{0}} \times 8\cancel{0}\cancel{0} \qquad \text{(cancelling by 100)}$$

$$= 240 \text{ tons}$$

Example 10.8. What is 55% of £27 300?

$$55\% \text{ of } £27\,300$$

$$= \frac{55}{1\cancel{00}} \times 27\,3\cancel{00} \qquad \text{(cancelling by 100)}$$

$$= 55 \times 273$$
$$= £15\,015$$

```
        273
         55
      _____
      1 365
     13 650
      _____
     15 015
      _____
```

10.9 Exercises: Percentages of Given Quantities

Calculate the following percentage parts:

1. 35% of £2800
2. 28% of £4200
3. 12½% of 3600 kg
4. 48% of 25 250 kg
5. 65% of 10 500 hectares
6. 88% of £19 250
7. 42% of 76 500 electors
8. 49% of £38 240
9. 82½% of 34 000 members
10. 62% of £7140

10.10 Discounts

One of the commonest uses of percentages is in the calculation of discounts. A discount is a reduction in the price of an article. The commonest types are trade discounts, cash discounts and settlement discounts, but they can also be used as a convenient way of offering customers special terms during a 'sale'.

Trade Discounts. Trade discount is offered by wholesalers to retailers who are in a particular trade. It represents the retailer's profit margin upon the article, which for convenience is referred to by its final retail price. Thus a publisher offering a textbook at a selling price of £4.50 to the final purchaser must offer the bookseller a supply at a cheaper price. To avoid difficulties in referring to the book at a range of prices, it is usual to offer a range of trade discounts. This might be 25%, 33⅓%, 45% or even 50% according to the size of the order placed. Thus for an order for 200 copies at a discount of 33⅓%, the invoice would read

	£
200 copies *Engineering for Today* at £4.50 =	900
Less 33⅓% trade discount	300
	£600

Cash Discounts. Cash discounts are offered as an inducement to the customer to pay in cash, thus reducing the risk of bad debts on a particular order. They are frequently 2½%, but 5% is not uncommon.

Settlement Discounts. These are offered to customers who are normally given a period of credit as an inducement to pay earlier rather than later. They are often called 'cash discounts', since they are very similar, and it is usual to specify the period within which discount is deductible. A typical statement might read

5% settlement discount cash 7 days, 2½% cash 30 days

The customer paying such a statement will adjust the total due by hand before writing out the cheque in settlement. Thus

	Total due	£600
Less 5% (cash 7 days)		30
Cheque herewith		£570

Example 10.9. A plumber orders a bath, sink unit and toilet suite from a wholesale builders' suppliers. The prices are £30, £24 and £48 respectively, less trade discount at 45%. What is the net price?

$$\text{Total price} = £30 + £24 + £48 = £102$$
$$\text{Discount} = 45\% \text{ of } £102$$
$$= \frac{45}{100} \times £102$$
$$= \frac{45^9}{100_{20}\,_{10}} \times £102^{51} \quad \text{(cancelling by 5 and 2)}$$
$$= \frac{£459}{10}$$
$$= £45.90$$
$$\text{Net Price} = £102 - £45.90$$
$$= £56.10$$

Example 10.10. A retailer pays a statement from a wholesaler after deducting 5% settlement discount. The amount of the debt shown on the statement was £429.50.

(a) What was the discount to the retailer (answer to the nearest penny)?

(b) What did the retailer actually pay?

(a) Discount = 5% of £429.50

$$= \frac{5}{100} \times £429.50$$

$$= \frac{£429.50}{20}$$

$$= £21.475$$

To the nearest penny this is £21.48

(b) The retailer therefore pays £429.50 − £21.48 = £408.02.

(*Note:* Remember that where a calculation works out exactly to $\frac{1}{2}$ the correction is done so as to make the desired figure an even number. Thus £21.475 = £21.48, but £21.465 would 'correct' to £21.46. In any set of numbers this evens out the error in the set to avoid bias.)

10.11   Exercises: Discounts

1. Calculate the following cash discounts (answers to the nearest penny):

(a) 5% of £30   (b) 5% of £185
(c) 5% of £125   (d) 5% of £2145
(e) 5% of £3875   (f) $2\frac{1}{2}$% of £80
(g) $2\frac{1}{2}$% of £120   (h) $2\frac{1}{2}$% of £75.60
(i) $2\frac{1}{2}$% of £125.60   (j) $2\frac{1}{2}$% of £2150

2. Calculate the following settlement discounts (answer to the nearest penny). In each case the discount is 5% cash 7 days or $2\frac{1}{2}$% cash 30 days. In each case the amount of the outstanding debts is given, and the time taken to pay.

(a) £50; 2 days   (b) £184; 27 days
(c) £62.50; 6 days   (d) £95.80; 4 days
(e) £133.64; 20 days   (f) £286.54; 24 days
(g) £1756.50; 1 day   (h) £1824.74; 5 days
(i) £726.50; 29 days   (j) £464.84; 28 days

3. Work out the total trade discount at 40% on the following goods supplied to a retailer:

24 'Speed-king' tricycles at £46.50 each
20 'Mobiltryke' tricycles at £18.50 each

4. Work out the trade discount offered in the following cases (answers to the nearest penny):

(a) $33\frac{1}{3}$% on £285   (b) 50% on £5750
(c) 40% on £550   (d) 30% on £364.50
(e) 25% on £49.65   (f) $33\frac{1}{3}$% on £726.50
(g) 45% on £2850   (h) 60% on £7250
(i) 15% on £4612.50   (j) 45% on £5184.50

10.12   One Quantity as a Percentage of Another

Frequently statistical calculations require us to state one quantity as a percentage of another. In examinations we compare the number of successful with the total number of candidates, to find the percentage who were successful. Similarly, a mailing to consumers might be evaluated on the basis of a percentage response. We might in the planning stages calculate certain percentage responses which we hoped to achieve from particular groups, and then when the responses begin to come in we can compare the actual response with the estimated response. In the latter case, to express the response received as a percentage of the mailing we proceed as shown below.

Rule for calculating one quantity as a percentage of another

(a) Write down the first quantity and rule a line under it.
(b) Write down the second quantity underneath the line (thus giving the first quantity as a fraction of the second).
(c) Multiply this fraction by 100, to make it a percentage.

Example 10.11. A mailing to 44 000 consumers is planned to achieve a 15% response. In fact 2560 responses are received. What was the planned objective, and what percentage was in fact achieved?

(a) Planned objective: 15% of 44 000

$$= \frac{15}{100} \times 44\,000$$

$$= 15 \times 440 \text{(cancelling by 100)}$$

$$= 6600$$

$$\begin{array}{r} 440 \\ 15 \\ \hline 2200 \\ 4400 \\ \hline 6600 \\ \hline \end{array}$$

(b) Actual response: 2560 replies
The fractional response is $\frac{2560}{44000}$
In percentage terms this is

$$\frac{2560}{44000} \times 100 \qquad \text{(cancelling by 1000 and} \atop \text{then by 4)}$$

$$= \frac{64}{11} \qquad \begin{array}{r} 5.81 \\ 11 \overline{\smash{)}\,64.00} \end{array}$$

Percentage achieved = 5.8%

10.13 Exercises: Calculating One Quantity as a Percentage of Another

Calculate the first quantity in the sums below, as a percentage of the second quantity (*answers where necessary correct to 2 decimal places*).

1. 250 as a percentage of 1750
2. 480 as a percentage of 3600
3. £520 as a percentage of £18 000
4. £960 as a percentage of £14 400
5. 360 kg as a percentage of 2 tonnes
6. 75 metres as a percentage of 5 kilometres
7. 245 Deutschmarks as a percentage of 5000 DM
8. 27 500 votes as a percentage of 75 000 electors
9. 41 500 votes as a percentage of 88 500 votes
10. 7860 replies as a result of 55 000 questionnaires

10.14 Mental Calculations: Multiplication of Decimals

It is important to be able to manipulate decimals mentally. We know that if we set down a multiplication of decimals sum the rules are:

(a) Ignore the decimal points at first; simply multiply the numbers.

(b) Fix the decimal point at the end by counting up the number of figures after the decimal points in both the multiplier and the multiplicand.

As a simple example, 0.2×0.4. Leaving out the noughts for the moment to show the fractions clearly, we have $.2 \times .4$. Ignoring the decimal points we have $2 \times 4 = 8$.

Counting up the figures after the decimal point in both the multiplier .4 and the multiplicand (the number to be multiplied) .2 we have one figure after the decimal point, making two figures in all. There will therefore be two figures after the decimal point in the answer. That means that the answer is not 8 but .08.

So $.2 \times .4 = .08$

Note: .08 is of course smaller than both .2 and .4. We would expect this because when we multiply proper fractions or decimal fractions we always get a smaller answer. For example

$$\frac{1}{2} \times \frac{1}{2} = \frac{1}{4}$$

$$\frac{1}{3} \times \frac{1}{3} = \frac{1}{9}$$

Or in this case $$\frac{2}{10} \times \frac{4}{10} = \frac{8}{100}$$

i.e. $.2 \times .4 = .08$
Similarly $.3 \times .3 = .09$
                                      $.4 \times .5 = .20 = .2$
                                      $.6 \times .6 = .36$
                                  $.08 \times .7 = .056$
                      $.03 \times .009 = .000\ 27$, etc.

10.15 Exercises: Multiplication of Decimals

1. Multiply the following mentally, and write down the answers:

(a) 0.3×0.1 (b) 0.4×0.3
(c) 0.5×0.7 (d) 0.9×0.08
(e) 0.6×0.25 (f) 0.8×0.08
(g) 0.04×0.012 (h) 0.03×0.005
(i) 0.06×0.07 (j) 0.009×0.02

2. Multiply the following mentally, and write down the answers:

(a) 1.2×0.3 (b) 1.3×0.4
(c) 1.5×0.06 (d) 1.5×0.04
(e) 2.75×0.2 (f) 2.85×0.03
(g) 0.003×1.8 (h) 0.05×0.0125
(i) 0.07×1.8 (j) 0.062×0.011

10.16   Mental Arithmetic Test

1. $1276 - 384 =$

2. $235 \times 7 =$

3. $4165 \div 5 =$

4. $300 \times 400 =$

5. £5.79 + £3.84 + £2.72 =

6. What will be the total cost of 12 articles at £7.95 each?

7. $\frac{5}{8} - \frac{2}{5} =$

8. $\frac{1}{2} \times \frac{1}{2} =$

9. How many centimetres in $1\frac{3}{4}$ metres?

10. How many days in 4 weeks?

11. Write 1925 in Roman figures.

12. What is 50% of £820?

13. $47 \times 500 =$

14. What is the cost of 12 × 15p stamps?

15. An article marked at £12.50 is sold at a discount of 10%. What is the final charge?

11
Value Added Tax

11.1 What is Value Added Tax?

On April 1, 1973, a new taxation system was introduced in the United Kingdom, replacing two other forms of taxation, purchase tax and selective employment tax, which were abolished on that date. Value added tax (VAT) was designed partly to bring the United Kingdom taxation system into closer alignment with Common Market systems, but it also spread taxation over a wider range of consumer products, making taxation fairer than before. The disadvantage of the system is that it requires about 1 500 000 businesses, many of them quite small, to keep VAT records. This means that VAT routines have become part of business calculations for every firm in the country.

The principle of VAT is that tax is levied on the value added to goods at every stage as they pass from the natural raw material stage to the finished product, and then onwards to the final consumer. Every middleman along the way buys goods and uses services which have already had some tax levied upon them. When he in turn sells goods or provides services, he levies tax on the price he charges his customers. The amount he is liable to pay over to the authorities is the difference between his 'output tax' levied on customers and the input tax levied upon him by his suppliers. It is directly related to the value he has added.

Imagine an oak tree cut down in a farmer's field, taken to a sawmill and cut into planks, sold to a manufacturer and turned into 500 coffee tables eventually retailed at £28.75 each including tax. The list of values added shown in Table 12.1 might be calculated. Tax has been levied at 15%. The notes below explain in detail how the tax is calculated.

Note: As the tax is 15%, the final selling price charged by each business in the chain of events is 115% of the tax-free price. Since 15% is not $\frac{15}{100}$ of this selling price but $\frac{15}{115}$ the VAT fraction used in the calculation is $\frac{15}{115}$, which cancels down to

$\frac{3}{23}$. The VAT fraction is a very important fraction, and has to be recalculated every time the rate of VAT is changed. For example, if the Chancellor of the Exchequer cut VAT to 10% tomorrow, the VAT fraction in any purchase would be $\frac{10}{110}$ of the selling price, which cancels down to $\frac{1}{11}$. Now study Table 11.1 carefully.

Table 11.1. Calculations—value added tax.

	Cost price free of tax £	Sale price free of tax £	Value added £	Final charge to customer (inc. 15% tax) £	Input tax £	Output tax £	Tax payable £
1. Farmer	0	500 (tree trunk)	500	575	0	75	75
2. Sawmill company	500	1 000 (sawn planks)	500	1 150	75	150	75
3. Furniture manufacturer	1 000	8 500 (coffee tables)	7 500	9 775	150	1 275	1 125
4. Retailer	8 500	12 500	4 000	14 375	1 275	1 875	600

Notes

(i) In each business the final charge to the customer includes 15% tax. This means that $\frac{3}{23}$ of the final charge is output tax, for which the businessman is accountable.

(ii) With the exception of the farmer, who is cutting down a gift of nature (a tree) the cost of the businessman's input is the price he pays to the previous businessman in the chain that leads to the final consumer. This again includes $\frac{3}{23}$ of the price as tax. This is his input tax.

(iii) The tax payable to Customs and Excise Department is the difference between output tax and input tax.

(iv) The effect of the tax is that the final consumers pay a total price of £14 375, of which £12 500 is the true value of the coffee tables they bought and £1875 is tax. The £1875 will be accounted for as shown in the *Tax payable* column above. It is not the businessman who pays the tax—that is paid by the consumer—but the businessman becomes an unpaid collection agent of HM Customs responsible for collecting the tax and paying it over to the Customs and Excise Department.

11.2 Selling Prices including VAT

When a trader or a manufacturer sells goods to a customer the selling price must be increased by the amount of value added tax. At the time of writing (1983) this is fixed at a standard rate of 15% on nearly all goods.

Some goods are zero-rated, which means that although they are taxed, the tax rate is zero. This might seem a strange statement, but it does mean that traders in these goods—particularly food and children's clothing—come within the VAT regulations and are able to claim back the VAT input tax they pay, even though they are not charging VAT output tax because the tax rate is 0%.

When calculating VAT at 15% the simplest way is to note that 10% = $\frac{1}{10}$ and 5% is half of that. The calculations for 15%

VAT on selling price are therefore very simple, as the following examples show:

Example 11.1. An item selling at £50 has to be increased by 15% VAT. What is its selling price, inclusive of VAT?

	£
Selling price free of tax	50.00
10% tax	5.00
5% tax	2.50
Selling price incl. 15% tax	£57.50

Example 11.2. An item selling for £850 has to be increased by 15% VAT. What is its selling price, inclusive of VAT?

	£
Selling price free of tax	850.00
10% tax	85.00
5% tax	42.50
Selling price incl. 15% tax	£977.50

Calculations for VAT at any rate

VAT rates can be varied very easily, which is one of the reasons why Chancellors like this kind of tax. Suppose the rate was changed to $18\frac{1}{2}$%. This is no clear fraction of a 100, and this cannot be worked simply in the head. Of course we should probably do the calculation with an electronic calculator these days, but the arithmetic required for awkward rates like this is very simple, as is shown in the following examples:

Example 11.3. A machine selling at £4350 has to be increased by $18\frac{1}{2}$% VAT. What is the final selling price?

	£	
Ordinary selling price	4350	
1% of selling price	43.50	(dividing by 100)
$18\frac{1}{2}$% of selling price =	43.50	(ignore the decimal points)
	× 18.5	
	21 750	× 5
	348 000	× 80
	435 000	× 100

Fixing the decimal point in the usual way £804.750

$$\text{Selling price} = £4350 + £804.75$$
$$= £5154.75$$

Example 11.4. An item selling at 16 pence has to be sold inclusive of VAT at $16\frac{3}{4}$%. What is the selling price, to the nearest penny?

		£	
Ordinary selling price	=	0.16	
1% selling price	=	0.0016	(dividing by 100)
$16\frac{3}{4}$% of selling price	=	0.0016	
		× 16.75	

(*Note:* $16\frac{3}{4} = 16.75$)

$$
\begin{array}{r}
80 \\
1120 \\
9600 \\
16000 \\
\hline
\end{array}
$$

Fixing the decimal point in the usual way   0.026800

$$\text{Selling price} = £0.16 + £0.026\ 88$$
$$= £0.16 + £0.03$$
$$= £0.19 \text{ to nearest penny}$$

11.3 Exercises: Selling Prices Inclusive of VAT

1. Given that the rate of VAT is 10%, what must a shopkeeper charge for goods which he intended to sell at the net of tax prices shown below?

(a) £100   (b) £120
(c) £225   (d) £360
(e) £1.50   (f) £1.90
(g) £0.20   (h) £0.40
(i) £850.50   (j) £375.80

2. Given that the rate of VAT is 15% what must a shopkeeper charge for goods which he intended to sell for the net-of-tax prices shown below (calculations to the nearest penny)?

(a) £60   (b) £72
(c) £85   (d) £16.50
(e) £35.75   (f) £42.50
(g) £275.50   (h) £849.50
(i) £0.84   (j) £0.48

3. What will a manufacturer have to charge for an £840 machine if VAT is at the rate of 21%?

4. What must a retailer charge for a bookcase at £38.50 if he has to add on VAT at $18\frac{1}{2}$% (calculations to the nearest penny)?

5. What must a wholesaler charge a retailer for an item he would sell net of tax at £17.58 if VAT is set at $12\frac{1}{2}$% (answer correct to the nearest penny)?

6. What will a car manufactured to sell at £3580 net of VAT cost when the VAT has been added at 18%?

7. VAT at $17\frac{1}{2}$% is added to a washing machine selling for £158. What is its price to the consumer?

8. A machine selling for £4850 net of VAT has VAT added at $16\frac{1}{4}$%. What is the full price to the consumer (answer correct to the nearest penny)?

11.4 'Net of VAT' Prices

When most goods are sold in the shops they are marked with the full charge to the retail customer, including VAT. In order to discover the 'net of VAT' price it is necessary to deduct a fraction which is called the **VAT fraction** by the VAT authorities. If we take a simple case it will be easy to follow the process, one of the most important points in business calculations.

Imagine that VAT is set at 10%.

10% is of course $\frac{10}{100} = \frac{1}{10}$, so we might think the VAT fraction would be $\frac{1}{10}$. This is *not* the case, because the VAT fraction is calculated on the selling price, not the net of VAT price. Consider the following points:

(a) The 'net of VAT' price is treated as 100%.
(b) VAT is added at 10% to find the selling price.
(c) Selling price is therefore 110% of the 'net of VAT' price.
(d) Of this 110% 10% is VAT.
(e) Therefore the VAT fraction is found as follows:

$$\text{VAT fraction} = \frac{10}{110} = \frac{1}{11} \qquad \text{(cancelling by 10)}$$

The VAT fraction is $\frac{1}{11}$ not $\frac{1}{10}$ of the selling price.

Consider the same thing with VAT at 15%:

$$\text{'Net of VAT' price} = 100\%$$
$$\text{'Net of VAT' price} + \text{VAT} = 100\% + 15\% = 115\% = \text{SP}$$

$$\text{VAT fraction} = \frac{15}{115} = \frac{3}{23} \qquad \text{(cancelling by 5)}$$

With VAT at 18% the calculation is

'Net of VAT' price = 100%
'Net of VAT' price + VAT = 118% = SP

$$\text{VAT fraction} = \frac{18}{118} = \frac{9}{59} \text{ (cancelling by 2)}$$

Clearly VAT fractions can be extremely awkward and give us some pretty nasty business calculations.

The ordinary customer does not need to bother too much about VAT fractions because all the customers are interested in is the total price to be paid for the article they wish to purchase. The businessman, by contrast, has to pay the VAT over to the collecting authority—which in the United Kingdom means HM Customs and Excise. Thus if the total sales by a retailer in one week are £11 726 and VAT is at the rate of 15%, what sum is due to the Customs authorities for VAT? We have already seen that with a rate of 15% the VAT fraction is $\frac{3}{23}$.

$$\text{VAT payable} = £11\ 726 \times \frac{3}{23}$$

$$= \frac{£35\ 178}{23}$$

$$
\begin{array}{r}
£ \\
1529.478 \\
23 \overline{)\ 35178} \\
23 \\
\hline
121 \\
115 \\
\hline
67 \\
46 \\
\hline
218 \\
207 \\
\hline
110 \\
92 \\
\hline
180 \\
161 \\
\hline
190 \\
184 \\
\hline
6
\end{array}
$$

$$= £1529.48$$

Clearly, most businesses use electronic calculators for such long division calculations, but the need to keep VAT records is still a time-consuming activity, and some people regard it as a good example of an uneconomic tax. This is especially true since the output tax the business collects from its customers is reduced by the amount of input tax the business has paid to its suppliers. Thus the VAT payable in the example quoted above (£1529.48) would not all be paid to HM Customs: the input tax paid to the suppliers has first to be deducted. In the United Kingdom only 24% of the tax collected is actually paid to Customs and Excise, the other 76% is deducted as input tax. We therefore have a type of tax where the amount of work involved in collection is large compared with the proceeds of collection. It is therefore a poor method of taxation, since a good tax is one with low costs of collection. This is an economic argument, and is more appropriate to an economics textbook. Readers who are interested might like to read a companion volume, *Economics Made Simple*.

Example 11.5. What will a trader need to pay over to the VAT authorities if his total sales in the accounting period (including 15% output tax charged to customers) are £345 000 and his total purchases (including 15% input tax paid to suppliers) are £230 460?

$$\text{Output tax} = \frac{3}{23} \times £345\,000$$
$$= 3 \times £15\,000 \qquad \text{(cancelling by 23)}$$
$$= £45\,000$$

$$\text{Input tax} = \frac{3}{23} \times £230\,460$$
$$= 3 \times £10\,020 \qquad \text{(cancelling by 23)}$$
$$= £30\,060$$

$$\text{Tax due} = £45\,000 - £30\,060$$
$$= £14\,940$$

11.5   Exercises on Output Tax

1. What will be the VAT fraction included in any sales price when the VAT rate is as shown below?

(a) 10%   (b) 20%
(c) 25%   (d) 15%
(e) 8%   (f) 12%
(g) 16%   (h) 18%
(i) 14%   (j) $15\frac{1}{2}$%

2. If articles are sold at the following prices when the VAT rate is 15% how much output tax is being charged to the customer in each case? (Answer correct to the nearest penny where necessary.)

(a) £23   (b) £460
(c) £48.30   (d) £73.60
(e) £60   (f) £580
(g) £424.50   (h) £320.49
(i) £5.85   (j) £126.50

3. What will be the total output tax collected from customers by businesses which have the following weekly takings (tax is reckoned at 10%)? (Calculations correct to the nearest penny where necessary.)

(a) £11 000   (b) £27 500
(c) £35 750   (d) £44 660
(e) £5954.75   (f) £6263.70
(g) £71 284.75   (h) £94 384.00
(i) £78 549.55   (j) £11 904.77

4. What will a trader need to pay over to the VAT authorities if his total sales (including the output tax he has charged to customers) are £276 000 in the accounting period and his total purchases (including the input tax he has paid) amount to £184 460 in the accounting period? Tax is levied at 15%.

5. What will a trader need to pay over to the VAT authorities if his total sales (including the output tax he has charged to customers) are £206 250 in the accounting period and his total purchases (including the input tax he has paid) amount to £130 306 in the accounting period? Tax is levied at 10%.

6. What will a trader need to pay over to the VAT authorities if his total sales (including the output tax he has charged to customers) are £2 317 424.50 in the accounting period and his total purchases (including the input tax he has paid) amount to £1 425 638.75 in the accounting period? Tax is levied at 20%. (Calculations to the nearest penny.)

11.6   Mental Arithmetic Text

Write down *the answers only* to these mental arithmetic calculations.

1. An item is to be sold at £2 + VAT at 15%. What will its selling price be?

2. $1725 + 495 + 3826 + 17 + 495 =$

3. $1295 - 380 =$

4. A machine sells at £250 less 5% cash discount. What is its final selling price?

5. What shall I pay for 5 bicycles at £34.50 each?

6. An item is to be sold at 40 pence + VAT at 20%. What will its selling price be?

7. What is ⅔ as a percentage?

8. How many centimetres in 5¼ metres?

9. What is the ratio between 7 days and 21 days?

10. Share £20 between three children so that A has twice as much as each of B and C

11. What year will be designated MM in Roman figures?

12. A motor car sells at £3600 + VAT at 15%. What will its selling price be?

13. 5 × 0.5 =

14. 12 tickets to a theatre cost £60. What will 17 cost?

15. A fence down one side of a plot of land has 14 panels costing £6 each and posts costing £2 each. If the labour charge is £20 what is the total cost of the fence?

12
Simple Interest

12.1 Interest—the Reward for the Use of Money

Money is of no use by itself, as Robinson Crusoe found on his desert island. His ship's treasure included a box of gold coins, but it was of no use to him. Money is only useful because in our money economy it can obtain goods and services. Therefore if someone has more than necessary to spend on goods and services for immediate use, it seems only sensible to lend it to someone else who can put it to good use. When I borrow money to expand my business what I am really borrowing is the power to purchase goods and services which I can make use of immediately, while the person who lent me the money loses the power to purchase goods and services. In return for this sacrifice of purchasing power it is usual for the borrower to pay **interest** on the money to the lender.

The **rate of interest** is expressed as a percentage, and it varies a good deal. Thus before the Second World War, for about 150 years, the Government of the United Kingdom was able to borrow at about $2\frac{1}{2}\%$ interest. In recent years it has been paying about 12% interest, almost five times as much, while many hire purchase contracts cost as much as 27–30%.

Interest is the reward paid to the lender for surrendering the present use of the money loaned, and for running the risk that the debtor will, for some reason, be unable to pay. Many loans today have life insurance cover built into them, so that any lender whose debtor dies can claim the money from an insurance company, and need not ask the debtor's family for repayment of the money loaned.

Interest can be of two types: simple interest and compound interest. As these names imply, the calculations concerned with compound interest are more difficult. Compound interest is dealt with later in this book.

The following terms are used in simple calculations:

(a) The **principal** is the sum borrowed, or in the case of a person lending money to a bank or financial institution, the sum deposited.

(b) The **rate** is the rate of interest payable per annum. It is always expressed as a percentage.

(c) The **term** is the time the loan is to run, expressed in years. Thus a loan for six months would be described as $\frac{1}{2}$ year, while a loan for one month would be $\frac{1}{12}$ of a year, and a loan for one day would be $\frac{1}{365}$ of a year. Leap year is ignored for interest purposes in these fractions.

12.2 Simple Interest on Loans Made for One Year

Because money is decimalised in most countries today it is very easy to do simple interest calculations, as shown in Example 12.1 below.

Example 12.1. What is the simple interest payable on a loan of £500 for 1 year at 12%?

First we calculate the interest at 1%. Then we multiply this answer by 12 to find the interest at 12%:

$$\text{Principal} = £500$$

$$\text{Interest at 1\%} = \frac{1}{100} \qquad\qquad = £5 \qquad\qquad \text{(dividing by 100)}$$

$$\text{Interest at 12\% (12 times 1\%)} \qquad = £60 \quad \text{(multiplying £5} \times 12)$$

Example 12.2. What is the simple interest payable on a loan of £850 for 1 year at 15%?

$$\text{Principal} = £850$$

$$\text{Interest at 1\%} = \frac{1}{100} \qquad = £8.50 \qquad \text{(dividing by 100)}$$

$$
\begin{aligned}
\text{Interest at 15\%} \qquad =\quad &8.50 \\
\times\quad &15 \\
\hline
&42.50 \quad \text{(5 times £8.50)}\\
&85.00 \quad \text{(10 times £8.50)}\\
\hline
£&127.50
\end{aligned}
$$

Example 12.3. What is the simple interest payable on a loan of £2750 for one year at $9\frac{1}{2}$%?

$$\text{Principal} = £2750$$

$$\text{Interest at 1\%} = \frac{1}{100} \qquad = £27.50 \qquad\qquad \text{(dividing by 100)}$$

Interest at 9%	=	247.50	(9 times £27.50)
Interest at $\frac{1}{2}$%	=	13.75	($\frac{1}{2}$ times £27.50)
Interest at $9\frac{1}{2}$%		£261.25	(adding the two lines above)

12.3   Simple Interest for a Number of Years

Using the method shown above, but dealing with a loan that lasts longer than one year, it is only necessary to multiply the 'interest for one year' by the term of the loan, as shown in the following examples:

Example 12.4. What is the simple interest on a loan of £1000 for 3 years at 11%?

$$\text{Principal} = £1000$$

Interest at 1% for 1 year = $\dfrac{1}{100}$	= £10	
Interest at 11% for 1 year (11 × 1%)	= £110	(11 times £10)
Interest for 3 years	= £330	(3 times £110)

Example 12.5. What is the simple interest on a loan of £2650 for $3\frac{3}{4}$ years at $8\frac{1}{2}$%? (Answer to the nearest penny.)

Here we must first find the interest at $8\frac{1}{2}$% for 1 year and then multiply it by $3\frac{3}{4}$. This is best done by multiplying the annual interest by 3, and then adding on $\frac{1}{2}$ a year's interest and $\frac{1}{4}$ of a year's interest.

Principal = £2650			
Interest at 1% for 1 year = $\frac{1}{100}$	=	£26.50	
Interest at 8% for 1 year (8 × 1%)	=	£212.00	(8 × £26.50)
Interest at $\frac{1}{2}$% for 1 year	=	£13.25	($\frac{1}{2}$ × £26.50)
Interest for 1 year	=	£225.25	
Interest for 3 years	=	675.75	(3 × £225.25)
Interest for $\frac{1}{2}$ year	=	112.625	($\frac{1}{2}$ × £225.25)
Interest for $\frac{1}{4}$ year	=	56.3125	($\frac{1}{2}$ × £112.625)
		£844.6875	
	=	£844.69	(to nearest penny)

12.4 Exercises: Simple Interest on Loans Made for One Year

1. Find the simple interest on the following loans, made for one year only:

(a) £500 at 8%   (b) £2700 at 11%
(c) £850 at 12%   (d) £1950 at 12½%
(e) £385 at 8%   (f) £3660 at 17%
(g) £1400 at 12¾%   (h) £4200 at 18½%
(i) £1850 at 15½%   (j) £3675 at 27%

2. Find the simple interest on these loans, correct to the nearest penny:

(a) £500 at 10% for 2 years
(b) £650 at 12% for 2½ years
(c) £720 at 14% for 3 years
(d) £1800 at 8½% for 3½ years
(e) £2350 at 11½% for 4 years
(f) £7500 at 15½% for 5½ years
(g) £18 250 at 12% for 6½ years
(h) £20 500 at 14½% for 2¾ years
(i) £25 800 at 16% for 3¾ years
(j) £36 500 at 20½% for 5¼ years

12.5 Finding Simple Interest by the Formula Method

In mathematics it is frequently helpful to use a formula, which expresses a simple calculation in a general form, using letters instead of numbers. Any calculation can then be performed by substituting for the general letters in the formula the actual figures for the calculation. The formula for simple interest may be expressed as follows:

$$\text{Interest} = \text{Principal} \times \frac{\text{Rate (per cent)}}{100} \times \text{Number of years}$$

The 100 appears in the equation because the rate of interest is always expressed as a percentage. This formula can be abbreviated to

$$I = \frac{PRN}{100}$$

Note: As with all mathematical formulae, where letters are written next to one another it is assumed that a multiplication sign has been left out. Thus the above formula really means

$$I = \frac{P \times R \times N}{100}$$

In solving any problem about simple interest the formula is written down first and the figures for the actual problem are then substituted into the formula in place of the letters. This is illustrated in Example 12.6.

Example 12.6. What is the simple interest on £5800 for 3 years at 12%?

The formula is

$$I = \frac{PRN}{100}$$

Substituting in the figures we have

$$I = \frac{£58\cancel{00} \times 12 \times 3}{1\cancel{00}}$$

$$= £696 \times 3$$

$$= £2088 \text{ interest}$$

Example 12.7. What is the simple interest on £7280 for $2\frac{1}{2}$ years at $13\frac{1}{2}$%?

$$I = \frac{PRN}{100}$$

$$= \frac{£7280 \times 13\frac{1}{2} \times 2\frac{1}{2}}{100}$$

$$= \frac{£7\cancel{280}^{182^{91}} \times 27 \times \cancel{5}^{1}}{1\cancel{00}_2{}_1 \times \cancel{2}_1 \times \cancel{2}_1}$$

$$= \frac{£91 \times 27}{1}$$

$$\begin{array}{r} 91 \\ \times 27 \\ \hline 637 \\ 1820 \\ \hline 2457 \\ \hline \end{array}$$

$$= £2457 \text{ interest}$$

12.6 Exercises: Finding Simple Interest by the Formula Method

1. Find the simple interest on each of the loans listed below, using the formula $I = \dfrac{PRN}{100}$.

(a) £800 loaned for 4 years at 12%
(b) £1500 loaned for 7 years at 8%

(c) £12 000 loaned for 3 years at 12%
(d) £20 000 loaned for 5 years at 15%
(e) £36 000 loaned for $2\frac{1}{2}$ years at $7\frac{1}{2}$%

2. Find the simple interest on each of the loans listed below, using the formula method. Answers correct to the nearest penny, where necessary.

(a) £720 borrowed for $2\frac{1}{2}$ years at $7\frac{1}{2}$%
(b) £550 borrowed for $3\frac{1}{2}$ years at 14%
(c) £1450 borrowed for $4\frac{1}{2}$ years at $12\frac{1}{2}$%
(d) £1640 borrowed for $2\frac{3}{4}$ years at 11%
(e) £2000 borrowed for $6\frac{1}{2}$ years at $8\frac{1}{2}$%
(f) £4800 borrowed for 6 months at 27%
(g) £5200 borrowed for 3 months at 24%
(h) £7500 borrowed for 15 years at $14\frac{1}{2}$%
(i) £6400 borrowed for 20 years at $13\frac{3}{4}$%
(j) £30 000 borrowed for 25 years at $17\frac{1}{2}$%

12.7   Solving Other Simple Interest Problems

While the question 'How much interest will be payable?' is the normal question in simple interest problems, it is possible to use the formula to find other unknowns. For example, questions could be posed in the following ways:

(a) What principal must have been invested if £200 was paid in interest in 4 years at 10% per annum?
(b) What rate of interest must have been charged if £200 was paid in interest in 2 years on £500 borrowed?
(c) How many years was the money borrowed for if a loan of £4000 at 5% incurs interest of £400?

In each of these cases we know the interest that is payable, but we have to find one of the other terms in the formula. In (a) it is the principal that is unknown, in (b) it is the rate of interest and in (c) it is the number of years. In order to solve for these unknowns we have to rearrange the formula, so that it begins with $P =$, $R =$ and $N =$. When rearranged the formula becomes

$$\text{(a)}\quad P = \frac{100I}{RN}$$

$$\text{(b)}\quad R = \frac{100I}{PN}$$

$$\text{(c)}\quad N = \frac{100I}{PR}$$

Note: The Rearrangement of Formulae

For the reader who wishes to know how these formulae are arrived at the explanation (which is really simple algebra) is as follows:

$$I = \frac{PRN}{100}$$

The original formula is $I = \dfrac{PRN}{100}$

This is an equation. An equation can be manipulated in the following ways. Consider the simple equation $2 = 1 + 1$

(a) We can turn it round the other way and it is still true (e.g. $1 + 1 = 2$).

(b) We can add the same thing to both sides and it is still true

e.g. $2 + 7 = 1 + 1 + 7$

(c) We can take the same thing from both sides and it is still true

e.g. $2 - \frac{1}{2} = 1 + 1 - \frac{1}{2}$

(d) We can multiply both sides by the same number and it is still true

e.g. $2 \times 3 = (1 + 1) \times 3$ or $6 = 6$

(e) We can divide both sides by the same number and it is still true

e.g. $2 \div 5 = \dfrac{1 + 1}{5}$ or $\dfrac{2}{5} = \dfrac{2}{5}$

In short, so long as we do the same thing to both sides of an equation it will still be a true equation.

Now, to find P from the formula $I = \dfrac{PRN}{100}$ we need to leave P on one side by itself. To do this we need to remove R, N and 100. We can remove R if we divide both sides by R

$$\frac{I}{R} = \frac{PRN}{100R} \qquad \text{(cancel the } R\text{'s on the right-hand side)}$$

$$\frac{I}{R} = \frac{PN}{100}$$

We can remove N in the same way

$$\frac{I}{RN} = \frac{PN}{100N} \qquad \text{(cancel the } N\text{'s on the right-hand side)}$$

$$\frac{I}{RN} = \frac{P}{100}$$

We can remove the 100 by multiplying both sides by 100

$$\frac{100I}{RN} = \frac{P \times 100}{100}$$ (cancel the hundreds on the right-hand side)

$$\frac{100I}{RN} = P$$

Turn the equation round the other way and we have our new formula

$$P = \frac{100I}{RN}$$

The same method will give us the other two formulae

$$R = \frac{100I}{PN} \text{ and } N = \frac{100I}{PR}$$

The solutions to the questions given above are now found as follows:

(a)
$$P = \frac{100I}{RN}$$

$$= \frac{100 \times 200}{10 \times 4}$$

Cancelling by 10 and 4 we have:

Principal Invested = £500

(b)
$$R = \frac{100I}{PN}$$

$$= \frac{100 \times £200}{£500 \times 2}$$

Cancelling by 100, 5, and 2 we have:

Rate payable = 20%

(c)
$$N = \frac{100I}{PR}$$

$$= \frac{100 \times 400}{4000 \times 5}$$

Cancelling by 100, 10, 4 and 5 we have:

Duration of loan = 2 years

Table 12.1. A ready reckoner for days.

	January	February	March	April	May	June	July	August	September	October	November	December
1	1	32	60	91	121	152	182	213	244	274	305	335
2	2	33	61	92	122	153	183	214	245	275	306	336
3	3	34	62	93	123	154	184	215	246	276	307	337
4	4	35	63	94	124	155	185	216	247	277	308	338
5	5	36	64	95	125	156	186	217	248	278	309	339
6	6	37	65	96	126	157	187	218	249	279	310	340
7	7	38	66	97	127	158	188	219	250	280	311	341
8	8	39	67	98	128	159	189	220	251	281	312	342
9	9	40	68	99	129	160	190	221	252	282	313	343
10	10	41	69	100	130	161	191	222	253	283	314	344
11	11	42	70	101	131	162	192	223	254	284	315	345
12	12	43	71	102	132	163	193	224	255	285	316	346
13	13	44	72	103	133	164	194	225	256	286	317	347
14	14	45	73	104	134	165	195	226	257	287	318	348
15	15	46	74	105	135	166	196	227	258	288	319	349
16	16	47	75	106	136	167	197	228	259	289	320	350
17	17	48	76	107	137	168	198	229	260	290	321	351
18	18	49	77	108	138	169	199	230	261	291	322	352
19	19	50	78	109	139	170	200	231	262	292	323	353
20	20	51	79	110	140	171	201	232	263	293	324	354
21	21	52	80	111	141	172	202	233	264	294	325	355
22	22	53	81	112	142	173	203	234	265	295	326	356
23	23	54	82	113	143	174	204	235	266	296	327	357
24	24	55	83	114	144	175	205	236	267	297	328	358
25	25	56	84	115	145	176	206	237	268	298	329	359
26	26	57	85	116	146	177	207	238	269	299	330	360
27	27	58	86	117	147	178	208	239	270	300	331	361
28	28	59	87	118	148	179	209	240	271	301	332	362
29	29		88	119	149	180	210	241	272	302	333	363
30	30		89	120	150	181	211	242	273	303	334	364
31	31		90		151		212	243		304		365

12.8   Exercises: More Difficult Problems on Simple Interest

1. In each of the following cases find the principal invested:

	Rate payable	Number of years	Interest earned
(a)	12%	3	£270
(b)	8%	$4\frac{1}{2}$	£432
(c)	$9\frac{1}{2}$%	$2\frac{1}{2}$	£593.75
(d)	$11\frac{1}{2}$%	6	£3174
(e)	$13\frac{3}{4}$%	$3\frac{1}{2}$	£866.25

2. In each of the following cases find the rate payable on the loan:

	Sum borrowed	Interest earned	Number of years
(a)	£1000	£280	2
(b)	£2400	£1200	4
(c)	£2650	£563.12$\frac{1}{2}$	$2\frac{1}{2}$
(d)	£5800	£5872.50	$3\frac{3}{4}$
(e)	£24 250	£49 106.25	15

3. In each of the following cases find out for how long the money was borrowed:

	Sum borrowed	Interest earned	Rate of interest
(a)	£760	£209	11%
(b)	£1580	£691.25	$12\frac{1}{2}$%
(c)	£2380	£1636.25	$13\frac{3}{4}$%
(d)	£7250	£11 400.62$\frac{1}{2}$	$18\frac{1}{2}$%
(e)	£14 000	£78 750	$22\frac{1}{2}$%

4. What sum of money must have been borrowed at 14% simple interest if the interest payable over $2\frac{1}{2}$ years amounted to £2975?

5. What rate of interest must have been payable if £25 000 borrowed for 3 months requires interest of £718.75 to be paid?

6. For how long must a sum of £18 000 have been invested at $9\frac{1}{2}$% if it earns interest of £2565?

12.9   Calculating Interest For Loan Periods Measured in Days

In many financial institutions interest is calculated in days. A simple ready reckoner for this is the chart shown as Table 12.1. The method of using the chart can be illustrated by several examples.

Example 12.8. Money is borrowed on 12 January and repaid on 23 May. How many days' interest is payable?

The chart tells us that 12 January is the 12th day of the year, and 23 May is the 143rd day of the year. (23 May is found by using the days of January as a guide. Running the eye across from the 23rd day of January we are looking at the 23rd day of each month, and the 23 May is seen to be the 143rd day of the year.) The calculation requires us to take one number from the other.

$$23 \text{ May} = \text{Day } 143$$
$$12 \text{ Jan} = \text{Day } 12$$

131 days of interest to pay

Example 12.9. Money is borrowed on 7 April and repaid on 20 November. How many days' interest is payable?

$$20 \text{ November} = \text{Day } 324$$
$$7 \text{ April} = \text{Day } 97$$

227 days of interest to pay

(*Note:* If a loan includes the leap year day 29 February one extra day must be added to the calculation.)

Example 12.10. Money is borrowed on 24 November 1983 and repaid on 28 March 1984. How many days' interest is payable?

1984 is a leap year so we need to add 1 extra day for 29 February. Also this calculation goes through the year-end. It must therefore be done in two parts.

$$31 \text{ December} = \text{Day } 365$$
$$24 \text{ November} = \text{Day } 328$$

37 days to end of year

In the New Year count all days to 28 March:

$$28 \text{ March} = \text{Day } 87$$
$$29 \text{ February} = \qquad 1 \text{ extra day}$$

125 days of interest to pay

Example 12.11. What interest is payable on a sum of £500 borrowed at 15% interest on 14 July and repaid on 13 October?

$$13 \text{ October} = \text{Day } 286$$
$$14 \text{ July} = \text{Day } 195$$

91 days

91 days is $\frac{91}{365}$ of a year.

$$I = \frac{PRN}{100}$$

$$= £5\cancel{0}\cancel{0} \times \frac{1\cancel{5}^{\,3}}{1\cancel{0}\cancel{0}} \times \frac{91}{3\cancel{6}\cancel{5}\,73}$$

Cancelling by 100 and by 5

$$= \frac{1365}{73}$$

$$
\begin{array}{r}
18.698 \\
73 \overline{)\, 1365.000} \\
73 \\
\hline
635 \\
584 \\
\hline
510 \\
438 \\
\hline
720 \\
657 \\
\hline
630 \\
584 \\
\hline
46
\end{array}
$$

$$= £18.70 \text{ interest due}$$

12.10 Exercises: Calculating Interest for Loan Periods Measured in Days

1. In each of the following cases how many days' interest is payable on money borrowed on the first date and repaid on the last date? None of the dates is in a leap year.

(a) 14 January–27 March   (b) 5 February–27 April
(c) 26 April–4 July   (d) 15 March–30 July
(e) 19 May–15 September   (f) 22 June–14 August
(g) 27 June–14 November   (h) 29 July–5 October
(i) 31 October–17 December   (j) 7 October–24 November

2. In each of the following cases how many days' interest is payable on money borrowed on the first date and repaid on the second date? None of the dates is in a leap year.

(a) 25 November–18 February   (b) 7 December–14 March
(c) 14 June–7 January   (d) 14 November–11 April
(e) 27 December–11 March   (f) 15 August–22 May
(g) 11 August–25 April   (h) 28 November–17 February
(i) 8 October–30 January   (j) 31 July–28 February

3. What interest is payable on £1500 borrowed at 12% on 4 January and repaid on 18 March? It was not a leap year.

4. What interest is payable on £2750 borrowed at $15\frac{1}{2}$% on 11 July and repaid on 4 December?

5. What interest is payable on £560 borrowed at $12\frac{1}{2}$% interest on 7 April and repaid on 24 January the following year?

6. What interest is payable on £3650 borrowed at $12\frac{3}{4}$% on 12 May and repaid on 11 July?

7. What interest is payable on £730 borrowed at 15% on 14 December and repaid on 22 January?

8. What interest is payable on £850 borrowed at 11% on 21 July and repaid on 14 December?

9. What interest is payable on £2500 borrowed at 17% on 10 May and repaid on 15 December?

10. What interest is payable on £1460 borrowed at 21% on 15 June and repaid on 10 July?

12.11   Mental Arithmetic: Simple Interest

Many simple interest sums can be calculated mentally if the rates of interest are not too complex and the numbers of years are also simple.

Thus the simple interest on £500 at 12% = £60 per year and for 3 years this would be £180. Such questions frequently appear in mental arithmetic papers in elementary examinations.

Certain common fractions of a year frequently feature in questions—for example, the following:

6 months = $\frac{1}{2}$ year	73 days = $\frac{1}{5}$ year
4 months = $\frac{1}{3}$ year	146 days = $\frac{2}{5}$ year
3 months = $\frac{1}{4}$ year	219 days = $\frac{3}{5}$ year
1 month = $\frac{1}{12}$ year	292 days = $\frac{4}{5}$ year

12.12   Questions on Simple Interest

Write down *the answers only* to these simple interest calculations:

1. What is the simple interest on £100 for 2 years at 15%?

2. What is the simple interest on £1000 at 12% for 3 years?

3. What is the simple interest on £500 at $8\frac{1}{2}$% for 2 years?

4. What is the simple interest on £800 at 8% for $2\frac{1}{2}$ years?

5. What is the simple interest on £300 at 15% for 6 months?

6. What is the simple interest on £450 at 10% for 3 months?

7. What is the simple interest on £650 at 20% for 73 days?

8. What is the simple interest on £2000 at $13\frac{1}{2}$% for 2 years?

9. What is the simple interest on £5000 at 12% for 4 months?

10. What is the simple interest on £10 000 at 15% for 219 days?

12.13 Mental Arithmetic Test

1. $274 + 362 + 498 + 241 =$

2. $476 \div 7 =$

3. £29.54 − £13.80 =

4. $1\frac{1}{5} - \frac{1}{3} =$

5. $\frac{3}{8} \times \frac{4}{5} \times \frac{2}{9} =$

6. How many pence in £100?

7. What is two thirds of £960?

8. A telephone call lasting 90 seconds costs 4p per 10 seconds. What is the charge for the call?

9. $0.5 \times 0.5 =$

10. How many centimetres in $3\frac{1}{2}$ metres?

11. A trader buys furniture for sale at £500. The trade discount is 40%. How much does he pay for it?

12. VAT is set at 15%. What is the VAT on an item selling normally at £150?

13. Share £1000 between Peter, Harry and John so that Peter and John have twice as much as Harry.

14. What is the simple interest on a loan of £2000 for 2 years at $12\frac{1}{2}$%?

15. What is the simple interest on £3500 for 3 years at 10%?

13
Simple Averages

13.1 The Origin of Averages

The word 'average' comes from the Arabic word for 'damage'. For a thousand years or more, since the first dhows sailed the Arabian Sea, it has been the custom for those whose goods were damaged or deliberately thrown overboard to lighten the ship in a storm to claim compensation from those whose goods survived because of the sacrifice. It is only fair that this should be so, since otherwise all would have been lost, including the ship itself. Even the ship-owner must join in compensating those who suffered. The sacrifice is called a 'general average sacrifice' and to compensate the losers the rest must make a 'general average contribution'. How is the amount decided? The answer is 'by equal shares, from all parties'. Whilst the calculation is quite simple, the valuation of the goods which arrived safely can be quite difficult, and special insurance staff called **average adjusters** are employed to carry them out.

13.2 Simple Averages

The word 'average' today means 'equally divided among all, to give a medial figure'. Thus a batsman who scores 100 runs in his first innings and 50 runs in his second innings has made an average score (when equally shared between the two innings) of 75 runs per innings. To find an average, we add up the quantities available, and divide the result by the number of occasions concerned. In the example above we have:

$$\text{Runs scored} = 100 + 50 = 150$$
$$\text{Number of innings} = 2$$

$$\text{Average score per innings} \quad \frac{150}{2} = \underline{\underline{75}}$$

Example 13.1. Five classes in a technical college have 32, 18, 24, 26 and 15 students respectively. What is the average membership of classes in the college?

$$\text{Total number of students} = 32 + 18 + 24 + 26 + 15 = 115$$
$$\text{Number of classes} = 5$$

$$\text{Average number per class} = \frac{115}{5} = \underline{23 \text{ students}}$$

Averages rarely come out to an exact number and we must usually be prepared to give the answer to some agreed level of accuracy. In Example 13.2 we give the answer correct to one decimal place.

Example 13.2. A cricketer scores as follows in six test-match innings: 84, 32, 0, 5, 27, 136. What was his average score per innings?

$$\text{Total runs scored} = 84 + 32 + 0 + 5 + 27 + 136 = 284$$
$$\text{Number of innings} = 6$$

$$\text{Average score} = \frac{284}{6} = 47.33$$

$$= \underline{47.3} \qquad \text{(correct to one decimal place)}$$

Example 13.3. Output at a cement works in a four-week period was as follows: week 1, 2875 tonnes; week 2, 3854 tonnes; week 3, 2988 tonnes; week 4, 3624 tonnes. What is the average weekly output, correct to the nearest tonne?

$$
\begin{array}{r}
\text{tonnes} \\
2\,875 \\
3\,854 \\
2\,988 \\
3\,624 \\
\hline
4\,)\,13\,341 \\
\hline
3\,335\tfrac{1}{4} \\
\hline
\end{array}
$$

Answer (to nearest tonne) = 3335 tonnes per week

13.3   Exercises on Simple Averages

1. Find the average of each of the following sets of data:

(a) 3, 7, 14

(b) 4, 7, 9, 8

(c) 36, 29, 25

(d) 14, 18, 23, 27, 33

(e) 138, 156

(f) 274, 326, 429

(g) 242, 316, 715, 298

(h) 1045, 2946, 3128

(i) 24 m, 32 m, 56 m, 27 m, 29 m, 84 m

(j) 7 kg, 15 kg, 35 kg, 19kg

2. Find the average of each of the following sets of data.

(a) £23.50, £42.60, £39.80

(b) 29 min; 33 min; 36 min 28 sec; 34 min 15 sec; 28 min 42 sec

(c) 5.8 litres, 4.7 litres, 3.35 litres, 1.65 litres, 8.55 litres

(d) 3209 kg, 4703 kg, 5185 kg, 2428 kg

(e) £750, £840, £380, £560, £480, £1000, £736

(f) £13 560, £14 920, £27 250, £24 325

(g) 385 tonnes, 295 tonnes, 476 tonnes, 185 tonnes, 274 tonnes

(h) 2075 tonnes, 3859 tonnes, 7163 tonnes

(i) 3 h 35 min, 2 h 29 min, 4 h 07 min, 3 h 11 min

(j) 4 h 04 min, 5 h 27 min, 5 h 13 min, 4 h 58 min

13.4 Weighted Averages

Sometimes in calculating averages one of the numbers involved may need to be given greater emphasis than others, and this is referred to as 'weighting'. The best example in real life is in the calculation of the Retail Price Index and other statistics. For example, if we are calculating what the average family spends each month on its requirements we may need to give a greater emphasis to expenditure on bread than on diamond rings. Families buy bread every day, but a diamond ring is a rare purchase—so rare that it might even be left out of the calculations altogether for the average family. We must 'weight' the index in favour of bread, and against diamond rings.

Example 13.4. In an examination in Business Studies a student scores as follows: Accountancy 78%, Economics and Economic History 56% in each case, Office Administration 42% and Principles of Management 31%. The pass mark for the examination is an average of 50% for all subjects. Should the student be passed, or failed?

(*Note:* The mark of 56% has to be counted twice, as it was scored in two subjects, i.e. its weight is 2.)

$$\text{Total marks scored} = 78 + (56 \times 2) + 42 + 31$$
$$\text{Number of subjects} = 5$$

$$\text{Average score} = \frac{78 + 112 + 42 + 31}{5}$$

$$= \frac{263}{5}$$

$$= 52.6\%$$

The student has passed the examination.

Example 13.5. In a junior tennis club the 24 members are aged as follows: 3 are 11 years old, 2 are 12 years old, 5 are 14 years old, 4 are 15, 5 are 16 and 3 are 17. The rest are 18 years old. What is the average age of the members in years (answer correct to the nearest year)?

Listing the members we have

Weight	Age in Years	Total
3	11	33
2	12	24
5	14	70
4	15	60
5	16	80
3	17	51
2	18	36
—		—
24		354

$$
\begin{array}{r}
14\frac{18}{24} \text{ years} \\
24 \overline{)\,354} \\
24 \\
\overline{114} \\
96 \\
\overline{18}
\end{array}
$$

Average age = 15 years

(*Note:* It would be incorrect to give the average age as 14 years 9 months, since we do not know the ages of the students in years and months we cannot give an answer in years and months. That would be more accurate than the figures given and used in the calculations.)

13.5　Exercises on Weighted Averages

1. Find the average marks per student obtained in an examination where 3 students scored 75% each, 2 scored 71%, the next 3 candidates scored 70%, 67% and 62% respectively. The remaining 4 candidates scored 51% each (answer correct to one decimal place).

2. When posting parcels the Post Department in a certain office sent off 5 parcels stamped at £2.20, 1 at £1.90, 3 at £1.75, 26 at £1.60 and 5 at £1.25. What is the average cost per parcel?

3. Find the average cost of each of the following sets of office furniture:
    (a) 4 chairs at £29.50 each and 3 chairs at £19 each.
    (b) 4 desks at £87.00 each and 6 desks at £123.50 each.
    (c) 24 waste-paper bins at £6.25 each and 12 waste-paper bins at £5.50 each.

4. Find the average weight of a container in the following consignments:
    (a) 1 container weighing 16 tonnes, 4 containers weighing 20 tonnes and 15 containers weighing 32 tonnes.
    (b) 3 containers weighing 12 tonnes, 7 containers weighing 15 tonnes, 9 containers weighing 21 tonnes and 1 container weighing 30 tonnes.

5. The capital employed by a construction firm is £19 710 000. The number of employees is 3650. In response to a demand from the trade unions for a wage increase management decides to calculate the average amount of capital employed per worker. What is this average figure?

6. A 10 000 metres race is 25 laps of a race track. These laps are timed as follows: 1 lap took 62 seconds, 3 took 65.4 seconds, 3 took 68.6 seconds, 5 took 69 seconds, 6 took 72 seconds and the rest took 72.3, 73.5, 74, 75.2, 75.4, 75.6 and 78 seconds respectively. What was the average lap time?

7. 30 recruits to the army were measured and their heights were found to be as follows: 1 measured 160 cm, 3 measured 163 cm, 2 measured 167 cm, 3 measured 170 cm, 5 measured 172 cm, 6 measured 174 cm, 4 measured 178 cm, 3 measured 183 cm, 2 measured 188 cm and 1 measured 191 cm. What was the average height of recruits? (Answer correct to the nearest tenth of a centimetre.)

8. An art gallery has the following groups of pictures insured: 5 valued at £10 000 each, 4 valued at £7800 each, 15 valued at £5000 each, 36 valued at £2500 and 20 valued at £1000. What is the average value of a picture?

13.6 The Average of Large Numbers

Averages are frequently set as mental arithmetic exercises, and in many cases are very easy. For example, what is the average of 5, 8 and 14? As there are three numbers, and they total 27, the average is 27 ÷ 3 = 9.

A more difficult question might be 'what is the average of 25 008, 25 005 and 25 014?' When finding the average of large numbers like this we can disregard a large part of each number. Since each of these numbers includes 25 000 we need only find the average of 8, 5 and 14. As explained above, the average of these is 9. So the average of the large numbers is 25 009.

Example 13.6. What is the average of 2856, 2860, 2862 and 2870?
Since all these numbers are bigger than 2856 we can just find the

average of the extra amounts. 2860 is 4 extra, 2862 is 6 extra and 2870 is 14 extra, making 24 extra in all. When this is shared up between the four numbers it means an average of 6 extra. Therefore

$$\text{Average} = 2856 + 6$$
$$= 2862$$

Check: We can always check an average by comparing those below average with those above average. There should be the same variation in total quantity below average as above average. In this example the average is 2862.

2856 is 6 below average
2860 is 2 below average
2862 is exactly average
2870 is 8 above average

Our answer is therefore correct since we have 8 below and 8 above average.

13.7   Exercises on Averages

1. Find the average of 7, 8 and 15
2. Find the average of 12, 16 and 17
3. Find the average of 40, 70, 80 and 90
4. Find the average of 25, 28, 32 and 39
5. Find the average of 22, 25, 26, 28 and 29
6. Find the average of 101, 103 and 105
7. Find the average of 812, 814, 826 and 828
8. Find the average of 10 106 and 10 140
9. Find the average of 20 026, 20 040 and 20 102
10. Find the average of 75 012, 75 024, 75 036, 75 048 and 75 080

13.8   Mental Arithmetic Test

1. $274 \times 7 =$
2. $1725 - 829 =$
3. £17.29 + £32.45 + £165.92 =
4. $1\frac{1}{4} + 2\frac{3}{8} + 1\frac{1}{2} =$
5. $1.25 \times 0.2 =$

6. 4725 ÷ 5 =

7. How many grams in 2½ kilograms?

8. A pamphlet costs 25p. How many can I purchase for £30?

9. What is the average of 2, 3, 4, 7, 11 and 15?

10. How many days in January?

11. A trader's VAT output tax is £1500. His input tax paid on goods purchased is £850. What must he pay over to Customs and Excise Department for VAT?

12. What is the simple interest on a loan of £4800 for 4 years at 7½%?

13. What is 75 as a percentage of 150?

14. The simple interest paid on £1000 at 12½% is £250. For how many years was the money borrowed?

15. What is the average of 3001, 3005, 3027 and 3035?

14
Cost Price and Selling Price

14.1 Mark-ups on Cost Price

Some people are producers, others are wholesalers or retailers. We are all consumers demanding supplies of food, clothing and countless other manufactured goods. Costs and prices are consequently of enormous interest to everyone.

For the producers—farmers, market gardeners, fishermen and manufacturers—their costs are the expenses of production, and we shall see in a later chapter what costing of their products involves. For wholesalers, who buy in bulk from the producers and sell in smaller quantities to the retailers, their cost prices are the prices paid to the producers for their products. They also have to meet overhead expenses, such as warehousing costs, transport costs, insurance premiums, etc. Retailers buy in small quantities from wholesalers and sell to the general public in very small quantities, single items in many cases.

Both these groups, the wholesalers and the retailers, operate by adding on a mark-up to their cost prices to achieve their selling prices. These mark-ups have to be substantial, because they have to cover all the overhead expenses and still leave a margin of pure profit for the trader as a reward for the effort involved. One of the most common causes of bankruptcy among small businesses is the tendency of traders to underestimate the mark-up they need to cover all their overhead expenses—particularly if items are slow-moving.

Mark-ups are nearly always calculated as percentages, and are based on the cost price. The formula is

Cost price + Mark-up = Selling price

Consider the following examples:

Example 14.1. A trader buys articles at £3 each and adds on 50% mark-up. What is his selling price?

$$\text{Cost Price} = £3$$
$$\text{Selling price} = £3 + (50\% \text{ of } £3)$$
$$= £3 + £1.50$$
$$= £4.50$$

Example 14.2. A retailer buys an item of furniture for £65 and adds on a 150% mark-up. What is his selling price?

$$\text{Cost price} = £65$$
$$\text{Selling price} = £65 + (150\% \text{ of } £65)$$
$$= £65 + £65 + £32.50 \quad (100\% + 50\%)$$
$$= £162.50$$

(This may seem a high mark-up, but if the item is a slow-moving one it must carry several months' overheads.)

Example 14.3 A confectioner buys chocolate bars at 12 pence each and adds on a 25% mark-up. What is his selling price?

$$\text{Selling price} = 12p + (\tfrac{1}{4} \text{ of } 12p) \qquad (\text{remember } 25\% = \tfrac{1}{4})$$
$$= 12p + 3p$$
$$= 15p$$

Many simple mark-up problems, like Example 14.3 above, can be solved mentally.

14.2 Exercises on Selling Prices after Mark-up

1. If mark-up is fixed at 50%, what will be the selling price of articles costing a retailer as follows?

(a) 60p   (b) 80p
(c) £1.00   (d) £2.00
(e) £2.30   (f) £5.20
(g) £3.20   (h) £6.30
(i) £4.50   (j) £10.50

2. If mark-up is fixed at 20%, what will be the selling prices of goods costing a retailer as follows?

(a) £3   (b) £6.50
(c) £10   (d) £27.00
(e) £15.60   (f) £18.50
(g) £25.30   (h) £48.80
(i) £500   (j) £620

3. If mark-up is fixed at 250% what will be the selling price of goods costing as follows:

(a) £1.50   (b) £1.80
(c) £3.40   (d) £5.60
(e) £7.20   (f) £12.50
(g) £18.50   (h) £24.00
(i) £350   (j) £720

14.3   Selling Prices and Margins

A mark-up is always calculated on cost price, but in many branches
of retail trade the same figure is looked at from a different point of
view. Frequently management does not wish its branch managers
to know what was the cost price of the goods they are selling. They
take the view that it is for head office management to decide what
measure of profit will be made: the manager's job is to see that he
achieves the correct price from the consumer. Goods are sent to the
branches not at cost price, but at selling price. The efficient manager
will achieve this full selling price from his customers. It is easy to
check on this, because if a spot check is done on the branch from
time to time, and the stock remaining on the shelves is counted (at
selling price), the manager must be able to account for every penny
of stock sent to him. Consider the following case:

Megabury Branch

Goods supplied to branch in year (at selling price) = £134 750		
Money banked by branch manager	= £85 950	
Stock on shelves (at selling price)	= £27 825	
Permitted discounts sanctioned by head office (fruit and vegetables)	= £3 850	
		£117 625
Shortfall		£17 125

Permitted discounts are cuts in selling prices made, with head
office permission, to clear stock which otherwise would go bad,
such as fruit and vegetables. The amount of the discount is notified
to head office who take it into account in their calculations of the
money the manager should be able to bank.

Since the stock on the shelves is valued at only £27 825, and
permitted discounts only total £3850, the manager must have sold
the rest. If he sold the goods at the price he was supposed to sell
them at, he should have banked not £85 950, but £17 125 more
than that. This is a very serious shortfall. The following questions
need to be asked:

(a) Is the manager stealing the money?
(b) Are the assistants stealing the money?

(c) Is someone stealing the stock (manager, assistants or shop-lifters posing as customers)?

(d) Have there been breakages of stock?

(e) Has stock gone bad and had to be thrown away? If so, why don't head office know about it?

There are many more questions that could be asked.

Business calculations are not just about manipulating numbers. The 'business' part of the term is just as important; we have to understand how business works; how head office controls branches, etc.

The **margin** of profit is that percentage which has to be deducted from selling price to find cost price. It is therefore the same as the mark-up, but viewed from a different direction:

$$\text{Cost price} + \text{Mark-up} = \text{Selling price}$$
$$\text{Selling price} - \text{Margin} = \text{Cost price}$$

There is obviously a connection between the two, which is explained later. First consider the following examples:

Example 14.4. A shopkeeper sells an article for £40 of which 25% is his profit margin. What did the article cost him?

Notes: (i) Here the margin of profit is worked out on the selling price and is given as 25% of £40. (ii) This margin then has to be subtracted from the selling price to find the cost price.

$$\begin{aligned}
\text{Selling price} &= £40.00 \\
\text{Margin} &= 25\% \text{ of } £40 \\
&= \tfrac{1}{4} \text{ of } £40 \\
&= £10 \\
\text{Cost price} &= \text{Selling price} - \text{Margin} \\
&= £40 - £10 \\
&= £30
\end{aligned}$$

Example 14.5. A trader sells an article for £165 of which $33\tfrac{1}{3}\%$ is profit. What was the cost price of the article?

$$\begin{aligned}
\text{Margin of profit} &= 33\tfrac{1}{3}\% \text{ of } £165 \\
&= \tfrac{1}{3} \text{ of } £165 \\
&= £55 \\
\text{Cost price} &= \text{Selling price} - \text{Margin} \\
&= £165 - £55 \\
&= £110
\end{aligned}$$

14.4 Exercises on Selling Prices and Margins

1. What was the cost price of each of the following articles, if the selling prices and the margin of profit are as shown?

(a) 80p : 50%	(b) 60p : 33⅓%
(c) £1.20 : 25%	(d) £2.50 : 60%
(e) £3.60 : 40%	(f) £5.50 : 50%
(g) £27 : 30%	(h) £56 : 25%
(i) £750 : 60%	(j) £1500 : 20%

2. A dealer sells an antique desk for £3400. It included a profit margin of 55%. What was its cost to him?

3. A jeweller sells a ring for £185, of which £5 was for cleaning the ring and 40% of the remainder was his profit margin. What did the ring cost him?

4. A dealer sells a fridge-freezer for £145, on which the profit margin was 30%. What did it cost him?

5. A trader sells a motor vehicle for £5250 on which the profit margin was 40%. What did it cost him?

14.5 The Link Between Mark-up and Margin

There is a link between mark-up (reckoned on the cost price) and margin (reckoned on the selling price). Consider the case of an item marked up from cost price at 33⅓%. Starting with cost price as 100% and adding 33⅓% profit we have

$$\text{Cost price} + \text{Profit} = \text{Selling price}$$
$$100\% \quad + \quad 33\tfrac{1}{3}\% \quad = \quad 133\tfrac{1}{3}\%$$

From the other point of view, if we are trying to move from the selling price to find the cost price, the figures must be reversed

$$\text{Selling price} - \text{Profit} = \text{Cost price}$$
$$133\tfrac{1}{3}\% \quad - \quad 33\tfrac{1}{3}\% \quad = \quad 100\%$$

The question is 'What percentage of 133⅓% is 33⅓%?' The answer is

$$\frac{33\tfrac{1}{3}\%}{133\tfrac{1}{3}\%} \times 100$$
$$= \tfrac{1}{4} \times 100$$
$$= 25\%$$

If we want to remove 33⅓% from the selling price it is not one third but one quarter of it: there are $4 \times 33\tfrac{1}{3}\%$ in 133⅓%. Put another way, we may say:

$\frac{1}{3}$ onto cost price = $\frac{1}{4}$ off selling price

This can be expanded into a table of relationships, as follows:

$$\frac{1}{2} \text{ on to cost price} = \frac{1}{3} \text{ off selling price}$$
$$\frac{1}{3} = \frac{1}{4}$$
$$\frac{1}{4} = \frac{1}{5}$$
$$\frac{1}{5} = \frac{1}{6}$$
$$\frac{1}{6} = \frac{1}{7}$$

etc., indefinitely

In each case the denominator of the fraction increases by 1. For example

Thus
$$\frac{1}{20} \text{ onto cost price} = \frac{1}{21} \text{ off selling price}$$
$$\text{Cost price} + \frac{1}{20} = 100\% + 5\% = 105\%$$
$$\text{Selling price} - \frac{1}{21} = 105\% - (\frac{1}{21} \text{ of } 105\%)$$
$$= 105\% - 5\% = 100\%$$

For percentages that do not easily change to this type of proper fraction (like 40%) we find the cost price by this formula:

$$CP = \frac{SP}{140} \times 100$$

i.e. the CP is $\frac{100}{140}$ of the SP.

Example 14.6. A merchant sells all articles at prices fixed by adding $33\frac{1}{3}\%$ on to the cost price. What did he pay for an item sold for £12?

$$33\frac{1}{3}\% = \frac{1}{3}$$
$$\frac{1}{3} \text{ on to cost price} = \frac{1}{4} \text{ off selling price}$$
$$\text{cost price} = £12 - (\frac{1}{4} \times £12)$$
$$= £12 - £3$$
$$= £9$$

Note: It is always helpful to check such calculations by working them back again to the starting point. Thus we have found the cost price by deducting the appropriate fraction from the selling price. If we now work forwards, starting with the cost price we have found and adding on the agreed mark-up, we should return to the selling price again. We can thus prove that our answer is correct.

Check: Cost price = £9
Selling price = £9 + $33\frac{1}{3}\%$ of £9 = £9 + £3 = £12

Example 14.7. A merchant prices all his goods at 60% above cost price. What did he pay for something he is selling for £36?

Selling price = £36

Cost price = $\dfrac{100}{160}$ × £36

$= \dfrac{5 \times 9}{2}$ (after cancelling by 10, 4 and 2)

$= \dfrac{45}{2}$

= £22.50

Check: Cost price   = £22.50

Selling price = £22.50 × $\dfrac{160}{100}$ = $\dfrac{£22.50 \times 8}{5}$ = £4.50 × 8

= £36

14.6   Exercises on the Link Between Mark-up and Margin

1. The following selling prices in a particular shop had all been arrived at by adding 50% on to cost price. What was the cost to the retailer of each of the items sold?

(a) £3   (b) £2.70
(c) £12   (d) £36
(e) £7.50   (f) £54.90

2. The following selling prices in a particular shop had all been arrived at by adding 33⅓% on to cost price. What was the cost price of each of the items sold?

(a) 60 pence   (b) £1.60
(c) £3.60   (d) £4
(e) £15.60   (f) £33.60

3. The following selling prices in a particular branch of trade were achieved by adding on the percentage mark-up shown to the cost price. What was the cost price of each of these items?

(a) 60p; 20%   (b) £2.25; 12½%
(c) £184; 33⅓%   (d) £8.40; 50%
(e) £56.50; 25%   (f) £240; 33⅓%
(g) £700; 16⅔%   (h) £55; 10%
(i) £720; 20%   (j) £1850; 25%

4. The following selling prices in certain retail trades were obtained by adding the percentage mark-up shown to cost price. What was the cost price of each of these items?

(a) 80p; 60%   (b) £5.80; 45%
(c) £6.50; 30%   (d) £27; 35%
(e) £46.50; 55%   (f) £27; 80%
(g) £35; 75%   (h) £66; 65%
(i) £75; 100%   (j) £6; 300%

5. A dealer sells a second-hand motor vehicle for £1088, which yields him a profit of 36% on cost price. What did he pay for the vehicle?

6. A property company sells a house for £35 500, which represents a 42% increase on the cost price. What did it pay for the property when purchased?

7. A jeweller sells a gold watch for £462, which represents a 68% mark-up on cost price. What did the watch cost him?

8. A shopkeeper retires and sells his business for £33 950, which represents a 94% profit on the price paid for it some years ago. What did it cost him originally?

14.7 Mark-downs

It frequently happens that a retailer marks down the price of articles on display with a view to clearing them from the shelves. One cause for such mark-downs is the deterioration in quality or appearance that comes with time—garments may fade, others become shop-soiled, films have a 'sell-by' date on them beyond which the manufacturer will not guarantee results, etc. To clear such items 'sales' are held and individual price tickets are marked down, or a general notice 'all goods reduced by $33\frac{1}{3}$% on marked prices' may signal the mark-down to customers. A few examples will illustrate the calculations required.

Example 14.8. A tailor has a suit for sale marked at £35 which is shop-soiled. He marks it down by $33\frac{1}{3}$%. What will its sale price be (correct to the nearest penny)?

$$
\begin{aligned}
\text{Mark-down} &= 33\tfrac{1}{3}\% \text{ of } £35 \\
&= \tfrac{1}{3} \times £35 \\
&= £11.666 \\
&= £11.67 \\
\text{Sale price} &= £35 - £11.67 \\
&= £23.33
\end{aligned}
$$

Example 14.9. An office equipment store decides to clear unpopular lines by marking down all stock. What will be the sale prices of articles whose original selling prices were as shown below, with the percentage mark-down as indicated?

(a) £4.50 : 20%
(b) £16.90 : 10%
(c) £83.50 : 40%

(a)   Mark-down = 20% of £4.50
                                 = $\frac{1}{5}$ × £4.50
                                 = 90 pence
            Sale price = £4.50 − 90 pence
                       = £3.60

(b)   Mark-down = 10% of £16.90
                                 = $\frac{1}{10}$ × £16.90
                                 = £1.69
            Sale price = £16.90 − £1.69
                       = £15.21

(c)   Mark-down = 40% of £83.50
                                 = $\frac{4}{10}$ of £83.50
                                 = 4 × £8.35
                                 = £33.40
            Sale price = £83.50 − £33.40
                       = £50.10

14.8   Exercises on Mark-downs

1. A shopkeeper's premises are damaged in a storm and stock is affected. He decides to clear it by a range of suitable mark-downs. What will be the storm-damaged price of articles whose original selling prices were as shown below? The percentage mark-down is indicated in each case.

(a) 52p; 25%   (b) £1.20; 40%
(c) £2.50; 20%   (d) £3.44; 12½%
(e) £5.70; 33⅓%   (f) £12.80; 30%
(g) £10.75; 20%   (h) £15; 25%
(i) £32; 15%   (j) £80; 35%

2. Shop-soiled items originally priced as shown below are to be marked down by the percentages shown to clear them from a particular store. What will be the new 'clearance sale' prices?

(a) £7.90; 50%   (b) £13.50; 50%
(c) £15; 60%   (d) £25.50; 40%
(e) £18; 75%   (f) £21.50; 60%
(g) £24; 15%   (h) £42; 35%
(i) £56; 62½%   (j) £85; 65%

14.9   Mental Arithmetic: Bills

A bill is an account for goods supplied or services rendered. One of the commonest business activities is making out bills. It is important to do such calculations mentally wherever possible, rather than relying upon the till to do all the workings for you. For example, consider the following items:

7 packets of detergent at £1.28 each

As we write the answer down as we go along, the mental processes are as follows:

Seven times 8 pence = 56 pence. Write down the 6 pence and remember the 50 pence to carry into the tenpence column.

6

Seven times 20 pence = 140 pence and 50 pence to carry = 190 pence. Write down the 90 pence next to the 6 pence and carry the 100 pence as £1 into the £1 column.

96

Seven times £1 = £7 and £1 makes £8. The answer is:

£8.96

Now consider 4 books at £1.65:

4 fives are 20 Write the 0 down and carry 2	0 —
4 sixes are 24 and 2 are 26 Write down the 6 and carry 2	60
4 ones are 4 and 2 are 6	£6.60

14.10 Simple Bill Calculations

What will be the cost of each of the following?

1. 3 bottles of milk at 26p per bottle
2. 4 packets of detergent at 89p per packet
3. 5 lever-arch files at £1.23 each
4. 12 books at £3.65 each
5. 7 filing cabinets at £89.50 per cabinet
6. 4 kg butter at £1.41 per kg
7. 9 photograph frames at £1.78 each
8. 7 projector bulbs at £3.85 each
9. 24 m^2 carpet at £7 per m^2

10. 3650 rhododendron bushes a £2.50 per bush

14.11 Mental Arithmetic Test

1. 1568 + 2342 + 796 =

2. 2952 ÷ 9 =

3. 130 × 300 =

4. What shall I pay altogether for 9 items at £1.67 each?

5. $\frac{1}{2} \times \frac{1}{4} =$

6. 6.25 ÷ 0.25 =

7. $1\frac{1}{4} + 2\frac{3}{8} + 4\frac{1}{2} =$

8. Change £75.75 to pence

9. A trader buys bicycles to retail at £150. The trade discount is $33\frac{1}{3}$%. What does he pay for a bicycle?

10. What is the average of 4, 7, 9, 12 and 18?

11. What is the cost of a straight fence of 6 panels, supported by posts, if the panels are £5 each and the posts £2 each? Labour, etc., costs £20

12. A retailer banks takings of £1800; 20% of this is his profit. How much profit did he make?

13. An item costing 35p is marked up by a retailer by 20%. What does it sell for?

14. 49 panels each 2 metres wide are erected as a fence on posts 10 centimetres wide. What is the total length of the fence in metres?

15. An item sells for £50 after being marked up by 25%. What was its cost price to the retailer?

15
Rates

15.1 Local Taxation

We all live and work in communities where a variety of services are provided by local government councils. To pay for these services some sort of local taxation has to be imposed. In the United Kingdom this takes the form of **rates**. Rates are levied on *fixed property*—land and buildings. The procedure is for all farms, factories, offices, shops, hotels, etc., and all residential property to be assessed for rates according to a **rateable value** fixed by the Inland Revenue Valuation Officer. The basis for calculating rateable value is as follows:

(a) What would the property have fetched per annum if it has been rented out at a given base date? This is called the **gross value**.

(b) What would the owner renting the property have had to pay out, on average, from the gross rent obtained, for repairs to the property during the year?

(c) Deducting (b) from (a) gives the **net value of the property to the owner**, which is used as the rateable value for the purpose of taxing the property owner.

It will be seen that this is a rather artificial calculation, since most householders have no intention of renting their property out, and the figure for 'average' repairs may not bear much relation to the actual cost of repairs in any one year. The property owner has a right of appeal to an independent rates tribunal if dissatisfied with the figures for rateable value notified to him by the local authority. A typical calculation for rateable value might be:

Property: Office block in city centre (nine suites of offices)

	Gross value	£30 000
Less	Repairs and maintenance	£10 000
	Rateable Value	£20 000

Aggregate Rateable Value

While individual property owners are interested in knowing the rateable value of their property, the local authority is concerned with the **aggregate rateable value** of all the property in its area. The method of levying rates is based upon the yield of a penny rate. This means *'one penny in the pound' for every £1 of rated property in the area.*

Suppose a town's aggregate rateable value is £25 million. A rate of one penny in the £1 will bring in 25 000 000 pence, which is £250 000. Knowing that a penny rate yields this amount, a local authority can easily decide how many pence in the £1 it needs to charge to cover all its expected costs in the year ahead.

15.2   Simple Rate Calculations

From the householders' point of view, once notified of the rateable value of the property and the rate payable in the pound, the calculation of local taxation is very simple. Consider the following examples:

Example 15.1. What will a ratepayer whose property has a rateable value of £240 pay in rates if the rate is fixed at 35 pence in the £1?

The ratepayer must clearly pay 35 pence for every £1 of rateable value (RV):

$$
\begin{array}{r}
\text{Rates payable} = \quad 240 \times 35\text{p} \\
\times\, 35 \\
\hline
1200 \\
7200 \\
\hline
= 8400 \text{ pence} \\
\hline
= £84 \\
\hline
\end{array}
$$

Example 15.2. A garage proprietor whose property is rated at £7800 RV is told that the rate is 57 pence in the £1. How much will he pay?

$$
\begin{aligned}
\text{Rate payable} &= 7800 \times 57 \text{ pence} \\
&= \frac{7800 \times 57}{100} \text{ pounds} \\
&= £78 \times 57 \qquad\qquad \text{(cancelling by 100)}
\end{aligned}
$$

$$\begin{array}{r} 78 \\ \times\ 57 \\ \hline 546 \\ 3900 \\ \hline \pounds 4446 \\ \hline\hline \end{array}$$

$$= \pounds 4446$$

Example 15.3. A city council has property in its area with a total RV of £275 620 000. What will a penny rate bring in?

Yield of a penny rate = 275 620 000 pence

$$= \frac{\pounds 275\ 620\ 0\cancel{0}\cancel{0}}{1\cancel{0}\cancel{0}} \qquad \text{(cancelling by 100)}$$

$$= \pounds 2\ 756\ 200$$

15.3 Exercises: Simple Rate Calculations

1. A council fixes the rates in its area at 27 pence in the £1. What will householders whose rateable values are as shown below pay in rates for the year?

(a) RV = £85   (b) RV = £120
(c) RV = £160   (d) RV = £235
(e) RV = £450   (f) RV = £850

2. A city council fixes the rates in its area at 85 pence in the £1. What will the following business premises, whose rateable values are as shown below, pay in rates each *half* year?

(a) Office £340 RV   (b) Cinema £2600 RV
(c) Garage £2450 RV   (d) Factory £8550 RV
(e) Warehouse £3800 RV   (f) Car park £7250 RV

3. Find the yield of a penny rate in each of the following areas, where the aggregate rateable values are as shown below. You should be able to do all these calculations mentally, so that only the answer needs to be written down.

(a) £274 500   (b) £382 000
(c) £2 745 350   (d) £3 965 280
(e) £27 360 700   (f) £36 854 620
(g) £137 720 480   (h) £295 721 540
(i) £745 464 620   (j) £795 362 730

15.4 Paying for Services on the Rates

Once the councillors know what a penny rate will bring in it is easy to fix the rates for the coming year so as to cover the budgeted expenditure.

Example 15.4. The Homeshire County budget shows expected expenditure of £14 455 000. A penny rate will raise £295 000. What rate must be charged in the pound?

Since one penny rate raises £295 000 the question is 'How many £295 000 are there in £14 455 000?'

$$\frac{14\ 455\ 000}{295\ 000}$$

$$= \frac{2891}{59} \qquad \text{(after cancelling by 1000 and then by 5)}$$

$$\begin{array}{r} 49 \\ 59\,)\overline{2891} \\ 236 \\ \hline 531 \\ 531 \\ \hline \cdots \end{array}$$

$$= 49$$

The rate set must be 49 pence in the £1 to raise the necessary money.

Example 15.5. A proposal to erect a leisure centre complex in Overstone City is costed at £3 500 000. A penny rate will raise £450 000. What rate will be necessary to build the leisure complex (Answer to the nearest penny)?

$$\text{Cost of complex} = £3\ 500\ 000$$
$$\text{Yield of a penny rate} = £450\ 000$$
How many times does £450 000 divide into £3 500 000?

$$\frac{3\ 500\ 000}{450\ 000}$$

$$= \frac{70}{9} \qquad \text{(cancelling by 10 000 and 5)}$$

$$= 7.7\dot{} \text{ times}$$

Therefore (to the nearest penny) a rate of 8p must be levied.

Example 15.6. A local authority has property in its area to an aggregate rateable value of £24 275 300. Its budget shows that services to be supplied will cost £8 324 720. What rate must be levied? (Answer to the nearest 0.1 of a penny.)

$$\text{Rate to be levied} = \frac{\text{Cost of services}}{\text{Yield of a penny rate}}$$

$$= \frac{£8\,324\,720}{£242\,753}$$

```
              34.29
242753 ) 8324720
         728259
         ———————
         1042130
          971012
         ———————
          711180
          485506
         ———————
         2256740
```

$$= 34.3 \text{ pence in the } £1$$

15.5 Exercises: Fixing the Rates

1. What rate in the pound must be levied in the five towns named below if the budgeted costs of services and the yields of a penny rate are as shown?

Town	Budgeted costs	Yield of 1p rate
A	£999 000	£37 000
B	£3 607 500	£55 500
C	£20 394 400	£275 600
D	£18 215 680	£325 280
E	£63 918 800	£726 350

2. What rate in the pound must be levied in the five counties named below if the aggregate rateable values of the property in the county and the budgeted costs of services are as shown? (Hint: Find the yield of a penny rate first.)

County	Budgeted costs	Aggregate RV
(a) V	£8 525 000	£27 500 000
(b) W	£13 387 500	£38 250 000
(c) X	£212 500 000	£250 000 000
(d) Y	£81 554 000	£148 280 000
(e) Z	£497 109 670	£720 448 800

3. A local authority has an aggregate rateable value of £558 000. What

rate in the £1 must be levied to pay for the following items (to nearest 0.1 of a penny)?

(a) A walkway alongside a local river, costing £7000
(b) A dust cart costing £17 500
(c) A flood-control scheme costing £120 000
(d) A school bus costing £14 750
(e) A sports pavilion costing £32 750

4. In a certain town the aggregate RV is £72 780 000. (a) What will a penny rate bring in? (b) What rate will it be necessary to levy if total budgeted expenditure for the year is £14 175 000? (Answer correct to the nearest tenth of a penny.)

5. In a certain town a proposed facility will cost £2 780 000 to build, while running costs in excess of income earned by admission charges are expected to cost £27 500 per annum. The aggregate rateable value of the property in the area is £24 000 000. (a) What rate must be levied if the building is to be paid for, and (b) what rate will be necessary each year to cover the running costs? Give your answer in each case correct to the nearest 0.1 of a penny.

15.6   Mental Arithmetic Test

Write down the answers only to these mental arithmetic questions:

1. $127 + 364 + 1295 + 726 =$

2. $2763 - 1518 =$

3. $495 \times 9 =$

4. $8720 \div 8 =$

5. $0.7 \times 0.3 =$

6. $19.5 \div 1.5 =$

7. $\frac{1}{2} + \frac{2}{3} + \frac{3}{4} =$

8. What is 20% of £5500?

9. $\frac{2}{3} \times \frac{9}{10} =$

10. Write 1980 in Roman figures

11. What is the average of 125, 175 and 195?

12. What is the simple interest on £3000 for 3 months at 16% per annum?

13. What shall I pay for 5 electronic calculators at £7.75 each?

14. A fence 30 metres long is to be erected from panels 2 metres wide at £5 per panel. How much will it cost if the posts cost £30 and the labour £20?

15. £9500 is shared between Peter, John and Mary so that Mary has twice as much as each of the boys. How much does Mary get?

16
Electricity, Gas and Water Charges

16.1 Public Utilities

Electricity, gas and water services are often called **public utilities**. Such industries have heavy capital costs, and tend therefore to be run as nationalised undertakings. They charge consumers on a variety of scales of charges, called **tariffs**. Sometimes there is a 'flat' tariff—the same to everyone—but more usually there is some sort of meter installed to measure the quantity of gas, electricity or water used.

The cost of laying gas and water pipes, or of bringing in electricity by cables, is high and it is only economic if all premises are connected. Some inducement may be offered to encourage all householders to use the supply. The chief objection by consumers is the cost, and for this reason it became customary to spread installation costs and the charges for appliances over a considerable period—several years in many cases. The result is that business calculations in this field usually involve additions to the quarterly bills for hire purchase, service charges, repairs and alterations.

16.2 Electricity Charges

Electricity charges in the United Kingdom are based on a standing charge per quarter year and a charge for each unit of electricity used. The standing charge is made to cover overhead costs related to the supply of electricity to premises. It is quite low; about £5 per quarter. The charge per unit recovers the costs of generating electricity, and yields a profit to the Board. The unit of electricity is a *kilowatt-hour*, the amount of electricity used by an appliance burning one kilowatt when it is switched on for one hour.

Besides the standing charge, consumers pay per unit according to the tariff selected. A standard tariff is charged to consumers for ordinary supplies, but off-peak supplies are cheaper. Typical off-peak appliances are storage heaters which heat up during the night and then give out their heat during the daytime when they are not using electricity. Business and industrial users frequently get cheaper rates if they take large quantities of electricity from the national grid.

An extract from a bill rendered to a typical consumer paying the standard rate is shown in Fig. 16.1.

METER READING		UNITS USED	UNIT RATE (pence)	AMOUNT £	STANDING CHARGE £	VAT CODE	TOTALS £
PRESENT	PREVIOUS						
14600	13377	1223	4.18	51 12	5 07	0	56 19

Fig. 16.1. An electricity bill.

Notes

(i) The difference between the two meter readings gives the number of units used in the period.

(ii) The unit rate, given in pence, is charged for each unit.

(iii) The standing charge is the same for all consumers in that type of property.

(iv) Supplies of electricity are zero-rated for value added tax.

(v) The total payable is due as soon as the bill is received by the consumer.

Example 16.1. A consumer using off-peak electricity at a cheaper rate is charged for 1223 units at a standard rate of 4.18 pence per unit, and 1492 cheap-rate units at 2.25 pence per unit. The standing charge is £5.07 and this consumer is also charged £11.65 for the seventh instalment (out of 20 instalments) on storage heaters supplied earlier.

$$
\begin{array}{lr}
 & £ \\
\text{Standard rate units used} = 1223 \times 4.18 \text{ pence per unit} = & 51.12 \\
\text{Cheap rate units used} = 1492 \times 2.25 \text{ pence per unit} = & 33.57 \\
\text{Standing charge} = & 5.07 \\
\hline
 & 89.76 \\
\text{Hire purchase charges (storage heaters—No. 7 of 20)} = & 11.65 \\
\hline
 & £101.41 \\
\end{array}
$$

(*Note:* The charge for storage heaters has been split into 20 payments, of which this is the seventh payment. With bills being rendered quarterly this means the payment is spread over five years.)

Calculations:

1223	1492
× 4.18 pence	× 2.25 pence
9784	7460
12230	29840
489200	298400
5112.14 pence	3357.00 pence
= £51.12	= £33.57

16.3 Exercises: Electricity Charges

1. The following consumers are all charged for electricity on the basis of a standing charge of £7.20 per quarter and a standard rate per unit consumed of 4.62 pence per unit. What will their bills be in the quarter shown? (Calculations correct to the nearest penny.)

Name	Units used in quarter	Other charges
(a) Mr A	1825	HP £16.50
(b) Mrs B	1162	—
(c) Miss C	275	Alterations £8.40
(d) Mr D	2426	HP £11.20
(e) Mr E	1832	—

2. The following consumers are charged for electricity at a standard rate of 4.48 pence per unit, and a standing charge of £6.05 pence. Meter readings and 'Other charges' are as shown below. What will be the balance owing on their accounts for the quarter? (Calculations correct to the nearest penny.)

Name	Meter readings Present	Previous	Other charges
(a) Mr V	21 742	20 305	HP £11.80
(b) Mrs W	38 295	36 172	Repairs £10.50
(c) Mr X	41 636	40 298	HP £17.50
(d) Miss Y	17 814	15 738	—
(e) Mr Z	9 916	8 777	Alterations £28.50

3. The following consumers are charged at both standard and off-peak rates for electricity used. The standing charge is £6.78 each, and 'Other charges' are shown. Calculate (correct to the nearest penny) the total electricity charges payable for the quarter concerned.

Name	Standard rate units charged (4.32 pence per unit)	Off-peak rates units charged (2.25 pence per unit)	Other charges
(a) Mrs P	842	1742	HP £27.50
(b) Mr Q	636	1595	HP £14.50
(c) Mrs R	725	862	Repairs £10.80
(d) Mr T	1425	2385	—
(e) Mr S	1106	2426	HP £11.80

4. The following business users of electricity pay a basic charge agreed with the Electricity Board, and then a standard rate of 4.28 pence per unit for an agreed quota of units. The rest of the electricity they use is much cheaper, based on a 'heavy-user' tariff at 1.75 pence per unit. Calculate the electricity charge for the quarter for each of them. (Calculations correct to the nearest penny.)

Name	Basic charge	Agreed quota	Total units used in quarter
(a) ABC Plc	£80	10 000	38 543
(b) DEF Plc	£100	15 000	49 750
(c) GHJ Plc	£250	18 000	63 239
(d) KLM Plc	£350	20 000	71 560
(e) NOP Plc	£400	25 000	85 990

16.4 Gas Charges

In the United Kingdom gas charges are based on the *therm*, the British unit of heat. As with electricity charges, a **standing charge** is imposed per quarter year, and the gas supplied is metered to determine the number of therms used. A variety of tariffs apply according to the type of user. There is a 'domestic rate' for householders, but those using gas for central heating may be supplied more cheaply after a basic quota of gas has been used. Once again appliances are frequently supplied on hire purchase, and charges for services are sometimes spread over a period of time to help less wealthy customers. In view of the danger, no charges are made for attending to gas leaks.

Business users and industrial customers using large quantities can negotiate special tariffs.

A typical account might appear as in Fig. 16.2.

Example 16.2. A consumer using gas for domestic and central heating purposes is charged a standing charge of £5.50; 25.5 pence per therm for the first 60 therms; and 21.25 pence per therm thereafter. Total consumption is 93 therms. He also pays £12.25 per quarter for a cooker. What will his quarterly bill amount to?

| READING OR INVOICE DATE | METER READING | | GAS SUPPLIED | | PRICE PER THERM | AMOUNT | VAT CODE | VAT CHARGES | HIRE PURCHASE |
	PRESENT	PREVIOUS	CUBIC FEET (HUNDREDS)	THERMS					CASH SETTLEMENT VALUE IF PAID WITHIN 14 DAYS
19 6	5127	5049	78						
19 6	METER EXCHANGE								
16 7	0027	0000	27						
		TOTAL		108.67					
		52.00 THERMS AT			24.600	12.79	A	0.00	
		56.67 THERMS AT			19.300	10.94	A	0.00	
		STANDING CHARGE				4.40	A	0.00	
		TOTAL VAT CODE A @ ZERO %				0.00			

Fig. 16.2. A gas bill.

Notes

(i) The difference between the two meter readings gives the quantity of gas used. In this case a faulty meter had to be exchanged on 19 June.

(ii) The volume used is changed to therms by taking account of the calorific value—not shown on this extract.

(iii) The therms are charged at two different rates, a quota of 52 therms at a standard rate and the rest at a cheaper rate.

(iv) The standing charge is then added.

(v) Gas is zero rated for value added tax purposes.

(vi) The total £28.13 is shown on the bottom of the bill—not shown in this extract.

		£
Standing charge	=	5.50
Therms at standard rate = 60 × 25.5 pence	=	15.30
Therms at cheap rate = 33 × 21.25 pence	=	7.01
Hire purchase charges		12.25
		£40.06

Calculations:

25.5	21.25
60	33
1530.0 pence	6 375
	63 750
= £15.30	701.25 pence
	= £7.01

16.5   Exercises: Gas Charges

1. The consumers listed below are charged for gas at a flat rate of 24.6 pence per therm used. There is a standing charge of £5.40 per quarter and charges for hire purchase, alterations, etc., during the quarter are as shown. Calculate the quarterly charges for each customer.

	Name	Therms used	Other charges per quarter
(a)	Mr G	145	HP £12.85
(b)	Miss H	47	HP £11.00
(c)	Mrs I	86	—
(d)	Mrs J	123	HP £14.58
(e)	Mr K	148	Installation £13.60

2. The consumers listed below pay a standing charge of £4.48 per quarter and then 28.5 pence for the first 55 therms. After that they pay 18.5 pence per therm. Other charges are as shown. Calculate the quarterly charges for each consumer.

	Name	Therms used	Other charges
(a)	Mr V	76	HP £9
(b)	Mr W	132	HP £8.50
(c)	Mrs X	105	Installation £17.25
(d)	Miss Y	29	Repairs £14.80
(e)	Mr Z	142	HP £17.50

3. The following industrial users of gas are charged for gas on the following basis: (a) a basic quarterly charge based upon the likely volume of gas used; (b) 25 pence per therm for the first 1000 therms; (c) 15.5 pence per therm for the remainder of supplies. The meter readings are as shown below. Calculate the charge for the quarter in each case.

Name	Basic charge per quarter	Meter readings Present	Previous
(a) Industrial Cement Plc	£250	27 142	21 676
(b) Crispmakers Plc	£500	39 816	28 594
(c) United Biscuit Co.	£850	72 594	43 726
(d) Car Body Repairs Plc	£680	69 316	54 262
(e) Iron Founders Plc	£850	72 168	47 377

16.6 Water Rates

Except for large industrial users of water, whose water is metered and charged accordingly, the water rates are based on three elements. First a local water authority responsible for delivery of water to premises, and for the quality of drinking water, levies an annual water rate. This is in two parts, a **standing charge** and a **water rate based upon rateable value**. Then an annual area water authority rate is added to the local rate to finance an area authority responsible for the collection of water, the control of reservoirs and the conservation of rivers and river catchment areas.

A typical account is shown in Fig. 16.3.

LOCAL WATER COMPANY CHARGES	RATE per annum	CHARGE	STANDING CHARGE	TOTAL DUE
WATER SUPPLY	R.V. = £142.50 at 5.600P	7.98	1.50	9.48
AREA WATER AUTHORITY CHARGES	12.600P	17.96		17.96
				27.44

Fig. 16.3. A bill for water rates.

Notes

(i) This property has a rateable value of £142.50.

(ii) The rate is fixed at 5.6 pence in the £1 for the local water authority and 12.6 pence in the £1 for the area water authority.

Example 16.3. A householder whose property has a rateable value of £126 is charged water rates on the basis of a standing charge of £1.50, a local water rate of 5.9 pence in the £1 and an area authority rate of 23.2 pence in the £1. What will the water charge be?

$$
\begin{array}{lr}
 & \text{£} \\
\text{Standing charge} = & 1.50 \\
\text{Local charge} = 126 \times 5.9 \text{ pence} = & 7.43 \\
\end{array}
$$

$$
\begin{array}{r}
126 \\
5.9 \\
\hline
1134 \\
6300 \\
\hline
743.4 \text{ pence}
\end{array}
$$

$$
\text{Area charge} = 126 \times 23.2 \text{ pence} = 29.23
$$

$$
\text{£38.16}
$$

$$
\begin{array}{r}
126 \\
23.2 \\
\hline
252 \\
3780 \\
25200 \\
\hline
2923.2 \text{ pence}
\end{array}
$$

16.7   Exercises: Water Rates

1. The following occupiers of premises all live in the same area where the water rates are based on a standing charge of £2.25, a local rate of 7.25 pence in the £1 and an area rate of 16.95 pence in the £1. Rateable values of their premises are as shown. What is the amount payable by each?

Name	RV	Name	RV
(a) Mr R	£240	(b) Mr U	£155
(c) Mr S	£295	(d) V W Plc	£1760
(e) T Co. Plc	£460	(f) XYZ Plc	£880

2. Calculate the water rate payable by the following occupiers of premises whose charges are calculated on the basis of a standing charge and rateable values and rates as shown.

Name	RV	Standing charge	Local rate	Area rate
(a) Mr A	£320	£2.80	5.8 pence in £1	16.5 pence in £1
(b) Mr B	£240	£3.50	6.4 pence in £1	18.9 pence in £1
(c) F.C. Plc	£560	£2.40	7.25 pence in £1	21.6 pence in £1
(d) RTS Plc	£720	£2.75	4.6 pence in £1	18.4 pence in £1
(e) Mrs C	£140	£3.25	5.4 pence in £1	19.5 pence in £1

16.8 Fahrenheit and Celsius Degrees of Temperature

Everyday measurements of temperature are today made in degrees
Celsius, on a scale which ranges from the freezing point of water at
0° Celsius to the boiling point of water at 100° Celsius. The Fahrenheit scale is still in use for many everyday purposes. This varies
from 32° for the freezing point of water to 212° for the boiling
point of water. It is still necessary therefore to be able to convert
temperatures measured on one scale into temperatures measured
on the other. The two scales are illustrated in Fig. 16.4.

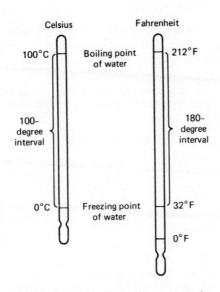

Fig. 16.4. The Fahrenheit and Celsius scales compared.

The link between the two scales is that there are 100 degrees on
the Celsius range and 180 degrees on the Fahrenheit range. These
two ranges are therefore in the ratio of 100:180 = 5:9. However,

since the Fahrenheit scale starts at 32° we also have to adjust for this starting point.

The rules are therefore as follows:

Changing Celsius to Fahrenheit

(a) Divide the Celsius figures by 5 and multiply by 9 (because there will be more Fahrenheit degrees than Celsius degrees).

(b) Add on 32 degrees for the higher starting point under the Fahrenheit system.

Example 16.4. The temperature at Jericho in the Dead Sea Valley is 50° Celsius. What is the equivalent in Fahrenheit?

$$\frac{50}{5} \times 9 = 10 \times 9 = 90°$$

Add on 32° for the higher starting point

$$= 90° + 32° = 122° \text{ F}$$

Changing Fahrenheit to Celsius

(a) Subtract 32° for the higher starting point under Fahrenheit.

(b) Divide the degrees left by 9 and multiply by 5 (because there will be fewer degrees under the Celsius system).

Example 16.5. A healthy human being has a body temperature of 98.4° Fahrenheit. What is the equivalent temperature in Celsius?

Deducting 32°, we have

$$98.4° - 32° = 66.4°$$

Adjusting this in the ratio 9:5, we have

$$\frac{66.4}{9} \times 5° \text{ C}$$

$$= \frac{332.0}{9} °C$$

$$= 36.88 °C$$

$$= 36.9 °C$$

16.9   Exercises: Converting Temperatures

In these mental arithmetic sums you may jot down the answers to each part of the calculation as you do it (do not write in this book unless it is your own property):

1. Change 25° Celsius to Fahrenheit.

2. Change 15° Celsius to Fahrenheit.

3. Change 32° Celsius to Fahrenheit.

4. Change 86° Fahrenheit to Celsius.

5. Change 113° Fahrenheit to Celsius.

6. Change 140° Fahrenheit to Celsius.

16.10 Mental Arithmetic Test

1. $274 \times 12 =$

2. $525 + 429 + 316 + 214 =$

3. How many theatre tickets at £7.50 can 1 buy for £30?

4. A team scores as follows in five football matches; 3; 1; 0; 7; 4. What is the average score?

5. $0.7 \times 0.4 =$

6. $1\frac{1}{2} + 2\frac{3}{4} + 3\frac{7}{8} =$

7. How many grams in 1 tonne?

8. 6 men take 5 days to plant out an ornamental garden. At the same rate how long will it take 4 men?

9. Change $7\frac{1}{2}$ minutes to seconds

10. VAT is imposed at 20% on motor vehicles. What will be the cost of a car whose 'free of VAT' price is £5500?

11. A gas bill is based on 30p per therm for 150 therms and a standing charge of £8.50. What is the amount payable?

12. A shopkeeper adds 25% to goods which cost him £15. What is the selling price?

13. A shopkeeper has added 25% to goods he sells for £20. What did they cost him?

14. What year is carved on a memorial stone reading MCMLXXXII?

15. My water rate is based on a standing charge of £5 and a rate of 25p in the £1 of my rateable value of £240. How much shall I pay?

17
Telephone and Telex Charges

17.1 Telephone Charges

Businesses today use the telephone system far more, and the postal system far less, than in former times. It is not cheap to use the telephone, expecially at peak periods. Between 9 am and 1 pm the charge is very high, depending on the distance called. For calls over 56 kilometres each unit used lasts only 10 seconds. Between 1 pm and 6 pm the unit lasts 15 seconds. The cost of a unit varies from year to year, but at the time of writing it is 4.3 pence per unit. So a peak period call costs 25.8 pence per minute, and an afternoon call costs 17.2 pence per minute. A call to America costs 92 pence per minute. These charges are subject to alteration and are only given as illustrations; for example a 5p charge per unit has been proposed.

Charges are levied as follows:

(a) Rental charges. These are charges for the use of equipment, such as telephone handsets, switchboards, callmakers (*which dial numbers automatically*), etc. They are called **recurring charges** because they are charged every quarter.

(b) Metered units charges. These are charges for the calls made. The meter clocks up the units used as each call is made, and takes account of the time of day. The meter ticks over more quickly at peak cost periods, charging more units for the same amount of time. Thus a one-minute long-distance call at mid-morning uses 6 units (25.8 pence) while the same time in the afternoon it uses 4 units (17.2 pence); at off-peak times it uses only $1\frac{1}{4}$ units and costs only 5.375 pence.

(c) Operator-controlled calls. These are more expensive than self-dialled calls because of the labour costs involved, and are listed and charged for each call.

(d) Directory charges. One's own local directory is supplied free of charge. Those requiring directories for other areas must pay a charge for each directory supplied.

A typical calculation is as shown below, based on a charge of 5 pence per unit.

Example 17.1

	£
Rental and other recurring charges	15.75
Metered units to 31 March 4827 at 5p	241.35
Operator calls to hand on 31 March 19 . .	
20 February	54
27 February	1.58
5 March	24
Total charges (exclusive of VAT)	259.46
VAT at 15%	38.92
	298.38
Directories supplied	2.56
Total payable	£300.94

(*Note:* Directories are zero rated for VAT.)

17.2 Exercises: Telephone Charges

1. What will be the charge for units used at 5 pence per unit in each of the cases below? (Ignore VAT.)

(a) 240 units   (b) 326 units
(c) 576 units   (d) 784 units
(e) 1856 units   (f) 2124 units
(g) 3784 units   (h) 5612 units
(i) 12 754 units   (j) 18 268 units

2. The five householders listed below pay the same recurring charges for rental of £15.75. Other items charged are shown below. All charges, including rental, pay VAT at 15%, except for directory charges which are zero-rated. Work out the total bill in each case, to the nearest penny if necessary.

	Name	Units used (5p per unit)	Operator-controlled calls (total)	Other charges
(a)	Mr A	484	£1.74	Directories £2.50
(b)	Mrs B	2165	£2.86	Repairs £3.80
(c)	Miss C	172	£1.95	Installation £29.50
(d)	Mr D	2345	£7.38	Directories £2.80
(e)	Mrs E	4825	£1.56	Directories £3.60

3. The five firms listed below pay telephone charges as shown. Calculate the total bill for each firm including VAT at 15% (except for directory charges). (Calculations, where necessary, correct to the nearest penny.)

Name	Rental £	Units at 5p	Operator calls (£)	Other charges
(a) XY Co. Plc	27.54	12 724	1.76	Installation £82.50
(b) Showbiz Plc	63.55	19 864	15.20	Directories £3.50
(c) Electrical Plc	45.65	5 868	0.54	Directories £8.25
(d) Compubooks Plc	38.75	7 265	1.65	—
(e) Telesell Plc	142.56	27 364	13.25	Directories £4.76

17.3   Telex Charges

A telex machine is a device which sends typewritten messages over the telephone network. An electronic typewriter in one office can be connected to a similar machine in any office throughout the world, switching it on and causing it to send out its 'answerback' code. As soon as the answerback code is received the typist can type the message which will appear on both the sending and the receiving machines. The clerk at the receiving end tears off the message, which is exactly like a telegram and sends it to the department which will be interested. Messages arriving overnight (a daytime message from the United Kingdom will arrive in Australia or Hong Kong in the middle of the night) are cleared by the telex clerk on arrival at the office next morning, and the matters can then be dealt with at once.

Charges for telex include **installation charges**, **rental charges** for the hire of the necessary equipment and **call charges** which are based either on 'units' or 'minutes'. Units are used for local calls within the United Kingdom and calls to Europe and North Africa. The unit gives a certain time for the transmission of messages—the time decreasing with peak periods and with distance. Thus a unit gives 60 seconds for local calls, but only 7.5 seconds for calls to Finland, and 6 seconds for calls to Tunisia. Minutes of time are used for calls to other countries around the world—for example, calls to Australia cost 90 pence per minute. This is quite economical for instantaneous delivery of messages. Sometimes calls are connected by the operator, and these are charged for at a special rate, with a minimum time of three minutes.

A typical calculation might be as follows:

Example 17.2

	£
Recurring charges: quarterly rental	210.00
Non-recurring charges: units used	
12 734 at 2½p per unit	318.35
Operator connections	4.75
	533.10
VAT at 15%	79.96
	£613.06

17.4   Exercises: Telex Charges

1. The offices listed below pay a telex rental charge of £275 per quarter and 2½ pence for each unit. Other charges are as shown below. Work out the total charge in each case, including VAT at 15%. (Calculations, where necessary, correct to the nearest penny.)

Office	Units used	Timed calls (£)	Operator calls (£)
A	7 265	27.56	3.56
B	5 898	186.95	17.26
C	12 426	172.65	19.85
D	15 284	585.24	27.58
E	18 249	385.60	16.54

2. The firms listed below pay a telex rental charge of £275 per quarter and 2½ pence per unit. Other charges are as shown below. Work out the total charge in each case, including VAT at 15%. (Calculations where necessary correct to the nearest penny.)

Firm's name	Units used	Timed calls (£)	Operator calls (£)
AB Plc	3 724	14.56	—
CD Plc	5 896	27.34	3.70
EF Plc	9 742	18.95	17.20
GH Plc	12 856	118.72	115.20
JK Plc	17 232	136.54	65.30

17.5   Mental Arithmetic: Significant Figures

Sometimes we are asked to say how many significant figures there are in a number. For example, consider the number 52 934. Each of these digits is significant—it means something. The 5 is 50 000, and the 2 is 2000 while the 4 is four units. If we are asked to give this correct to the nearest thousand we need only look at the 5 and the 2, 52 thousand. As the 2 thousand is followed by 934 (almost another thousand) we should—to give it *correct* to the nearest thousand—say 53 000. We must put in the three 0's to make sure that everyone realises the place value of the five and the three.

A difficulty now arises if we use this figure in any calculation. For example, suppose we were told that 27 335 lorries were sold last year, and that the figure of 53 000 given above was the number of cars sold. If we add these two figures together we get 80 335 vehicles altogether. The question now is 'How significant is each of the figures in 80 335?' Since the 53 000 figure was correct to the nearest thousand, we cannot really believe any figures below the thousand figure. The 335 appears to be accurate, but it is not, because the 000 we added it to in 53 000 was not accurate. We can never get a significant (meaningful) answer from adding together inaccurate figures. So the significant figures are 80, and the answer is only sensible if we treat it as 80 000.

Example 17.3. A figure of 24 236 is added to a figure which has been corrected to the nearest hundred as 3800. What is the result of adding these figures together and how many figures are significant in the answer?

$$
\begin{array}{r}
24236 \\
+\ 3800 \\
\hline
28036 \\
\hline
\end{array}
$$

Because the 3800 was correct to the nearest 100 we do not know what the figures were in the last two places. Therefore only the figures 280 are really significant in the answer and we should give it as 28 000 (or 280 hundreds).

Example 17.4. Add together the figures 39 729 and 50 000. The latter figure has been given correct to the nearest ten thousand: it only has one significant figure, the 5. Before we can add 39 729 to this figure we should express it also correct to the nearest ten thousand, which is 40 000. Therefore:

$$
\begin{array}{r}
40\ 000 \\
+\ 50\ 000 \\
\hline
90\ 000 \\
\hline
\end{array}
$$

The answer has only 1 significant figure, the 9.

17.6   Exercises: Significant Figures

In each of the sums below one figure is given correct to the nearest thousand. Give the answer to the sum with the same number of significant figures.

1. 27 352 + 38 000 =
2. 42 000 + 37 890 =
3. 17 830 + 18 000 =
4. 129 000 + 114 743 =
5. 138 286 +   72 000 =

17.7   Mental Arithmetic Test

1. 2475 ÷ 5 =
2. 8174 × 9 =
3. 1.2 ÷ 0.6 =
4. 5.75 × 0.02 =
5. What is $16\frac{2}{3}$% of £1260?
6. A chapter in a book is headed LIV. What is this in Arabic numbers?
7. 'All stock marked down 25% on listed prices' reads a sale notice. What shall I pay for an appliance listed as £184.60?
8. What is the simple interest on £6000 for 2 years at $12\frac{1}{2}$%?
9. Divide £28 500 by 8
10. $4\frac{1}{2} + 2\frac{3}{5} + 1\frac{7}{10} =$
11. A retailer marks up a £700 diamond ring by 30%. What is its selling price?
12. Telephone calls to America cost 94p per minute. What shall I pay for a call lasting $4\frac{1}{2}$ minutes?
13. Share £18 000 between four people in the ratios 3:3:2:1
14. Change 68° Fahrenheit to Celsius
15. Telephone charges are 4p per unit + 15% VAT. What shall I pay if I use 10 000 units?

18
Motor Vehicle Calculations

18.1 Motor Vehicle Expenses

Every business today has motor vehicles of one sort or another for the delivery and collection of goods and the use of sales representatives and managers. The costs are not inconsiderable: a single heavy lorry may cost as much as £1500 in road tax per annum and a set of new tyres may be well over £1000. The chief expenses may be listed as follows:

(a) The capital cost of the vehicle itself, spread over the vehicle's lifetime.

(b) The running costs, including petrol, oil, servicing and repairs.

(c) Road fund licence charges.

(d) Insurance charges. A driver must be insured against all 'third party' claims. These are claims made for injury to other people and damage to property owned by others. It is usual to cover one's own vehicle against fire and theft, so that a common type of policy is called **'third party, fire and theft'**. **Comprehensive policies** also cover the driver himself and his vehicle. (The word 'comprehensive' means 'including much', but it may not cover every possible loss.)

In calculating motor vehicle expenses we must of course take account of all these costs, but it is not very helpful to know just what the total cost for the year is: we need to know how effective the vehicle is in serving the firm. Consider two vehicles, with details as follows:

Vehicle A—Total cost £24 000 in the year. Kilometres run = 48 000.

Vehicle B—Total cost £8500 in the year. Kilometres run = 4000.

Vehicle B's costs are lower, but how efficient was it? Let us find the cost per kilometre.

Vehicle A—Cost per kilometre = $\dfrac{£24\,000}{48\,000}$ = £0.50 = 50 pence

Vehicle B—Cost per kilometre = $\dfrac{£8500}{4000}$ = £2.125

Clearly the first vehicle is much more economical, since it is used very intensively. The other vehicle must be idle much of the time.

Example 18.1. A heavy goods vehicle incurs costs in a particular year as follows: depreciation £3200, road tax £540, insurance £280, repairs and spare parts £1460. It covers 50 000 kilometres in the year, running 4 kilometres per litre of fuel at 36 pence per litre. Find:

(a) The total running costs incurred.
(b) The average cost per kilometre (to nearest tenth of a penny).

(a) We may add up the costs as follows:

		£
Depreciation		3200
Road tax		540
Insurance		280
Repairs and spare parts		1460
Fuel $\dfrac{50\,000}{4} \times 36$ pence		
$= 50\,000 \times 9$		
$= 450\,000$ pence $=$		4500
Total running costs		£9980

(b) Average cost per kilometre

$\dfrac{9980 \times 100}{50\,000}$ (changing £9980 to pence)
            (dividing by the kilometres run)

$= \dfrac{998}{50}$ pence

$= \dfrac{99.8}{5}$ pence

$= 19.96$
$= 20.0$ pence (correct to nearest tenth of a penny)

18.2 Exercises: Motor Vehicle Expenses

1. Find (i) the total running costs per annum and (ii) the running cost in pence per kilometre of the five vehicles listed below. Fuel is 35 pence per litre (costs per kilometre in pence correct to one decimal place).

Tax	Depreciation	Insurance	Repairs	Kilometres run	Kilometres per litre
(a) £100	£480	£94	£240	24 000	8
(b) £180	£420	£162	£180	42 000	6
(c) £240	£2800	£180	£360	56 000	5
(d) £620	£4400	£225	£840	90 000	4
(e) £880	£5100	£360	£720	102 000	4

2. A firm has a small fleet of six cars whose running costs are as shown below, against the names of the representatives who use them. Fuel is 38 pence per litre. (i) What are the running costs of each car? (ii) What is the running cost per kilometre of each car? (Answer correct to the nearest tenth of a penny.) From these results decide which vehicle gives the most economical service to the firm.

Name of representative	Depre- ciation (£)	Tax (£)	Insurance (£)	Repairs (£)	Kilometres run	Kilometres per litre
Mr Smith	960	70	145	£65.50	18 000	18
Mr Jones	840	70	162	£82.50	20 000	16
Miss Green	1250	70	98	£125.40	24 000	12
Miss Johnson	860	70	115	£174.80	33 000	11
Mrs Wilde	720	70	165	£186.50	54 000	9
Mr Mortimer	1340	70	185	£234.50	36 000	8

3. At the beginning of the year, a businessman bought a car for £4250. The tax for the year was £70 and the insurance premium was £158.50. Petrol cost 38 pence per litre and the car (which averaged 12 kilometres per litre) was driven a total of 25 000 kilometres during the year. At the end of the year the car was sold for £3000. Calculate (a) the total cost of the year's motoring and (b) the average cost per kilometre, correct to the nearest 0.1p.

4. The expenses of running a car during a recent year were as follows: tax £70, insurance £144.50, depreciation £680, maintenance £184.50. The driver had to pay the first £50 of an accident claim he was forced to make. During the year he travelled 22 000 kilometres with an average petrol consumption of 8 kilometres per litre. If the cost of petrol was 38 pence per litre calculate (a) the total cost of the year's motoring, and (b) the average cost per kilometres in pence correct to one tenth of a penny.

5. The costs of running a motor vehicle in a certain firm are agreed to include one fifth of the original purchase price as depreciation, as well as the actual costs recorded on the vehicle cost sheet over the year. One particular vehicle, which cost £15 250, has the following costs recorded: road fund licence £325, insurance £285, hazardous goods insurance £500, servicing £380, repairs £658, diesel fuel £540, tyres £420, share of overhead £350.

(a) Find the total cost for the year.
(b) Express each of the costs listed as a percentage of the total cost (calculations correct to one decimal place).
(c) Find the cost per kilometre run, the distance covered in the year being 36 000 kilometres (calculations correct to one decimal place).

18.3 Speed, Time and Distance

There is a relationship between the distance that we travel on any journey, the speed we travel at and the journey time. This is usually expressed in a simple formula

$$\text{Distance} = \text{Speed} \times \text{Time}$$

or more briefly

$$D = ST$$

(*Note:* In all such calculations we must think of speed in terms of average speed for the journey.)

Example 18.2. A heavy goods lorry travels for $6\frac{1}{4}$ hours at an average speed of 60 kilometres per hour. How far does it travel?

$$
\begin{aligned}
D &= ST \\
&= 60 \times 6\tfrac{1}{4} \\
&= 360 + 15 \\
&= 375 \text{ kilometres}
\end{aligned}
$$

Like all formulae, this can be rearranged to help us find other unknowns. Consider the questions below:

(a) A heavy goods vehicle travels 350 km in 7 hours. What was its average speed for the journey?

(b) A heavy goods vehicle sets off on a journey of 450 km and averages 60 km/h. How long does it take?

In (a) the unknown is the speed for the journey and in (b) the unknown is the time taken.

Rearranging the formula $D = ST$ to find these two unknowns, we have

$$S = \frac{D}{T}$$

$$\text{Speed} = \frac{\text{Distance}}{\text{Time}}$$

and

$$T = \frac{D}{S}$$

$$\text{Time taken} = \frac{\text{Distance}}{\text{Speed}}$$

The answers are therefore as follows:

(a)
$$S = \frac{D}{T}$$
$$= \frac{350}{7}$$
$$= 50 \text{ km/h}$$

(b)
$$T = \frac{D}{S}$$
$$= \frac{450}{60}$$
$$= \frac{45}{6}$$
$$= 7\frac{1}{2} \text{ hours}$$

Example 18.3. A supersonic aircraft flies a distance of 5600 km. Over the open sea it travels at an average speed of 2000 km/h, for $2\frac{1}{4}$ hours. The rest of the journey is made at a speed of 825 km/h. What time does it land if it took off at 11.30 am? (*Note:* Ignore changing time zones around the world.)

Distance travelled at supersonic speed $= 2000 \times 2\frac{1}{4}$ km
$$= 4500 \text{ km}$$
Balance of journey to be covered $= 5600 \text{ km} - 4500 \text{ km}$
$$= 1100 \text{ km}$$

Time taken is found by $T = \dfrac{D}{S}$
$$= \frac{1100}{825}$$
$$= \frac{44}{33} \quad \text{(cancelling by 25)}$$
$$= \frac{4}{3}$$
$$= 1\frac{1}{3} \text{ hours}$$

$\therefore$ Total time taken $= 2\frac{1}{4} \text{ h} + 1\frac{1}{3} \text{ h}$
$$= 3\frac{3 + 4}{12} \text{ h}$$
$$= 3\frac{7}{12} \text{ h}$$
$$= 3 \text{ h } 35 \text{ min}$$

$\therefore$ Landing time $= 11.30 \text{ am} + 3 \text{ h } 35 \text{ min}$
$$= 15.05 \text{ h or } 3.05 \text{ pm}$$

Example 18.4. A cyclist travels at 20 km/h for $2\frac{1}{2}$ hours and then at 16 km/h for $3\frac{1}{2}$ hours. (a) What was the total distance cycled? (b) What was the average speed for the whole journey? (Answer correct to 1 decimal place.)

(a)
$$D = ST$$

$$\text{Distance for part I} = 20 \times 2\tfrac{1}{2}$$
$$= 50 \text{ km}$$
$$\text{Distance for part II} = 16 \times 3\tfrac{1}{2}$$
$$= 56 \text{ km}$$
$$\text{Total distance} = 50 + 56 \text{ km}$$
$$= 106 \text{ km}$$

(b)
$$S = \frac{D}{T}$$

$$= \frac{106}{6} \text{ km/h}$$

$$= 17\frac{4}{6} \text{ km/h}$$

$$= 17\frac{2}{3} \text{ km/h}$$

$$= 17.66 \text{ km/h}$$

$$= 17.7 \text{ km/h}$$

18.4   Exercises: Speed, Time and Distance

1. In each of the following calculations find the missing element (the distance, the time or the speed):

Journey	Average speed (km/h)	Time	Distance (kilometres)
A	64	3 h 45 min	?
B	88	5 h 30 min	?
C	58	7 h 45 min	?
D	?	5 h	480
E	?	3 h 40 min	176
F	72	?	612
G	52	?	247
H	?	3 h 30 min	235.2
I	73.6	?	312.8
J	36	14 h 20 min	?

2. A cyclist travels 187 kilometres in $8\frac{1}{2}$ hours. What is his average speed in kilometres per hour?

3. A motorist drives for $2\frac{1}{2}$ hours at an average speed of 64 kilometres per hour and $4\frac{1}{2}$ hours at an average speed of 48 kilometres per hour. (a) How far does he travel? (b) What is his average speed for the whole journey? (Answer correct to 1 decimal place.)

4. A cyclist travels for $3\frac{3}{4}$ hours at a speed of 18 km/h and then for $1\frac{3}{4}$ hours at 24 km/h. (a) What was the total distance covered? (b) What was the average speed for the whole journey? (Answer correct to one decimal place.)

5. A motorist travelled 160 kilometres at an average speed of 64 km/h and then joined a motorway to travel at 96 km/h for a distance of 144 kilometres. (a) What was the total journey time? (b) What was the average speed for the whole journey?

6. A motorcar rally requires drivers to cover the 2232-kilometre course at an average speed of 72 km/h: 448 kilometres of the course is in towns where speed limits apply. If the cars can only average 56 km/h in these towns how fast must they average on the rest of the journey to achieve the specified average overall? (Answer to the nearest 0.1 of a kilometre per hour.) (*Hint:* Find how many hours it takes to travel through the towns. Find how many hours' travel is permitted to achieve the average speed laid down for the whole journey. The balance of the distance has to be covered in the balance of the time.)

7. A motorcar rally requires drivers to cover a course 5760 kilometres long at an average speed of 80 km/h: 312 kilometres are in towns where speed limits apply and drivers can only average 52 km/h. How fast must they travel on the rest of the journey to achieve the specified average overall? (Answer correct to 0.1 of a kilometre per hour.)

18.5   Exercises: Speeds and Distances

Do these calculations mentally:

1. A car travels at an average speed of 56 km/h for $2\frac{1}{4}$ hours. How far does it go?

2. A lorry travels at an average speed of 72 km/h for $7\frac{1}{2}$ hours. How far does it go?

3. A journey of 384 kilometres is expected to be covered at an average speed of 64 km/h. How long will the journey take, allowing 30 minutes for a rest period on the way?

4. A journey of 420 kilometres is expected to be covered at an average speed of 56 km/h. How long will it take allowing for two rest periods of 20 minutes each?

5. A journey of 360 kilometres is made at an average speed of 80 km/h. How long does it take?

18.6 Mental Arithmetic Test

1. $3216 \times 9 =$

2. £275.60 + £321.45 + £675.30 =

3. £475.20 − £276.80 =

4. $3\frac{1}{5} + 2\frac{2}{3} =$

5. $0.5 + 0.75 + 0.125 + 0.5 =$

6. How many litres in $5\frac{1}{2}$ kilolitres?

7. What shall I pay altogether for 7 articles at £1.84 each?

8. What is the simple interest on £500 for 6 months at 10%?

9. A call to America costs 84p per minute. How much for a 9-minute call?

10. What shall I pay for 35 therms of gas at 40p per therm?

11. What is 75% of £30 000?

12. Electricity is 3p per unit. What shall I pay for 1780 units?

13. An article costing £144 is marked up by 25%. What will its selling price be?

14. The rateable value of my house is £250. Rates are 60p in the £1. What must I pay?

15. A cyclist travels 70 km in $3\frac{1}{2}$ hours. What is his average speed?

19
Simple Costing

19.1 Pricing Goods and Services

Whenever goods are supplied, or services are performed, there is a pricing problem to be overcome. The trader who buys goods to sell again has only to add on his mark-up, as already described in Chapter 14. The manufacturer has a more difficult task, for the materials he manufactures are built into the finished product either to meet the needs of the particular job—**job costing**—or as part of a process—**process costing**. A person who provides services, like a building contractor, freight forwarder or a repairer will usually use job-costing or work to an agreed contract and use a method called **contract costing**.

Simple costing usually involves the use of some type of **cost sheet**, on which the details of costs incurred can be noted. From the cost sheet the actual price to be charged for the job can be calculated.

19.2 Cost Sheets

A simple cost sheet is ruled to provide adequate space to record the various types of costs which are incurred on any particular job. There will usually be space for materials used and for components 'bought-in' to be used as required. Thus a commercial vehicle-body builder might use materials like timber, sheet alloy, etc., but might buy in components like lighting fittings or refrigeration machinery for use in the vehicles under construction. Other departments, machine shops, foundries, etc., may perform parts of the work, and service departments like the transport department may need to charge their costs to the contract or job in hand. When the job is complete, and time has been allowed for all the cost centres concerned to send in their charges, the cost clerk will proceed to draw up a summary of costs which will give the grand total of costs to be recovered.

One further point here is that the costs charged must include an element of **overheads**. Consider a component, like an electric motor, used in a particular assembly. Suppose it 'cost' £15.80 when purchased. This is not the only cost to be incurred, for forms had to be completed; suppliers had to be found making this kind of component; orders placed; delivery arranged; the motors had to be unpacked and stored, etc. All these costs are **overhead costs**, and must all be recovered when the job or contract is priced and paid for by the customer. Usually each department will have an 'oncost' percentage added to its charges to recover the overheads of the department concerned. Thus a department charging costs of £32 with an overhead oncost of 50% will charge £32 + £16 = £48 for its services.

When the summary is complete the cost sheet will be passed to the accounts department, who will invoice the customer for the job. The final charge will of course include a profit element for the firm, which may be based on a percentage of the total costs—just like a mark-up for an ordinary trader. At other times it will be based on what the market can bear: the accountant will charge a round price which gives a good profit, but not such a high profit that the customer will go elsewhere next time. An example of a typical cost sheet is given in Fig. 19.1.

19.3 Exercises: Simple Costing

Make a number of copies of the cost sheet in Fig. 19.1 and use them to record the costs for the following jobs performed by Prefabricators Plc for the customers named. What was the total charge to the customer in each case?

1. Serial number 0001, Job number 284, Light Engineering Plc, 24 Somers Way, London E5 2TS. Telephone 01-008 3124. Job description: spiral staircases. Materials: steel rod, £38.50; brass rod, £72.85; bolts, etc., £8.54. Foundry charges: spiral assemblies 84 at £5.80 each. Drawing Office: plans, £45.80. Transport charges: £39.50. Other charges: quality control, £23.50; painting shop, £38.50. Profit to be based on 40% of total costs.

2. Serial number 0002, Job number 285, Rail Enthusiasts Club, Glen Railway Station, Aberdovey. Telephone 0436-012. Job description: admission turnstiles. Materials used: steel bars, £38.50; steel sheet, £42.50; sand and cement, £15.80. Foundry charges: £31.64. Machine shop charges: drilling, £12.85; shaping, £7.56; turning, £14.25. Drawing office: plans, £35.80. Transport Dept.: delivery, £28.50. Other charges: paint shop, £28.50; inspection and testing, £18.50. Profit to be based on 45% of total costs.

3. Serial number 0003, Job number 286, Interior Fitting Co., 2401 High Street, Southampton. Telephone 0703-01245. Job description: staircases

Cost sheet serial number: Customer's name and address:

Telephone number: Job number: Job description:

Materials used	F	£	p	Components used	F	£	p	Foundry charges	F	£	p	Machine shop charges	F	£	p	Cost summary	£	p
																Materials		
																Components		
																Foundry		
																Machine shop		
																Drawing Office		
																Packing Dept.		
																Transport Dept.		
Total				Total				Total				Total				Other charges		
Add oncost at 50%				Add oncost at 50%				Add oncost at 200%				Add oncost at 150%				Total costs		
Total to summary				Total to summary				Total to summary				Total to summary				Add profit		
																Invoice total		

Drawing office	F	£	p	Packing dept.	F	£	p	Transport dept.	F	£	p	Other charges	F	£	p	Final Report: Note here any problems connected with this order.
Total				Total				Total				Total				
Add oncost at 100%				Add oncost at 75%				Add oncost at 100%				Add oncost at 200%				
Total to summary				Total to summary				Total to summary				Total to summary				

Fig. 19.1. A simple cost sheet. (*Note:* this illustration may be copied for class use.)

and safety rails. Materials: timber, £62.50; brackets and bolts, £8.84; safety rails, £48.50. Components: Lewis balustrades, 4 sets at £18.50. Machine shop charges: £17.55, drilling. Packing Dept.: crates, etc., £15.80. Other charges: painting shop £25.80. Profit to be based on 25% of total costs.

4. Serial number 0004, Job number 287, Luminex Ltd, 2734 High Street, Great Tenby, Derbyshire. Job description: exhibition stands. Materials used: steel framework, £84.50; light alloy sheet, £164.85; nuts, bolts, etc., £17.20. Components: Zorro lighting units, £34.50; Visi-shelf units, 12 at £15.80 each. Drawing office: plans, £138.50. Transport Department, £34.90. Other charges: electrician, £34.50. Profit to be based on 28% of total costs.

19.4 Mental Arithmetic: Simple Costing

Do these calculations mentally:

1. Costs of £24.50, £36.20 and £8.44 are incurred on a certain job. What is the total cost incurred?

2. Costs of £35.60, £72.80 and £15.40 are incurred on a certain job, but subsequently a refund of £5.95 is made on the second of these expenses. What was the final cost involved?

3. Costs of £40, £60 and £80 are incurred on a job. Then overhead costs are added at 50% of costs incurred. What are the total costs?

4. Overheads are fixed at 150% on cost. What is the overhead charge on costs of £84.00?

5. Overheads are fixed at 75% on cost. What is the overhead charge on costs of £164?

6. Profits are fixed at 25% on costs of £180. What is the charge for the job?

7. Profits are fixed at 30% on costs of £220. What is the charge for the job?

8. Costs on a particular contract are £1800. To this 50% is added for overheads, and to the final total 20% is added for profit. What is the final charge for the contract?

19.5 Mental Arithmetic Test

1. $17 + 26 + 384 + 2716 + 495 =$

2. $27\,000 \times 90 =$

3. $\frac{3}{8} \times \frac{2}{3} =$

4. $909 \times 0.3 =$

5. Change 73 850 grams to kilograms

6. Share up £1650 equally among 15 people. How much does each get?

7. An article costs £10.20. How much must I pay for 250?

8. What is the average of 27, 31 and 44?

9. A house is rated at £375 rateable value. What will I pay if rates are £1.10 in the £1?

10. What is $66\frac{2}{3}$% of £660?

11. How many days altogether in January and February, 1988?

12. An article selling for £500 has been marked up by $33\frac{1}{3}$%. What did it cost?

13. A chapter in a book is headed XLIX. What chapter is it in Arabic numbers?

14. A motorcar travels at an average speed of 42 km/h for $5\frac{1}{4}$ h. How far does it travel?

15. The costs of a contract amount to £2350. Profit is added at 20%. What is the price charged to the customer?

20
Wages and Commission

20.1 Wages and Salaries

Wages and salaries are the rewards paid to labour for its part in a firm's activities. Under the Payment of Wages Act, 1960, wages must be paid in cash, unless the employee agrees to be paid by cheque or by transfer into a bank account. The terms 'wages' and 'salaries' have the same meaning, but 'wages' is usually applied to hourly-paid or weekly-paid staff, while 'salaries' is used for employees paid monthly.

There are many ways of calculating wages, of which payments by the hour, week or month are the commonest. There are also piece-rate systems, in which the employee is paid for each unit of output (piece) produced; bonus systems which pay the employee an extra sum for output over and above a standard set task; commission based upon quantity sold, and many more.

With most weekly paid and monthly paid staff the hours worked may vary without the payment of overtime or deductions for undertime—though excessive overtime will usually be compensated in some way. With hourly paid staff overtime is usually paid at an agreed rate, time and a third, time and a half or double time (at weekends) being common proportions. A great many employers have now adopted a system of flexible working hours which permits employees to some extent to choose which hours they work. Some like to start early in the day; others prefer to arrive late and work on into the evening. Special clock-recording systems record the arrival and departure of staff and a list of hours worked will eventually be produced for the Wages Department. The information may even be produced on a floppy disc for direct entry into a computer system. From these records the pay can be calculated.

The first stage in calculating pay is therefore finding the gross pay, that is the pay without any **deductions**. Deductions are explained later.

20.2   Calculating Gross Wages

The traditional way of recording hours of work for hourly-paid workers was by 'clocking in and clocking out'. A timing device is placed at the factory gate with clock cards arranged in racks on either side of the clock. An employee entering the factory takes his card from the 'out' rack, puts it into the clock to be stamped and replaces it in the 'in' rack. The result is a clock card similar to the one shown in Fig. 20.1.

Name: J. Gardner					
Clock No. 278					
Week No. 1		Commencing 4 April			
Day	In	Out	*Less* Lunch-time	Hours worked	Overtime payable
Mon. a.m.	08.00		$\frac{1}{2}$	$8\frac{1}{2}$	$\frac{1}{4}$
Mon. p.m.		17.00			
Tue. a.m.	07.59		$\frac{1}{2}$	$8\frac{1}{2}$	$\frac{1}{4}$
Tue. p.m.		17.00			
Wed. a.m.	08.00		$\frac{1}{2}$	$9\frac{1}{2}$	$\frac{3}{4}$
Wed. p.m.		18.00			
Thur. a.m.	07.30		$\frac{1}{2}$	$10\frac{1}{2}$	$1\frac{1}{4}$
Thur. p.m.		18.30			
Fri. a.m.	08.14		$\frac{1}{2}$	$8\frac{1}{4}$	$\frac{1}{8}$
Fri. p.m.		17.00			
Sat. a.m.	08.00		$\frac{1}{2}$	$8\frac{1}{2}$	$8\frac{1}{2}$
Sat. p.m.		17.00			
Sun. a.m.	09.00		–	$3\frac{1}{2}$	$3\frac{1}{2}$
Sun. p.m.		12.30			
Overtime rates	Total			$57\frac{1}{4}$	$14\frac{5}{8}$
Weekdays $1\frac{1}{2}$	Add overtime			$14\frac{5}{8}$	
Weekends 2					
	Hours payable			$71\frac{7}{8}$	

Fig. 20.1. A clock card.

Notes

(i) A normal working day is 8 hours.

(ii) Employees clock in and out only once a day, but $\frac{1}{2}$ hour is deducted for meals which are taken in the canteen.

(iii) Since overtime is at time and a half on weekdays, overtime is calculated by paying the employee for any extra time and overtime equal to half the extra time.

(iv) At weekends, when overtime is at double-time, the employee is paid for the hours worked and overtime for that numbers of hours as well.

(v) Clock hours are calculated to the nearest quarter of an hour.

Example 20.1. An employee works $47\frac{1}{2}$ hours per week, of which $7\frac{1}{2}$ hours was overtime at time and a half. His rate of pay is £1.85 per hour. What is his gross wage?

$$\text{Total hours payable} = 47\frac{1}{2} + (\tfrac{1}{2} \text{ of } 7\frac{1}{2})$$
$$= 47\frac{1}{2} + 3\frac{3}{4}$$
$$= 51\frac{1}{4} \text{ hours.}$$

Gross pay $= 51\frac{1}{4} \times £1.85$

$$
\begin{array}{r}
51.25 \\
1.85 \\
\hline
256\ 25 \\
4100\ 00 \\
5125\ 00 \\
\hline
94.81\ 25 \\
\end{array}
$$

$$= £94.81$$

20.3 Exercises: Calculating Gross Wages

1. Calculate the gross pay for the 10 members of staff whose clock records show hours of work as follows. All staff work a normal week of 40 hours, and overtime is paid at time and a half (answer correct to nearest penny).

	Name	Hours Worked	Extra hours payable	Rate of pay
(a)	Mr Black	$47\frac{1}{2}$	?	£1.70
(b)	Mr Gray	45	?	£1.65
(c)	Mr White	40	—	£1.30
(d)	Mrs Green	49	?	£1.50
(e)	Miss Brown	$48\frac{1}{2}$	?	£1.80
(f)	Miss Smith	$44\frac{1}{2}$	?	£2.10
(g)	Miss Plumber	40	—	£1.30
(h)	Mr Baker	62	?	£1.95
(i)	Mr Cook	$65\frac{1}{2}$	?	£1.60
(j)	Mrs Barber	$48\frac{1}{2}$	?	£1.55

2. Calculate the gross pay for the 10 members of staff whose clock records show hours of work as follows. All staff work a $37\frac{1}{2}$-hour week. Overtime is calculated at time and a half on week days and double time at weekends. (Calculations correct to the nearest penny.)

	Name	Hours worked	Of which weekend working was	Extra hours payable	Rate of pay
(a)	Mr A	$37\frac{1}{2}$	—	—	£1.95
(b)	Mr B	$42\frac{1}{2}$	—	?	£1.80
(c)	Mrs C	$37\frac{1}{2}$	—	—	£1.85
(d)	Mrs D	46	4	?	£1.95
(e)	Miss E	$45\frac{1}{2}$	4	?	£1.45
(f)	Miss F	51	7	?	£1.75
(g)	Mr G	53	7	?	£1.60
(h)	Mr H	47	4	?	£1.30
(i)	Mrs I	$46\frac{1}{2}$	—	?	£1.95
(j)	Mr J	$39\frac{1}{2}$	—	?	£2.20

20.4   Commission

Commission is money paid as a reward for services which bears a simple percentage relationship to the value of business transacted. Many agents are rewarded by a commission, perhaps 5% of the value of the deal arranged. Many salesmen are paid a basic salary which by itself would not enable the employee to enjoy a very good standard of living, but this is supplemented by a commission related to the sales made.

The following types of commission are used:

(a) **Straight commission.** The reward is based on a simple percentage rate of the value of the sales made or business transacted.

(b) **Graduated commission.** The reward is graduated, either in increasing steps or decreasing steps. Thus an agent might earn 10% on the first £5000, 5% on the next £5000 and $2\frac{1}{2}$% thereafter. The bigger commission at the start encourages the agent to set out in business.

(c) **Volume commissions and value commissions.** Volume commissions are paid on the number of articles sold (£10 per machine, for example). Where a whole range of items is being sold this is inconvenient and it is better to base the commission on the total value of the goods sold.

(d) **Bonuses.** Where a salesman is paid a basic salary it is usual to allocate a quota to be sold before commission becomes payable. This quota can be varied to suit the problems being faced—some areas may be more difficult markets than others, for example. Once the quota of sales has been made commission starts on the balance, the bonus being fixed as a percentage of the extra sales made.

20.5   Calculating Commission

Straight commission. This is very simple to calculate. It is merely a percentage rate of the value of business transacted.

Example 20.2. An employee is paid a basic wage of £50 per week plus a commission of 5% of sales. In week 23 of the financial year he makes sales of £950. What is his gross pay for the week?

$$\text{Commission} = 5\% \text{ of } £950$$
$$= \tfrac{1}{20} \times £950$$
$$= \frac{£95}{2} \qquad \text{(cancelling by 10)}$$
$$= £47.50$$

$$\text{Therefore Gross pay} = £50 + £47.50$$
$$= £97.50$$

Graduated commission. Here the commission payable is made up of two or more parts. A cut-off point is laid down for each rate of commission payable.

Example 20.3. An employee is paid a basic salary of £60 per week, followed by a commission of $2\tfrac{1}{2}\%$ on the first £1000 of sales and 5% thereafter. What will she earn in a week when sales total £4700?

$$\text{Commission on the first } £1000 = 2\tfrac{1}{2}\% \text{ of } £1000$$
$$= \tfrac{1}{40} \times £1000$$
$$= £25$$

$$\text{Commission on the balance} = 5\% \text{ of } £3700$$
$$= \tfrac{1}{20} \times £3700$$
$$= £185$$

$$\text{Gross Pay} = £60 + £25 + £185$$
$$= £270$$

20.6   Exercises: Commission

1. Calculate the commission payable to an agent on the following deals:

(a)   10% on £7250
(b)   10% on £5 335.50
(c)   5% on £485
(d)   5% on £1850
(e) $2\tfrac{1}{2}\%$ on £7640
(f) $2\tfrac{1}{2}\%$ on £19 800

(g)   1% on £175 500   (h)   1% on £1 million
(i)   ½% on £2 420 000   (j)   ¼% on £80 million

2. A salesforce is remunerated by a basic salary of £80.00 for which each salesman is expected to achieve a certain quota of sales which reflects the area in which he works. After this quota has been achieved each unit sold brings in a commission of £4.50. Calculate the gross pay of each of the employees listed below.

	Name	*Quota (in units)*	*Actual sales (in units)*
(a)	Mr A	25	29
(b)	Mr R	15	27
(c)	Mr T	18	32
(d)	Mr W	30	58
(e)	Mr Y	36	84

3. Sales staff in a store earn a basic monthly salary plus graduated commission related to the sales made and taking account of the department in which they work. What will each of the following staff earn?

	Basic salary	*Rate of initial commission*	*Limit*	*Higher rate of commission*	*Sales in month*
(a)	£120	1%	£5 000	5%	£8 800
(b)	£135	2%	£8 000	5%	£9 200
(c)	£140	2%	£10 000	5%	£12 700
(d)	£150	2½%	£15 000	10%	£17 200
(e)	£160	2½%	£15 000	10%	£16 900

4. An auctioneer is paid an attendance fee of £10, and then takes a commission of 5% on the first £350 of goods sold, and 10% thereafter. Sales total £722. What was his total fee?

5. An auctioneer is paid an attendance fee of £50, and then takes a commission of 2½% on the first £850 of goods sold, and 5% thereafter. Sales total £8250. What was his total fee?

6. A commission agent takes 1% of the first £25 000 of sales arranged, and ¼% thereafter. If he sells altogether £282 500 of goods, what was his total commission?

7. A commission agent takes 2% of the first £20 000 of sales arranged, and ½% thereafter. If he sells altogether £175 580 of goods what was his total commission?

20.7   Deductions from Wages

Besides the employee, other parties are interested in the wages payable. Chief of these is the Inland Revenue Department, which is interested in securing the income tax and social security contributions of the employee. Many trade unionists agree to have their trade union contribution deducted by the employer and sent to the trade union headquarters direct. Many charities persuade employers to offer their employees a similar direct facility for the collection of charitable contributions of a very nominal sort. A penny from each employee per week may seem a negligible contribution to Dr Barnardo's Homes, but a firm with 50 000 employees can send a cheque for £500 every week to the charity.

Another common voluntary deduction is the 'Save As You Earn' scheme by which the employee asks the employer to deduct a fixed sum weekly for saving in Government savings schemes.

The result is that an employee's **gross wage** is reduced by a number of **compulsory deductions** (income tax, national insurance contributions and pension contributions) and then by a further series of **voluntary deductions** (trade union contributions, charitable contributions and savings). The balance left is called the **net pay**, which actually goes into the pay packet or is transferred into the employee's bank account.

Employers must keep proper records of wages paid and deductions from gross pay. There are many simple wages systems of which two are illustrated in the following pages.

20.8 A Simple Wages Book

The simplest type of Wages Book is shown in Fig. 20.2 and is explained in the accompanying notes (see pages 176 and 177).

20.9 Exercises: Simple Wages Books

Rule up a wages book similar to the one in Fig. 20.2, and make entries for the following firms. Wages details for employees are shown for Week 1 of the financial year. (*Note:* In Week 1 of the financial year 'Gross Pay for tax purposes' and 'Gross Pay to date for tax purposes' are the same.) Bring out the totals payable for wages, tax, etc.

1. T. Roberts and Co. Employee details are as follows:

Name	Basic pay	Other pay	Super-annuation	Tax-free pay	Tax due
	£	£	£	£	£
A.B.	85.50	3.20	4.40	13.65	21.00
C.D.	102.60	15.40	5.90	34.25	23.10
E.F.	73.50	8.50	4.10	25.60	15.60
G.H.	64.70	4.20	3.40	17.50	14.40

No.	Name of employee	Earnings week 5 May 4-10					Tax details to date							Deductions						Net pay	Refunds, etc.	Amounts payable	Employee's National Insurance
		Basic pay	Overtime	Other	Gross pay	Super-annuation	Gross pay for tax purposes	Gross to date for tax purposes	Tax-free pay	Taxable pay to date	Tax due to date	Tax paid	Refunds (if any)	Tax	National Insurance	T.U.	Charity	SAYE	Total deducts				
		(i)	(ii)	(iii)	(iv)	(v)	(vi)	(vii)	(viii)	(ix)	(x)	(xi)	(xii)	(xiii)	(xiv)	(xv)	(xvi)	(xvii)	(xviii)	(xix)	(xx)	(xxi)	(xxii)
1	A. Smith	56.00	–	5.00	61.00	3.05	57.95	275.70	82.75	192.95	57.60	46.80	–	10.80	4.49	0.41	0.03	–	15.73	42.22		42.22	7.94
2	B.Taylor	65.25	3.25		68.50	3.42	65.08	318.50	110.50	208.00	62.40	49.60	–	12.80	5.04	0.41	0.02	–	18.27	46.81		46.81	8.91
3	C. Baker	72.40	–	17.50	89.90	4.50	85.40	426.30	251.00	175.30	52.50	43.20	–	9.30	6.62	0.41	0.01	5.00	21.34	64.06		64.06	11.70
4	D. Porter	48.20	–	22.30	70.50	3.52	66.98	328.20	123.00	205.20	61.50	63.50	2.00	–	5.19	0.41	0.02	3.00	8.62	58.36	2.00	60.36	9.17
		241.85	3.25	44.80	289.90	14.49								32.90	21.34	1.64	0.08	8.00	63.96	211.45	2.00	213.45	37.72

Figures for management to use in controlling costs and fixing selling prices

Due to Inland Revenue (less refund of £2.00)

Due to trade union

Due to charity

Due to National Savings Office

Due to employees in wage packets or to bank accounts

Due to Inland Revenue

Fig. 20.2. A simple wages book.

Notes

(i) The first section shows earnings of various sorts, totalled to give the gross pay.

(ii) From this gross pay superannuation is deducted to give the gross pay for tax purposes. The employee will draw this amount, less the deductions.

(iii) Working out the tax deductions can be a little difficult. The stages are:

(a) What did the employee earn this week, after superannuation? (Column VI)

(b) What is the gross pay to date after superannuation? (Column VIII)

(c) How much of this is tax free? We have to look at Tax Table A from the tax office to find this out. (Column VIII)

(d) That gives us the total taxable pay to date (column VII minus column VIII). (See column IX)

(e) What is the tax on this amount? We need to look at Tax Table B to find this out. (Column X)

(f) We look at the employee's record last week. How much tax has been paid so far this year? Clearly Smith has to pay some more this week, and so must Taylor and Baker, but Porter has paid too much and is entitled to a refund.

(iv) Finally the tax, national insurance and other deductions are totalled to give column XVIII, from which the net pay (Column XIX) can be calculated. Porter, who is entitled to a refund, has this added to the net pay, to give the amount payable. (Column XXI)

(v) The employer's national insurance contribution, which is payable for each employee employed, is now entered in column XXII.

(vi) The cashier now goes to the bank to draw the payroll money and makes up the wage packets. Alternatively, those who have agreed to be paid by cheque have the money transferred into their bank accounts.

(vii) Once a month the employer will pay the Inland Revenue, the trade union, etc., the sums due.

(Continued)	National Insurance	Trade union	Charity	SAYE	Employer's National Insurance
	£	£	£	£	£
A.B.	6.53	0.50	0.15	5.00	11.54
C.D.	8.69	0.50	—	—	15.36
E.F.	6.03	0.50	0.15	5.00	10.15
G.H.	5.07	0.50	0.10	—	8.96

2. M. Davies and Co. Employee details are as follows:

Name	Basic pay	Other pay	Super-annuation	Tax-free pay	Tax due
	£	£	£	£	£
R.S.	96.50	4.60	6.07	8.25	25.80
T.U.	74.50	5.40	4.79	14.80	18.00
V.W.	126.20	32.80	9.36	32.70	34.80
Y.Z.	132.50	46.50	10.74	17.30	45.00

(Continued)	National Insurance	Trade union	Charity	SAYE	Employer's National Insurance
	£	£	£	£	£
R.S.	7.36	0.65	0.25	—	13.01
T.U.	5.82	0.65	—	5.00	10.29
V.W.	11.60	0.65	—	5.00	20.50
Y.Z.	13.04	0.65	0.15	15.00	23.05

20.10   The Kalamazoo Wages System

Some three million people in the United Kingdom alone are paid their wages weekly or monthly using the Kalamazoo Wages System. This system is an example of **simultaneous records**, a system which avoids copying errors by preparing several sets of records simultaneously using carbon or NCR (no carbon required) paper. A few words of explanation are helpful. To keep proper records of wages three things are required:

(a) a **pay advice note** which shows the employee exactly how the pay has been calculated. This is used to make up the wage packet, and enables the employee to check the pay on receipt. Sometimes the packet has small holes in it so that coins can be counted, and the notes can be checked, before opening the packet.

(b) A **payroll** which lists all payments made for the week or month, and which is the firm's record retained in a special loose-leaf binder.

(c) An individual **employee's record card**, which lists all the employee's pay for the year. In any query about pay we can produce this record to discuss it with the employee. We do not want to produce the payroll, for this would enable the employee to see what other staff earn.

In the Kalamazoo system a flat board, called a **copy-writer** is used as a backing sheet as shown in Fig. 20.3. It has a row of studs at the top over which the various documents can be placed. First comes a set of ten wages advice notes. On top of this is placed the NCR coated payroll form. Then the individual's record card is placed over the top of the payroll form. The week's pay is then entered on the record card. Naturally the entry is copied onto the payroll form and the advice note because of the NCR coating. When the entry is complete the wages clerk takes the next employee's record card, and positions it over the next clean column on the payroll—a few studs up from the previous entry. The perforations in the forms can be seen in Fig. 20.3 and in Fig. 20.4. Fig. 20.3 shows how the system works. The final result is a full set of records, (a), (b) and (c) as explained above. A pay advice note is shown in detail in Fig. 20.4.

Notes

(i) The week or month number is shown and the date it commences.

(ii) There are six lines for types of earning, such as basic wage, overtime, commission, etc. One of these lines is for statutory sick pay. The total of these gives the gross pay.

(iii) Superannuation is then deducted, because it is not taxable.

(iv) The gross pay for tax purposes is then used to find the tax payable—using the Tax Tables provided by the Inland Revenue.

(v) The deductions are then listed, which gives the net pay.

(vi) There are then two lines for any additions to net pay—such as refunds of tax overpaid or expenses incurred. This gives the total amount payable.

(vii) The employer also needs to know what the total cost was for National Insurance—in this case the employer had to pay £18.51, making £29.01 in all.

20.11 Exercises: Kalamazoo Wages Systems

(*Note:* To complete a full set of Kalamazoo wages records it is essential to have the correct stationery and invent imaginary names, code numbers, etc. Schools and colleges wishing to purchase such stationery should approach the Education Department of Kalamazoo Ltd, Mill Lane, Northfield, Birmingham, B31 2RW. For the purpose of the exercises below it is suggested that pay advice notes similar to Fig. 20.4 should be ruled up.)

Complete wages advice notes for the four employees shown on page 183 whose pay details are as follows:

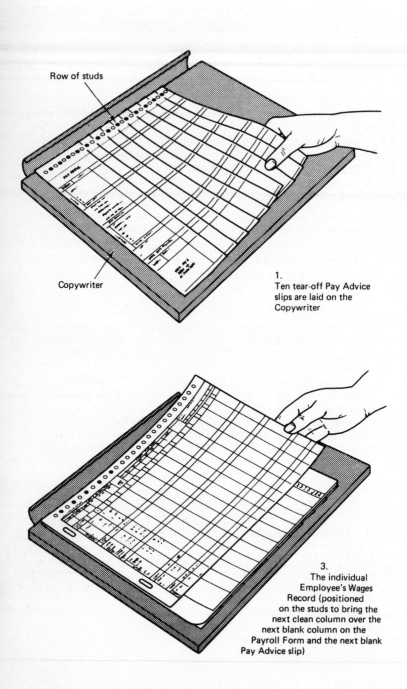

Row of studs

Copywriter

1.
Ten tear-off Pay Advice
slips are laid on the
Copywriter

3.
The individual
Employee's Wages
Record (positioned
on the studs to bring the
next clean column over the
next blank column on the
Payroll Form and the next blank
Pay Advice slip)

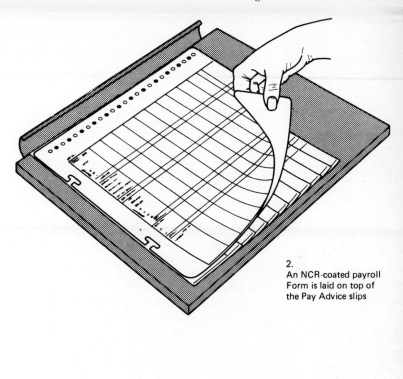

2.
An NCR-coated payroll
Form is laid on top of
the Pay Advice slips

4.
The torn-off Pay Advice slips
folded once to go into the
pay packets. If paid in cash
the money is inserted in the
same envelope

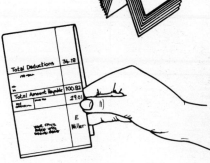

Fig. 20.3. The Kalamazoo wages system.

(Reproduced by courtesy of Kalamazoo Ltd)

Place over cone

Pay Advice

Week or Month No.	Date	14	10/7
Earnings			
Details			
A		100	40
B		5	00
C			
D			
E			
SSP		29	60
Gross Pay		135	00
Superannuation			
Gross Pay less Superannuation		135	00
Gross Pay to Date for Tax Purposes		2085	00
Tax Free Pay		853	30
Taxable Pay to Date		1231	70
Tax Due to Date		369	30
Tax Refund			
Deductions Tax		22	20
*N.I. Contribution (Employee)		10	48
1		–	50
2		1	00
3			
4			
5			
6			
7			
Total Deductions		34	18
Net Pay			
F			
G			
Total Amount Payable		100	82
N.I. Contribution (Employer)			
N.I. Total (Employer and Employee)		29	01
H			
*Contracted-out Contribution included above			

Your Pay is made up as shown above

Miller K.E.

Kalamazoo business systems T-18303 ©

Fig. 20.4. A Kalamazoo pay advice slip.

(Reproduced by courtesy of Kalamazoo Ltd)

	1 A.B.	*2 C.D.*	*3 E.F.*	*4 G.H.*
Week	1	7	9	16
Date	12.4.19..	24.5.19..	7.6.19..	26.7.19..
Earnings A	66.50	122.50	79.80	84.60
Earnings B	4.55	3.80	17.24	16.60
Gross pay	?	?	?	?
Superannuation	3.55	6.32	4.85	5.06
Gross pay for tax purposes	?	?	?	?
Gross pay to date for tax purposes	? (*Note:* It is week 1)	836.50	902.60	1582.50
Free pay	26.15	189.70	297.90	553.60
Taxable pay to date	?	?	?	?
Tax due to date	12.30	193.80	181.20	308.40
Tax paid up to last week	—	202.90	166.70	291.20
Tax	?	? (*careful*)	?	?
N.I. Contribution	5.23	9.30	7.14	7.21
Charity	0.25	0.15	0.15	0.20
Total deductions	?	?	?	?
Net pay	?	?	?	?
Refunds (if any)	?	?	?	?
Total amount payable	?	?	?	?
N.I. contribution (employer)	9.25	16.44	12.63	13.17
N.I. Total	?	?	?	?

20.12 Mental Arithmetic Test

1. $274 + 382 + 726 + 109 =$

2. $2742 - 1387 =$

3. $295 \times 5 =$

4. $270 \times 300 =$

5. What is the VAT at 15% on an item costing £350?

6. Find the average of 27, 38 and 43.

7. What is 23% of £5000?

8. The rateable value of property in a town is £17 500 000. What will 1 penny rate bring in?

9. How far do I go if I average 48 kilometres per hour for $3\frac{1}{2}$ hours?

10. What is the commission on £8000 at 7%?

11. What interest shall I earn in 2 years at $9\frac{1}{2}$% on £1000?

12. $0.5 \times 0.8 =$

13. $0.36 \div 0.9 =$

14. What shall I pay for 7 items at £3.84 each?

15. What will the discount be on an invoice of £450 at $7\frac{1}{2}$%?

21
Hire Purchase

21.1 The Nature of Hire Purchase

When families and businesses need expensive items of household or business equipment, but do not have the necessary purchase money, it is quite usual today to obtain the goods on **hire purchase.** As the name implies the goods are only on hire to the family, or business, until the terms in the contract about the payments have been fulfilled. When the last payment is made the 'hire' becomes a 'purchase', and the ownership of the goods passes to the customer.

All such transactions in the United Kingdom are controlled by regulations made under the Consumer Credit Act, 1974, which are supervised by the Director General of Fair Trading. Many safeguards have been built into the regulations to prevent hardship to hire purchasers—who have in the past sometimes become overcommitted on hire purchase debt. One safeguard is shown below, a box (printed in red) on all hire purchase agreements.

> This document contains the terms of a hire purchase agreement. Sign it only if you want to be legally bound by them.
>
> Signature of Hirer ....
>
> The goods will not become your property until you have made all the payments. You must not sell them before then.

Fig. 21.1. A safeguard in a hire purchase agreement.

21.2 The Elements in an HP Agreement

These are as follows:

(a) A fixed percentage of the purchase price, called the **deposit,** is payable at once.

(b) The **balance due** is payable over a period of time called the

term of the hire, **with interest**. Usually the retailer will not have enough capital to finance this loan to the customer, which will be made by a finance company. The finance company simply pays the retailer the balance of the money due and the loan is made to the customer by the finance company once the **hire purchase agreement** is signed.

(c) Interest is added at a *flat rate* for the duration of the hire. Thus if the flat rate of interest is $12\frac{1}{2}\%$ for two years, 25% will be added to the balance due, to give the total amount outstanding when the agreement is signed. The flat rate of interest is convenient and simple, but it hides the true annual rate of interest, because the money is being repaid all the time. This need not concern us here, but the true rate is actually about twice the flat rate.

(d) The monthly (or weekly) **instalments** payable can then be calculated. Sometimes the final instalment is increased by a nominal amount, the payment of which signals the transfer of ownership to the purchaser.

Example 21.1. A typical transaction would be as follows: Retailer A.B. offers a suite of dining-room furniture for £420 cash, or on hire purchase. The terms of the hire are: (a) a deposit of 20% of the cash price; (b) 24 monthly instalments commencing one month after the purchase; (c) interest added at 15% per annum; (d) the final instalment to be increased by 50 pence for the purchase of the hired goods.

$$
\begin{aligned}
\text{Cash price} &= £420 \\
\text{Deposit} &= 20\% \text{ of } £420 \\
&= \tfrac{1}{5} \times 420 \\
&= £84 \qquad \text{(cancelling by 5)}
\end{aligned}
$$

$$
\begin{aligned}
\text{Balance due} &= £420 - £84 \\
&= £336
\end{aligned}
$$

$$
\begin{aligned}
\text{Interest payable} &= £336 \times 30\% \ (15\% \times 2 \text{ yrs}) \\
&= £33.60 \times 3 \\
&= £100.80
\end{aligned}
$$

$$
\begin{aligned}
\text{Total payable under agreement} &= £336 + £100.80 \\
&= £436.80
\end{aligned}
$$

$$
\begin{aligned}
\text{Monthly instalment} &= \frac{£436.80}{24} \qquad \text{(24 months)} \\[2mm]
&= \frac{£109.20}{6} \qquad \text{(cancelling by 4)} \\[2mm]
&= £18.20 \text{ per month}
\end{aligned}
$$

$$\text{Weekly instalment} = \frac{\pounds 436.80}{104} \qquad (52 \text{ weeks} \times 2)$$

$$= \pounds 4.20$$

$$\begin{array}{r} 4.20 \\ 104 \overline{)\ 436.80} \\ 416 \\ \hline 208 \\ 208 \\ \hline \end{array}$$

(*Note:* The final instalment in each case will be 50 pence greater, i.e. £18.70 pence on the 24th month or £4.70 pence on the 104th week.)

21.3   Exercises: Hire Purchase

1. Find (i) the deposit payable and (ii) the balance to pay in each of the following hire purchase transactions:

	Purchase price	Deposit rate
(a)	£54	15%
(b)	£60	$33\frac{1}{3}\%$
(c)	£85	20%
(d)	£120	30%
(e)	£285	20%

2. Find the amount of each monthly instalment in the hire purchase agreements listed below (answers correct to the nearest penny where necessary):

	Cash price of goods	Deposit payable	Rate of interest per annum	No. of years
(a)	£100	20%	15	1
(b)	£340	10%	15	1
(c)	£500	20%	$12\frac{1}{2}$	1
(d)	£235	20%	15	2
(e)	£375	$33\frac{1}{3}\%$	20	2

3. Find the monthly instalment payable for each of the hire purchase transactions listed below (answers correct to the nearest penny, if necessary):

	Cash price of goods	Fraction payable as deposit	Rate of interest (% per annum)	No. of years
(a)	£100	$\frac{1}{5}$	$12\frac{1}{2}$	1
(b)	£200	$\frac{1}{4}$	15	1
(c)	£250	$\frac{1}{5}$	$12\frac{1}{2}$	2
(d)	£400	$\frac{1}{10}$	$12\frac{1}{2}$	2
(e)	£500	$\frac{1}{5}$	15	2
(f)	£240	$\frac{1}{3}$	10	2
(g)	£380	$\frac{1}{4}$	$12\frac{1}{2}$	3

(h)	£450	$\frac{1}{5}$	10	3
(i)	£650	$\frac{1}{5}$	15	3
(j)	£860	$\frac{1}{10}$	15	3

4. Find the *weekly* instalment payable for each of the hire purchase transactions listed below (answers correct to the nearest penny where necessary):

	Cash price of goods	Deposit payable £	Rate of interest (% per annum)	No. of years
(a)	£100	10	15	1
(b)	£140	30	15	1
(c)	£450	50	$12\frac{1}{2}$	2
(d)	£640	60	$12\frac{1}{2}$	2
(e)	£760	80	15	2
(f)	£480	96	15	$2\frac{1}{2}$
(g)	£500	100	15	$2\frac{1}{2}$
(h)	£750	150	18	3
(i)	£1000	200	$12\frac{1}{2}$	3
(j)	£1250	250	15	3

21.4   Mental Arithmetic: Hire Purchase

Do these calculations mentally:

1. A bicycle costing £80 requires a 20% deposit. How much is that?

2. A suite of furniture costing £560 requires a 20% deposit. How much is that?

3. What would a $33\frac{1}{3}$% deposit on a car costing £4800 amount to?

4. A 30% deposit is placed on a £1250 motorcycle. What is the balance to pay?

5. A $16\frac{2}{3}$% deposit is required on a dining-room suite costing £660. What is the balance to pay?

6. Interest at $12\frac{1}{2}$% for two years is added to a balance to pay of £480. How much is now payable?

7. Interest at 15% for three years is added to a balance to pay of £1000. How much is now payable?

8. Interest at 10% for three years is added to a balance to pay of £800. How much is payable altogether?

9. Interest at $12\frac{1}{2}$% is added to a balance to pay of £400. The total is repayable over 1 year. How much is payable each month?

10. After interest has been added the total payable on a hire purchase agreement is £1040. Repayments are made weekly over one year. How much is payable per week?

21.5 Mental Arithmetic Test

Do these calculations mentally.

1. $425 \times 12 =$

2. $1750 \div 25 =$

3. What is the total cost of 5 items at 95 p and 3 items at £1.25 each?

4. $\frac{3}{4} \div 1\frac{1}{2} =$

5. VAT is charged at 15%. What will be the VAT on a vehicle priced at £3500 before VAT?

6. $3.75 + 4.5 + 3.84 + 4.26 =$

7. How many days from 24 May to 3 July inclusive?

8. What is the average of 36, 44, 60 and 64?

9. What is the interest on a loan of £7000 for 3 years at 8%?

10. What is 60% of £20 000?

11. A man works 40 hours per week at £1.95 per hour. What is his total wage?

12. Share a bequest of £30 000 between A, B and C so that A gets three times as much as B and C.

13. A garage is rated by the rating authority at £4000 rateable value. The rates are fixed at £1.20 in the £. How much must the proprietor pay?

14. A project costs £2500 for materials, £3160 for labour, £195 for design costs and £485 for setting up and testing. What is the total cost?

15. A car costs a deposit of £1000 and 36 monthly payments of £60. What is its total price on hire purchase?

22
Foreign Exchange Calculations

22.1 Foreign Money

Every nation-state has its own currency, unless it is linked to a 'great nation' and uses the currency of that nation. The money in use is designated as legal tender, which means that it may be offered in payment of any debt in the country concerned and must be accepted by the creditor as satisfaction for the debt. There is usually a main coin (or note) divided into smaller denominations. Most countries have a **centesimal** system, with each unit of currency divided into 100 smaller coins. Thus there are 100 cents in a United States dollar and 100 pence in £1 sterling. A few countries have a **millesimal** system, with 1000 small coins in the larger unit of currency. Thus the Bahrain dinar is divided into 1000 fils. A few countries—perhaps because of inflation over the years—have discarded any smaller denominations and the smallest coin available is the unit. Notable examples are the Italian lira (2200 lire = £1) and Japanese yen (370 yen = £1). A list of the more important currencies is given in Table 22.1.

Table 22.1. The major currencies of the world.

Country	Unit of currency	Smaller coins
Argentina	New peso	100 old pesos
Australia	A. dollar	100 cents
Austria	Schilling	100 groschen
Belgium and Luxembourg	Franc	100 centimes
Brazil	Cruzeiro	100 centavos
Canada	C. dollar	100 cents
Denmark	Krone	100 oere
France	Franc	100 centimes
Germany (Western)	Deutschmark	100 pfennigs
Greece	Drachma	100 lepta

Country	Unit of currency	Smaller coins
India	Rupee	100 paise
Italy	Lira	
Japan	Yen	
Kenya	Shilling	100 cents
Kuwait	Dinar	1000 fils
Malaysia	Ringgit	100 cents
Netherlands	Guilder	100 cents
New Zealand	NZ dollar	100 cents
Nigeria	Naira	100 kobo
Norway	Krone	100 oere
Pakistan	Rupee	100 paisa
Peru	Sol	100 centavos
Portugal	Escudo	100 centavos
Saudi Arabia	Riyal	20 qursh
Spain	Peseta	100 centimes
Sierra Leone	Leone	100 cents
South Africa	Rand	100 cents
Sweden	Krona	100 oere
Thailand	Baht	100 satang
United Kingdom	Pound sterling	100 pence
USSR	Rouble	100 kopeks
USA	Dollar	100 cents

In the exercises which follow the exchange rates have deliberately been chosen at random since they are liable to fluctuate. For current exchange rates consult the financial pages of your daily newspaper.

The rule for converting British currency to foreign currency is *'Multiply the number of pounds sterling to be exchanged by the rate of exchange.'*

Example 22.1. A businessman leaving for a business trip to Madrid exchanged £500 for pesetas at London Airport. The rate of exchange is £1 = 183 pesetas. How many pesetas will he receive?

$$£1 = 183 \text{ pesetas}$$
$$£500 = 183 \times 500$$
$$= 91\,500 \text{ pesetas}$$

(*Note:* It is always advisable to do a rough estimate on such calculations. Call 183 only 180: $5 \times 180 = 900$; $500 \times 180 = 90\,000$. Is our answer roughly 90 000? Yes it is, so we have clearly received the correct amount of Spanish currency.)

Example 22.2. A British tourist takes £200 to the USA, which she exchanges at the rate £1 = $1.93. How many dollars will she receive?

$$£1 = \$1.93$$
$$£200 = \$1.93 \times 200$$
$$= \$386$$

Example 22.3. Change £325 to Japanese yen at £1 = 405 yen.

$$£1 = 405 \text{ yen}$$
$$£325 = 405 \times 325$$

	405
	325
	2 025
	8 100
	121 500
= 131 625 yen	131 625

22.2   Exercises: Converting Sterling to Foreign Currency

Change the following amounts of sterling into the currencies shown, at the rate of exchange given for that currency:

1. £300 to United States dollars at £1 = $1.95
2. £500 to Deutschmarks at £1 = DM4.38
3. £700 to French francs at £1 = F11.01
4. £525 to yen at £1 = 426.5 yen
5. £630 to Spanish pesetas at £1 = 185.6 pesetas
6. £780 to Portuguese escudos at £1 = 125.6 escudos
7. £435 to Kuwaiti dinars at £1 = 0.52 dinars
8. £585 to Dutch guilders at £1 = 4.74 guilders
9. £729 to Singaporean dollars at £1 = S$3.86
10. £695 to Australian dollars at £1 = $A1.68

22.3   Converting Foreign Currency to Sterling

The rule for converting foreign currency to Sterling is '*Divide the amount of foreign currency by the rate of exchange*'.

Example 22.4. A British holidaymaker returns from Spain with 4650 pesetas. The rate of exchange is £1 = 186 pesetas. How much sterling will be received by the traveller?

$$186 \text{ pesetas} = £1$$
$$4650 \text{ pesetas} = \frac{£4650}{186}$$

$$
\begin{array}{r}
25 \\
186 \overline{)\,4650} \\
372 \\
\hline
930 \\
930 \\
\hline
\cdots
\end{array}
$$

$$= £25$$

Example 22.5. A French couturier arrives at London Airport with 5505 French francs. The rate of exchange is £1 = F11.01. How much British money will be received?

$$11.01 \text{ francs} = £1$$
$$5505 \text{ francs} = \frac{5505}{11.01} \text{ pounds}$$

$$
\begin{array}{r}
500 \\
1101 \overline{)\,550500} \\
5505 \\
\hline
\cdots
\end{array}
$$

$$= £500$$

Example 22.6. A British salesman has just sold 5000 refrigerators to Nigeria at a price of 128 Naira each. The Nigerian currency will be paid in six months' time. On the forward exchange market the six-months' forward rate of exchange is £1 = N1.6. How much will the British firm receive for the Nigerian currency if it arranges a forward contract for the total purchase price?

$$
\begin{aligned}
\text{Total purchase price} &= 5000 \times 128 \text{ N} \\
&= 640\,000 \text{ N} \\
1.6\text{N} &= £1 \\
640\,000\text{N} &= \frac{£640\,000}{1.6} \\
&= \frac{£6\,400\,000}{16} \\
&= £400\,000
\end{aligned}
$$

22.4   Exercises: Converting Foreign Currency to Sterling

Change the amounts of foreign currency shown below to pounds sterling, at the rates of exchange given:

	Foreign currency	*Rate of exchange*
1.	3787.5 Austrian schillings	£1 = 30.3 schillings
2.	1114.7 Danish krone	£1 = 14.2 krone
3.	312 deutschmarks	£1 = 4.8 deutschmarks
4.	20 952 yen	£1 = 432 yen
5.	73.8 Irish punt	£1 = 1.23 punt
6.	709.2 United States dollars	£1 = $1.97
7.	769.25 South African rands	£1 = 1.81 rands
8.	24 440 Singapore dollars	£1 = S$3.76
9.	49 452 Saudi Arabian riyals	£1 = 6.34 riyals
10.	77 625 Swiss francs	£1 = 3.45 Swiss francs

22.5   Exercises: Foreign Currency

Do these calculations mentally:

1. How many pounds sterling for $414 at £1 = $2.07?

2. How many pesetas for £50 at £1 = 185 pesetas?

3. How many Swiss francs for £300 at £1 = 3.47 Swiss francs?

4. How many pounds sterling for 6000 naire at £1 = N1.5?

5. How many Escudos for £250 at £1 = 130 Escudos?

6. A 100-dollar bill is changed into sterling at £1 = $2.50 to pay a bill of £18.50 at a restaurant. What change will be received, in sterling?

7. Change £1000 to deutschmarks at 4.75 DM to the pound

8. Change £800 to Dutch guilders at 4.7420 guilders to the pound

9. Change 21 840 Hong Kong dollars to pounds sterling at £1 = $HK10.92

10. Change 32 700 Greek drachma to pounds sterling at £1 = 109 drachma

22.6   Mental Arithmetic Test

Do these calculations mentally:

1. 475 + 382 + 726 + 15 =

2. £1700.56 − £590.60 =

3. $275.76 \div 0.9 =$

4. What is $16\frac{2}{3}\%$ of 120 metres?

5. What is four fifths of £800?

6. How many 250 g packets of tea can be made up from $10\frac{1}{2}$ kg?

7. A motor scooter retails at £480. A trader is given 25% trade discount. How much does he pay for a scooter?

8. French francs are 10.25 to the £1. How many shall I get for £200?

9. A washing machine costs a deposit of £29.50 and 12 monthly instalments of £12.50. What is the total cost?

10. Reduce £55 by 20%

11. A retailer adds 150% to all goods purchased to find his selling prices. What will he charge for an item costing £5?

12. What is the simple interest on £10 000 for 2 years at 20%?

13. A dispatch rider travels 150 km in $2\frac{1}{2}$ hours. What is his average speed?

14. The rate of exchange for US dollars is $1.63 = £1. How many shall I get for £200?

15. A contract is earning 4800 German marks at a time when DM2.4 = £1. How much will the contract earn in £ sterling?

23
Lengths, Areas and Volumes

23.1 Introduction—a Three-Dimensional World

We live in a three dimensional world: all objects in that world have three dimensions or measurements. They are, **length, breadth** and **height**. The word **width** is sometimes used instead of 'breadth', and when an object is flat (one of its dimensions is small) we speak of its **thickness** rather than its height. The page of this book has length, breadth and thickness. In many cases this third dimension can be ignored for practical purposes. Thus when carpeting a room we need concern ourselves only with the length and breadth of the room, for the thickness of the carpet will not affect the **area** to be covered. An area is a two-dimensional shape. **Squares** and **rectangles** are regular-shaped areas, but many areas are irregular. For example, a parking area behind a factory may be of any shape, and when we carpet rooms we usually have to allow extra material for recesses, bays, etc.

Three-dimensional figures are called **solids**. If all the faces of a solid are rectangles it is called a rectangular solid. If all the faces of a solid are squares, the object is called a **cube**. Rectangular solids which are not cubes are often called **cuboids**, which means 'having the form of a cube'.

The branch of mathematics concerned with lengths, areas and volumes is **mensuration**, or measuring. In order to measure we need units of known length. Today these units are metric units—the metre, centimetre, millimetre and kilometre being the most common units used. They are recognised worldwide as SI units, as explained in Section 7.1.

The metre measures length. To measure areas we need a measure which has two dimensions: the unit used is the **square metre** (written m^2). Similarly, to measure volumes we need measures that have three dimensions, like the **cubic metre** (written m^3).

23.2　Rectangles and Squares

A rectangle is a shape which has four straight sides each of which is at right angles to the sides adjacent to it. A square is a special case of a rectangle because its four sides are all of equal length. Other rectangles have opposite pairs of sides of equal length. If this were not so, the angles could not be right angles.

To calculate the areas of rectangles and squares we use the formula:

$$Area = Length \times Breadth$$

which is abbreviated to

$$A = l \times b$$

This is illustrated in Fig. 23.1

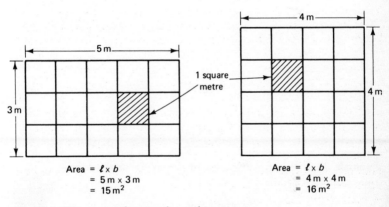

$$
\begin{aligned}
Area &= l \times b \\
&= 5\,m \times 3\,m \\
&= 15\,m^2
\end{aligned}
\qquad
\begin{aligned}
Area &= l \times b \\
&= 4\,m \times 4\,m \\
&= 16\,m^2
\end{aligned}
$$

Fig. 23.1. The areas of rectangles and squares.

The answer to this type of calculation will always be in square units, such as square metres, square millimetres, etc. Large areas of land are measured under the metric system in hectares. The **table of square measure** is given in Table 23.1.

Table 23.1. Table of square measure.

100 square millimetres	= 1 square centimetre
100 square centimetres	= 1 square decimetre
100 square decimetres	= 1 square metre
100 square metres	= 1 are
100 ares	= 1 hectare
100 hectares	= 1 square kilometre

In abbreviated form this reads as follows:

100 mm²	=	1 cm²
100 cm²	=	1 dm²
100 dm²	=	1 m²
100 m²	=	1 a
100 a	=	1 ha
100 ha	=	1 km²

(*Note:* Remember that only certain symbols in the metric system have capital letters. Most symbols have small letters, and symbols do *not* need an 's' added to the plural.)

To calculate the areas of squares and rectangles we use the formula given in Fig. 23.1.

Example 23.1. What is the area of a table-top 2.5 metres long and 1.8 metres wide?

$$\text{Area} = l \times b$$
$$= 2.5 \text{ m} \times 1.8 \text{ m}$$

```
        2.5
    ×   1.8
    _____
      20 0
      25 0
    _____
      4.50
    _____
```

$$= 4.5 \text{ m}^2$$

Example 23.2. What is the area of a playing field 120 metres long and 85 metres wide?

$$\text{Area} = l \times b$$
$$= 120 \text{ m} \times 85 \text{ m}$$

```
        120
    ×    85
    _____
        600
      9 600
    _____
    10 200 m²
    _____
```

$$= 1 \text{ ha } 2 \text{ a (one hectare two ares)}$$

Example 23.3. A rectangular playground has an area of 1176 square metres. If it is 42 metres long how broad is it?

The formula for an area is

$$\text{Area} = \text{length} \times \text{breadth}$$

If we know the area and the length we must rearrange the formula to find the breadth. We have already learned how to rearrange formulae (see page 107). Using this method to rearrange the formula $A = l \times b$ we need to leave b by itself on one side of the equation. To do this we have to divide that side of the equation by l, because then the l will cancel out

$$\frac{l \times b}{l} \qquad \text{(the } l\text{'s will cancel, leaving } b\text{)}$$

If we are going to do this to one side of the equation we must do it to the other side of the equation. So, beginning again

$$A = l \times b$$

Dividing both sides by l, we have

$$\frac{A}{l} = \frac{l \times b}{l} \text{ (the } l\text{'s now cancel out on the right-hand side)}$$

We are left with

$$\frac{A}{l} = b$$

As any equation can be written down the other way round we can write

$$b = \frac{A}{l}$$

or

$$\text{Breadth} = \frac{\text{Area}}{\text{Length}}$$

We can now solve Example 23.3.

$$\text{Breadth} = \frac{\text{Area}}{\text{Length}}$$
$$= \frac{1176 \text{ m}^2}{42 \text{ m}}$$

$$= 28 \text{ m}$$

```
        28
42 ) 1176
     84
     ---
     336
     336
     ...
```

(*Note*: Similarly, Length $= \dfrac{\text{Area}}{\text{Breadth}}$ or $l = \dfrac{A}{b}$.)

23.3 Exercises: Areas of Squares and Rectangles

1. Calculate the areas of squares whose sides have the following lengths. Refer to Table 23.1 to ensure that you use the correct units for your answers.

(a) 5 cm   (b) 8 cm
(c) 27 cm   (d) $1\frac{1}{2}$ m
(e) $2\frac{3}{4}$ m   (f) 25 m
(g) 100 m   (h) 150 m
(i) 300 m   (j) $2\frac{1}{2}$ km

2. Find the area of rectangles whose dimensions are as follows:

	Length	Breadth		Length	Breadth
(a)	12 cm	7 cm	(b)	36 cm	17 cm
(c)	60 cm	24 cm	(d)	95 cm	25 cm
(e)	120 m	80 m	(f)	250 m	60 m
(g)	$2\frac{1}{2}$ m	$1\frac{3}{4}$ m	(h)	$3\frac{1}{2}$ m	$2\frac{1}{2}$ m
(i)	2 km	$1\frac{3}{8}$ km	(j)	5.8 km	2.3 km

3. Find the length of rectangles whose areas and breadths are as given below:

	Area	Breadth		Area	Breadth
(a)	132 cm²	6 cm	(b)	84 cm²	3.5 cm
(c)	280 m²	14 m	(d)	405 m²	15 m
(e)	1728 m²	36 m	(f)	594 m²	18 m

4. Find the breadth of rectangles whose areas and lengths are as given below:

	Area	Length		Area	Length
(a)	156 cm²	13 cm	(b)	340 cm²	20 cm
(c)	720 m²	36 m	(d)	551 m²	29 m
(e)	2295 m²	85 m	(f)	1748 m²	46 m

23.4 Areas of Irregular Figures based on Rectangles

Many rooms have irregular shapes which are based upon rectangles. An L-shaped configuration is commonly used in buildings, while working areas for machines are often constructed as annexes to a main office or factory. The areas of such irregular shapes can often be found by dividing the shapes into two or more rectangles. An example of such an irregular figure is given in Fig. 23.2.

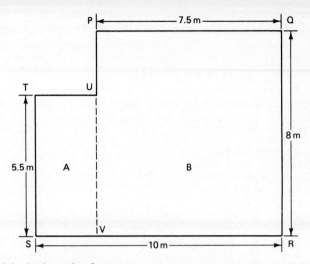

Fig. 23.2. An irregular figure.

The irregular shape in Fig. 23.2 may be divided into two regular figures by a dividing line drawn from U parallel to the side TS, to join the side RS at V. We now have two rectangles A and B. We can therefore find the areas of these two rectangles and by adding them together find the area of the whole figure. What is not absolutely clear from the diagram is the length of some of the sides entering into the calculations we are about to do. We can see that rectangle B is 8 m long and 7.5 m wide. Rectangle A is 5.5 m long, but how wide is it?

Because we know that opposite sides of rectangles are equal in length we can see that the total length opposite side SR must be 10 m, because SR is 10 m long. Since PQ is 7.5 m the rest of the length (TU) must be 10 m − 7.5 m = 2.5 m.

Therefore rectangle A is 5.5 m long and 2.5 m wide.

$$\begin{aligned}
\text{Area of figure} &= \text{Area of A} + \text{Area of B} \\
&= (5.5 \text{ m} \times 2.5 \text{ m}) + (8 \text{ m} \times 7.5 \text{ m}) \\
&= \quad 5.5 \qquad\qquad + \; 60.0 \text{m}^2 \\
&\quad\;\; 2.5
\end{aligned}$$

$$\begin{aligned}
&27\,5 \\
&110\,0 \\
\\
&13.75 \text{ m}^2 \qquad\qquad + 60.0 \text{ m}^2 \\
\\
&= 73.75 \text{ m}^2
\end{aligned}$$

Sometimes an irregular figure is caused by inner areas within a larger rectilinear figure. In Fig. 23.3 a central flowerbed is surrounded by a grass area 2 m wide. The area of this grass border can be found in two ways. In the first method the area of the whole garden is found and the area of the central flowerbed is deducted from it. In the second method the irregular area of grass is divided into four small rectangles. The areas of these can be found and added together.

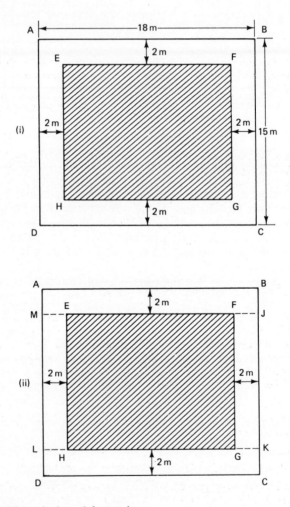

Fig. 23.3. Flowerbeds and footpaths.

Method 1

$$\text{Area of whole garden ABCD} = 18 \text{ m} \times 15 \text{ m}$$

$$
\begin{array}{r}
= 18 \\
\times 15 \\
\hline
90 \\
180 \\
\hline
270 \text{ m}^2 \\
\hline\hline
\end{array}
$$

$$
\begin{aligned}
\text{Area of flower bed EFGH} &= 14 \text{ m} \times 11 \text{ m} \\
&= 154 \text{ m}^2
\end{aligned}
$$

(*Note*: To find the measurements of the flower bed we must deduct 4 m from each side of the garden, since the grass is 2 m wide at *each* end.)

$$
\begin{aligned}
\text{Area of grass} &= 270 \text{ m}^2 - 154 \text{ m}^2 \\
&= 116 \text{ m}^2
\end{aligned}
$$

Method 2. The grass may be divided into four rectangles. ABJM and LKCD are similar in size, and measure 18 m × 2 m. FJKG and MEHL are also similar in size and measure 11 m × 2 m.

$$
\begin{aligned}
\therefore \quad \text{Total area} &= (18 \text{ m} \times 2 \text{ m}) \times 2 + (11 \text{ m} \times 2 \text{ m}) \times 2 \\
&= 72 \text{ m}^2 + 44 \text{ m}^2 \\
&= 116 \text{ m}^2
\end{aligned}
$$

23.5 Exercises: Areas of Irregular Figures

1. Fig. 23.4 shows some irregular figures. The dimensions are given in metres in enough detail to enable you to calculate the area of each figure. Find the area in each case. (*Hint:* It is helpful if the shape is copied roughly onto your workpaper and the measurements written in. The figure should then be marked off into rectangles and any missing dimensions can be calculated. Then use the formula Area = $l \times b$ to find the areas of each part.)

2. An office measures 5.5 m by 3.4 m, but it has attached on one side a machine section for photocopying which measures 2.5 by 3.5 m. What is the total area of the premises?

3. A classroom is 8 metres square, but it has a washroom facility on one side which measures 3.5 by 2.25 m. What is the total area of the room?

4. Fig. 23.5 shows proposed layouts for formal gardens planned in a leisure complex. Find the area of the paving required for the shaded areas in each plan. All measurements are given in metres.

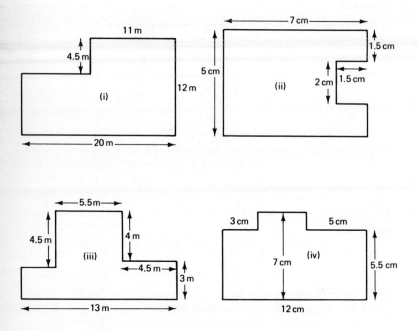

Fig. 23.4. Some irregular figures.

5. In Fig. 23.5d the paths are to be paved with square blocks of side 0.5 m. (a) How many blocks will be required? (b) What will be the cost of paving the footpaths if the blocks are 60p each, the labour is £80, and sand and other materials cost in all £35.80.

23.6   Perimeters of Rectangles

The **perimeter** of a rectangle is the distance all the way round its edge. Perimeters can be important—for example, when fencing in a garden, or a field, or when framing pictures.

A rectangle has two pairs of opposite sides, and both members of each pair of sides are the same length. In the case of a square, all four sides are the same length. We can therefore say:

$$\text{Perimeter of a square} = 4 \times \text{length}$$
$$\text{Perimeter of rectangles} = (2 \times \text{length}) + (2 \times \text{breadth})$$

or
$$\text{Perimeter} = 2 \, (\text{length} + \text{breadth})$$

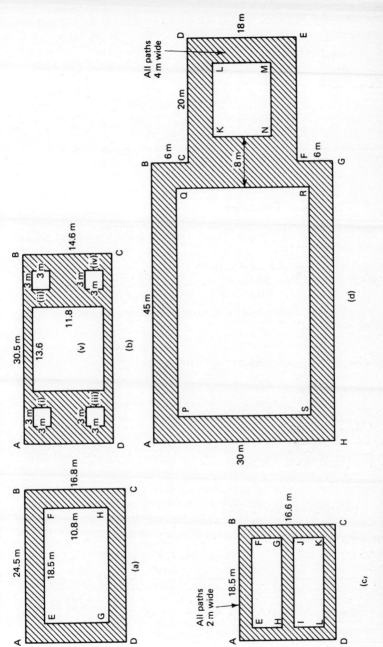

Fig. 23.5. Formal gardens.

Example 23.4. An allotment is 40 m long by 22 m wide. What is its perimeter?

$$\begin{aligned} \text{Perimeter} &= (2 \times 40 \text{ m}) + (2 \times 22 \text{ m}) \\ &= 80 \text{ m} + 44 \text{ m} \\ &= 124 \text{ m} \end{aligned}$$

or

$$\begin{aligned} \text{Perimeter} &= 2(40 \text{ m} + 22 \text{ m}) \\ &= 2 \times 62 \text{ m} \\ &= 124 \text{ m} \end{aligned}$$

23.7   Exercises on Perimeters

1. Find (i) the perimeters and (ii) the areas of squares whose sides are as shown below:

(a) 5 cm   (b) 8 cm
(c) 24 cm   (d) 36 cm
(e) 3 m   (f) 100 m

2. Find (i) the perimeters and (ii) the areas of rectangles whose sides are as shown below:

	Length	Breadth		Length	Breadth
(a)	4 cm	3 cm	(b)	6 cm	4 cm
(c)	7 cm	4 cm	(d)	9 cm	6 cm
(e)	12 m	8 m	(f)	16 m	12 m
(g)	23 m	15 m	(h)	28 m	18 m
(i)	32 m	20 m	(j)	42 m	24 m

23.8   The Walls of a Room

A particular case of a perimeter exercise concerns calculations about the walls of rooms. When decorating and redecorating calculations about the quantity of paint, wallpaper, etc., required make us consider the total surface area of walls, ceilings, etc.

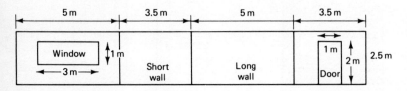

Fig. 23.6. The walls of a room.

Fig. 23.6 shows the walls of a room, opened out into a long figure. The room is 5 m long by 3.5 m wide, and it is 2.5 m high. In such a diagram the walls of the room, both length and breadth, become one long measurement, and the height of the room becomes the other dimension.

$$\text{Length of diagram} = 5\,\text{m} + 3.5\,\text{m} + 5\,\text{m} + 3.5\,\text{m}$$
$$= 17\,\text{m}$$
$$\text{Breadth of diagram} = \text{height of room} = 2.5\,\text{m}$$
$$\therefore \quad \text{Area of walls} = 17\,\text{m} \times 2.5\,\text{m}$$
$$= 42.5\,\text{m}^2$$

From this area we must deduct the areas of the window and the door if we are to discover the area of wall to be painted or papered.

$$\text{Area of window} = 3\,\text{m} \times 1\,\text{m}$$
$$= 3\,\text{m}^2$$
$$\text{Area of door} = 2\,\text{m} \times 1\,\text{m}$$
$$= 2\,\text{m}^2$$
$$\therefore \quad \text{Area to be painted} = 42.5\,\text{m}^2 - 5\,\text{m}^2$$
$$= 37.5\,\text{m}^2$$

23.9 Exercises: The Walls of a Room

1. What is the area of the walls of a room 5 m × $3\frac{1}{2}$ m and 2.5 m high, if the area of the doors and windows is 6.5 m²?

2. A room is 6 m long by $4\frac{1}{2}$ m wide. (a) What is the area of the ceiling? (b) The room is 2.75 m high: what is the area of the walls, allowing 3.5 m² for windows and 1.5 m² for *each* of the two doors?

3. Find the area of the walls of a room 15 m long, 10.5 m wide and 3 m high if the area of the windows and doors altogether totals 9 m².

4. (a) What will be the area of the walls of a room 7.5 m long by 4.5 m wide and 3.5 m high, if the door and windows measure in total 5.25 m²? (b) What will be the cost of painting the walls if paint can only be purchased in tins which give a coverage of 20 m² and which cost £1.75 per tin?

5. (a) What will be the area of the walls of a room 17 m long by 8.25 m wide and 3.5 m high, if the doors and windows measure in total 8.75 m²? (b) What will be the cost of painting the wall if paint can only be obtained in tins costing £2.35 each, giving a coverage of 25 m²?

6. A room is 18 m long by 12.5 m wide (a) What will be the area of the ceiling? (b) What will it cost to paint it if the paint can only be purchased in tins giving a coverage of 50 m² or 25 m²? The larger tins cost £3.35 each, the smaller tins £2 each.

23.10 Volumes of Cubes and Cuboids

We have seen that a volume is a measure of three-dimensional space. Three-dimensional figures are known as **solids**. If the solid is contained by squares it is called a **cube**. If it is contained by other rectangle shapes it is said to be **cuboid**. It is convenient to measure volume by cubic measures, such as the cubic metre (m^3), the cubic centimetre (cc or cm^3), or the cubic decimetre (known by its other name of a litre). The term **cubic capacity** is frequently used to describe the internal space available—for example, in a refrigerator, or the boot of a car. Engine capacity is often given in cubic centimetres, or for bigger cars in litres. Thus a 3.5 litre engine has a cubic capacity of 3500 cc.

The volume of a cuboid is found by the formula

$$\text{Volume} = \text{Length} \times \text{Breadth} \times \text{Height}$$

Example 23.5. What is the volume of a crate measuring 2.2 m by 1.8 m by 0.95 m?

$$\begin{aligned} \text{Volume} &= l \times b \times h \\ &= 2.2\,\text{m} \times 1.8\,\text{m} \times 0.95\,\text{m} \end{aligned}$$

$$\begin{array}{r} 2.2 \\ \times \quad 1.8 \\ \hline 176 \\ 220 \\ \hline 3.96 \\ \times \quad 0.95 \\ \hline 1\,980 \\ 35\,640 \\ \hline 3.7620 \\ \hline \end{array}$$

$$= 3.762\,\text{m}^3$$

Example 23.6. What is the volume of a warehouse 60 m long, 23.5 m wide and 9.8 m high?

$$\begin{aligned} \text{Volume} &= l \times b \times h \\ &= 60\,\text{m} \times 23.5\,\text{m} \times 9.8\,\text{m} \\ &= 1\,410 \times 9.8 \\ &= 13\,818\,\text{m}^3 \end{aligned}$$

$$\begin{array}{r} 1\,410 \\ 98 \\ \hline 11\,280 \\ 126\,900 \\ \hline 13\,818.0 \\ \hline \end{array}$$

Example 23.7. A container is 12.5 m long and of square cross section 2.5 m × 2.5 m. These are the internal measurements. What is its volume? How many cubic crates side 0.5 m will fit into the container?

Volume = $l \times b \times h$
= 2.5 m × 2.5 m × 12.5 m
= 78.125 m³

$$
\begin{array}{r}
2.5 \\
\times \quad 2.5 \\
\hline
125 \\
500 \\
\hline
6.25 \\
\hline
\end{array}
\qquad
\begin{array}{r}
6.25 \\
\times \quad 12.5 \\
\hline
3\ 125 \\
12\ 500 \\
62\ 500 \\
\hline
78.125 \\
\hline
\end{array}
$$

The number of crates that will fit in can be discovered by two methods.

Method I The crates will fit in as follows

25 crates down the long side
5 crates across the container
5 crates deep (i.e. piled high)

Number of crates = 25 × 5 × 5
= 625 crates

Method II Here we find how many crates would fit in by dividing the volume of 1 crate into the total volume of 78.125 m³:

Volume of 1 crate = 0.5 m × 0.5 m × 0.5 m
= 0.125 m³

Number of crates = $\dfrac{78.125}{0.125}$

= $\dfrac{78\ 125}{125}$

$$
\begin{array}{r}
625 \\
125 \overline{)\ 78\ 125} \\
750 \\
\hline
312 \\
250 \\
\hline
625 \\
625 \\
\end{array}
$$

= 625 crates

(*Note:* From these alternative methods of working it may be seen that the first method gives a simple multiplication sum; the second gives a rather difficult division sum.)

Example 23.8. Find the volume of the cuboid object shown in Fig. 23.7.

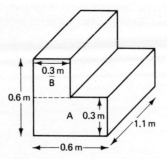

Fig. 23.7. A cubiod.

As with irregular plane figures based on rectangles, we can imagine this cuboid split into two rectangular solids, A and B.

Volume of Part A
$$= 0.6 \text{ m} \times 0.3 \text{ m} \times 1.1 \text{ m}$$
$$= 0.18 \times 1.1$$
$$= 0.198 \text{ m}^3$$

Volume of Part B
$$= 0.3 \text{ m} \times 0.3 \text{ m} \times 1.1 \text{ m}$$
$$= 0.09 \times 1.1$$
$$= 0.099 \text{ m}^3$$

$$\therefore \quad \text{Volume of cuboid} = 0.198 \text{ m}^3 + 0.099 \text{ m}^3$$
$$= 0.297 \text{ m}^3$$

23.11   Exercises: Volumes of Cubes and Cuboids

1. Find the volumes of cubes which have sides as follows:

(a) 4 cm   (b) 7 cm
(c) 15 cm   (d) 20 cm
(e) 1.5 m   (f) 2.3 m

2. Find the volumes of the cuboids which have dimensions as listed below:

	Length	Breadth	Height
(a)	17 cm	8 cm	4 cm
(b)	23 cm	11 cm	8 cm
(c)	1.3 m	0.8 m	0.5 m
(d)	2.5 m	1.5 m	1.2 m
(e)	7.3 m	2.8 m	1.8 m
(f)	12.5 m	3.6 m	2.4 m

3. Find the volume of each of the cuboids shown in Fig. 23.8

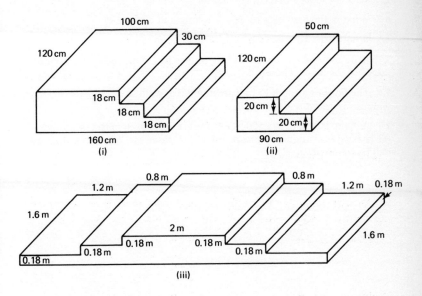

Fig. 23.8. More cuboids.

4. How many cubes with a side of 2 cm will fit into a packing case which has internal dimensions of 30 cm × 20 cm × 12 cm?

5. How many cubes with a side of 3 cm will fit into a crate with internal dimensions of 3 m × 1.5 m × 1.2 m

23.12 Mental Arithmetic Test

Write down the answers only to these questions:

1. Change £2.84 to pence

2. Write 3840 halfpence in sterling

3. What is $33\frac{1}{3}$% of £120?

4. Add two thirds of £60 to half of £50

5. How much is 5 per cent of £1200?

6. Change MCMVII to Arabic numbers

7. Multiply 0.1 by 0.1 and then multiply the answer by 0.1

8. What is $\frac{7}{12}$ of $\frac{4}{5}$?

9. Write down the number 'ten million and one'

10. What is 40 as a percentage of 8000?

11. What is the area of a room 23 m long and 8 m wide?

12. What is the volume of a cube of side 1.2 m?

13. How many 6 cm cubes will fit into a box with internal dimensions 36 cm × 24 cm × 12 cm?

14. The floor of a room has an area of 480 m² and its length is 30 m. How wide is the room?

15. A field is 100 m × 120 m. A farmer intends to erect 4 strands of barbed wire all round it, except for a 2 m gateway. What length of wire will be required?

24
Circles and Cylinders

24.1 The Circumference of a Circle

A circle is a plane figure bounded by one line, each point of which is equidistant from a fixed point called the centre of the circle. It is marked out with a pair of compasses, which are opened out to a suitable dimension which becomes the **radius** of the circle. The leg bearing the sharp steel point is fixed into the paper, and marks the **centre** of the circle. The other leg bearing the pencil or other marking device is then rotated round the centre to mark out the **circumference** of the circle. If a line is drawn from the circumference at one point, through the centre, to the circumference again it is called the **diameter** and will be two radii long.

We may say

$$\text{Diameter} = \text{two radii}$$
$$D = 2r \qquad \text{(in abbreviated form)}$$

When we draw in a diameter, we divide the circle into two equal **semicircles**. Since very ancient times the circle has been divided up into 360 degrees, written 360° for short. This is a relic of the Ancient Babylonian number system based on 60 and 360.

There is a constant relationship between the diameter of a circle and the circumference. It cannot be expressed as an exact amount, but for all practical purposes the circumference is taken as 3.141 59 times as long as the diameter. This is an awkward ratio to remember, and in mathematics we use the Greek letter π as a symbol for this ratio. (π is pronounced 'pie'.) The ratio 3.141 59 : 1 is actually very close to $3\frac{1}{7}$, so that in elementary calculations it is usual to use $3\frac{1}{7}$ or 3.14 as being accurate enough for π. If using a calculator it is advisable to use 3.141 59 unless instructed otherwise.

The formula for finding the circumference of a circle is therefore:

$$\text{Circumference} = \pi D$$
or
$$\text{Circumference} = 3\tfrac{1}{7} \times D$$
or
$$\text{Circumference} = 3.14 \times D$$

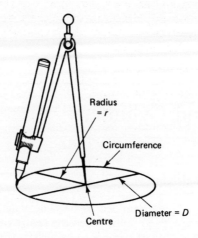

Fig. 24.1. Drawing a circle.

As the diameter is equal to twice the radius *r* we could substitute 2*r* for *D*. Since it is usual to put the number first, we then have

$$\text{Circumference} = 2\pi r$$

Example 24.1. Find the circumference of a wheel which has a diameter of 56 cm (use $\pi = 3\tfrac{1}{7}$).

$$\begin{aligned}
\text{Circumference} &= \pi D \\
&= 3\tfrac{1}{7} \times 56 \text{ cm} \\
&= \frac{22}{7_1} \times \overset{8}{\cancel{56}} \text{ cm} \\
&= 176 \text{ cm}
\end{aligned}$$

Example 24.2. Find the circumference of a circle which has a radius of 7 cm (use $\pi = 3\tfrac{1}{7}$).

$$\begin{aligned}
\text{Circumference} &= 2\pi r \\
&= 2 \times 3\tfrac{1}{7} \times 7 \text{ cm} \\
&= 2 \times \frac{22}{7_1} \times 7^1 \text{ cm} \\
&= 44 \text{ cm}
\end{aligned}$$

Example 24.3. How far will a bicycle go if its wheels revolve 500 times on the journey and have a radius of 33 cm? (Use $\pi = 3.14$.)

On each revolution the bicycle travels a distance equal to one circumference of its wheels. After 500 revolutions it will have travelled 500 times that distance.

$$\text{Circumference} = 2\pi r$$
$$= 2 \times 3.14 \times 33 \text{ cm}$$
$$\text{Distance travelled} = 500 \times 2 \times 3.14 \times 33 \text{ cm}$$
$$= \frac{5\cancel{0}\cancel{0} \times 2 \times 3.14 \times 33}{1\cancel{0}\cancel{0}} \text{ m}$$
$$= 31.4 \times 33 \text{ m}$$

$$\begin{array}{r} 31.4 \\ 33 \\ \hline 942 \\ 9420 \\ \hline 1036.2 \\ \hline \end{array}$$

$$= 1036.2 \text{ m}$$

24.2 Exercises: The Circumferences of Circles

1. Find the circumferences of circles with diameters as shown below (take $\pi = 3\frac{1}{7}$).

(a)	7 cm	(b)	21 cm
(c)	$3\frac{1}{2}$ cm	(d)	$10\frac{1}{2}$ cm
(e)	14 cm	(f)	12 cm
(g)	18 cm	(h)	33 cm
(i)	35 cm	(j)	42 cm

2. Find the circumferences of circles with radii as shown below (take $\pi = 3\frac{1}{7}$).

(a)	7 cm	(b)	$10\frac{1}{2}$ cm
(c)	14 cm	(d)	28 cm
(e)	12 cm	(f)	20 cm
(g)	35 cm	(h)	70 cm
(i)	30 cm	(j)	45 cm

3. Find how far the following vehicles go when their wheels, whose diameters are given, revolve the number of times shown (use $\pi = 3.14$).

	Diameter of wheel	Number of revolutions
(a)	50 cm	500
(b)	60 cm	1000
(c)	100 cm	1000
(d)	200 cm	2500
(e)	210 cm	5000

24.3   The Area of a Circle

Surface area has to be measured in square units—for example, square centimetres or square metres. It is obvious that this will not be easy when finding the area of a circle, which will not divide up easily into squares. We can only demonstrate this area by a diagrammatic rearrangement of a circle from its component parts.

The method adopted is shown in Fig. 24.2. A circle is marked out, and is then divided into eight equal parts. One of these parts is then divided in half (marked 8(i) and 8(ii) in the diagram). The circle is then cut up and re-arranged as shown in the diagram, in a nearly rectangular shape, but with two sides of the rectangle with wavy edges.

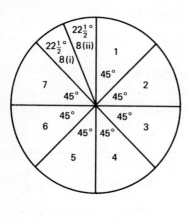
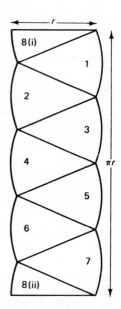

Fig. 24.2. Finding the area of a circle.

We now have to use our imagination. Suppose we had cut the circle up into 16 parts, not eight: the wavy edge of the rectangle would have been less wavy, a mere ripple. Had we been able to cut the circle into 32 parts, or 64 parts, etc., the ripple would eventually have been so reduced that we effectively had a straight line. The circle has been rearranged into a rectangle. The area of a rectangle is of course Length × Breadth. What are the dimensions of this rectangle? Its breadth is clearly r, the radius of the circle. The length of the rectangle is half the circumference of the circle, which is half $2\pi r$—in other words, $1\pi r$, or just πr. So we have

$$\text{Area of circle} = \pi r \times r$$

$r \times r$ is usually written as r^2, so

$$\text{Area of circle} = \pi r^2 \text{ (pie } r \text{ squared)}$$

Example 24.4. Find the area of a circle radius 7 cm (use $\pi = 3\frac{1}{7}$).

$$\text{Area} = \pi r^2$$
$$= 3\frac{1}{7} \times r \times r$$
$$= \frac{22}{7_1} \times 7^1 \times 7$$
$$= 154 \text{ sq. cm}$$

154 sq. cm is best written 154 cm².

Example 24.5. Find the area of a circle radius 63 cm (use $\pi = 3\frac{1}{7}$).

$$\text{Area} = \pi r^2$$
$$= \frac{22}{7_1} \times 63^9 \times 63$$
$$= 198 \times 63$$

$$\begin{array}{r} 198 \\ \times 63 \\ \hline 594 \\ 11\,880 \\ \hline 12\,474 \\ \hline \end{array}$$

$$= 12\,474 \text{ cm}^2$$

Note: A square metre is a unit of square measure which has 100 cm along each side of the square. There are therefore $100 \times 100 = 10\,000$ cm² in a square metre. So the answer to Example 24.5 above could be written.

$$= 1 \text{ m}^2 \ 2474 \text{ cm}^2$$

Example 24.6. Find the area of a circle diameter 21 cm (use $\pi = 3.14$).

As the radius is half the diameter, $r = 10.5$ cm.

$$\text{Area} = \pi r^2$$
$$= 3.14 \times 10.5 \times 10.5$$

$$\begin{array}{r} 10.5 \\ \times 3.14 \\ \hline 420 \\ 1\,050 \\ 31\,500 \\ \hline 32.970 \\ \times 10.5 \\ \hline 164\,850 \\ 3\,297\,000 \\ \hline 346.185\,0 \\ \hline\hline \end{array}$$

$$= 346.185 \text{ cm}^2$$

24.4 Exercises: The Areas of Circles

1. Find the area of the circles whose radii are given below (use $\pi = 3\frac{1}{7}$).

(a)	7 cm	(b)	$3\frac{1}{2}$ cm
(c)	14 cm	(d)	21 cm
(e)	49 cm	(f)	63 cm

2. Find the area of the circles whose diameters are given below (use $\pi = 3\frac{1}{7}$).

(a)	14 cm	(b)	28 cm
(c)	7 cm	(d)	21 cm
(e)	10 m	(f)	$17\frac{1}{2}$ m
(g)	15 m	(h)	50 m
(i)	100 m	(j)	120 m

3. Find the area of the circles whose radii are given below (use $\pi = 3.14$).

(a)	3 cm	(b)	5 cm
(c)	9 cm	(d)	15 cm
(e)	20 cm	(f)	50 cm

In the following calculations give the answer correct to the nearest square centimetre if necessary:

(g)	90 cm	(h)	1.25 m
(i)	3.25 m	(j)	4.5 m

24.5 Surface Areas and Volumes of Cylinders

A cylinder is a solid with a circular base and parallel sides. It is important in everyday life because of the prevalence of canned foods, drinks, etc. Millions of tin cans are made every day. There are two aspects of this from the calculations point of view: (a) how much sheet metal does it take to make a can—in other words, what is the surface area? (b) What is the volume of good contained in the can?

The dimensions of a typical can are shown in Fig. 24.3.

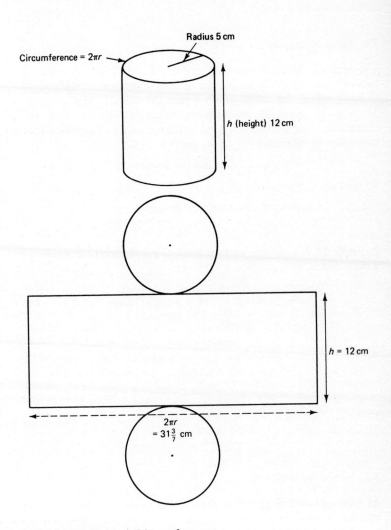

Fig. 24.3. A cylinder and its surface area.

Notes

(i) Two circular plates form the two ends of the cylindrical can.

(ii) The sides of the can are made from a single flat sheet, whose measurements are as follows:

(a) The width of the sheet is the height of the can.

(b) The length of the sheet is the same as the circumference of the circles it is to enclose—in other words, $2\pi r$.

(iii) These diagrams should help us to follow the calculations involved in making cylindrical cans.

The Surface Area of a Cylinder

The area of the circles at each end is of course πr^2. As there are two of them we must double the area of sheet metal required.

The area of the sheet which forms the sides of the cylinder is $2\pi r \times h$. To avoid the use of a multiplication sign we adopt from algebra the rule that any symbol written directly alongside another symbol is to be multiplied by it, so

$$\text{Area of the walls of the cylinder} = 2\pi rh \text{ (i.e. } 2 \times \pi \times r \times h)$$

So we have

$$\text{Surface area of a cylinder} = 2\pi rh + 2\pi r^2$$

Example 24.7. Find the surface area of a cylinder 12 cm high and with a radius of 5 cm (use $\pi = 3.14$).

$$\text{Surface area} = 2\pi rh + 2\pi r^2$$

$$
\begin{aligned}
2\pi rh &= 2 \times 3.14 \times 5 \text{ cm} \times 12 \text{ cm} \\
&= 120 \times 3.14 \text{ cm}^2 \\
&= 376.8 \text{ cm}^2
\end{aligned}
$$

3.14
120

376.80

$$
\begin{aligned}
2\pi r^2 &= 2 \times 3.14 \times 25 \text{ cm}^2 \\
&= 50 \times 3.14 \text{ cm}^2 \\
&= 157 \text{ cm}^2
\end{aligned}
$$

3.14
50

157.00

$$
\begin{aligned}
\text{Surface area} &= 376.8 \text{ cm}^2 + 157 \text{ cm}^2 \\
&= 533.8 \text{ cm}^2
\end{aligned}
$$

The Volume of a Cylinder

As with all volumes there are three dimensions: the length, breadth and height. The height of the cylinder is clear, but the length and breadth are controlled by the size of the circles which make up the end plates. The volume of a cylinder is found by multiplying the area of these end circles by the height:

$$\text{Volume of a cylinder} = \pi r^2 h$$

This volume will be expressed in cubic measure, e.g. cubic centimetres (cm^3).

Example 24.8. What is the volume of a cylinder 12 cm high with a radius of 5 cm (use $\pi = 3.14$)?

$$\begin{aligned}
\text{Volume} &= \pi r^2 h \\
&= 3.14 \times 5 \times 5 \times 12 \text{ cm}^3 \\
&= 3.14 \times 300 \text{ cm}^3 \\
&= 942 \text{ cm}^3
\end{aligned}$$

24.6 Exercises: Surface Areas and Volumes of Cylinders

1. Find the volumes of the cylinders whose heights and radii are as given below (use $\pi = 3\frac{1}{7}$).

	r	h
(a)	3 cm	7 cm
(b)	$3\frac{1}{2}$ cm	10 cm
(c)	5 cm	14 cm
(d)	7 cm	15 cm
(e)	14 cm	20 cm

2. Find the volumes of the storage drums whose heights and radii are as given below (use $\pi = 3.14$). (*Note:* There are 100 cm in 1 m. Therefore there are $100 \times 100 \times 100$ cubic centimetres in 1 cubic metre, i.e. $1\,000\,000 \text{ cm}^3 = 1 \text{ m}^3$.)

	r	h
(a)	20 cm	50 cm
(b)	50 cm	1.2 m
(c)	75 cm	1.5 m
(d)	1 m	1.5 m
(e)	1.25 m	2 m

3. Find the total surface area of a cylinder of radius 7 cm and height 8 cm (use $\pi = 3\frac{1}{7}$).

4. Find the total surface area of a cylinder of radius 10 cm and height 14 cm (use $\pi = 3\frac{1}{7}$).

5. Find the total surface area of a cylinder of radius 50 cm and height 150 cm (use $\pi = 3.14$).

24.7 Exercises on Circles

Do these calculations mentally, using $\pi = 3\frac{1}{7}$.

1. What is the circumference of a circle whose radius is 7 cm?

2. What is the circumference of a circle whose radius is 49 cm?

3. What is the circumference of a circle whose diameter is 21 cm?

4. What is the circumference of a circle whose diameter is 35 cm?

5. What is the area of a circle radius 2 cm?

6. What is the area of a circle radius $3\frac{1}{2}$ cm?

7. What is the area of a circle radius 10 cm?

8. What is the formula for the volume of a cylinder?

9. What is the formula for the surface area of a cylinder?

10. What is the volume of a cylinder radius 7 cm and height 10 cm?

24.8 Mental Arithmetic Test

Do these calculations mentally:

1. $3725 - 2816 =$

2. $5992 \div 8 =$

3. $1\frac{3}{5} + 2\frac{1}{4} + 1\frac{1}{2} =$

4. $0.125 \div 0.25 =$

5. How many Portuguese escudos at 185 Escudos = £1 shall I get for £300?

6. How many days from 27 November to 21 January inclusive?

7. What is three sevenths of £140?

8. Items costing £30 are marked up by 75%. At what price do they sell?

9. What is $66\frac{2}{3}\%$ of £330?

10. Costs on a project are £3200 and overheads are 40% on this figure. What is the total cost?

11. What year was MDCCCLI?

12. What is the average of 12 760, 12 765 and 12 767?

13. The aggregate rateable value of all the property in a city is £595 000 000. How much will a penny rate bring in?

14. What is the circumference of a circle radius $3\frac{1}{2}$ cm (use $\pi = 3\frac{1}{7}$)?

15. What is the area of a circle radius 7 m (use $\pi = 3\frac{1}{7}$)?

25
Stocks and Shares

25.1 Introduction

Stocks and shares are securities issued to investors who subscribe capital to companies, or lend money to companies, local authorities, central government or nationalised institutions. The securities can be transferred from one owner to another through the work of a stock exchange. The two most famous stock exchanges are at Throgmorton Street in the City of London and Wall Street in New York City. There are many more all over the non-communist world.

Imagine Mrs A who has some shares in ICI, but wishes to have cash instead. She phones a stockbroker to sell them for her. Within a few minutes he visits the floor of the Stock Exchange and sells them at the best price obtainable. At the same time the National Coal Board wishes to invest pension money for miners' pensions. It buys the ICI shares five minutes later for a price slightly above the price received by Mrs A. These transactions will be settled a few days later on Settlement Day—which takes place once a fortnight. Mrs A will have her money (less small charges called **brokerage**, for the broker's services); the miners' pension funds will receive the share certificate and ICI will register the change of ownership.

The two words 'stocks' and 'shares' are almost interchangeable today, but historically 'shares' were issued first, and later were **consolidated** into stock. Shares, when issued, have a nominal value (nominal means 'in name only') called the **par value**. Thus a company may issue £1 shares, or 50 pence shares, but as soon as these begin to be traded on the Stock Exchange the actual **market value** may be above par, or below par, according to the market's view of the company's trading situation. Thus a £1 share might sell for £1.25, which is above par (sometimes called **at a premium**), or for 98 pence, which is clearly below par (or **at a discount**).

Stocks do not have a par value, the value of the stock is written on the certificate, but for convenience sake all calculations are done using £100 units of stock. Thus if a certain type of Government stock (gilt-edged stock) was selling at below par (say 95) this means that £100 stock would only fetch £95 if sold on the market that day.

After the end of each financial year the directors of companies decide what part of the profits should be distributed to the share-holders. They recommend this to the shareholders at the **annual general meeting** and if the recommendation is accepted a **dividend** is paid. The word 'dividend' means 'the amount divided among' the shareholders.

Many stocks are 'fixed interest' securities representing loans made to companies or to nationalised institutions and governments. Such stocks as Treasury $8\frac{3}{4}$% 1997 Stock mean that money originally loaned to the United Kingdom treasury at $8\frac{3}{4}$% will be repaid in 1997. Persons owning such stock will receive an interest payment—usually twice a year at $4\frac{3}{8}$% of the amount of stock they hold.

25.2 Simple Share Dealings

The easiest way to understand simple share dealings is to consider the commoner types of transaction. The following examples will help.

Example 25.1. Mr A sells 500 £1 shares in Excalibur Industries which are standing at £1.83. How much will he receive, if brokerage charges are £4.50?

$$\text{Total received} = 500 \times £1.83 - £4.50$$

$$\begin{array}{r} £1.83 \\ \times\, 500 \\ \hline £915.00 \end{array}$$

$$= £915 - £4.50$$
$$= £910.50$$

Note: The broker deducts his charges from the money received for the sale of shares before sending the balance due to Mr A.

Example 25.2. Mrs B buys 1725 £1 shares at 97 pence each, and pays brokerage charges of £7.25. What will she pay altogether?

Total payable = 1725 × £0.97 + £7.25 brokerage

$$
\begin{array}{r}
1725 \\
0.97 \\
\hline
12\,075 \\
155\,250 \\
\hline
1673.25 \\
\hline
\end{array}
$$

= £1673.25 + £7.25
= £1680.50

Note: This time the broker adds on his charges and asks Mrs B to pay both the sum due for the shares and his charges. When her cheque arrives the broker will send her the share certificate for the amount she has purchased.

Example 25.3. Mr C sells 12 000 £1 shares purchased at par some time ago for their current market price £1.27 each. What profit did he make (ignore brokerage).

Profit made = 12 000 × 27p
= 120 × £27

$$
\begin{array}{r}
120 \\
27 \\
\hline
840 \\
2400 \\
\hline
3240 \\
\hline
\end{array}
$$

= £3240

25.3 Exercises: Simple Share Dealings

1. Find the cost of the following sets of shares. Brokerage in each case is £7.50.

(a) 200 £1 shares at £1.25 each

(b) 300 £1 shares at £1.45 each

(c) 500 £1 shares at 94p each

(d) 1200 £1 shares at 57p each

(e) 550 £1 shares at £1.73 each

(f) 850 £1 shares at £2.97 each

(g) 720 50p shares at 63p each

(h) 640 50p shares at 44p each

(i) 1730 10p shares at 15.5p each

(j) 1520 10p shares at 9.5p each

2. What will the seller receive in each case below for the shares sold?

	No. of shares sold	Sale price	Brokerage charges
(a)	300	£2.43	£15
(b)	500	47p	£4.50
(c)	750	£1.37	£12.83
(d)	2000	£4.95	£123.75
(e)	3850	£1.88	£90.48

3. What profit (or loss) was made in each of these cases, where shares were purchased at one price and sold later (ignore brokerage charges):

	No. of shares	Purchase price	Sale price
(a)	500	£2.29	£2.85
(b)	800	£1.85	£1.99
(c)	2500	£0.14	£0.16
(d)	2250	£1.32	£2.11
(e)	8500	£5.65	£4.99

25.4   Stocks

As explained above, in calculations it is usual to envisage £100 stock as the basic unit. If a stock is below par £100 stock will cost less than £100 and if it is above par £100 of stock will cost more than £100. A stock at $27\frac{3}{4}$ costs £27.75 for £100 of stock, and a stock at $112\frac{1}{2}$ costs £112.50 for £100 of stock. Brokerage is either added to or deducted from these figures. Thus if brokerage is $\frac{1}{4}$% a person selling the first stock above would actually receive $27\frac{1}{2}$, the broker deducting $\frac{1}{4}$ from the price. A person buying the second stock would pay $112\frac{3}{4}$, the broker adding $\frac{1}{4}$ for his services.

Many stocks are fixed-interest stocks, in which the earnings from the stock are known at the time of issue and represent the rate of interest prevailing at the time. Thus 'Old Consols', a British Government stock first issued in 1745, earn $2\frac{1}{2}$% interest. Suppose interest rates today are $12\frac{1}{2}$%. It will not be sensible to pay more than £20 for £100 of Old Consols, since the £100 of stock will only pay £2.50 interest in the year. If I pay £20 for it I earn £2.50 on an investment of £20, which is $12\frac{1}{2}$% interest, the 'fair' rate of interest prevailing today.

Students of commerce and economics might like to note that this is the cause of much of the excitement on stock exchanges when governments change interest rates (or these days manipulate the interest rates covertly behind the scenes). If interest rates alter, the prices of fixed interest stocks change immediately, and millions of transactions take place.

Example 25.4. An investor buys £6400 of Old Consols at $17\frac{3}{4}$. Brokerage is $\frac{1}{4}$%. (a) How much will she pay? (b) What interest will she receive in the first six months at $2\frac{1}{2}$ per cent per annum?

(a)   Price payable = $17\frac{3}{4} + \frac{1}{4}$ = £18 per £100 of stock.
                £6400 = 64 × £100 of stock.

$\therefore$ Amount payable = 64 × £18

$$
\begin{array}{r}
64 \\
18 \\
\hline
512 \\
640 \\
\hline
£1152 \\
\hline
\end{array}
$$

                 = £1152

(b) Interest earned *each six months* is $1\frac{1}{4}$% per £100 of stock:

       Interest earned = 64 × £1.25
                    = £64 + £16 (64 × $1\frac{1}{4}$)
                    = £80

You should now try Question 1 of Section 25.5 (Exercises) on page 230.

Example 25.5. The financial director of an investment trust buys £10 000 of British 7% Treasury Stock at $55\frac{3}{4}$. Brokerage is $\frac{1}{4}$%. (a) What interest does this earn a year? (b) What is the yield on the investment?

(a)   £10 000 of stock is 100 × £100

Since every £100 pays £7 interest, the total interest earned is

$$100 \times £7 = £700$$

(b) The yield on the investment is the percentage rate of interest earned on the investment. This is not the same as the nominal rate of interest on the stock, because in this case the stock is well below par. First we must find the cost of the stock, to discover how much was invested.

   Cost of Stock = $55\frac{3}{4} + \frac{1}{4}$ brokerage = £56 per 100
   Sum invested = 100 × £56 (because 100 lots of £100 were purchased)
                   = £5600

$$\text{Yield on investment} = \frac{\text{Interest earned}}{\text{Sum invested}} \times 100$$

$$= \frac{700}{5600} \times 100$$

$$= \frac{700}{56}$$

```
          12.5
  56 ) 700
       56
       ──
      140
      112
      ──
      280
      280
      ──
      ...
```

$$= 12.5\%$$

You should now try Question 2 of Section 25.5 (Exercises).

Institutional Investors

Institutional investors are firms like life insurance companies, pension fund managers, investment trusts and such organisations as trade unions. They collect funds from members and those wishing to be insured, which are invested for use later when required. The stocks and shares they buy are called a **portfolio** of shares, and the aim is to have a **balanced portfolio** with some safe shares, some risky shares, etc. They have constantly to vary their holdings of stocks and shares as these change in value. To hold shares which are no longer giving a good return on capital invested reduces the funds available for pensioners, for example. A typical calculation of this sort is given below.

Example 25.6. A pension fund investment portfolio at present includes £8400 of 8% Exchequer stock which originally cost £4120 and which is currently fetching $96\frac{1}{4}$ on the market. It is proposed to sell it and buy 13% Treasury Stock at $62\frac{3}{4}$. (a) What will be the change in income? (b) What will be the change in yield? Brokerage is $\frac{1}{4}\%$ in each case. (Calculate yields correct to one decimal place.)

First let us find the income and the yield on the original stock.

Interest earned $= 84 \times £8$ (£8 on each £100 of stock)
$$= £672$$

$$\text{Yield} = \frac{\text{Interest earned}}{\text{Original cost}} \times 100 \text{ per cent}$$

$$= \frac{672}{4120} \times 100 \text{ per cent}$$

$$= \frac{6720}{412} \qquad \text{(cancel this by 4)}$$

$$= \frac{1680}{103}$$

```
              16.31
103 ) 1680
      103
      ___
      650
      618
      ___
      320
      309
      ___
      110
```

$$= 16.3\%$$

Now we must find how much new stock can be purchased if the old stock is sold.

Sale of old stock provides $84 \times £96$ (£96¼ less brokerage ¼ per £100)

```
        84
      × 96
      ___
       504
      7560
      ____
      8064
```

$$= £8064$$

When £8064 is spent on the new stock at $62\frac{3}{4}$ per £100 (brokerage is ¼)

$$\text{New stock purchased} = \frac{£8064}{63} \times 100$$

$$= \frac{896}{7} \times 100 \qquad \text{(cancelling by 9)}$$

$$= £12\,800 \qquad \text{(cancelling by 7)}$$

Now we can find the income and the yield on the new stock.

Interest received = £13 per £100 of stock
= 128 × £13

$$\begin{array}{r} 128 \\ 13 \\ \hline 384 \\ 1280 \\ \hline 1664 \\ \hline \end{array}$$

= £1664

$$\text{Yield} = \frac{\text{Interest received}}{\text{Cost of investment}} \times 100$$

$$= \frac{1664}{8064} \times 100$$

$$= \frac{208}{1008} \times 100 \qquad \text{(cancelling by 8)}$$

$$= \frac{26}{126} \times 100 \qquad \text{(cancelling by 8)}$$

$$= \frac{13}{63} \times 100 \qquad \text{(cancelling by 2)}$$

$$\begin{array}{r} 20.63 \\ 63 \overline{)\,1300} \\ 126 \\ \hline 400 \\ 378 \\ \hline 220 \end{array}$$

= 20.6%

Therefore the new stock provides a better yield (20.6% instead of 16.3%), and hence a better income (£1664 instead of £672).

25.5   Exercises: Calculations with Stocks

1. Find (i) the cost to the investor of each of the stocks listed below and (ii) the income received each year by the stockholder. (Where necessary give the answer correct to the nearest penny.)

	Amount purchased	Rate of interest	Purchase price	Brokerage payable
(a)	£500	16%	$102\frac{5}{8}$	$\frac{3}{16}$
(b)	£1250	9%	$17\frac{3}{8}$	$\frac{3}{8}$
(c)	£5000	$11\frac{3}{4}$%	$56\frac{3}{4}$	$\frac{1}{4}$

(d)	£6500	$12\frac{1}{2}\%$	$73\frac{1}{4}$	$\frac{1}{4}$
(e)	£10 000	$9\frac{7}{8}\%$	$111\frac{1}{4}$	$\frac{1}{4}$

2. Find (i) the cost to the investor of each of the purchases of stock listed below; (ii) the income received each year in each case; (iii) the yield on the money invested (correct to one decimal place).

	Amount of stock purchased	Rate of interest payable	Price including brokerage
(a)	£5000	$8\frac{1}{2}\%$	68
(b)	£6500	$12\frac{1}{4}\%$	$102\frac{1}{2}$
(c)	£8750	$14\frac{1}{2}\%$	112
(d)	£10 000	$10\frac{1}{2}\%$	94
(e)	£12 500	$2\frac{1}{2}\%$	$22\frac{1}{2}$

3. Find the change in income when 1000 shares paying a dividend of 16p per share are sold at a price (after brokerage charges) of £1.65 each and the proceeds used to buy Treasury 7% Stock at $49\frac{3}{4}$ (brokerage $\frac{1}{4}\%$).

4. What will be the change in income when £1700 of 8% stock is sold at $50\frac{1}{4}$ and the proceeds invested in 12% stock at 106? Brokerage $\frac{1}{4}\%$ in each case.

5. What will be the change in income when £7500 8% Exchequer stock is sold at $74\frac{3}{4}$ and used to buy 12% Treasury Stock at $99\frac{3}{4}$? Brokerage is $\frac{1}{4}\%$ in each transaction.

6. A pension fund buys £10 000 of 7% Treasury Stock at $55\frac{3}{4}$, and £25 000 $11\frac{1}{4}\%$ Exchequer Stock at $85\frac{1}{4}$. What will the total investment cost, and how much income will be received? Brokerage is $\frac{1}{4}\%$ in each case.

7. A trade union invests subscriptions from its members by buying 8000 shares in Micromethods Plc at £2.45 per share and £25 000 Old Consols at $17\frac{7}{8}$. Brokerage is 5p per share and $\frac{1}{8}\%$ on the Old Consols. The shares pay a dividend of 42p per share and the Old Consols pay $2\frac{1}{2}\%$. (a) What is the total investment made? (b) What is the income in the first year?

8. A pension fund investment portfolio at present includes £10 000 of 8% Treasury Stock, which is fetching $82\frac{1}{4}$ on the Stock Exchange. It is proposed to sell it and replace it with shares in International Freighters Ltd at £1.59 per share. Brokerage is $\frac{1}{4}$ on the stock and 5p per share. In the present year International Freighters paid 20p dividend per share, and it is expected that the same dividend will be paid in the coming year. (a) Calculate the change in income and say whether you approve of the proposal to change over to the shares. (b) What would the yield be on the new investment? (Calculation correct to one decimal place.)

25.6 Mental Arithmetic Test

1. $84 \times 25 =$

2. $3875 \div 125 =$

3. 2.74 + 3.875 + 5.8 =

4. Change 50% to a common fraction

5. $\frac{1}{2} \times \frac{3}{4} \times \frac{8}{9}$ =

6. Share up £8000 so that Tom gets twice as much as both Dick and Mary.

7. Two porters on an expedition carry loads in the ratio of 2 : 1. If the total load to be carried is 48 kilograms how much will the stronger man carry?

8. A table costs £120 + 15% value added tax. What is the price to the consumer?

9. What is the simple interest on £350 at 8% for 2 years?

10. What is the average of 8, 10, 12, 14, 16 and 18?

11. What shall I pay for 7 gold fountain pens at £18.45 each?

12. A penny rate fetches £8500. What rate must residents pay for a library costing £85 000?

13. An investor spends £8200 on stock at $81\frac{7}{8}$ (brokerage $\frac{1}{8}$). How much stock will he receive?

14. Shares pay a dividend of 7% on the nominal value of £1. If I have 350 shares what dividend shall I receive?

15. What is the yield on a $7\frac{1}{2}$% stock selling on the stock exchange at $49\frac{3}{4}$ (brokerage $\frac{1}{4}$)?

26
Keeping Accounts

26.1 What is an Account?

An 'account' is a page in a book called 'the ledger', which is the main book of account in every business. Such books may be a collection of loose-leaf pages which can be arranged in alphabetical order and are then locked into a binder for security reasons. This is called a **loose-leaf ledger**. These days they may also be kept in the memory bank of some computer, and can be called forward to a visual display unit (VDU) if necessary.

If you open an account with anyone—say a bank or a fashion house—all it means is that they go to the next clean page in their ledger, write your name and address on it, and record on that page anything that happens between you and them. You will be given an **account number**, called in business a **folio number** (from the Latin *folium*—a page) and any transaction between you and them will be recorded on that account. The keeping of this type of account is described more fully later in this chapter. First we must look at the layout of such an account.

			Amount		Credit Side			Amount	
Debit Side					Credit Side				
Date	Details	Folio	£	p	Date	Details	Folio	£	p

L1
Dr.   Cr.

Fig. 26.1. A page from the ledger.

26.2   Debits and Credits

The layout of a traditional account is shown in Fig. 26.1, and explained in the notes below.

Notes

(i) The page is divided down the middle.

(ii) The left-hand side of the page is called the debit side, or debtor side, which is abbreviated to Dr.

(iii) The right-hand side of the page is called the credit side, or creditor side, and is abbreviated to Cr.

(iv) The folio number (page number) is written in the top right-hand corner of the page where it can be seen easily as the ledger is opened. In this case it is L1, page 1 in the ledger.

(v) The folio columns on each side are used to record the page numbers where the 'double entry' would be found for the entry shown on that line. This is explained later.

(vi) The name of the account is written on the top line of the page. This might be the name of a person (John Brown A/C) or of a real thing (an asset like Typewriters A/C) or of an expense (Telephone Expenses A/C) or of a profit (Commission Received A/C).

(vii) The exercises in this chapter require the use of ledger paper, which is available at any reputable stationer's shop. Alternatively, the reader may rule up a few pages as shown above.

When we keep accounts the most important guide to what to do is the name of the account, written on the top line. If this says Thomas Blenkinsop then it is Thomas Blenkinsop that we think about and we ask ourselves 'What happened to Thomas Blenkinsop? Did he receive money, or goods or services? Or did he give money, or goods or services?'

The rules are:

Debit the receiver of money, goods or services.
Credit the giver of money, goods or services.

26.3   A Simple Account: The Cash Account

Of the different types of accounts mentioned in note (vi) under Fig. 26.1 the simplest to consider is an asset account. One of these is the cash account, a busy account which is in use every hour of every day. When keeping this account, we are only concerned with money and the amount of it that we have in the till, for a till cannot receive or give goods and services. When we keep the cash account we ask ourselves 'Did the cash box receive money or did it give money?' If it received money we enter the amount received on the debit side, and if it gave money we enter the sum paid out on the credit side. Fig. 26.2 shows a simple cash account with some debit and credit entries. After studying this and the notes below it, try the exercises in Section 26.4.

Dr.							L1 Cr.
			CASH ACCOUNT				
19. . Aug 1	To Balance	b/d	£ 43.28	19. . Aug 1	By Postage	L17	£ 4.25
4	" Cash Sales	L87	127.80	1	" R. Lark	L5	8.07
5	" R. Poynter	L76	15.50	2	" Stationery	L19	3.50
6	" Cash Sales	L87	184.65	3	" Travelling	L21	8.40
6	" M. Lee	L49	25.50	4	" Bank	L2	100.00
				4	" M. Lowe	L38	16.25
				5	" Stationery	L19	4.25
				6	" P. Smith	L35	26.60
				6	" Balance	c/d	225.41
		£	396.73			£	396.73
19. . Aug 8	To Balance	b/d	£ 225.41				

Fig. 26.2. A simple cash account.

Notes

(i) The balance in the cash box on 1 August was £43.28.

(ii) On that day the till gave £4.25 for postage stamps and also gave £8.07 to R. Lark. (We must have owed R. Lark this money for goods or services supplied.) Credit the cash account for giving the money.

(iii) Similarly, money was paid out for stationery, travelling expenses and to two more creditors, M. Lowe and P. Smith during the week.

(iv) On 4 August and again on 6 August the cashier added up all the cash received and entered it on the cash account as cash sales.

(v) During the week R. Poynter and M. Lee paid us in cash for goods or services supplied and these moneys were received by the cash account (debit the cash account in each case).

(vi) On 4 August the cashier transferred £100 to the bank account—credit the cash account. Of course the bank account would receive the money, so it would be debited. The folio number L2 tells us that the bank account is page 2 in the Ledger, and if we turn to that page we will find the other half of this entry. In book-keeping there are always two accounts affected, one gives and the other receives. All the other folio numbers similarly tell us where the double entry is for each entry made.

(vii) At the end of the month the account is balanced off. The two sides are totalled and the difference between them is found. This is the '*balance in hand*'. The total that has come into the cash box is £396.73. The total that has gone out is £171.32. The difference is £225.41. This is written in on the right-hand side, to make the two sides balance, and then brought down to the debit side as the balance in hand (c/d stands for 'carried down', b/d stands for 'brought down').

(viii) Any spare lines on one side or the other are filled in by a large Z so that nobody can later write anything in on those lines.

26.4 Exercises: Simple Cash Accounts

You should now try to keep the cash account for each of the exercises below. You will need some ledger paper, ruled as shown in Fig. 26.1. This can be purchased from any stationer's shop. You should head each exercise cash account, and as you make each entry ask yourself: 'What happened to the cash account. Did it receive money (debit the receiver) or did it give money (credit the giver)?'

1. R. Martinson is in business and keeps a simple cash account. In the week commencing Sunday, 4 July, the figures were:

5 July. Balance brought down £28.50. Drew £30 from bank to place in cash box. Paid for postage £4.25. Paid for travelling expenses £24.25.

6 July. Paid M. Lee the amount due to him £14.20. Paid for plumbing repairs £13.75 (repairs account). Received from T. Prendergast £8.85. Cash sales totalled £134.65, and entered in cash account.

7 July. M. Driver paid Martinson the sum of £8.80 due to him and J. Pawley also paid £5.50. Cash sales totalled £165. Paid £7.25 for packing materials. Banked £150.

8 July. Paid £48.50 for supplies to resell. (Call this 'purchases'. In business anything the business buys to sell again is called 'purchases' and a record is kept in the purchases account. Anything sold is called 'sales' and a record is kept in the sales account.) Paid £13.25 to a local farmer for produce (purchases). Cash sales totalled £127.50. Banked £80.

9 July. Paid for postage £3.50. Paid for rent £42. Cash sales totalled £320. Received £15.70 from T. Simpson. Paid Wages £58.50. Balanced off account and brought the balance down ready for next week. Balance agrees with cash in hand so no problems seem to have arisen.

2. M. Lawrence keeps a cash account in which he makes entries each day, balancing the account off at the close of work every day. Enter the following items on 24 April:

    (a) Balance in hand at start of day £174.56.
    (b) Paid into bank £150.00.
    (c) R. Brown paid £37.25 due from him, in cash.
    (d) Bought goods for resale (purchases) £42.50.
    (e) Paid M. Lunday £3.84 due to her, in cash.
    (f) Paid T. Bell's account £4.75 in cash.
    (g) Paid postage £17.00.
    (h) Paid travelling expenses £15.25.
    (i) Cash sales for day £325.50.

Balance off the account and bring the balance down, dating it 25 April.

3. Tahira Muhammadu, a dressmaker, keeps a cash account in which she makes entries each day, balancing the account off at the close of work. Enter the following items on 14 October:

    (a) Balance in hand at start of day £275.52.
    (b) Paid into bank £200.00.
    (c) M. Ajakaiye paid £13.80 due from him, in cash.
    (d) Bought goods for resale (purchases) £38.25.
    (e) Paid T. Lawrence £5.85 due to her for goods supplied earlier.
    (f) Paid M. Richards account £17.80 in cash.
    (g) Paid for accessories (purchases) £13.95.

(h) Paid for belts and buckles (purchases) £27.85.

(i) Cash sales for day £321.16.

4. H. Ginsell is in business and keeps a simple cash account. In the week commencing Sunday, 17 September, the figures were:

Monday. Balance brought down £3.55. Cash sales totalled £84.50. Paid for postage £4.75. Paid for travelling expenses £8.25.

Tuesday. Paid A. Clothier the amount due to him £14.85. Paid for lock repairs £7.80. Received from T. Mohammed £82.45. Cash sales totalled £76.85.

Wednesday. M. Leeley paid Ginsell the sum of £29.45 due to him and T. Barker paid him £3.25. Cash sales totalled £136.50. Paid £4.50 for packing materials. Banked £100.

Thursday. Paid local farmer for supplies £85 (call this purchases). Paid £7.50 to R. Sims. Cash sales totalled £48.50.

Friday. Paid for postage £8.25. Paid for rent £50.00. Cash sales totalled £236.85. Received £4.50 from R. Marshall. Paid wages £57.25. Balanced off account and brought the balance down ready for next week. Balance agrees with cash in hand so no problems seem to have arisen.

26.5 Simple Bank Accounts

A bank account is commonly understood as meaning an account opened with a bank, and kept in the bank's records as part of the bank's ledger. This is of course true, but such an account is kept from the bank's point of view. All business persons must have bank accounts in their own books kept from their point of view and not from the bank's.

For example, consider Mrs Anne Johnson, who is starting in business as an interior decorator. Suppose she puts £500 into the Hallamshire Bank to open an account with them. The bank account she opens will receive the money, so in her records she debits the bank account. This is shown in Fig. 26.3 above. (Note that the Hallamshire Bank will at once open an account for Mrs Johnson, but it will not be called 'bank account'. It will be called Mrs A. Johnson Account, and as she has given them £500 they will credit her account with £500.)

From Figs. 26.2 and 26.3 we can see that there is very little difference between keeping a cash account and a bank account. One keeps a record of cash received and spent, the other keeps a record of cheques received and paid. At the end of the week when the accounts are balanced off we can check the cash balance shown on the cash account with the cash in hand in the till. To check the correctness of the bank account is not so easy. We have to ask the bank for a bank statement. This is usually done once a month, and the bank account can then be compared with the bank statement.

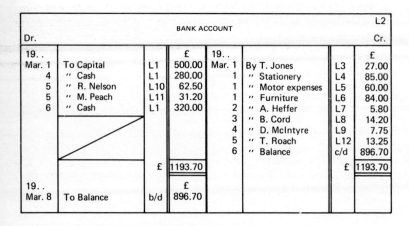

Fig. 26.3. A simple bank account.

Notes

(i) On 1 March Mrs Johnson puts £500 into the bank account, which receives the money and therefore has to be debited. This is called 'capital'.

(ii) The same day she writes out certain cheques to pay money to T. Jones and to pay for stationery, petrol and furniture.

(iii) On the debit side Mrs Johnson banks cash from takings on 4 March and 6 March, and cheques from two customers on 5 March.

(iv) Various sums are paid out on 2, 3, 4 and 5 March.

(v) On the last day of the week the bank account is balanced off and the balance brought down ready for the start of work the following week.

26.6   Exercises: Simple Bank Accounts

1. On 1 January A. Rust starts in business as a grocer with capital of £5000 which he enters in his bank account. The same day he pays out £1750 by cheque for a major delivery of stock from Wholesale Groceries Plc. He also pays £1280 to Instore Freezers Ltd for display cabinets, and £240 to Cash Electronics Plc for an electronic till. Other entries in the week are as follows:

Jan. 2. Banked £184 from the till (enter as 'To cash').
Jan. 3. Paid A. Farmer for goods £36.50. Banked cash from till £136.
Jan. 4. Banked cash from till £262.50.
Jan. 5. Paid Wholesale Groceries Plc £325.50 for goods supplied. Also banked cash from till £375.50
Jan 6. Paid R. Tyler £25.80 for salad vegetables.

Make these entries in a simple bank account. Balance off the account and bring down the balance.

2. Enter the following items in the simple bank account of A. Coleby. At the end of the week balance off the account and bring down the balance.

July 14. Balance at bank at start of week £2875.55. Paid to United Butchers Plc £325.50. Paid to Offal Suppliers Ltd £275.90. Banked cash from tills £495.

July 15. Banked cash from tills £732.

July 16. Received cheque from Long Riding County Council £462.50. Banked cash from tills £385.

July 17. Paid United Butchers Plc £786.50. Banked cash from tills £723.55.

July 18. Paid Offal Suppliers Ltd £228.50. Banked cash from tills £779.95. Paid wages £484.27.

3. Tom Raybould runs a skip service for building sites. Enter the following items in his bank account, which on the 15 November had an opening balance of £742.50:

Nov. 15. Paid A. Liquidator £350 for 20 skips from a bankrupt's stock. Banked cheque for £32.50 from Anne Occupier.

Nov. 16. Banked cash takings £35. Paid Inland Revenue £84.60.

Nov. 17. Banked cheque received from Rubbish Clearers Plc £285.

Nov. 18. Banked cash takings £15 and cheque from T. Horwich £37.50.

Nov. 19. Paid Urban District Council £75.50. Banked cash takings £22.50.

Nov. 20. Paid wages by cheque £68.

Balance off the account ready for next week and bring down the balance.

26.7 Mental Arithmetic Test

1. $1472 + 3854 + 2716 =$

2. $824 \div 8 =$

3. $200 \times 1900 =$

4. £172.50 − £38.95 =

5. £17.20 + £19.35 + £16.75 + £14.82 =

6. How many $\frac{1}{4}$ kg cartons of currants can be made up from 480 kg of currants?

7. What is the average of 7, 12, 15 and 22?

8. Change £200 to dollars at £1 = $1.85

9. How many seconds in $3\frac{1}{2}$ minutes?

10. An item usually sold at £1000 is sold on hire purchase for a deposit of £100 and 24 monthly payments of £50. How much interest was paid altogether?

27
Petty Cash and the Imprest System

27.1 The Work of the Petty Cashier

While the cashier keeps the main books of account, including the cash account and bank account described in Chapter 26, it is convenient to appoint a young person to keep account of petty cash. Petty means small or unimportant, from the French word *petit*. There are many occasions in business, such as the purchase of postage stamps, the payment of bus fares, etc., where it is inappropriate to bother the cashier for the trifling sums required. It is usual to ask the person in charge of post to keep a small float of money for these purposes. To keep control of the system a sum of money called the **imprest** (or float) is provided. Usually it is sufficient to cover petty expenditure for one week, and therefore a sum of between £30 and £50 would be adequate for most small offices. When the imprest is almost all used, or at the end of the week, the petty cashier totals the petty cash book, and takes it to the chief cashier. The cashier checks the book and restores the money spent, so that the petty cashier starts again with the agreed imprest.

27.2 Keeping the Petty Cash Book

Although the sums involved are small it is essential to keep control of them. Half the cases where money is stolen in offices concern thefts from petty cash. The system requires a **petty cash voucher** to be presented for every amount spent. Whenever possible this voucher is obtained from outside the business, preferably in the form of a bill or till receipt from the shop where the purchase was made. Where this is not possible—as with train fares, etc.—an internal voucher is made out requesting the reimbursement of the money spent, and signed by a manager who thus has the opportunity to check the amount.

The petty cash book is ruled in the same way as any other account, with a debit and credit side, but since very few entries need to be made on the debit side it is reduced to a single column. All the details are entered on the right-hand side, but any debit entries are made in the debit column. The credit entries are on the right-hand side, but this is extended into a series of analysis columns, where all similar items that can be collected together in the week, such as the sums spent on postage, travelling expenses, etc., are assembled. The end column is used for entries that cannot be collected together. The whole system is explained in Fig. 27.1.

27.3 Exercises: The Petty Cash Book

Obtain a supply of suitable petty cash paper or rule up a few pages similar to Fig. 27.1. Then make the following entries on the paper:

1. Rule up a petty cash book with five analysis columns; Sundry Expenses, Fares, Stationery, Postage and Ledger Accounts. Enter the following items:

May 1. Drew imprest £40.00 from the chief cashier; paid for envelopes £2.25; postage stamps £4.35; fares £1.55.
  2. Paid for paper £2.50; paid P. Stevenson £8.25.
  3. Paid fares £1.32; cleaning materials £3.25.
  4. Paid stationery £1.83; paid P. Bryant £2.60.
  5. Paid for cleaning materials £2.34; collected telephone money £16.36.
  6. Paid for ball of string £0.98. Paid part-time cleaner's wages £12.50.
  7. Paid for sundry items for office use £3.84.

Balance off the book and restore the imprest. Invent suitable folio numbers and petty cash voucher numbers.

2. Enter the following items in a petty cash book with five analysis columns, for Postage, Fares, Office Sundries, Cleaning, and Ledger Accounts. Invent appropriate folio numbers and petty cash voucher numbers.

Oct. 25. Drew petty cash imprest £50.00; paid postage £4.50.
  26. Paid fares £6.80; paid excess postal charges £0.26 and a creditor, T. Lyons £8.27.
  27. Paid for soap £1.55; bought envelopes £3.80; bought cleaning materials £2.72.
  28. Paid R. Smith £3.50; member of staff purchased redundant typewriter for £10; paid fares £4.30.
  29. Paid M. Cox £3.80; paid cleaner's wages £15; paid refreshment materials £2.82.

Balance the book and restore the imprest. Enter suitable folio numbers and petty cash voucher numbers.

3. Enter the following items in a petty cash book kept on the imprest

Dr. £ p	Date	Details	PCV	Total £ p	Postage £ p	Travelling Expenses £ p	Cleaning £ p	Sundry Expenses £ p	Stationery £ p	Folio Nos.	Ledger A/cs £ p
50.00	19.. July 5	Imprest from cashier	CB 27								
	5	Rail fares	1	5.60		5.60					
	5	Postage	2	2.48	2.48						
	6	Cleaning expenses	3	3.65			3.65				
	6	Bus fares	4	2.40		2.40					
	6	Envelopes	5	1.00					1.00		
17.80	7	Telephone calls	L.3	—							
	7	Wrapping paper	7	1.50					1.50		
	7	Postage	8	2.35	2.35						
	7	Sundries	9	0.85				0.85			
	8	Travelling expenses	10	7.25		7.25					
	8	M. Carter	11	4.50						L13	4.50
	8	Postage	12	0.80	0.80						
	8	Furniture	13	13.50						L27	13.50
		Totals	—	45.88	5.63	15.25	3.65	0.85	2.50		18.00
		Balance	c/d	21.92	L.5	L.6	L.7	L.8	L.9		
£67.80				£67.80							
21.92	July 12	Balance	b/d								
28.08	12	Restored imprest	C.B. 29								

Fig. 27.1. The petty cash book.

Notes

(i) The petty cash book is divided into two unequal parts, with the debit side reduced to a single column as shown.

(ii) The credit side has not only the 'Details' column, and a credit column headed 'Total', but the rest of the page is made up of analysis columns which enable us to analyse the expenses. The last column is used for any items which cannot be analysed but must be kept separate. This column has a Folio Nos. column alongside so that postings can be made to the accounts separately.

(iii) At the start of the week the petty cashier draws the imprest from the chief cashier and enters it on the debit side, because the petty cash book is receiving money. The page in the main cashbook CB27 is shown in the petty cash voucher column.

(iv) Entries are made for each payment as it occurs, on the credit side since the petty cash book is giving money. The entry is entered twice, once in the 'Total' column and once in an analysis column.

(v) Notice that the petty cashier collects money for private telephone calls from members of staff. As these are receipts the £17.80 is entered on the debit side.

(vi) The payments to M. Carter and for furniture have to go to M. Carter's A/C and Furniture A/C respectively, and these are entered in the end column marked 'Ledger A/cs'.

(vii) At the end of the week a line is ruled across the credit side and all the columns are added. The analysis columns should then be cross-totted to ensure that they agree with the total. The balance can then be calculated and both sides ruled off as shown.

(viii) The petty cashier then presents the book for checking to the main cashier and the imprest is restored to £50. The money required is only £28.08, not £45.88 (the amount spent). This is because £17.80 collected from staff is available in the till.

(ix) The entries L3, L5, L6, L7, L8, L9, L13 and L27 are the folio numbers of the entries in the ledger which are made to complete the book-keeping. This cannot be explained in detail—it is really part of book-keeping, not business calculations.

(x) The petty cash vouchers are numbered and filed, and the reference numbers are written in the PCV column.

(xi) You should now rule up or duplicate some paper of the sort illustrated here and try some of the exercises in Section 27.3 on page 241.

system with an imprest of £50. Use analysis columns for Postage, Office Sundries, Bus Fares, Refreshments and Ledger Accounts.

July 1. Opening balance from previous week £15.87; drew cash to restore imprest to £50; paid for stamps £9.50; sealing wax £0.75.

    2. Paid bus fares £0.66; paid D. Burns £4.85; paid for string and wrapping paper £1.85.

    3. Paid postage £2.30; collected telephone money from staff £5.65; paid for coffee and sugar £3.28.

    4. Paid M. Wrenn £7.25; paid bus fares £0.88.

    5. Paid for office stationery £4.25; paid refreshment materials £2.85.

Balance off the book, bring down the balance and restore the imprest. Invent suitable folio numbers and petty cash voucher numbers.

4. Enter the following items in a petty cash book kept on the imprest system. At the end, balance off the book and restore the original imprest. Use analysis columns for Fares, Postage, Sundry Expenses, Stationery, and Ledger Accounts. Invent appropriate folio numbers and petty cash voucher numbers.

June 7. Drew imprest from cashier £50.00.

    8. Paid fares £1.65; paid postage £3.25.

    9. Paid for refreshments £4.50; paid for stationery £2.30; paid for railway fares £7.00.

    10. Paid fares £2.50; paid for sealing wax and spirit £2.95.

    11. Postage stamps £2.35; paid fares £3.85; member of staff purchased duplicator surplus to requirements for £12.50; paid A. Thomas £8.50.

    12. Paid fares £2.50; paid cleaner £13.50; paid dustman £1.

5. R. Bull employs a cashier who keeps a petty cash book on the imprest system. It has five analysis columns for Postage, Travelling, Stationery, General Expenses and Ledger Accounts. Rule special petty cash paper and record the following week's transactions, inventing appropriate folio numbers and petty cash vouchers numbers:

Dec. 17. Drew imprest of £50.00 from cashier; paid postage £3.50; paid M. Long's account £7.25.

    18. Paid fares £1.80; paid for envelopes £2.55; collected from staff for private telephone calls £7.23.

    19. Paid for fares £1.95.

    20. Paid postage £2.35; paid P. Carter's account £17.25.

    21. Paid fares (chauffeur) £3.20; sundry expenses £1.25.

Rule off the book, bring down the balance in hand, and restore the imprest to £50.00.

27.4 Mental Arithmetic Test

1. Add together 17, 12, 26 and 48

2. Take 4216 from 5000

3. $3267 \div 9 =$

4. $27\,000 \div 125 =$

5. Seven children are 5, 6, 8, 9, 11, 14, and 17 years old respectively. What is their average age?

6. $\frac{3}{4} + \frac{1}{2} + \frac{3}{8} =$

7. $7\frac{1}{3} - 3\frac{1}{4} =$

8. $0.25 \times 0.5 =$

9. What is 14 as a percentage of 42?

10. What is the perimeter of a rectangle 17 m long by 14 m wide?

11. What is the simple interest on £750 at 10% for 3 years?

12. How many shares at £1.25 each shall I buy for £500?

13. What is the VAT on a bicycle costing £80 if the VAT charge is 15%?

14. How many days in the year 1986?

15. How many days from 19 May to 4 July inclusive?

28
Depreciation

28.1 Assets and 'Fair Wear and Tear'

Every business requires assets, of which land and buildings, plant and machinery, furniture and fittings and motor vehicles are typical examples. An asset is an item purchased for long-term use in the business, extending over a period of years. Thus postage stamps are not usually considered assets of the business, for within a few days we stick them on a letter and post them in the pillar box. Stationery, advertising brochures and similar things are other examples of items with a short life, which may be called by the general name 'consumables'—things that get used up in the course of business and are just regarded as an expense the business has to bear.

Even though assets last a long time they do wear out, and eventually have to be replaced. This means that their value gradually declines. As anyone who buys a new car or motorcycle soon discovers, its value declines fairly quickly. Most businesses do not expect a motor vehicle to last more than five years, and industrial vehicles subject to heavy use might only have a life of three years. We must find some way of writing this loss off the assets as they decline in value, otherwise we shall have the asset accounts saying that the asset is worth its original price, when in fact it is worth much less. The process is called 'depreciation', and it takes account of 'fair wear and tear' over the lifetime of the asset. Thus a vehicle involved in a crash, and becoming a 'write-off', would not be the subject of depreciation, but would have to be written off the books by another procedure.

There are many methods of depreciation, but the three commonest methods are (a) the **straight-line** (or equal-instalment) method, (b) the **diminishing balance** method and (c) the **revaluation** method. The calculations are very simple.

28.2 The Straight-line Method (or Equal-instalment Method)

Under this method we write off the same amount each year, using the estimated life time and the estimated residual (scrap) value of the asset. For example, consider a car costing £4000 estimated to have a useful life of five years and a trade-in value at the end of the five years of £800. This means that over five years it will decline in value by £3200 (£4000 − £800 = £3200 loss in value). Dividing this by five, we find that the loss each year is £640. On the last day of each year the accountant writes off £640 of the book value.

The formula for finding how much to write off each year is therefore:

$$\frac{\text{Original cost} - \text{Residual value}}{\text{Lifetime in years}}$$

$$= \frac{£4000 - £800}{5}$$

$$= \frac{£3200}{5}$$

$$= £640 \text{ per year}$$

When these entries are made in the ledger accounts—the motor vehicle account, for example—they will be as shown in Fig. 28.1.

Motor Vehicles A/c

19_1		£	19_1		£
Jan. 1	To Bank A/c	4000	Dec. 31	By Depreciation	640
				,, Balance	3360
		£4000			£4000
19_2			19_2		£
Jan. 1	To Balance	3360	Dec. 31	By Depreciation	640
				,, Balance	2720
		£3360			£3360
19_3		£			
Jan. 1	To Balance	2720	*etc.*		

Fig. 28.1. Depreciation by the straight-line method.

At the end of five years the value of the vehicle will be reduced to £800 and we shall then trade it in for a new one, and hope to persuade the salesman to give us £800 allowance on the old vehicle. Of course there may be some final adjustment to be made at this time, as depreciation cannot be estimated with absolute accuracy.

28.3   Exercises: The Straight-line Method

1. Calculate the amount to be written off each year from the asset accounts listed below:

Asset account	Original Cost	Estimated lifetime in years	Residual Value
(a) Motor car A/c	£7500	5	£1500
(b) Furniture A/c	£3800	15	£800
(c) Typewriters A/c	£1650	8	£250
(d) Plant and machinery A/c	£38 000	10	£2500
(e) Heavy goods vehicles A/c	£24 000	6	£3000

2. The plant and machinery account of Wheeler Brothers Ltd shows assets of £27 600. All the machines were purchased on 1 January of this year, and depreciation is to be over a period of 8 years, with an estimated residual value of £4200. (a) Calculate the annual depreciation by the straight-line method. (b) Show the plant and machinery account for the first two years.

3. A farmer depreciates agricultural machinery using a plant register in which each machine is recorded and depreciated separately on the straight-line method. He has a combine harvester that cost £36 000 on 1 July this year. It has an estimated life time of 15 years and a residual value of £1500.
(a) Calculate the annual depreciation for a full year. (b) Calculate the depreciation for 31 December *this* year. (c) Show the combine harvester account for 31 December Year 1, Year 2 and Year 3.

28.4   The Diminishing Balance Method

Under the straight-line method an equal amount is written off every year. Some people regard this as unsatisfactory, because repairs to assets usually increase as the years go by, and this means that the total cost for the use of the asset is not spread evenly over the lifetime. Compare Year 1 and Year 5 of the lifetime of the motorcar referred to earlier:

Year 1. Depreciation £640, servicing £100, repairs £0. Total £740

Year 5. Depreciation £640, servicing £180, repairs £260. Total £1080

To equalise charges over the years we can write off more for depreciation in the early years, when repair bills are small, and write off less in the later years, as repair bills grow. This is the diminishing balance method. A percentage figure is chosen which will give somewhere near the required result, and this is written off the 'diminishing balance' of the asset each year.

Suppose we imagine the same vehicle as in 28.1 above, costing £4000 with a residual value after five years of £800. A depreciation rate of 25% will give us somewhere near the correct figure (but by this method we cannot get accurately to an expected final trade-in value in many cases unless we choose quite difficult percentage figures).

In the first year we shall write off 25% of £4000 = £1000. This leaves a diminishing balance of £3000. Notice that the amount written off in the first year is much more than in the first year by the straight-line method (but of course the first year of a vehicle's use usually means very low repair bills).

In the second year we write off 25% of the diminishing balance, which is 25% of £3000 = £750. This leaves a balance of £2250. The next year we shall write off 25% of £2250 = £562.50. It is usual to write off correct to the nearest pound, so we would write off £562. (Remember we correct to the nearest *even* whole number if we have an exact half; £563 would be incorrect.) The whole lifetime is shown in Fig. 28.2.

Motor Vehicles A/c

19_1		£	19_1		£
Jan. 1	To Bank a/c	4000	Dec. 31	By Depreciation	1000
				,, Balance	3000
		———			———
		£4000			£4000
19_2		£	19_2		£
Jan. 1	To Balance	3000	Dec. 31	By Depreciation	750
				,, Balance	2250
		———			———
		£3000			£3000
19_3		£	19_3		£
Jan. 1	To Balance	2250	Dec. 31	By Depreciation	562
				,, Balance	1688
		———			———
		£2250			£2250

19_4		£	19_4			£
Jan. 1	To Balance	1688	Dec. 31	By Depreciation		422
				,, Balance		1266
		£1688				£1688
19_5		£	19_5			£
Jan. 1	To Balance	1266	Dec. 31	By Depreciation		316
				,, Balance		950
		£1266				£1266
19_6		£				
Jan. 1	To Balance	950				

Fig. 28.2. Depreciation by the diminishing balance method.

28.5 Exercises: The Diminishing Balance Method

1. Calculate the amount to be written off in each of the following cases, in the first three years of the asset life, by the diminishing balance method (calculations correct to nearest pound).

	Asset Account	Original cost 1 January	Percentage rate used
(a)	Heavy machinery a/c	£3500	25%
(b)	Motor vehicles a/c	£6400	$33\frac{1}{3}$%
(c)	Furniture and fittings a/c	£4800	20%
(d)	Typewriters a/c	£4250	25%
(e)	Printing press a/c	£68 000	20%

2. A business buys an electronic computer on 1 January for £15 000, which it depreciates at $12\frac{1}{2}$% per annum on the diminishing balance method. Show the asset account for the first three years.

3. A motorcar costing £4650, purchased on 1 July 19_1 is depreciated by 25% per annum on the diminishing balance method. Do the calculations as at 31 December for the years 19_1 and 19_2 and show the asset account for those two years (calculations to the nearest £1).

28.6 The Revaluation Method

Some assets do not wear out evenly over the years but change in value in rather different ways. For example, a farmer's herds may increase in value in some years and decrease in value in others. Loose tools, such as are used to make plastic utensils, toys, etc., are very expensive to produce and are being added to (made in the tool room) and discarded (scrapped as of no further use or interest to customers) month by month. In these cases the best procedure is to value the stock at the end of the year. If the herd, or stock of tools, has declined in value there is a loss which may be called 'depreciation'. If it has increased in value there is a profit which is called 'appreciation'. This is more appropriate to book-keeping than to business calculations but is mentioned here to complete the picture of elementary depreciation methods.

28.7 Mental Arithmetic Test

1. £3.65 + £2.75 + £1.40 =

2. Take £5.95 from £20

3. $\frac{2}{3} \times \frac{3}{4} \times \frac{1}{2} =$

4. $0.5 \times 0.25 =$

5. £75.65 ÷ 5 =

6. 25 000 × 300 =

7. How many litres are there in 2.54 kilolitres?

8. What is the profit on 48 items purchased for £1.75 each and sold for £2.35 each?

9. Tickets are sold for three concerts: 720, 680 and 763 people attend. What was the average attendance?

10. What is the formula for finding the area of a circle?

11. What is the formula for finding the surface area of a cylinder, not counting the two ends?

12. How many days in January, February and March altogether, in a leap year?

13. Share up £28 000 among three partners in the ratio $1\frac{1}{2}:1:1$

14. A car costing £5500 with a life of five years and a trade-in value at the end of £1500 is to be depreciated on the straight-line method. How much will be written off each year?

15. A lorry costing £16 000 with a life of 10 years and an estimated trade in value of £1600 is to be depreciated by the straight-line method. How much will be written off each year?

29
Compound Interest

29.1 What is Compound Interest?

Compound interest is the system of interest used in long-term investments for pensions and similar purposes. With simple interest, discussed in Chapter 12, the interest earned is paid over to the lender as a reward for permitting the borrower to use the lender's money. With compound interest any interest earned is added to the amount invested and in turn earns interest in the years ahead. This is generally the system used when an institutional investor, such as a building society, investment trust, unit trust, insurance company or bank, collects money from the general public. Savers who invest money with firms like this earn compound interest. An example will explain the effect.

Consider an investment of £1000 at 10% compound interest. The money is invested on 1 January and interest is added on 31 December each year.

		£	
Year 1	1 January	1000	
	31 December	100	Interest (10%)
		1100	Total
Year 2	31 December	110	Interest (10%)
		1210	Total
Year 3	31 December	121	Interest (10%)
		1331	Total
Year 4	31 December	133.10	Interest (10%)
		1464.10	Total
Year 5	31 December	146.41	Interest 10%
		1610.51	Total

Year 6	31 December	161.05	Interest 10%
		1771.56	Total
Year 7	31 December	177.16	Interest 10%
		1948.72	Total
Year 8	31 December	194.87	Interest 10%
		2143.59	Total

As these figures show, the original investment has more than doubled itself in eight years with an interest rate of 10%. If left in for 20 years the £1000 would become £6727. This is why pension funds, if left in for a whole working life, can yield very large sums. For example, a young person contributing £1000 a year to a pension from age 20 to age 65 would be entitled to a pension of £169 750 per year from age 65. This seems an enormous sum, and it illustrates how large sums of money become when accumulated with compound interest over a great many years.

29.2 The 'Practice' Method of Compound Interest

Compound interest has to be worked out on a rather lengthy method, called the 'practice method', or we can use a formula. The practice method depends upon taking an easy figure, and from it finding the harder figures that are usual in business life. The best way to follow the method is to study one or two examples. As usual the sum invested is called the **principal.**

Example 29.1. What will a principal of £5000 invested on 1 January 19_1 amount to in 3 years at 12% compound interest?

The method is to find 1%, which is easy, since it is one hundredth of £5000 = £50. Then work out 11% from this and when added on to the 1% we have 12%. We must do this every year for three years, as follows:

		£	
Principal invested at 1 January 19_1	=	5000.00	
Interest at 1%	=	50.00	
,, ,, 11%	=	550.00	(11 times the 1% line)
Amount at end of Year 1		5600.00	
Interest at 1%	=	56.00	
,, ,, 11%	=	616.00	(11 times the 1% line)
Amount at end of Year 2		6272.00	
Interest at 1%	=	62.72	
,, ,, 11%	=	689.92	(11 times the 1% line)
Amount after three years		£7024.64	

Example 29.2. What will a principal of £5840 invested for 3 years become at 8½% interest?

This time we can work out 8½% interest by taking 1%, 7% and ½%.

		£	
Principal invested at start	=	5840.00	
Interest at 1%		58.40	
,, ,, 7%	=	408.80	(7 times the 1% line)
,, ,, ½%	=	29.20	(½ times the 1% line)
Amount at end of Year 1		6336.40	*Note:* There is an
Interest at 1%	=	63.364	extra figure—as we
,, ,, 7%	=	443.548	are working correct to
,, ,, ½%	=	31.682	two decimal places we
			need to calculate to
Amount at the end of Year 2		6874.994	three places.
Interest at 1%	=	68.750	
,, ,, 7%	=	481.250	
,, ,, ½%	=	34.375	
		£7459.369	
	=	£7459.37	

29.3   Exercises: Easy Compound Interest by the 'Practice' Method

1. What will the following investments become if invested for 3 years at 12% compound interest (calculations to the nearest penny):

(a)	£500	(b)	£600
(c)	£750	(d)	£1200
(e)	£1500	(f)	£2000
(g)	£5000	(h)	£6500
(i)	£7400	(j)	£12 800

2. What will the following sums become if invested for the number of years shown at the rates of compound interest given in the table below (calculations to nearest penny):

	Principal	Rate of compound interest	Number of years
(a)	£600	8%	2
(b)	£750	9%	2
(c)	£1600	12%	2
(d)	£2400	15%	3
(e)	£3000	11½%	3
(f)	£3500	8½%	3
(g)	£4200	9½%	3

(h)	£6000	$10\frac{1}{4}\%$	4
(i)	£6500	$12\frac{1}{2}\%$	4
(j)	£7800	$14\frac{3}{4}\%$	4

29.4 The Formula Method for Compound Interest

Calculating compound interest by the practice method can be very tedious if the investment is held for a long time. Instead we can use the formula below:

$$A = P(1.0r)^n$$

Where A is the amount the principal becomes in n years, P the principal, r the rate per cent and n the number of years.

Suppose the rate of interest is 9% then $1.0r = 1.09$.

If the rate of interest is $11\frac{1}{4}\%$ then $1.0r = 1.1125$.

Example 29.3. What will an investment of £8000 amount to in 6 years at $13\frac{1}{2}\%$ compound?

$$A = £8000 \times (1.135)^6$$

To multiply 1.135 by itself 6 times is a time-consuming task, and we must either use an electronic calculator or logarithms. These days calculators are usually used, and the answer can be arrived at in a few seconds:

$$A = £8000 \times (1.135)^6$$
$$A = £17\,102.72$$

Example 29.3. What will an investment of £8000 amount to in 3 years' time at 10% per annum, interest being added half-yearly?

Note: When interest is added half-yearly the 'compound' interest on the interest is intensified. The first half-year a half-year's interest is added to the sum invested—i.e. 5% in this example. This interest earns interest in the second half-year so that the sum invested grows more quickly. The effect is the same as having half the rate of interest for twice as many years, i.e. 5% interest for 6 years.

$$A = £8000 \times (1.05)^6$$
$$= £10\,720.76$$

Had interest been added only once a year the answer would have been £10 648, showing the extra growth that results from half-yearly compounding to be £72.76.

29.5   Exercises: Compound Interest Calculations by the Formula Method

You will need an electronic calculator or logarithms for these calculations.

1. Use the formula method to calculate the amount that will accumulate in the following long-term investments. They are envisaged as being made on 1 January in Year 1 with interest added on 31 December each year.

	Principal	Annual rate of interest	Number of years
(a)	£4000	11%	3
(b)	£6000	$12\frac{1}{2}$%	3
(c)	£2500	$14\frac{1}{2}$%	4
(d)	£8500	$15\frac{1}{2}$%	5
(e)	£30 000	$16\frac{3}{4}$%	10

2. Use the formula method to calculate the amount that will accumulate in the following long-term investments, where interest is added to the principal *half-yearly*, at the *annual rate* shown below.

	Principal	Annual rate of interest	Number of years
(a)	£2000	10%	3
(b)	£5000	14%	4
(c)	£3500	$12\frac{1}{2}$%	5
(d)	£6800	$15\frac{1}{2}$%	6
(e)	£12 500	$16\frac{3}{4}$%	8

29.6   Mental Arithmetic Test

1. $3854 - 2538 =$

2. $3654 \div 18 =$

3. $3.5 \div 0.2 =$

4. $\frac{2}{3} + \frac{1}{4} + \frac{1}{8} =$

5. $1\frac{1}{5} \div \frac{6}{10} =$

6. What discount will be deducted if 5% is deducted from a cash price of £245?

7. What is the compound interest altogether on £100 invested for 2 years at 10% per annum.

8. Cheap overnight electricity costs 4 pence per unit. How much shall I pay for 850 units?

9. Five workers work 40 h, 43 h, 45 h 30 min, 47 h 30 min and 54 h respectively in a week. What is the average working week?

10. What commission will a salesman earn on sales of £45 500 if commission at 4 pence in the £1 starts after sales of £20 000 have been reached.

30
An Introduction to Statistics

30.1 The Nature of Statistics

The word 'statistics' was originally applied to the collection of numerical facts by the State. Such areas as population, tax revenue, government expenditure and agricultural output were initially covered with a view to finding out how the economy could be influenced and what social trends were developing. The facts collected were called 'data', a word which means 'starting points'. Today we use this word frequently because so many of our activities use the 'data processing' made possible by computers and microcomputers. We start with the 'data' we have collected, and process it in various ways to give us totals, averages, future projections, etc. The meaning of statistics has broadened to include not only a set of numerical data, but also the processes used in the collection, presentation, analysis, and interpretation of these data.

It is convenient to divide statistics into two parts:

(a) Descriptive statistics
(b) Analytical statistics

Descriptive Statistics

This term is applied to any statistics which are collected and arranged in some suitable order so that they can be presented in tabular or diagrammatic form to throw light upon the state of affairs in the field under consideration. In dealing with most human, economic or scientific problems it is helpful to know the true situation. How many people are involved? What expenditure is being envisaged? What is the likely cost of present proposals? Who is most affected by the problem? Such matters call for a clear description in statistical form. Hence, a table showing the number of registered unemployed from 1971 to 1982 falls within the field of descriptive statistics (see Table 30.1).

Table 30.1. UK Registered unemployed, 1971–1982.

1971	806 800	1981	2 520 400
1972	875 600	1982	2 916 900
1973	618 800		
1974	614 900		
1975	977 600		
1976	1 358 800		
1977	1 483 600		
1978	1 475 000		
1979	1 390 500		
1980	1 816 900		

(*Source: Monthly Digest of Statistics.* Monthly averages to nearest 100)

Analytical Statistics

These attempt to reach conclusions and make pronouncements on
the basis of the information made available by descriptive statistics.
It may be possible to make statements about why the totals of
registered unemployed were as they appeared in the 1971–82 table.
Measures taken during the decade might be linked to the changes
in unemployment in subsequent periods and their effectiveness
assessed. The cost of the measures might be set against the benefits
to reveal the most cost-effective policies for the future. Such analysis
makes use of techniques to be discussed later, such as averages and
trends.

30.2   Collecting Data—Census Forms and Questionnaires

Statistics used by investigators are of two types: **primary** and **secondary**. Primary statistics are collected by the investigator when he
searches out new information. Secondary statistics are those which
an investigator obtains from other sources. Most of these will be
published statistics and the Government is an active supplier of
information in this form.

Of course, at some stage all statistics have to be collected from
original sources. Such collection involves the investigator in a
number of decisions. The following are points which have to be
considered when about to embark upon an inquiry:

(a) What is the precise purpose of the inquiry?

(b) What definitions must we lay down if the investigators are to
be clear about the classification of the responses they receive?

(c) How is the inquiry to be conducted and how can we make it
as foolproof as possible? This usually requires the preparation of a
questionnaire or a census form.

As an illustration of such a series of decisions, consider Fig. 30.1, which was designed to conduct a traffic survey on a road going through a particular housing estate. Such an inquiry is called a **census**, since every vehicle passing through will be included in the data collected. In other inquiries, called **sample surveys**, only a selection of the relevant data will be obtained. In this census the answers to questions (a)–(c) above might be:

(a) The precise purpose of the inquiry is to find out exactly what traffic uses the road through the estate. Residents complain about the volume of heavy goods traffic and the public service through-traffic run by tour operators and excursion organisers. Is there real cause for complaint, or not?

(b) We decide to define heavy goods vehicles as 'large goods vehicles carrying containers, or enclosed vehicles such as removal vans or large distribution vans destined for depots and warehouses'. Small vans and hire-drive vans, caravanettes, etc., will all be treated as 'cars and vans'.

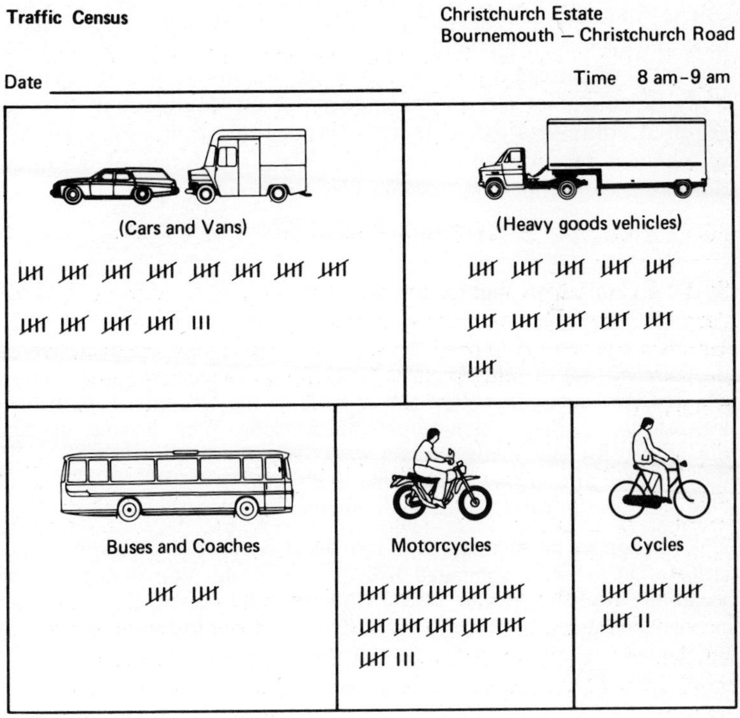

Fig. 30.1. A traffic census.

Buses and coaches are to be recorded as such only if they have 13 seats or more. Minibuses with 12 seats only are to be classed as 'cars and vans'.

The term 'motorcycles' includes scooters and mopeds.

(c) It seems best to conduct the survey over a full working day, from 6 am to midnight. An hour at a time is considered enough for a stint as 'census-taker'. A rota is prepared to cover each census period, and staff are trained to use the 'five-barred gate' system shown in Fig. 30.1. This system records the first four vehicles by upright lines, and the fifth vehicle as a cross bar, as on a five-barred gate. The resulting records are easy to count up in fives.

Questionnaires. The Consumers' Association is an official body which conducts investigations into matters of interest to consumers. Its publications are issued under the general title *Which?*, since their aim is to help consumers select the best buy in a particular range of goods or services. Every school and college should receive these publications, and readers are urged to consult *Which?* to discover the range and variety of statistics available.

The Association collects data from volunteers who have actually used the type of equipment or service being investigated, and from this mass of information draws helpful conclusions for the general body of consumers. A recent enquiry about 'Holidays in France' required volunteers to complete a 10-page questionnaire, one page of which is reproduced in Fig. 30.2. Note the design of the questionnaire, to permit easy response by the holiday maker.

30.3 Exercises on Inquiry Forms

1. You are proposing to conduct an inquiry among your classmates about their use of 'out of school/college time'. You particularly wish to know whether they have a part-time job or work in the home in an equivalent way because, perhaps, both parents are working. What hobbies do they pursue and for how many hours a week? What recreational activities do they indulge in and how much time is given to each activity per week? Design a form to carry out such an inquiry.

2. You propose to do a census at your local car park to assess the popularity of British cars compared with foreign rivals. You wish to record separately British, German, Italian, French and Japanese cars. All other cars will be classed as 'Other foreign'. Draw up a census form to be used in the inquiry.

3. Draw up a questionnaire to be used in an inquiry about student incomes. The inquiry proposes to discover how much the average student has to live on each week, and what this income is spent on.

HAVE YOU BEEN TO ANY OTHER PARTS OF FRANCE?

WE WOULD LIKE TO GET A FULL PICTURE OF WHAT YOU LIKE AND DON'T LIKE ABOUT FRANCE. TO HELP US WITH THIS WE WOULD BE GRATEFUL TO GET BRIEF DETAILS ABOUT ANY OTHER AREAS WHICH YOU HAVE VISITED IN THE LAST 3-4 YEARS. EACH OF THE FOUR COLUMNS ON THIS QUESTIONNAIRE CAN GIVE US BASIC INFORMATION ABOUT YOUR VIEWS ON ANOTHER AREA. PLEASE FILL IN ONE OR MORE COLUMNS TO TELL US ABOUT OTHER PLACES YOU HAVE BEEN TO IN FRANCE.

CARD 4
(1)(2)(3)(4)
8 5 4 6
(5)-(12) AS CARD 1

AREA/REGION 1

Q1. Which region of France did you visit? SEE Q5 OF THE WHITE QUESTIONNAIRE. PLEASE WRITE IN. (13)

______________________ (14)

Q2. When did you make this visit?
PLEASE WRITE IN YEAR, AND MONTH HOLIDAY BEGAN.

(15) (16) (17)

Year: 19 ☐☐ Month: ____________

Q3. What did you particularly enjoy or like about your stay in this area? PLEASE WRITE IN DETAILS.

(18)

(19)

(20)

Q4. And what did you dislike about your stay in this area? PLEASE WRITE IN DETAILS.

(21)

(22)

(23)

Q5. On the whole, how much did you enjoy your holiday in this area? (24)

PLEASE TICK ONE BOX

Very much .... ☐ 1
Quite a lot .... ☐ 2
Not very much ...... ☐ 3
Not at all .... ☐ 4

Q6. And summing up, how would you rate it as a place for a holiday? (25)

PLEASE TICK ONE BOX

Excellent .... ☐ 1
Good .... ☐ 2
Fair .... ☐ 3
Poor .... ☐ 4
Bad .... ☐ 5

Q7. And overall, do you think this area is good value for money? (26)

Yes .... ☐ 1
No .... ☐ 2

AREA/REGION 2

Q1. Which region of France did you visit? SEE Q5 OF THE WHITE QUESTIONNAIRE. PLEASE WRITE IN. (27)

(28)

____

Q2. When did you make this visit?
PLEASE WRITE IN YEAR, AND MONTH HOLIDAY BEGAN.

(29) (30) (31)

Year: 19 ☐☐ Month: ____________

Q3. What did you particularly enjoy or like about your stay in this area? PLEASE WRITE IN DETAILS

(32)

(33)

(34)

Q4. And what did you dislike about your stay in this area? PLEASE WRITE IN DETAILS.

(35)

(36)

(37)

Q5. On the whole, how much did you enjoy your holiday in this area? (38)

PLEASE TICK ONE BOX

Very much .... ☐ 1
Quite a lot .... ☐ 2
Not very much ...... ☐ 3
Not at all .... ☐ 4

Q6. And summing up, how would you rate it as a place for a holiday? (39)

PLEASE TICK ONE BOX

Excellent .... ☐ 1
Good .... ☐ 2
Fair .... ☐ 3
Poor .... ☐ 4
Bad .... ☐ 5

Q7. And overall, do you think this area is good value for money? (40)

Yes .... ☐ 1
No .... ☐ 2

Fig. 30.2. A questionnaire.
(Reproduced by courtesy of *Which?* magazine)

4. A fashion magazine proposes to do a census at a local youth centre about the colours preferred by young people. All members will be asked questions as follows:

(a) If you could buy a completely new rigout for yourself, what colour would you choose?

(b) If you were dating a member of the opposite sex for a day out next weekend, what colour would you like them to wear?

A note will also be made of the colour of the clothing the member is wearing at the time of the inquiry. Design a form which could be used to record the answers on the five-barred gate system.

30.4 Rounding Data after Collection

In statistics we are trying to present a picture of the matter under investigation which will be clear, simple to understand and as accurate as we can get it. From these points of view consider the following statistic.

'There are at present 17 265 171 drivers in the United Kingdom'

What can we say about this statistic? Is it clear, and simple to understand? No, for the mind cannot really envisage it. Once you have 17 million drivers in your mind it is not very easy to imagine another 265 171. Is it accurate? Here again we must reply 'No', for in fact every minute of the day someone dies, and others pass their driving tests and become 'drivers'. The figure of 17 265 171 is an example of what statisticians call 'spurious accuracy', we just cannot know if it is right.

For this reason, in statistics it is usual to 'round' numbers off to a stated degree of accuracy. In rounding we use the same rules we have already learned for rounding off decimal fractions. Anything over half-way rounds up to the next highest number; anything less than half rounds down to the lowest number. Thus

> 17 265 171 rounds down to 17 million
> 17 825 382 rounds up to 18 million
> 17 500 000 being exactly half way, is rounded to
> make the next figure an even number,
> i.e. 18 million

(So a figure of 16 500 000 will be rounded down to 16 million, not rounded up to 17 million because 17 is an odd number.)

Example 30.1. Round off the following figures to the nearest million pounds and rewrite the table in its new form.

Gross value of production in the United Kingdom, 19—

	£
Primary industries	12 766 654 264
Manufacturing	41 744 285 961
Building and construction	17 802 631 419
Service trades	39 185 423 367
Public services	38 354 500 000
Total	149 853 495 011

The numbers are to be rounded off to the nearest million. This means that the last six figures will be left out of the final table, but they may help us to decide whether we need to round 'up' or round 'down'.

Consider 'Primary industries'. The last six figures are 654 264, which is more than half a million—round up to £12 767 million.

Manufacturing: the last six figures are less than half a million—round down to £41 744 million.

Building and construction: 631 419 is more than half a million—round up to £17 803 million.

Service trades: 423 367 is less than half a million—round down to £39 185 million.

Public services: 500 000 is exactly half a million—round to make an *even number of millions*—so we round down to £38 354 million.

The new table will therefore read as follows:

Gross value of production in the United Kingdom, 19—

	£ millions
Primary industries	12 767
Manufacturing	41 744
Building and construction	17 803
Service trades	39 185
Public services	38 354
Total	149 853

A Special Note about Rounding

Whenever we round numbers to a given degree of accuracy we must introduce slight errors into the rounded figures. For example, compare the following addition sums:

Actual numbers	Rounded to nearest 10
31	30
37	40
45	40
113	110

Actual numbers	Rounded to nearest 10
31	30
37	40
46	50
114	120

In the second set of figures 114, when rounded to the nearest 10, comes to 110, but the sum of the rounded figures 30 + 40 + 50 = 120. This sort of total often finishes up with a small error and we frequently find in statistical publications the phrase 'Totals do not agree because of rounding'.

30.5   Exercises on Rounding

1. An investigation into the enrolment at various secondary schools shows the following number of pupils enrolled:

School A   942   School B   886   School C   837   School D   1142
School E   1050   School F   1829   School G   1750   School H   1632
School I   721   School J   882   School K   636   School L   1945

Round the numbers off to the nearest 100 in each case and present the result in a table, in alphabetical order, i.e.

Pupils in Secondary Schools

School A =
School B =
etc.

Total the rounded figures at the end of the table.

2. Output of a particular component by 10 trainee engineers is given as follows in units:

Mr A   27   Mr B   36   Miss C   45   Mr D   83
Mr E   13   Miss F   67   Mr G   59   Mr H   47
Mr I   32   Mr J   18

Round the outputs off to the nearest 10 units and present in a table in descending order in the form:

Output per Trainee

Mr D   80
Miss F   ?
etc.

Where two trainees have the same rounded output, place the one with the higher real output first.

3. Unofficial calculations for the population of the United Kingdom in three census years were as follows:

	Total	*Males*	*Females*
1961	52 809 231	25 525 760	27 283 471
1971	55 566 269	26 983 329	28 582 940
1981	55 930 088	27 201 326	28 728 762

It is decided to present these figures in millions, rounded off correct to one decimal place (e.g. 52.8 millions). Round the figures accordingly and present in a new table headed:

Population of the United Kingdom (millions)

4. Tonnages of iron ore shipped from a port in Western Australia to Japan are given in the following monthly table:

	Tonnes		Tonnes		Tonnes
January	582 606	February	536 856	March	724 085
April	498 364	May	724 720	June	667 500
July	648 795	August	721 505	September	495 721
October	565 990	November	638 428	December	720 500

Round these off to the nearest 1000 tonnes, and present them in a single-column table, totalled to give the shipments for the year. Head the table:

Iron Ore Shipments to Japan ('000 tonnes)

5. Add the following numbers to find the total, then round the total off to the nearest thousand: 7 256 + 11 271 + 13 898 + 14 252 + 16 500 + 8 694.

6. Subtract 275 840 from 385 279 and round the answer to the nearest hundred.

30.6   Mental Arithmetic Test

1. $3864 \div 12 =$

2. $25.95 \div 0.5 =$

3. $1\frac{1}{2} + 2\frac{1}{4} + 3\frac{7}{8} =$

4. How many days are there from 4th July to 5th September, inclusive?

5. $17\,450 \times 9 =$

6. $2800 \times 400 =$

7. How many seconds in $2\frac{3}{4}$ minutes?

8. What is the average of 7, 8, 12, 16 and 22?

9. An item is sold for 60 pence after adding $33\frac{1}{3}\%$ to cost price. What was the cost price?

10. A factory is rated at £24 000 and rates are 25 pence in the £1. How much must the owner pay in rates?

11. What will 20 theatre tickets cost at £6.25 each?

12. How many 2 cm cubes will fit into a box 8 cm $\times$ 6 cm $\times$ 4 cm?

13. Round off 27 289 to the nearest thousand

14. $0.2 \times 0.8 \times 0.3 =$

15. What shall I get for £150 if I turn them into French francs at F8.5 = £1?

16. What is the area of a circle radius 7 cm? Take $\pi = 3\frac{1}{7}$

17. What will be the freight charge for a crate 2 m $\times$ 2 m $\times$ 1 m at £38.50 per cubic metre?

18. Round off 28 500 000 to the nearest million

19. What is the circumference of a bicycle wheel 63 cm in diameter? Use $\pi = 3\frac{1}{7}$

20 A salesman earns a basic salary of £240 a month plus a commission of 5% on sales of £6400. What were his total earnings?

31
The Presentation of Statistics: Classification and Tabulation

31.1 Classification of Data

The problem with a statistical inquiry is that we finish up with a mass of data in a very disorganised form—files of completed census forms or questionnaires that have been answered. To present this data in a simple form we must first sort it out into a number of classes. This is called 'classification' of data.

Imagine an inquiry into the fishing industry, which collects figures about the fish caught every day for every boat, from every port involved in fishing. There would soon be so many sheets of statistics, that rather than clarify the situation they would only confuse it. To reduce the huge amount of detail available we must classify the catches into groups of similar or related items. For example, we might find that, of the fish landed, some were haddock, some cod, some mackerel, some herring, etc. It is useful to know how much of each type of fish has been caught. Therefore it would be in order to classify (i.e. group together) the species of fish caught. This also reduces the number of classes. Instead of each fish being an individual, there are only half-a-dozen or so classes for all the millions of fish caught. This makes the handling of the information much easier.

There are a few rules for classifying data, so that we know easily which class to put a particular item into. These are:

(a) *Classes should be few in number*. It is a mistake to have too many classes, for we have to compare them with one another, and this becomes difficult if there are too many of them.

(b) *There must be enough classes to include every item in the data*. Our fishing inquiry may prove that haddock, cod, mackerel and herring are the four chief classes but there will be hundreds of other fish caught, from tiny dabs to huge sharks. Usually we need a class called 'Other varieties' or some similar heading, so that the unusual items can be collected together.

(c) *Classes should not overlap*. If we classify fish by weight, and have classes 0–1 kg, 1–2 kg, 2–3 kg, etc., we shall not know where to classify a fish of exactly 1 kg. Does it go in Class 1, or Class 2? Does a fish of exactly 2 kg go in Class 2 or Class 3? To prevent this sort of overlapping, the classes should have been called

Class 1   Under 1 kg
Class 2   1 kg but under 2 kg
Class 3   2 kg but under 3 kg

Clearly now a 1 kg fish goes in Class 2, and a 2 kg fish goes in Class 3.

Example 31.1. A fishing port has five ships fishing one particular day in July. The catches were as follows:

Ship A   227 plaice, 346 herring, 2 skate, 4 conger eels, 27 soles.
Ship B   386 herring, 474 mackerel, 3 skate, 1 shark, 152 soles, 168 plaice.
Ship C   324 plaice, 486 herring, 286 mackerel, 3 crabs, 2 lobsters, 1 skate.
Ship D   284 herring, 362 mackerel, 42 soles, 4 skate.
Ship E   386 plaice, 998 mackerel, 4284 herring, 2 skate, 48 soles.

Arrange these catches in classes.

Note: Clearly we must have classes for plaice, herring, mackerel and soles. We might have a class for skate, since all ships caught some skate, but in view of the small numbers it seems hardly worthwhile. If we put these in a general class of 'Other fish and crustacea' we can put the crabs and lobsters in this class too.

Rough Classification

Plaice	227 + 168 + 324 + 386	= 1105
Herring	346 + 386 + 486 + 284 + 4284	= 5786
Mackerel	474 + 286 + 362 + 998	= 2120
Soles	27 + 152 + 42 + 48	= 269
Other fish and crustacea	2 + 4 + 3 + 1 +	
	3 + 2 + 1 + 4 + 2 =	22
		9302

Final Classification

Fish Caught by Westport Vessels: Friday 27 July

Herring	5786
Mackerel	2120
Plaice	1105
Soles	269
Other fish and	22
crustacea	
	9302

Placing them in this order is not necessary, but it clarifies which was the most common variety, etc.

31.2   Exercises in Classification

1. A quality control department in an electric light-bulb factory tests every thousandth bulb to see how long it lasts. Twenty bulbs burn for the following lengths of time:

41 hours; 475 hours; 38 hours; 276 hours; 11 hours
139 ,, ; 438 ,, ; 786 ,, ; 1726 ,, ; 274 ,,
286 ,, ; 72 ,, ; 149 ,, ; 325 ,, ; 721 ,,
 17 ,, ; 5 minutes; 285 ,, ; 486 ,, ; 49 ,,

It is decided to classify these into five groups: (a) under 100 hours; (b) 100–249 hours; (c) 250–499 hours; (d) 500–749 hours; (e) 750 hours and over.

   Using the five-barred gate system record the data in the groups and then write out the five classes showing how many in each class. What does the data tell you about the quality of these light bulbs?

2. Recruits to the armed forces are weighed on joining the service. The weights in kg are as follows for 30 recruits:

70 kg	68 kg	81 kg	72 kg	71 kg
64 kg	71 kg	65 kg	69 kg	60 kg
78 kg	78 kg	76 kg	71 kg	66 kg
74 kg	75 kg	70 kg	72 kg	59 kg
59 kg	64 kg	72 kg	76 kg	73 kg
68 kg	67 kg	69 kg	85 kg	71 kg

Group them into classes as follows: (a) under 60 kg; (b) 60 kg but under 65 kg; (c) 65 kg but under 70 kg; (d) 70 kg but under 75 kg; (e) 75 kg but under 80 kg; (f) 80 kg and over.

   Use the five-barred gate system to allocate the recruits to classes and then write out the list of classes showing the numbers in each class. What does this tell you about the weight of recruits?

3. The wages paid to 30 hotel staff in a year are given as follows in £ sterling:

1785	2250	3860	2540	3275
3060	2036	3570	8250	3500
4600	6285	3160	3850	2900

4050	3850	2350	1985	3760
3658	2950	4175	3125	4250
7250	4850	4145	2360	4350

Arrange them in five classes; (a) under £2000; (b) £2000–£2999; (c) £3000–£3999; (d) £4000–£4999; (e) £5000 and over, using the five-barred gate system. Then write out a table showing the numbers in each class.

4. The ages in completed years of blood donors at a blood transfusion centre on a particular morning were as follows:

21	27	36	23	42	56	64
22	20	25	26	31	25	36
63	27	22	56	24	47	64

30	64	29	21	43	36	40
28	37	42	43	33	49	38
54	36	63	48	22	27	24
28	29	30	55	52	23	46

One further donor was aged 62. Classify these donors into age groups, 5 years to a group, starting with the group aged 20–24 years.

31.3   Tabulation

After data has been classified the results must usually be made available to those interested in some suitable presentation. One of the simplest methods of presentation is in tabular form; the data are presented in a table which sets out clearly the results of the inquiry. Countless tables are published in official publications such as the *United Kingdom Monthly Digest of Statistics*, the *Annual Abstract of Statistics*, the *Balance of Payments Pink Book* and the *National Income and Expenditure Blue Book*.

When presenting tables, it is usual to follow the lay-out given in Fig. 31.1 and described in the notes below it. Table 31.1 then shows a typical table.

Notes

(i) A table should always have a clear title, which states exactly what the information within the table sets out to show.

(ii) Unless it is obvious, the left-hand column heading will describe what

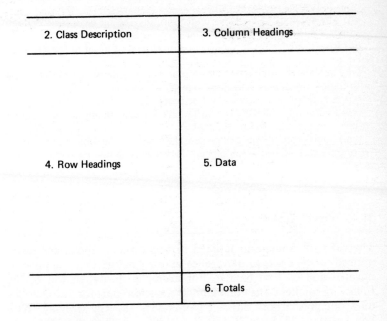

1. TITLE

2. Class Description	3. Column Headings
4. Row Headings	5. Data
	6. Totals

7. Footnotes

8. Source notes

Fig. 31.1. A general plan for tabular presentation.

Table 31.1. Membership of working-men's clubs.

Membership	Number of clubs
Under 200	68
200–499	185
500–999	1027
1000–1499	130
1500–1999	27
Over 2000	10
Total	1447

Footnote: Working-men's clubs are those excluding variety clubs.
Source Note: Workers' Gazette, Issue 2079.

is listed in the column below. For example, a table of industrial production might indicate at the top 'Type of Industry', and below this heading the various industries would be listed.

(iii) The columns of statistics under scrutiny should have clear column headings indicating what the columns represent.

(iv) Row headings for the collected data should be listed in the left-hand column.

(v) The data themselves should appear at (5), ordered according to the information which it is desired to extract.

(vi) Any totals necessary should be presented.

(vii) Footnotes, which explain variations or points of importance, should be given immediately below the table.

(viii) Sources should be given where the origin of the table is some other set of published statistics, and acknowledgements should be made if necessary.

31.4   Simple Tables

The rules of tabulation outlined in Section 31.3 above are easily applied to some sets of data, since by their nature they are uncomplicated and easy to handle. For example, the tabulation of the following catches of fish in a United Kingdom port for 1–7 October does not present any difficulties: Sunday, 187 kg; Monday, 2008 kg; Tuesday, 2775 kg; Wednesday, 1090 kg; Thursday, 2050 kg; Friday, 1720 kg; Saturday, 1928 kg. Table 31.2 below is a simple way of presenting this information more effectively.

Table 31.2. Catches of fish—1–7 October.

Day	Weight caught (kg)
Sunday	187
Monday	2008
Tuesday	2775
Wednesday	1090
Thursday	2050
Friday	1720
Saturday	1928
Total	11 758

31.5   Exercises: Simple Tabulation

1. Gas consumption in millions of therms is given as follows in a report of a nationalised body: 1st quarter, 6197; 2nd quarter, 4611; 3rd quarter, 3882; 4th quarter, 9639. Present this information in tabular form to bring out the total annual consumption.

2. The following information from an agricultural research project refers to: (a) cows and heifers in milk; (b) cows in calf but not in milk; (c) heifers in calf with first calf; (d) bulls; (e) all other cattle and calves. Present the data, given in thousands, to show the information in tabular form, and the total of this type of livestock. The figures are:

(a) 8756 (b) 1218 (c) 889 (d) 48 (e) 12 726.

3. A trade journal gives the following figures for sales of floorcoverings: (a) refers to carpets and rugs and (b) to linoleum and plastics. You are asked to round off the figures in each case to thousands of square metres, and present them in a table showing the sales of each type, the total quarterly sales and the total annual sales. The figures are: 1st quarter, (a) 38 474 353 square metres, (b) 19 284 852 square metres; 2nd quarter, (a) 37 891 453 square metres, (b) 16 658 391 square metres; 3rd quarter, (a) 41 884 723 square metres, (b) 14 686 948 square metres; 4th quarter, (a) 38 816 849 square metres, (b) 24 326 824 square metres.

4. Exports are listed in five categories. These are (a) Foods, beverages and tobacco; (b) Fuels; (c) Industrial materials; (d) Finished manufactures; (e) Other transactions. You are asked to round the figures off to the nearest £m and present them in tabular form for Year 1 and Year 2 to bring out the annual totals. The figures are: (a) Year 1 £3 094 276 153, Year 2 £4 993 463 218; (b) Year 1 £1 724 858 300, Year 2 £5 652 721 494; (c) Year 1 £6 239 434 721, Year 2 £8 738 346 829; (d) Year 1 £4 174 059 628, Year 2 £6 386 995 240; (e) Year 1 £424 736 284, Year 2 £595 106 396.

31.6 More Complex Tables

Simple tables of the type described above appear every day in newspapers and magazines. A more advanced type of table presents the simple material in table form, but then adds further statistics calculated from the simple statistics. These are called **derived statistics** because they are derived from the original data. They often take the form of averages, or percentages. Consider the following example:

Example 31.2. The 400 candidates in a particular examination were awarded marks as follows: 17 achieved more than 90%, 24 were given marks between 81% and 90%; 42 were in the group 71–80, 108 in the 61–70 group and 18 in the 51–60 group; 128 scored marks between 41 and 50, 38 had marks in the 31–40 group and 25 scored 30 or less marks. Show these marks in tabular form, and also the percentage of candidates in each group of marks.

The table looks as follows:

Examination Results

Marks out of 100	Number of candidates	Percentage of candidates
Over 90	17	4.25
81–90	24	6.0
71–80	42	10.5
61–70	108	27.0
51–60	18	4.5
41–50	128	32.0
31–40	38	9.5
30 or less	25	6.25
Total	400	100.0

Note: Since there are 400 candidates the percentage of each group is found as follows, using the 'over 90' group as an example: 17 students out of 400 were in this group. As a percentage this is:

$$\frac{17}{400} \times 100$$
$$= \frac{17}{4} \times 1 \qquad \text{(cancelling by 100)}$$
$$= 4.25\%$$

In fact, each of the numbers of candidates, when divided by 4, gives us the percentage of candidates, in this simple example.

31.7 Cumulative Frequency Tables

A table such as that shown in Example 31.2 is sometimes called a 'frequency distribution' because it shows how frequently an item of a particular size appears in the statistics. It is sometimes helpful to have a 'cumulative frequency' column, as shown in Example 31.2. Here the examining body may have a policy which says that only half the candidates at most can be allowed to pass the examinations and become fully qualified. Where does this point occur? Rewriting the table, with extra columns, to give both the cumulative frequency and the cumulative percentages, we have:

Examination Results

Marks out of 100	Frequency	Cumulative frequency	Percentage of candidates	Cumulative percentage
over 90	17	17	4.25	4.25
81–90	24	41	6.0	10.25
71–80	42	83	10.5	20.75
61–70	108	191	27.0	47.75
51–60	18	209	4.5	52.25
41–50	128	337	32.0	84.25
31–40	38	375	9.5	93.75
30 or less	25	400	6.25	100.0
Total	400	400	100.0	100.0

Since only half the candidates (200) or 50% are to be allowed to qualify the pass mark must be somewhere in the 51–60 mark range: 9 out of the 18 candidates in this range are to be allowed to pass, so the pass mark will be decided by looking at the distribution of marks in this group.

31.8 Exercises on More Complex Tables

1. A professional organisation has 10 000 candidates sitting for its final examinations. Of these 3 scored 100%, 195 scored 90–99%, 286 scored 80–89%, 894 scored 70–79%, 1859 scored 60–69%, 1956 scored 50–59%, 2553 scored 40–49% and 2250 scored less than 40%. Four candidates were taken ill and their cases will be reviewed separately. Arrange these figures in a table showing the numbers of students in each group, and the percentage of candidates in each group (correct to one decimal place).

2. Weekly turnover for 40 shops in a pedestrian precinct is found to be as below. Arrange these in a table using classes of 'under £2500', £2500–4999, £5000–7499, £7500–9999 and £10 000 or over. Also show in your table the percentage of shops in each group (correct to one decimal place). Turnover (£):

240	346	7215	6584	989	2100
1370	1475	4800	17 250	5500	4975
2650	3800	2980	7500	15 900	2950
1880	4860	13 500	3350	1925	3290
3450	4940	8500	1820	4375	17 000
1224	25 000	4950	1840	32 000	1775
2960	1700	1416	7790		

3. The wages (in £s) paid to 50 women in a factory in a particular week are given as follows:

£	£	£	£	£
41	42	52	44	72
57	56	48	45	46
69	38	72	49	47
51	28	50	56	44
48	55	44	82	45
49	73	46	74	28
54	48	47	48	72
48	52	49	36	75
66	55	69	52	46
69	53	84	60	56

Group the data into seven classes starting with the 20–29 group, and present the results in tabular form, including the percentage of women in each wage group. Why would it be wrong to specify classes as 30–40, 40–50, 50–60, etc.?

4. An earnings survey reveals that earnings (in £) per hour in a certain works were as below. You are asked to present the information as a table grouped into eight classes, starting with the £51–£60 class. Include in your table a cumulative frequency column.

54	73	91	69	100
72	84	93	95	100
62	58	74	67	120
99	81	96	102	120
64	74	99	120	76
86	94	65	75	66
77	82	102	106	130
88	105	124	124	106
79	106	78	130	79
97	106	89	107	89

31.9 Mental Arithmetic Test

1. 3584 × 9 =

2. 20 756 + 32 165 + 72 814 =

3. What is one third of 27 840?

4. 7.25 ÷ 0.5 =

5. 3000 × 400 × 600 =

6. $\frac{3}{8} + \frac{3}{4} + \frac{2}{3}$ =

7. What is the average score of a batsman who scores 27, 15, 29, 112 and 2?

8. What is 15% of £450?

9. 3 items cost £7.50. How much for 5?

10. An office block has a rateable value of £6400. What will the rates be at 30p in the £1?

11. What is the lowest common multiple of 2, 3 and 5?

12. How many millimetres in 12.75 metres?

13. Round off 27 924 to the nearest thousand

14. How many posts are required to support a straight fence of 30 m if the panels of fencing are 2 m wide?

15. £1 = 2000 lire. What shall I pay in sterling for 12 tyres at 16 000 lire each?

16. A penny rate in a town brings in £50 000. What will be the rate charged to raise funds for a swimming pool which is to cost £600 000?

17. What is the surface area of all the sides of a cube, which has a side of 3 cm?

18. Round off 16 500 000 to the nearest million

19. Express $27\frac{1}{2}$% as a fraction

20. A man leaves half his property to his wife, one third to his eldest son and his three other children divide the rest equally. What will each of these three children receive if the total estate is £54 000?

32
Pictorial Representation of Statistical Data

32.1 Introduction

It is generally accepted that pictures, diagrams and graphs are convenient methods of conveying simple ideas of a statistical nature, even to those who are largely uninterested in statistics as a science. Frequent use of pictures, diagrams and graphs is made on television, in the press and in magazines to pass on information relating to the cost of living, the level of unemployment, the cost of building society mortgages, etc.

This chapter deals with some of the more regularly used pictures and diagrams, whilst the slightly more complicated matter of graphs forms the subject of Chapter 33.

32.2 Pictograms

Pictograms are the simplest pictorial representations. Simple outline figures are used to represent quantities or values. For example, if the statistics relate to the changing level of unemployment over 10 years, the pictogram could be drawn as a number of human outlines, each one representing a given level of registered unemployed. Similarly, Fig. 32.1 illustrates the population of developing countries by income groups, with each human figure representing 100 million people.

A more complex pictogram, which includes both pictures and numerical data, is shown in Fig. 32.3.

Care must be taken when designing pictograms that a false impression is not created. For example, where the height of an illustration is used to depict increasing quantities, the area of the

	Total population (in millions)
Low-income countries *Less than US$ 265 per capita*	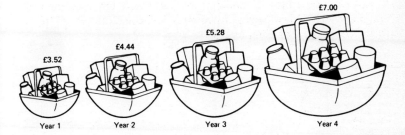 1,132
Lower middle-income countries *US$ 265–520 per capita*	292
Intermediate middle-income countries *US$ 521–1,075 per capita*	386
Upper middle-income countries *US$ 1,076–2,000 per capita*	121

Fig. 32.1. Developing countries: population by income groups.

(Reproduced by courtesy of Finance and Development)

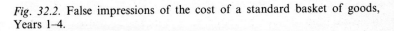

Fig. 32.2. False impressions of the cost of a standard basket of goods, Years 1–4.

diagram also changes, but not in the same proportion. An unscrupulous presenter might take advantage of this to convey a false impression. Fig. 32.2 illustrates the difficulty, with the basket for Year 4 appearing to be much more than twice as large as the basket for Year 1.

The tendency of diagrams and graphs to mislead is a problem which we must always bear in mind with pictorial representation.

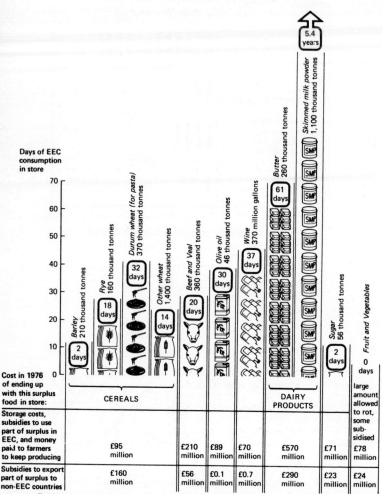

Fig. 32.3. Food mountains and wine lakes under the Common Agricultural Policy.

(Courtesy of *Which?* magazine)

32.3 Exercises: Pictograms

1. The following data have to be displayed in pictorial form. Choose an appropriate symbol and draw a pictogram.

Colour television sets in use
in United Kingdom (thousands)

1966	0
1968	100
1970	500
1972	1300
1974	6800
1976	9500
1978	10 800
1980	13 000

2. The volume of traffic can be measured by discovering the number of vehicles per mile of roads. A comparison of traffic densities in a number of countries produced the following results:

Country	Number of vehicles per road-mile
United Kingdom	61
West Germany	51
Netherlands	51
Italy	49
Belgium	36
France	26
Sweden	20

Using a motor vehicle as a symbol to represent every 10 cars, draw a pictogram to illustrate the set of statistics.

3. The profits of a famous bank are used as follows:

How the profits were used.	£m
Taxation payable	133
Dividends to shareholders	23
Minority shareholders	12
Kept in reserves	100
	£m268

Using piles of pennies as your symbol, illustrate how many pence in each £1 are used for each of these purposes.

4. Using a road sign directing traffic to the M1 Motorway as your symbol, with each road sign standing for 250 kilometres of motorway, draw a pictogram to illustrate the growth of motorways as shown in the table below.

Motorway growth in the United Kingdom (kilometres)

1964	500
1968	900
1972	1500
1976	2750
1980	3200

(*Source: Annual Abstract of Statistics*)

32.4   Bar Charts

Bar charts seek to relate information to the horizontal or vertical length of a bar or thick line. They are of two main types: those which compare statistics for a given period of time and those which compare them over a succession of periods.

For example, in Fig. 32.4 an ice-cream firm has investigated the popularity of different flavours of ice-cream by collecting statistics about the value of sales in a given week in one particular seaside resort. The statistics collected and presented in a bar chart in this way might lead to a decision to reduce the variety of flavours offered, or to an advertising campaign to promote less popular flavours. The preparation of such a chart presents a few problems, including:

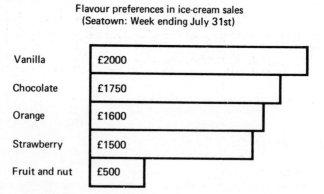

Fig. 32.4. A bar chart.

(a) Scale. A scale must be chosen which enables the graphics designer to represent the data clearly on the size of paper to be used.

(b) Length of bar. The length of bar in each case must be calculated to represent the correct fraction of the full scale chosen. Thus the £1750 bar in the diagram must be $\frac{1750}{2000} = \frac{7}{8}$ of the length of the longest bar.

(c) Shading, colour, etc. In some bar charts it might be desirable to pick out the bars in particular cross-hatchings or colours to present a clearer picture.

(d) Title, source details, etc. A suitable title, explanation of source material and date or dates (if required) should be added to the diagram, and the lettering and layout should be stylish and well-presented.

In Fig. 32.5 the vertical bar chart shown gives a clear indication of the number of vehicles in use in Great Britain over the given time range.

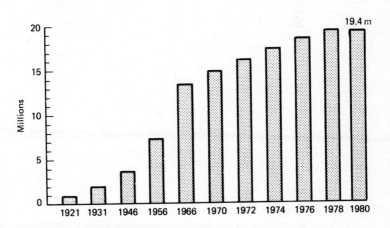

Fig. 32.5. A vertical bar chart: vehicles in use in Great Britain, 1921–80.

32.5 Percentage Bar Charts

A percentage bar chart is one in which the total body of statistics collected (100 per cent) is divided up into its component parts to show each part *as a percentage of the whole*. This is most useful where the total set of statistics has some special significance. This special method of presentation is often used in profit statements to show how the profits made have been allocated. For example, taking each £1 of profit it might be that 52 pence went in corporation tax, 12 pence to ordinary shareholders, 8 pence to preference shareholders, 5 pence to minority shareholders, and 23 pence into general reserves. Such a set of statistics could easily be displayed using a percentage bar chart.

In Fig. 32.6 the annual expenditure of an average household is broken down into its percentage component elements of expenditure.

Item	£	% (to nearest 0.5%)
Food	1 225	41
Housing	375	12.5
Heat and light	300	10
Transport	300	10
Entertainment	150	5
Clothes	150	5
Other	500	16.5
Total	3 000	100

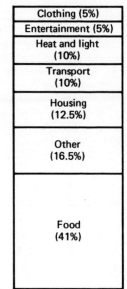

Fig. 32.6. A percentage bar chart: annual expenditure of an average household.

32.6   Exercises: Bar Charts

1. In four years the investment funds used by United Kingdom companies were obtained from the following sources:

	Profits ploughed back (£m)	Bank borrowing (£m)	Overseas borrowing (£m)	Other (£m)
Year 1	4000	1000	1000	500
Year 2	5000	3000	2000	500
Year 3	7000	5000	3000	1000
Year 4	8000	4000	3500	2000

Draw a vertical bar diagram to illustrate the figures, and show the total invested in each of the four years.

2. Figures for one-year's world fibre output in millions of tonnes were as follows:

Country or bloc	Natural fibre	Man-made fibre
United Kingdom	0.5	1.0
Other West Europe	1.5	2.0
USA	1.5	3.5
Communist Bloc	2.0	5.0
Third World	3.5	4.5

Draw a bar chart to illustrate these outputs. Use shading or colours to distinguish natural and man-made fibres.

3. Reductions in pupil-teacher ratios are shown in the following table. Draw a bar chart to illustrate the changes.

Pupils per teacher in primary schools
(England and Wales only)

Year	Number of pupils per teacher
1921	48
1931	43.5
1951	39
1961	36
1971	31.5
1981	27

(*Note:* In 1941 wartime disruption prevented the collection of statistics.)

4. A multinational company selling soft drinks made 'profits' of £350 million last year. Of this £175 million was used to pay its employees; £43.75 million was taken by the Government as taxation; £77 million was paid in interest and dividends to those who provided the company's capital and the rest was reinvested in new plant, etc. Calculate those parts as a percentage of the total and draw a percentage bar chart to illustrate the statistics.

32.7 Histograms

These are diagrams which display frequency distributions. Here a vertical block is drawn to represent each class interval. Provided the horizontal scales are equal (i.e. the blocks are of equal width), the height of each of the blocks is able to represent the frequency.

The greater the frequency of the group, the higher the block. Where class intervals are equal, as in Fig. 32.7, the width of the block is immaterial so long as all are the same width and may be chosen to suit the space available. The rules for drawing a histogram with uniform class intervals are as follows:

(a) Select a width of class interval which is appropriate for the size of paper to be used and the number of rectangles (class intervals) to be drawn. The class intervals will be marked along the horizontal axis and the frequency per class interval up the vertical axis.

(b) At the midpoint of each class interval, mark in a height above the horizontal axis which is proportional to the frequency of that particular class interval. Draw a horizontal line at this height equal to the width of the class interval.

(c) Now draw in the sides of the rectangles by joining up the ends of these lines to the horizontal axis. The result is a series of adjacent rectangles. The areas of the rectangles are proportional to the frequencies of their respective classes. In this particular case we can see that the total earnings are represented by the total area of the histogram.

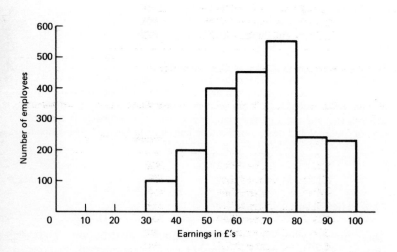

Fig. 32.7. A histogram: weekly earnings of engineering apprentices and craftsmen.

32.8   Exercises: Histograms

1. Employees' wages in the New Town area are shown below for the first week in June. Draw a histogram to illustrate the data.

Class range	Percentage of population with earnings in the group
Over £20 and under £30	4.5
Over £30 and under £40	7.5
Over £40 and under £50	15.5
Over £50 and under £60	20.0
Over £60 and under £70	34.0
Over £70 and under £80	12.0
Over £80 and under £90	5.0
Over £90 and under £100	1.5
	100.0

2. Property values in Seatown were found to be as follows in a survey:

Price range	Number in class
£12 000 and under £15 000	250
£15 000 and under £18 000	3500
£18 000 and under £21 000	4500
£21 000 and under £24 000	3500
£24 000 and under £27 000	1750
£27 000 and under £30 000	125

Draw a histogram to illustrate these statistics.

3. The price of motor vehicles sold by a distributor in one year were as follows:

Price	Number in Class
£2000 and under £3000	360
£3000 and under £4000	400
£4000 and under £5000	440
£5000 and under £6000	160
£6000 and under £7000	120
£7000 and under £8000	80
£8000 and under £9000	60

Draw a histogram to illustrate the data.

4. Cattle auctioned in a country market fetched the following prices:

Price range	Number in class
£80–£99.99	120
£100–£119.99	150
£120–£139.99	75
£140–£159.99	250
£160–£179.99	130
£180–£199.99	35

Draw a histogram to illustrate this data.

32.9   Pie Charts

One of the simplest methods to represent the way in which a whole statistical collection breaks down into its component parts is to use the 'pie' diagram. A pie is a circular culinary delicacy, and we are familiar from childhood with the advantages to be enjoyed by securing a larger slice of pie than other members of the family. The pie chart depicts the component parts of any set of statistical data as slices of pie.

The complete circle represents the whole set of data. Any subdivisions within the set are then shown by subdividing the circle in proportion. In Fig. 32.8, for example, the 'One-person pensioner index' gives a weighting of 442 parts in 1000 to food. The General Index, by contrast, gives food a weighting of 278 parts in 1000, since food does not form as large a proportion of total expenditure in general households. What share of the pie diagram should be given to 'Food' in these two pie-charts? There are 360° in a circle, and therefore the calculations are as follows:

$$\text{Pension Index:} \quad \text{Food} = \frac{442}{1000} \times 360°$$
$$= \underline{\underline{159.1°}}$$

$$\text{General Index:} \quad \text{Food} = \frac{278}{1000} \times 360°$$
$$= \underline{\underline{100.1°}}$$

In Fig. 32.8 the 'food' slices of the total pies have therefore been drawn with 159.1° and 100.1° respectively.

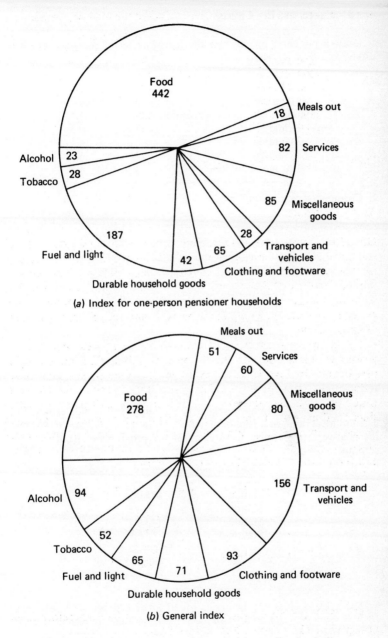

(a) Index for one-person pensioner households

(b) General index

Fig. 32.8. Pie charts showing the weights used in retail price indices.
(Source: Economic Progress Report)

32.10   Exercises: Pie Charts

1. Draw a pie chart to illustrate the following set of statistics, which is taken from *Social Trends*.

Families in Great Britain, 19. .

All families	100
Families with no dependent children	51.9
1 child	20.5
2 children	16.5
3 children	6.9
4 or more children	4.2

2. Consumers' expenditure in 19. . is given as follows, in £ million:

Food	12 500
Drink and tobacco	7500
Housing, fuel and light	8300
Clothing	5100
Cars and motor cycles	6500
Durable household goods	3600
Other goods	4500
Other services	3000
	51 000

Draw a pie diagram to illustrate the figures provided.

3. The following information relates to the number of people expected to listen to local radio in a 12-month period. Draw a pie diagram to illustrate the relative attractiveness to listeners of the programmes from the four stations.

Expected radio audiences

Station 1	125 000
Station 2	120 000
Station 3	140 000
Station 4	15 000
	400 000

4. The average student's income is found to be £20 per week, of which £3.50 is spent on books, £8.50 on food, £2.20 on liquid refreshment, £3.20 on materials, stationery, etc. The rest is unclassified, covering a huge range of items required by individual students. Draw a pie chart to illustrate this expenditure.

32.11   Conclusion about the Presentation of Data

In Chapter 31 and again in this chapter, reference has been made to the dangers that statistics may be distorted either deliberately or inadvertently. Diagrams, charts and graphs are amongst the easiest of statistical tools to use dishonestly, and since they are more easily understood than other presentations they may therefore delude a larger number of people. Deliberate distortion aside, enthusiastic individuals with a point of view to express which they believe to be in the public interest may unwittingly bring biased, incorrectly presented data forward in the genuine belief that it is correct. You should appraise all your own work critically, and also the presentations put before you by others, to detect shortcomings.

32.12   Mental Arithmetic Test

1. $72\,324 \div 12 =$

2. $47.55 \div 0.005 =$

3. $3\frac{3}{5} \div 2\frac{1}{4} =$

4. Round off 7365 correct to the nearest hundred

5. $380 \times 700 =$

6. What is the volume of a steel block 1 m × 2 m × 30 cm?

7. What did a furniture retailer pay for a cabinet sold for £600 after being marked up 50% on cost price?

8. Three students are 17 years old and two are 22 years old. What is their average age?

9. A pound is worth 8.2 francs. What will a British tourist receive for £50?

10. A theatre has 1460 seats. The average seat costs £3.50. How much is taken if the house is full?

11. What is the simple interest on £450 for 3 years at 9%?

12. How many seconds in $3\frac{1}{2}$ minutes?

13. A bicycle wheel 63 cm in diameter rotates 100 times. How far has the bicycle travelled, in metres (use $\pi = 3\frac{1}{7}$)?

14. A salesman earns a basic salary of £200 per month and a commission of 5% on sales of £4880. What is his total pay for the month?

15. Change $\frac{13}{40}$ to a percentage

16. What will be the profit on 60 items purchased for £4.50 each and sold for £6.25 each?

17. A wall 16 m long by 2 m high is to be painted at £1.50 per square metre. What will it cost?

18. An engineer is paid for 45 hours work at £2.20 per hour. What is his total wage?

19. A car costs £1500 deposit and 36 monthly payments of £80 each. What is the total HP price?

20. Alice is to get twice as much as Harry, who is to get twice as much as John in the division of an inheritance between them. The sum to be divided is £4900. How much will Alice get?

33
Graphs

33.1 Introduction

Pictograms, bar charts and histograms are all ways of presenting data in a form which can be easily understood. A graph is another way of presenting data. It displays the relationship between two sets of data, one of which is varying with the other.

Suppose we think of sales of a certain product during the year: the months will be changing—January, February, March, etc.—in the usual way, but the sales will be changing month by month. The changes may be seasonal. Thus we shall sell more umbrellas and raincoats in January than in June in the United Kingdom, while in Australia the situation will be reversed. One of the variables, months, is independent of the other, but the sales is a dependent variable, it depends upon which month we are talking about what the sales will be.

Graphs are widely used in the press, in business life and on television to illustrate a huge range of data.

33.2 Constructing a Graph

Graphs are drawn on squared paper, since this makes it very easy to *'plot'* the points on the paper which are to be used to illustrate the observed data. To plot these points we need some starting places, and these are called **axes**. They are lines drawn on the graph paper at right angles to one another. The horizontal axis is called the 'x axis' and the vertical axis is called the 'y axis'. The point where they cut one another is called the **'origin'** O. They are drawn in a little way from the edge of the paper so that we can label the axes with some simple explanation that will assist understanding. We might for example, label the x axis 'Months' and the y axis 'Sale of umbrellas (thousands)'. Each axis is also labelled with the units being used, and a scale is chosen to enable the full range of data to be shown, as large as possible. In Fig. 33.1 we have 12 months in the year so we have to choose a scale which will enable us to show the 12 months across the *x* axis. The sales of umbrellas are shown up to 100 000. If sales had been one million umbrellas, we should have needed a different scale (or a piece of paper ten times as big).

To plot a point on the graph we position it in relation to the two axes. For example, if the sales in August are 10 000 umbrellas, we can plot this by starting from August on the x axis and 10 000 on the y axis. These two pieces of information, when paired off together on the map, give a unique point, which can be marked with a dot, or a tiny cross indicating the spot where the two statistics intersect. Every point on a graph can be identified as different from all other points by referring it to the two axes. Thus the point labelled P in Fig. 33.1 can only mean that in April (a notoriously showery month) sales of umbrellas were 70 000.

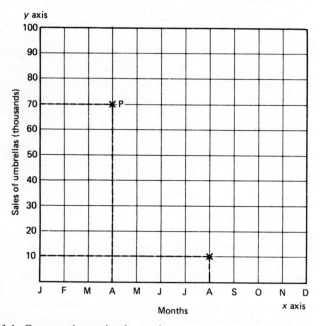

Fig. 33.1. Constructing a simple graph.

Notes

(i) The axes are drawn at right angles to one another, meeting at O, the origin of the graph. (In this graph it is the same as J for January.)

(ii) The axes are labelled with the name of the variables ('Months' and 'Sales of umbrellas') and the units being used (thousands on Y axis).

(iii) The points are plotted on the graph by using the values given in the table supplied or found in the statistical enquiry which is being carried out. Each pair of related facts, such as the fact that in August 10 000 umbrellas were sold gives a unique point on the graph. The point may be marked by a tiny dot, but preferably by a small cross made by two short lines inter-secting at the exact spot. In such graphs the points are clearly picked out, and the curves joining up the points may be discontinuous to give greater emphasis (see *Fig. 33.2.*).

33.3 Simple Graphs

The simplest form of graph merely presents the data in pictorial form rather like the bar charts and pictograms referred to in Chapter 32. A **time series**, such as a temperature chart showing a record of a patient's temperature over a period of time, or a sales chart such as the one shown in Fig. 32.2, presents a simple picture of the changes as they occur. We can tell how sales change from month to month, by a glance at the chart.

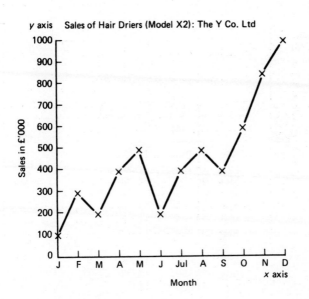

Fig. 33.2. A simple time series graph.

Note: The use of a discontinuous line in this sort of chart pinpoints the actual sales figures for each month, and clearly shows the rise and fall of sales.

33.4 Exercises: Simple Graphs

1. The following information relates to the total sales (value) of a supermarket chain over a 12-month period. Using a suitable scale record the information in the form of a graph.

Month	Sales (£)
1	270 000
2	200 000
3	240 000
4	300 000
5	320 000
6	400 000
7	410 000
8	400 000
9	420 000
10	440 000
11	410 000
12	500 000

2. The following sales for the year were achieved by the two departments of a town-centre store. Plot these on a graph, using a suitable scale.

Sales of Supertraders Plc

	Groceries (£)	Greengroceries (£)
Jan.	28 250	12 750
Feb.	24 250	11 500
Mar.	36 500	16 500
Apr.	33 750	14 750
May	34 500	15 500
Jun.	37 250	18 000
Jul.	25 000	13 250
Aug.	28 750	14 500
Sep.	34 000	18 500
Oct.	42 500	20 250
Nov.	43 500	21 000
Dec.	56 000	23 500

3. Mechanical Parts Ltd make two models of a particular machine, the 'Junior' model and the 'Senior' model. Sales during the year are given below. You are asked to record these figures, *and total sales*, on a graph, labelling all parts of the graph as necessary.

Mechanical Parts Ltd: sales during year 19—

	Jan. (£)	Feb. (£)	Mar. (£)	Apr. (£)	May (£)	Jun. (£)
Junior	5000	5500	7000	8000	8500	9000
Senior	14 000	13 500	12 000	13 000	11 000	8000

	Jul. (£)	Aug. (£)	Sept. (£)	Oct. (£)	Nov. (£)	Dec. (£)
Junior	8500	7000	9500	10 000	10 500	12 000
Senior	8500	3500	4000	4500	4000	5000

33.5 Straight-line Graphs

The simple graph of sales in Fig. 33.2 rose and fell in line with quantity sold—it was a zigzag line. However, some graphs, where the data are in a special relationship, consist of straight lines. Such a graph arises where one set of data varies directly with changes in the other set of data.

For example, in Fig. 33.3 (a) the cost of a particular product is plotted against the number of units required, up to a total of 10. Each unit is £3.50, and there is a direct relation between the cost of a particular order and the number of units ordered. The result is a straight-line graph passing through the origin (since when no units are ordered there is nothing to pay).

Such a straight-line graph can be drawn by plotting a single point—for example, 8 units cost £28. The point thus plotted, when joined to the origin of the graph 0, goes through all the points where other costs can be found—for example, 3 units cost £10.50. If the straight line is extended it will continue to pass through all the points where numbers of units and costs are matched—for example, 10 units cost £35.

A straight-line graph of this sort can be used very easily as a ready reckoner. This particular straight-line graph can be used to read off the total cost of any number of units from 1 to 10. To do this we draw a horizontal line across from the number of units required (say 4 units) until it intercepts the graph. We then drop a

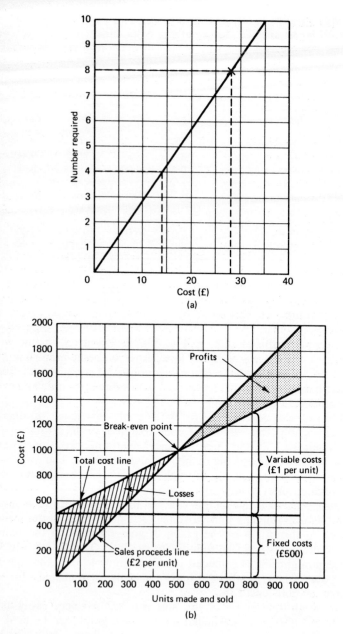

Fig. 33.3 (a) A straight-line graph used as a ready reckoner. (b) A break-even chart.

perpendicular from that point on to the price axis, where we find that 4 units cost £14 altogether.

Reading off values in this way is called **interpolation**—finding the intermediate terms in the known range of a series from the values already known. If we were to extend the straight line and find values outside the range already given, it would be called **extrapolation**.

Many straight-line graphs pass through the origin, where both variables are zero. For example, in Fig. 33.3(a) there is no charge if no units are purchased. *This is not always the case*, and a straight-line graph may intercept one of the axes at some point. In the break-even chart in Fig. 33.3(b) certain fixed costs of an output of a certain product are incurred before any output can be produced at all. This might include costs of jigs and tools to be used in manufacture, or design costs incurred before even a prototype product is produced. The cost of manufacture will therefore start with these fixed costs (£500 in the graph) and the other variable costs which vary directly with output must be borne in addition as output commences. The cost line therefore does not pass through the origin but intercepts the price axis at the £500 mark. By contrast, the proceeds from the sale of the output do start at the origin. Since selling price is fixed at a sufficiently high level to achieve a profit eventually, the 'sales proceeds' line is steeper than the cost line. The two lines therefore intersect at the break-even point. At this point the total costs incurred are covered by the sales proceeds and every unit sold after this point will yield a profit.

33.6 Exercises: Straight-line Graphs

1. (a) Labourers on a road gang earn £3 an hour. Draw a graph of the amounts earned using 15 hours, 30 hours and 45 hours worked as plotting points.

(b) Now read off from the graph how much will be earned for 42 hours' work.

2. (a) A farm worker earns £1.50 an hour. Draw a graph of earnings using 18, 36 and 54 hours worked as plotting points.

(b) Now calculate: (i) the amount earned for 37 hours worked; (ii) find out how many hours have been worked when his earnings are £67.50.

3. (a) A salesman receives 35p commission on every item he sells. Draw a graph to show his earnings up to maximum sales of 2000 items.

(b) Calculate what commission he receives when he sells 1750 units.

33.7   The Z Chart

A Z chart is so-called because when completed it looks like a capital Z. The chart is designed to show up three aspects on the same diagram:

(a) Current figures—for example, current sales or current output.

(b) Cumulative figures—for example, total sales or output to date this year.

(c) A moving annual total—which shows the total for the previous year.

Each month the annual total is increased by the current month's sales and reduced by deducting the sales of the same month a year ago. A typical set of figures is shown in Example 33.1 and the Z chart is drawn in Fig. 33.4.

(*Note:* The moving annual output shown in January is the total for February–December of the previous year and the January figure of the current year.)

Example 33.1

Output of refrigerator units: X Co. Ltd

Month	Output in units Last year	This year	Cumulative output	Moving annual output
Jan.	110	120	120	1655
Feb.	110	115	235	1660
Mar.	120	135	370	1675
Apr.	160	180	550	1695
May	150	145	695	1690
Jun.	115	140	835	1715
Jul.	125	125	960	1715
Aug.	140	135	1095	1710
Sep.	140	165	1260	1735
Oct.	155	185	1445	1765
Nov.	165	200	1645	1800
Dec.	155	190	1835	1835

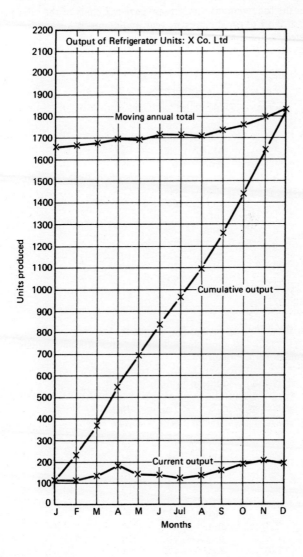

Fig. 33.4. The Z chart.

33.8   Exercises: Z Charts

1. From the following information prepare a Z chart of the sales performance of Alpha Ltd for the present year and comment on the year's results as revealed by the diagram.

	Sales (£'000)	
	Last year	*This year*
Jan.	56	75
Feb.	54	78
Mar.	58	82
Apr.	62	85
May	66	91
Jun.	66	93
Jul.	71	96
Aug.	73	98
Sep.	75	105
Oct.	78	108
Nov.	80	112
Dec.	81	115

2. From the following figures for output by the Heavy Components Co. Ltd draw up a Z chart showing the present year's production achievements, and comment on the diagram.

Output in units

	Last year	*This year*
Jan.	27	45
Feb.	24	43
Mar.	28	27
Apr.	40	15
May	42	0
Jun.	44	0
Jul.	33	0
Aug.	35	38
Sep.	46	58
Oct.	48	64
Nov.	50	72
Dec.	51	74

3. From the following information prepare a Z chart of the sales of Gargantua (Royston) Plc for the present year and comment on the company's sales performance.

Sales
(£m)

	Last year	This year
Jan.	26	38
Feb.	30	40
Mar.	32	42
Apr.	38	40
May	52	60
Jun.	58	66
Jul.	51	70
Aug.	60	81
Sept.	62	75
Oct.	38	39
Nov.	39	40
Dec.	32	38

33.9 Mental Arithmetic Test

1. $123 + 368 + 742 + 495 =$

2. $7246 - 3859 =$

3. $4275 \times 9 =$

4. $18\,720 \div 12 =$

5. $0.08 \times 0.02 =$

6. $0.08 \div 0.02 =$

7. How many millimetres in $2\frac{1}{2}$ metres?

8. What is the formula for the area of a circle?

9. What is the approximate temperature of a healthy human being in degrees Celsius?

10. What is the simple interest on £500 for 3 years at 12%?

11. What is the compound interest on £1000 for 2 years at 15%?

12. What shall I pay for 200 £1 shares selling at 94p per share?

13. How many minutes are there in $7\frac{1}{2}$ hours?

14. What is the cost per unit of a component, if 3000 units are made from brass costing £260 at a labour cost of £340?

15. Five houses are bought by a development company for a total of £80 000, and £16 000 is spent on repairs. They are then sold for £24 000 each. What profit was made?

16. What shall I pay for 4 packets of detergent at 64½p per packet?

17. Share up £9600 in the proportions 3:2:1.

18. What will be the profit on 40 items purchased for £12.50 each and sold for £15 each?

19. What is the hourly rate of pay of an employee who earns £84 for 40 hours?

20. A telephone call costs 4p for 10 seconds. If the call lasts 10 minutes, what is the charge for the call?

34
The Mean, Median and Mode

34.1 Measures of Central Tendency

Any statistical enquiry results in a mass of data. While each piece of information is of interest, its relation to the whole set of data is more important. Thus, in examining electric light bulbs to see how long they last, the fact that one out of 3000 went 'pop' the moment it was put into the lampholder is interesting, but is it very significant? If the other 2999 each burnt for more than 500 hours it would seem that this particular bulb was not typical of the whole group. A particular statistic therefore may prove to be of no significance. Similarly, the presentations of data using pictograms, bar charts, etc., while they display the statistics well, do not summarise the statistics in any way, or indicate which are more significant than the rest. To summarise data we need to average them in some way, and see how the actual data vary from the average figure.

Because these operations tend to reduce the significance of extreme values and stress the 'middle' ones, the processes are often referred to as **measures of central tendency**. In everyday life phrases like 'average attendance' or 'average score' are commonly used, and they do give a quick, clear impression of a particular situation. Thus the information that a batsman scored 1, 94, 72, 13, 8, 5, 7, 149, 186, 22 and 145 runs in matches played in the first two months of the cricket season is of great interest, but rather confusing. To say that his average score over 2 months was 63.8 gives a clearer picture of his ability. We have already studied simple averages and weighted averages in Chapter 13 of this book, so the reader will already be familiar with these simple 'measures of central tendency'.

Treating data in this fashion can be extremely useful. Where comparison has to be made between different sets of figures, it is more convenient to take a single (representative) figure from each set as the basis of comparison than to utilise every figure available. For example, a comparison of wage rates amongst the four largest United Kingdom car manufacturers would be exceptionally difficult if each worker's wage was included in the presentation. Instead, for comparison, a figure representative of each plant, trade or firm is taken.

The three most commonly used measures of central tendency are:

(a) The arithmetic mean
(b) The median
(c) The mode

Let us consider each of these in turn.

34.2 The Arithmetic Mean

This is the simple average most commonly used in everyday life and already considered in Chapter 13 of this book. It is what most people would understand when the word 'average' is mentioned. It is found by adding up the values of the variable (the scores in the cricketing example mentioned earlier) and dividing by the number of items (the innings played). A further instance is given in Example 34.1 below. It refers to the earnings of an insurance broker for the first 10 weeks of the financial year. The arithmetic mean is found by adding the set of earnings and dividing by the number in the set.

Example 34.1. Earnings of an insurance broker:

	19— Week ending	£
April	7	120
	14	100
	21	90
	28	160
May	5	140
	12	100
	19	110
	26	130
June	2	160
	9	110
Number of weeks	10	Total 1220

Clearly the mean earnings are £1220 ÷ 10 = £122 per week.

Information of this sort is called 'ungrouped data' to distinguish it from information which has been sorted out into a slightly more coherent form, in groups. Had this information, for example, been sorted out into groups in which the salary earned was recorded in groups of £50 each (£0–49, none; £50–99, 1; £100–159, 7; £150–199,

2) it would have presented different problems in finding the arithmetic mean.

In business statistics, as the data is only a part (sample) of all such data, we use the sign $\bar{x}$ to represent the arithmetic mean of the sample.

For ungrouped data a formula for the arithmetic mean would be

$$\bar{x} = \frac{\Sigma x}{n}$$

where $\bar{x}$ is the arithmetic mean, x is each of the measurements or values, n is the number of measurements or values, and Σ (sigma) means 'the sum of'.

(*Note:* by using Σ the notation $\frac{x_1 + x_2 + x_3 + x_4}{n}$ is avoided.)

Using this notation for Example 34.1, we have

$$\bar{x} = \frac{\Sigma x}{n}$$

$$= \frac{£1220}{10}$$

$$= £122$$

34.3   Exercises: Arithmetic Means of Simple Series

Using the formula given in Example 34.1 above, find the arithmetic mean of the following sets of statistics:

1. Electricity consumed during the quarter in a certain factory was as follows:

Jan.	27 284 units
Feb.	35 266 units
Mar.	41 928 units

Find the mean monthly consumption.

2. The ages of students attending an evening course, to the nearest year, are as follows: 17, 18, 18, 18, 19, 19, 22, 24, 25, 27, 27, 28, 38, 54 and 63. What is the mean age?

3. A library issues books as follows: Monday 742 books, Tuesday 1529 books, Wednesday 2472 books, Thursday 495 books and Friday 1246 books. Only 237 books were issued on Saturday. What is the mean issue per working day? (Answer correct to one decimal place.)

4. Five mills produce the following outputs of cloth in a particular week: 72 856 metres; 49 263 metres; 17 256 metres; 29 254 metres and 86 276 metres. What is the mean output?

5. An experimental crop of wheat from seven plots of land produces the following outputs:

(a) 224 kg	(e) 495 kg
(b) 330 kg	(f) 532 kg
(c) 75 kg	(g) 184 kg
(d) 176 kg	

What was the mean output?

34.4   The Arithmetic Mean from a Frequency Distribution

In a simple series the individual items may occur only once, and their frequency is therefore one. In a mass production world many business statistics involve frequencies greater than one. Thus a garage might sell 7 'Apollo' cars, 15 'Hermes' traveller models and 23 'St Christopher' touring vehicles. With such a frequency distribution the arithmetic mean must take into account not only the value of an item, but also the number of times that item occurs.

The formula must now become

$$\bar{x} = \frac{\Sigma f x}{n}$$

where $\bar{x}$ is the arithmetic mean, x the values of the individual items, f the frequency (i.e. the number of cases of each value), n the total number of items (i.e. the sum of the frequencies ($n = \Sigma f$)), and Σ 'the sum of'. This is illustrated in Example 34.2.

Example 34.2. What is the mean value of the policies sold by the XYZ agency, whose sales are given in the frequency distribution below (answer to nearest penny)?

Value of policy (£) (x)	Number of policies sold (f)	Product (f × x)
10	165	1650
20	290	5800
30	105	3150
40	92	3680
$n = \Sigma f =$ 652		$\Sigma f x = 14\,280$

$$\bar{x} = \frac{\Sigma f x}{n}$$

$$= \frac{£14\,280}{652}$$

$$= £21.90$$

34.5   Exercises: The Arithmetic Mean from a Frequency Distribution

1. A fish farm has 120 ponds. Find the mean surface area of the ponds from the following frequency distribution (answer correct to one decimal place).

Surface area (square metres)	Number of ponds
65	25
70	40
75	28
80	14
85	13

2. The following table illustrates the annual bonus to be paid by a firm to a number of its employees. What is the mean value of the bonus paid?

Bonus (£)	Number of employees
900	7
800	15
600	8

3. The weight of timber taken from 48 trees is as shown below. Arrange the information in a frequency distribution and calculate the mean weight of timber (answer to the nearest kg).

Weight of timber (kg)

1000	1200	1000	1100	1400	1300
1200	1200	1000	1100	1100	1000
1100	1200	1100	1400	1300	1100
1200	1300	1400	1500	1000	1400
1400	1100	1200	1300	1400	1200
1300	1200	1400	1300	1100	1100
1200	1300	1200	1200	1100	1200
1100	1200	1200	1300	1300	1000

4. Below are listed the sums taken at a box office for tickets sold one morning. From the information draw up a frequency distribution and from it find the mean price per ticket sold (correct to the nearest penny).

£1.60	£2.50	£2.50	£3.50
£2.50	£1.60	£3.50	£3.50
£3.50	£2.50	£1.60	£1.00
£5.00	£5.00	£3.50	£3.50
£1.60	£3.50	£3.50	£2.50

34.6 The Median

The median is defined as the value of the middle item of a distribution, when the items are arranged in ascending order of size.

For ungrouped data the method of calculation of the median is very simple. The procedure is:

(a) Arrange the data in order of size, i.e. so that they run from the smallest to the largest. Such an arrangement is called an **array**.

(b) Find the middle item. The formula for finding the middle item is

$$\frac{n + 1}{2}$$

where n is the number of items. Hence where there are seven items

$$\frac{n + 1}{2} = \frac{7 + 1}{2} = 4$$

The fourth item would give us the medium value. We know this to be the case since in an array of seven there are three items on either side of the fourth one—it is therefore in the middle.

Where the number of items is even it is not possible to isolate an actual item which is the middle one. Thus where there are eight items in an array

$$\frac{n + 1}{2} = \frac{8 + 1}{2} = 4\tfrac{1}{2}$$

The middle item is now the $4\tfrac{1}{2}$th item and it is necessary to find the average of the fourth and fifth items to find the median value.

(c) Find the value of the middle item.

Note: Statisticians sometimes refer to the 'median' item. Strictly speaking this is not correct. The median is, by definition, the *value* of the middle item in an array. In an array with an odd number of items the median value will coincide with the middle item in the array. In an array with an even number of items it will be the average of the two middle items. The danger is that a student may say that in an array of 27 numbers, 14 is the median. It is of course the *value* of the fourteenth number in that array that is the median.

Example 34.3. The salaries after tax of seven bank employees (per month) are £178, £220, £230, £150, £280, £275, £270. Find the median salary.

(a) Arrange the data in order of value:

1	2	3	4	5	6	7
£150	178	220	230	270	275	280

(b) Find the middle item. With seven items this is the fourth

$$\frac{n + 1}{2} = \frac{7 + 1}{2} = 4$$

(c) Find the median value. The value of the fourth item is £230.

$$\therefore \quad \text{median value} = \underline{\underline{£230}}$$

If an extra salary of £290 were added there would be no single median item. It would then be necessary to find the average value of items 4 and 5.

Example 34.4. The monthly salaries after tax of eight bank employees are given as £178, £220, £230, £150, £280, £275, £270, £290; find the median salary.

(a) Arrange the data in order of size:

1	2	3	4	5	6	7	8
£150	178	220	230	270	275	280	290

(b) Find the middle item:

$$\frac{n + 1}{2} = \frac{9}{2} = 4\tfrac{1}{2}$$

There is no single item: 4 and 5 are 'in the middle'.

(c) The median value will be the average of these items

$$= \frac{£230 + 270}{2}$$

$$= \frac{£500}{2}$$

$$= \underline{\underline{£250}}$$

34.7 Exercises: The Median

1. Calculate the median life of an electric light bulb based on the following nine examples: (a) 236 hours, (b) 11 hours, (c) 248 hours, (d) 25 hours, (e) 1294 hours, (f) 728 hours, (g) 5 hours, (h) 1 hour, (i) 483 hours.

2. Farmer Brown's hens laid as follows in one year: Lucy 236 eggs; Speckly 320 eggs; Mary 156 eggs; Crooked Leg 184 eggs; Dainty 156 eggs; Brownie

84 eggs; Polynesia 203 eggs; Margaret 225 eggs. Calculate the median output.

3. The orders received from the representatives of Cosmetics Ltd are as follows for the month of July:

	£		£
Mr A	8 540	Mr F	15 230
Mr B	12 720	Miss G	27 460
Mr C	16 230	Mr H	14 250
Mrs D	18 710	Mrs Y	1 850
Miss E	5 950		

Calculate the median value.

4. The orders received from the representatives of Icepack Ltd are as follows for the month of June:

	£		£
Mr A	18 540	Mr F	8 417
Mr B	12 760	Miss G	19 325
Mr C	29 250	Mr H	28 612
Mrs D	13 286	Mrs Y	14 713
Miss E	48 716	Mrs J	8 450

Calculate the median value.

34.8 The Mode

The mode is defined as that value in a set of figures which occurs most often. To arrive at the mode, then, one needs only to find the item having the greatest frequency.

When working with ungrouped data this merely necessitates counting the frequencies to discover which one predominates.

Example 34.5. Weekly contributions to pension fund of employees:

Contribution (£)	Number of employees
1	11
2	18
3	29
4	16
5	10
6	3

The most common payment—made by 29 employees—is £3; therefore this is the modal contribution.

Sometimes it is possible to have bimodal statistics. Had there been 29 people paying £5 per week it would have been a bimodal series.

34.9 Exercises: The Mode

1. In the following cricket scores which is the modal score for each batsman?

Batsman A: 27, 0, 14, 162, 27, 5, 27, 16, 17.
Batsman B: 5, 15, 38, 5, 72, 91, 106, 4, 3, 0, 5.
Batsman C: 27, 14, 36, 7, 21, 9, 19, 36.

2. In the following lists of bowling performances which is the modal performance for each bowler?

Bowler A: Wickets taken 4, 3, 1, 4, 4, 5, 3, 1, 2, 4, 5.
Bowler B: Wickets taken 2, 2, 2, 0, 1, 7, 3, 2, 2, 1, 5.
Bowler C: Wickets taken 5, 1, 4, 7, 1, 1, 3, 2, 3, 3, 4.

3. Houses in Newtown have the following number of bedrooms. Which is the modal-sized house?

Number of rooms	1	2	3	4	5	6
Frequencies	27	272	1954	825	430	36

4. Containers moving through a certain port are found to weigh as follows:

Weight in tonnes	Number of containers	Weight in tonnes	Number of containers	Weight in tonnes	Number of containers
12	114	19	206	26	136
13	127	20	138	27	127
14	163	21	139	28	142
15	165	22	187	29	156
16	234	23	165	30	165
17	217	24	234	31	139
18	219	25	144	32	234

What is the modal weight for containers passing through the port?

34.10 Which is the Best 'Average' to Use?

The arithmetic mean is the main average used because it is readily understood, fairly easy to calculate, takes into account all the data, and is capable of algebraic manipulation. However, there are certain sets of data for which the arithmetic mean does not fulfil its function of adequate representation. Consider the following illustrations:

(i) Imagine there is an enquiry into the average age of students at a college, classified according to whether they are day-release or evening. The following results might occur: arithmetic average age of day-release students 20 years; arithmetic average age of evening-class students, 20 years. Obviously the mean age is identical but the day-release average may have been computed from a class of 150 students each one aged 20 years, and the evening-class average from a class of 100 students of which 90 were each aged 17 years and 10 each aged 47 years. Clearly, the mean age of 20 is not representative of the evening class but is representative of the day-release group. Therefore if data contain extreme items, the arithmetic mean will tend to distort and incorrectly describe the situation.

(ii) The arithmetic average number of children per household might easily be calculated at 2.2 for Great Britain. Many students might find such a figure unrealistic, since obviously no family actually has 2.2 children. The mean number of legs per dog in the United Kingdom may be approximately 3.99, but this conjures up a strange picture of a dog. Clearly the mode conveys the best impression of a dog, and in that enquiry would be the best average to choose.

In the two cases above, to a greater or less extent, the arithmetic mean would appear to be unsatisfactory as a means of description and the median would probably be a better choice since:

(i) In the case of data with extreme items the median will not be affected by them and will possibly be more representative. Returning to our two classes of students, the median ages would be 20 for the day-release group and 17 for the evening group—a more accurate picture of the situation.

(ii) The median number of children per household in Great Britain is 2, which is a more realistic indication of the average family than 2.2.

Unfortunately, one of the characteristics of the median which is particularly useful in some circumstances, that of concentrating on the middle item, is a disadvantage in the majority of cases, because, in the main, all data relevant to the problem should be taken into account. Also the median is unsuitable for further mathematical calculation.

The mode is of limited use, because although it has some of the advantages and all of the disadvantages associated with the median, there is, in addition, the difficulty of distributions which have no mode or two modes (bimodal). For example, the data 2, 3, 8, 9, 12 and 13 have no mode; the data 2, 3, 3, 3, 5, 7, 8, 8, 8, 9 and 10 have two modes, 3 and 8.

In summary, it is a good rule-of-thumb guide to use the arithmetic mean in all those cases where it adequately represents the data. Where this is not the case, the median is usually the best alternative.

34.11   Mental Arithmetic Test

1. $47.5 + 32.26 + 187.55 + 24.927 =$

2. £186.55 − £38.78 =

3. £5000 × 700 =

4. £17 856 ÷ 9 =

5. How many $2\frac{1}{2}$ litre bottles can be filled from a barrel holding 6000 litres?

6. Increase 2400 by $33\frac{1}{3}\%$.

7. How many days are there from January 4 to March 11 inclusive, in a leap year?

8. Three boxes hold 27, 36 and 24 items respectively. What are the average contents?

9. What is two thirds of 720?

10. Gas is sold at 25p per therm. How much for 108 therms?

11. Electricity is sold for a standing charge of £4.68 and 3p per unit. A family uses 1200 units. What is the total bill?

12. A cargo valued at £200 000 is insured by Lloyds at a premium of £2.50 per £1000. What is the total premium?

13. Peter runs $1\frac{1}{2}$ kilometres. Malcolm runs half as far as Peter. Paul runs half as far as Malcolm. How many metres does Paul run?

14. A football pitch is 75 m × 100 m. What is its area?

15. A container measures $2\frac{1}{2}$ m × $2\frac{1}{2}$ m × 12 m. What is its volume?

16. A housewife pays £12.00 deposit and 24 monthly instalments of £6.50 for a tumble drier. What is the total hire purchase cost?

17. How many days were there altogether in the years 1980 and 1981?

18. An item costing £250 has VAT added at 15%. What is the total charge?

19. What is the area of a circle radius 7 cm? (Use $\pi = 3\frac{1}{7}$)

20. An inheritance of £66 000 is shared between X, Y and Z so that Z gets twice as much as Y and three times as much as X. How much does Z receive?

35
Introduction to Double Entry Book-keeping

35.1 The Double Entry System

In Chapter 26 we learned how to keep simple accounts. In this chapter we will look at the whole pattern of book-keeping, or accounting, to see how accounts are used to keep records of every aspect of a business, and to produce eventually the profits of the business and a Balance Sheet showing the state of affairs of any enterprise.

The chart which is the chief feature of this chapter shows clearly how the double entry system of book-keeping works. This method of keeping books so that the businessman knows his exact financial position at any given time is explained in the diagram, and in the sections of text below. Later in Chapter 38 we shall see how this whole double entry procedure is computerised, so that huge organisations such as banks, industrial companies and service industries can keep track of all their affairs. At this stage let us take a very quick look at Fig. 35.1 on pages 321–1 to pick up the general framework of book-keeping. The numbers 1 to 5 are guideways through the diagram.

35.2 The Original Documents (1)

Every transaction that takes place, whether it is a purchase, a sale, a return, a payment, or some other type of transaction has an original document. These documents are called invoices, credit notes, statements, receipts, petty cash vouchers, or they may be formal agreements like a hire purchase document or a legal contract. Even mere letters of complaint require some action to be taken.

35.3 The Books of Original Entry (2)

When you have a document you first record it in a book of original entry. These books may be Journals, that is Day Books or Cash Books like the Three-column Cash Book or the Petty Cash Book. We may also have Bill Books to record bills of exchange, Consignment Books to record consignments and other specialised books. These days books keep a record of the documents received in *chronological order*.

35.4 Posting the Day Books to the Ledger (3)

When we have entered our Original Documents in the Day Books we then post the transactions into the Ledger, which is the main book of account. Every transaction will appear twice, and this gives us the name 'double entry book-keeping'. In every transaction that takes place in business life two accounts are affected in opposite ways. One receives value and the other gives value. As we saw in Chapter 26, the left-hand side of an account, which is called the debit side, is the side where the account receives value, and the right-hand side of an account, which is called the credit side, is the side where the account gives value. The rule is:

Debit the account that receives goods or services or money; Credit the account that gives goods or services or money.

Suppose we pay out £500 by cheque for a microcomputer. The Bank Account has given £500 (credit Bank Account) and the Office Machinery Account has received a microcomputer (debit Office Machinery Account with £500). If we pay salaries in cash £2800, Cash Account has given £2800 (credit the Cash Account) and Salaries Account has received £2800 (debit the Salaries Account). Actually, of course, we gave the salaries to the employees but the record of salaries paid is kept in the Salaries Account and will be used later to work out our profits.

With double entry book-keeping then, every entry from the day books to the Ledger will be a double entry; one account will be receiving value and another giving it. For this reason the entries will be a debit entry in one account and a credit entry in some other account. Hundreds, even thousands, of accounts may be involved, but if we do our double entry carefully the total entries on the debit side will exactly balance the total entries on the credit side. This is the way we check the books, by taking out a Trial Balance.

35.5   The Trial Balance (4)

The Trial Balance is what its name implies; an attempt to discover whether the books really do balance. If they do not we know that someone has made a mistake somewhere, and we must discover it.

To take out a Trial Balance we must look at every account in our Ledger, and there may be thousands of them. Each account will be in one of three positions:

(a) It may have a debit balance outstanding.
(b) It may be clear—having no outstanding balance.
(c) It may have a credit balance outstanding.

We usually do a Trial Balance at least once a month, taking the opportunity to 'tidy up' accounts where we can, and bringing all the debit balances into a list of debit balances, and all the credit balances into a list of credit balances. These two columns of balances should come exactly equal, and we may conclude that if they do, it is fairly certain we have done our book-keeping well. The idea of the Trial Balance is the most important idea in book-keeping by the double entry system, and the whole of the final accounts at the end of the year depends upon it.

Book-keeping to the Trial Balance level is the first stage of accounting knowledge, which most people can learn very easily in about 15–20 hours of instruction or self-study. One often sees advertisements reading 'Book-keeper to Trial Balance level required'. If you want to develop a full understanding of book-keeping so that you can respond to such an advertisement you need to work through a companion volume to this one, *Book-keeping Made Simple* by Geoffrey Whitehead.

35.6   Final Accounts—the Trading Account (5a)

We are now ready to find out whether our business is profitable or running at a loss. To discover this we first do a simple Trading Account. This shows whether we are selling at a profit. We find our sales figure from the Sales Account; we find our purchases figure from our Purchase Account. After one or two adjustments, chiefly connected with opening and closing stocks, we discover the cost of the goods sold. A few more little matters help us discover the Cost of Sales, which is not quite the same as the Cost of Goods Sold, since, it includes a few expenses. Then Sales minus Cost of Sales gives us our overall profit—called in book-keeping the **Gross Profit.**

35.7 Final Accounts—the Profit and Loss Account (5b)

In this second half of our Final Accounts we start with the Gross Profit and deduct from it all overhead expenses. We add items of profit which are not part of normal trading, such as commissions or rents received. This leads us to the clear profit or clean profit – called in book-keeping **Net Profit**. This Net Profit is the reward of the businessman for his efforts, and is added to his Capital Account.

With partnership enterprises, and with limited companies, the Net Profit has to be shared among the partners, or shareholders. This is done in a section of the Profit and Loss Account, called the **Appropriation Account.** We give the profit to the appropriate persons in the appropriate proportions according to the **partnership agreement**, or the resolution passed at the **annual general meeting** of the company.

35.8 The Balance Sheet (5c)

When we have prepared the Final Accounts and added the profit to the owner's Capital Account (or perhaps deducted the loss from the owner's Capital Account) we have established what degree of success the business has achieved, and all we need to do now is summarise the final position of the business by drawing up a Balance Sheet which shows the assets and liabilities of the firm.

This is the general pattern of double entry book-keeping.

35.9 Computerisation of Double Entry Book-keeping

Computers are electronic machines which can be programmed to do many routine activities. Since book-keeping to the Trial Balance level is a routine and repetitive process it is relatively easy to instruct the computer how to keep book-keeping records to the Trial Balance. The more difficult level of work is the work to Final Accounts level. It is not usual to program a computer to do this as the cost of writing the programs is much greater. Some awkward decisions have to be made at this level which a human being can do much more easily than the computer programmer can prepare a program. Some people do go to the extra expense involved, but it is hardly necessary.

The computerisation of book-keeping is explained fairly simply in Chapter 38.

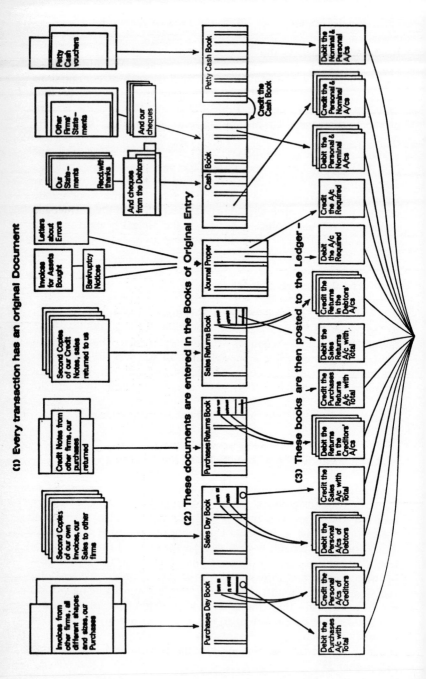

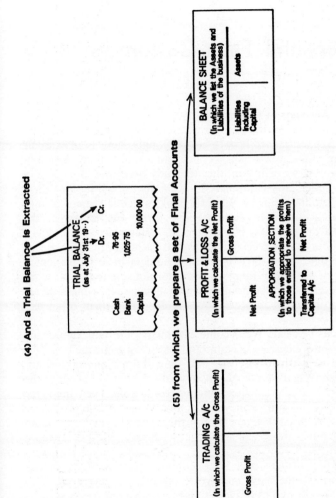

Fig. 35.1. Double entry book-keeping.

36
Bankers and Their Customers

36.1 The Accounts of Customers

In Chapter 26 we learned how to keep accounts using as an example
the keeping of a simple Cash Account and a simple Bank Account.
In this chapter we will continue to study accounts, but as it is
helpful to understand computerised accounts we will look at them
this time from the point of view of a bank, which is keeping a huge
number of accounts in computerised form. For example, the
Barclaycard organisation has over eight million account holders,
each of whom has to receive a statement each month. This means
that every day some 400 000 account holders have to be sent a
statement of account. Imagine the enormous amount of work
involved, even with a computer, in producing such a mass of accounts, putting them into envelopes and posting them off, every
working day.

First let us be clear. We become customers of a bank by putting
our money into a current account and accepting a cheque book for
use should we wish to pay our bills or withdraw any money for
personal use. When we put our money into the current account the
relationship created is a **debtor–creditor relationship**. The bank is the
debtor (it owes us our money back) and we are **creditors** (people
who are owed money). Every month the bank will send us a statement of account, and it will show that we have a credit balance on
our account.

Suppose we wish to spend more money than we have in our
account and ask the bank manager to sanction an **overdraft**. This
means we are allowed to draw out more than we put in. As soon as
we do so our credit balance disappears, and becomes a debit balance. We are now debtors of the bank, and the bank is our creditor.
We shall have a debit balance on our account. The roles of debtor
and creditor have been reversed.

Let us look at a simple account kept on a computerised system.
This is often called a '**running-balance account**'. Because a computer

works so fast it can do a new balance calculation every time any activity occurs on an account, whereas by traditional methods the balance on an account was usually worked out only once a month. A typical running balance account is shown in Fig. 36.1 and described in the notes below it.

G. M. Glover Esq.,
The Granary,
10245 Burnham Road,
Latchingford,
Essex.
SS42 1MA

Helpful Bank Plc,
Burnham Branch,
2164 High Street,
Burnham,
Essex.
SS69 5TT

19 . .   Sheet 205   Account No. 17856844

		DEBIT	CREDIT	BALANCE
				Credit C Debit D
DEC 16	**BALANCE**			1706.78C
19	200078	9.00		1697.78C
22	200077	109 00		1588.78C
23	PGO Tax 111.94		274.17	1862.95C
24	200079	2305.00		442.05D
29	200081	160.00		602.05D
29	Loan		1000.00	397.95C
30	Sundries		425.68	823.63C
19 . .				
JAN 14	200080	44.00		779.63C
16	**BALANCE**			779.63C

Fig. 36.1. A 'running-balance' Current Account

Notes
   (i) At first the account is in credit, the bank owing Glover a balance of £1706.78.
   (ii) The debit entries are all cheques drawn by Glover, and the cheque numbers are shown. They are deducted from the balance, because Glover has received the money (debit the receiver) and has paid it over to the payee named on his cheque.
   (iii) One of these cheques is so large (£2305) that it pushes the account 'into the red' (in the olden days debit balances were written in red ink). It is an overdrawn Current Account with a debit balance.
   (iv) To correct this overdraft a loan is arranged of £1000. This will mean the opening up of a separate Loan Account (which will of course be debited as Glover has received the loan) but it means that the Current Account can be credited with £1000 which repays the overdraft and leaves a credit balance of £397.95.
   (v) The entry on 23 December is a pension transfer from an official government pension department. The credit transfer means the bank has effectively received a further deposit from Glover.

(vi) The word 'sundries' refers to sundry cheques (or cash) deposited by the customer. This increases the balance owed to him by the bank.

You should now try some of the exercises below, considering them from the point of view of the bank, since they are running-balance accounts.

36.2   Exercises: Running-balance Current Accounts

1. Account of T. Naples. Balance carried forward on 21 September 19 . . £3275.67 credit. The following transactions then occurred:

Sept. 22   Cheque paid 803112 £132.65
      23   Cheque paid 803114 £9.56
      25   Credit received from Bank of England (gilt-edged dividend) £32.75
      28   Credit transfer—salary for month £247.57
      29   Cheque paid 803113 £326.75
      30   Cheque paid 803115 £19.27
Oct.   1   Loan arranged (credit to this account) £5000
       4   Cheque paid 803116 £6250
      17   Sundries paid in by customer £235.56

2. Account of Byron & Partners. Balance carried forward on 9 June 19 . . £428.56 credit. The following transactions then occurred:

June 12   Cheque paid 716552 £17.25
     14   Sundries banked by customer £141.42
     15   Cheque paid 716524 £642.50
     16   Cheque paid 716523 £131.50
     17   Dividend (Holcombe Industries) received £42.50
     19   Cheque paid 716526 £17.24
     29   Salary credited by transfer £284.50
     30   Cheque paid 716527 £85.00
July 4   Cheque paid 716525 £16.65
     11   Interest charged £3.25

3. Account of Sheila Cruise. Balance carried forward on 16 May 19 . . £23.85 debit. The following entries then take place:

May 17   Cheque paid 589501 £142.60
    18   Charges (overdraft marked) £3.50
    21   Cheque paid 589502 £165.70
    23   Funds deposited £86.50
    26   Cheque paid 589503 £236.56
    31   Bank giro transfer £5287.65
June 3   Cheque paid 589504 £100.00
    14   Cheque paid 589505 £272.36
    15   Sundry deposits £27.65

36.3 Understanding Double Entries: A Bank's Double Entries for its Customers

If you understand double entries you will always be able to see what is happening in any set of accounts, whatever the business. Every transaction that ever takes place requires a double entry; one account will be debited and another account will be credited. The account that receives value will be debited and the account that gives value will be credited, but we must remember what business we are dealing with since a set of accounts is always the accounts of a particular business. Thus in Fig. 36.1 the account of Mr Glover is a current account, part of the book-keeping of the Helpful Bank Plc. In considering some double entries in this account, we have to consider them from the Bank's point of view.

Double Entry No. 1   19 December: A cheque for £9.00 made out by Glover to Sailing Magazines Ltd.

(a) The entry in Glover's Account is a debit entry, since Glover has received back the £9.00 previously deposited with the bank. However, he has not actually received it back, he has told us to pay it to Sailing Magazines Ltd.

(b) When we clear this cheque into Sailing Magazines Ltd's Account we will credit it in their account, since in fact they are giving it to the bank as a deposit—the transfer is a deposit in their account—credit the giver. So the double entry is:

Debit Glover, who has received back the use of his money; debit the receiver. Credit Sailing Magazines Ltd, who have paid in the cheque as a deposit; credit the giver.

Of course, in fact Sailing Magazines Ltd, may not bank with us, but with Lloyds, or Barclays, etc. In that case we shall have to credit Head Office with the £9.00, and they will in turn give it to the Head Office of Lloyds, or Barclays, as the case may be, and they will credit it to Sailing Magazines Ltd's Account.

Other cheques in Glover's account (Fig. 36.1) would have similar double entry explanations.

Double Entry No. 2   23 December: The Government pension organisation is paying a pension to Glover of £274.17 (after deducting tax of £111.94). That last piece of information is not part of the double entry, it is just advice to the pensioner. We will ignore it. The double entry is:

(a) A credit in Glover's Account for £274.17. Careful thinking is required here. The pension office is paying this money to Glover by depositing it in the bank for him, so Glover is really giving the money to the bank for safe-keeping (credit the giver). The double entry for this is in the pension office's account, where the total paid in pensions for the weeks is debited. As this is an official fund it will be in an account at the Bank of England, which has relayed the payment through to the Helpful Bank Plc. Therefore, as far as the Helpful Bank is concerned, the debit entry will be in the Bank of England's Account at Head Office, as part of the total pensions paid out that month to customers who bank at the Helpful Bank.

Therefore the double entry is:

Debit Bank of England Account which has received the use of this money. Credit Glover, who has given the pension to the Bank for safe-keeping by setting up the credit transfer arrangement for his pension, to this account.

Double Entry No. 3   29 December: A loan of £1000 has been credited to G. M. Glover's account. The double entry here is fairly simple. When a bank makes a loan to a customer, the customer, of course, receives the money and we need to debit the customer's account. However, we have to imagine that the customer at once puts the £1000 in his Current Account, and uses it to clear his overdraft and leave a small balance (in this case £397.95). Therefore the entry in the Current Account is a credit entry. Where, then, is the debit entry? The answer is we must open up a second account, a Loan Account which is debited with the £1000, as the customer is a debtor for that amount. The double entry is:

Debit G. M. Glover Loan Account £1000 (Debit the receiver). Credit G. M. Glover Current Account £1000 (Glover has given the money to the bank to clear his overdraft. Credit the giver).

A little more is said about Loan Accounts in the next section.

Double Entry No. 4   30 December: Sundries are deposited by Glover £425.68. Actually this is a payment to Glover by a customer, Piedmont Garages Ltd, for work done rewiring their premises. Although Glover is retired, he still does the odd job when he can find it. Piedmont Garages Ltd also banks with the Helpful Bank Plc, so we can deal with this double entry in our branch. Glover has given the money to the bank as a deposit, so his account has been credited. Piedmont Garages Ltd, have received back some of the money deposited in their Current Account, and we must debit the receiver. The double entry therefore is:

Debit Piedmont Garages £425.68; debit the receiver. Credit G. M. Glover £425.68; credit the giver who has given us these funds for safe keeping.

Cyclical Billing in Accounting

You may wonder why this account, which is clearly for one month, starts on 16 December and ends on 16 January. It would surely be more sensible to start on 1 December and end on 31 December. The explanation is that big organisations like banks could not possibly deal with millions of customers on the same day, and send out all their statements of accounts on the last day of the month. They have to do some accounts every day. With about 20 working days in a month they need to send out 5% of all accounts each day. With five million accounts (and most banks have about that number) this means 250 000 accounts have to be sent out every day. This is called cyclical billing, everyone gets treated in turn.

You should now try some of the exercises below. Pretend you work for Helpful Bank Plc and explain the double entries in each case.

36.4 Exercises: Double Entries for Bankers' Customers

In each of the following questions explain the double entry from the point of view of the Helpful Bank Plc which is recording the transaction.

1. Mrs K. Johnston deposits cash £246.50. (Cash Account receives the money on the Bank's behalf.)

2. Mr T. Charles pays in a cheque from the Atlantic Building Society for £4200. Atlantic Building Society have an account at our branch.

3. Sara Patel pays in two cheques, one from A. Kadar for £220.00 and another from Wool Processors Ltd, for £84.56. Both Kadar and Wool Processors Ltd bank at another branch of our bank.

4. A cheque drawn by a customer M. Lopez for £223.95 arrives from the clearing house. It is paid to the Embassy of Mexico, which banks at Midland Bank Plc.

5. A cheque drawn by a customer, Peter Brown, arrives from the clearing house in favour of T. Marshall, who banks with the Bristol branch of Barclays. The cheque is for £172.78.

6. A direct debit entry from the Bolsover District Council, who have an account with our branch, asks us to debit a customer, T. Smith, who is a ratepayer with £326.50 for rates.

7. A credit transfer for salary from Gigantic Engineers Plc asks us to credit their employee M. Leighton with a salary of £856.24. Gigantic Engineers Plc banks at Lloyds in Manchester.

8. A dividend payment of £125.50 from Progressive Products Plc in favour of a customer C. Thomas comes through as a bank giro (credit transfer). Progressive Products Plc bank at the Bank of Scotland in Edinburgh.

9. A customer Julie Hoyle, who is an author, receives a giro transfer to her account for Public Lending Rights (PLR) for £385.00. The PLR authorities bank at the Tyneside branch of Helpful Bank Plc. (Be careful—do not be misled by the phrase 'receives a giro transfer'.)

10. Nirala Restaurant Ltd, is credited with a transfer of £2856.40, which is the value of Barclaycard takings paid in the previous week to the local Barclays branch, now cleared for payment.

36.5   Double Entries for General Business Purposes

The accounts of customers are a special case of double entry bookkeeping and are rather more difficult than the simple double entries required in everyday accounting. The best way to get a full understanding of double entries for ordinary business purposes is to understand the three classes of accounts. These are:

(a) Personal Accounts.
(b) Nominal Accounts.
(c) Real Accounts.

36.6   Personal Accounts

These are the accounts we keep in our books of the persons with whom we deal, who may be either debtors (people who owe us money for goods or services supplied) or creditors (people to whom we owe money for goods or services supplied to us, or for loans made to us). We have just seen in sections 36.3 and 36.4 that bank customers are creditors because they have deposited money with the bank, although they can be debtors if they are overdrawn.

Before looking at the accounts of a typical debtor and a typical creditor, let us just mention one personal account that is a little unusual. This is the Capital Account. When people go into business they contribute certain assets to the business to get it started. Very often this is in the form of money, so it is a common idea that capital is money. In fact capital can be in any form—tools, motor vehicles, furniture, stocks and land and buildings may all be brought in as assets at the start of a business. Assets of this type are all 'real' accounts, as we shall see later, because you can actually use, touch and handle the assets—they are real things. The total value of the assets contributed is the capital that the proprietor has provided and which the business now owes back to him. This is the figure that goes in the Capital Account, which is the personal account of the proprietor, who is a creditor of the business. Here is a typical Capital Account, and the real accounts showing the assets contributed. They have been shown in traditional form, rather than in running balance form. Notice that all the assets are debit balances on the accounts, but the Capital Account of the proprietor has a credit balance because it is the personal account of a creditor.

Capital A/c (William Bloggs)		L1
	19 . .	£
	Jan 1 Sundry assets	57 240.00

Premises A/c		L2
19 . .	£	
Jan 1 Capital	35 000.00	

Fixtures and Fittings A/c		L3
19 . .	£	
Jan 1 Capital	3 240.00	

Motor Vehicles A/c		L4
19 . .	£	
Jan 1 Capital	7 500.00	

Stock A/c		L5
19 . .	£	
Jan 1 Capital	8 500.00	

Bank A/c		L6
19 . .	£	
Jan 1 Capital	2 600.00	

Cash A/c		L7
19 . .	£	
Jan 1 Capital	400.00	

Fig. 36.2. Double entries on starting out in business.

Notes
   (i) Notice that all the assets are debit entries. Debit the receiver. Each of these accounts has received value from the proprietor. Where is the double entry for all these accounts?

(ii) Clearly it is in the Capital Account of the proprietor. The business owes him back the money he has contributed, to the total value of £57 240.

(iii) When will this capital be returned to the proprietor? The answer is that we do not know, but the most likely times are:

(a) if he discontinues the business or

(b) if he dies—when the heirs will inherit the business. Sometimes serious difficulties arise if the proprietor dies suddenly. This may bring the business to an abrupt stop, with heirs who are not interested claiming their share of the inheritance and any unfortunate employees being made redundant.

The Personal Account of a Debtor

Here is the personal account of a debtor Anna Machin, who runs a boutique. We supply her regularly with ladies' fashion goods, which she pays for once a month on receiving a monthly statement. Notice the various debits and credits. Then try to answer the questions below the account. An important point when trying to understand accounts in anyone's books is this. Books are kept from the point of view of the firm or company whose records they are. You have to think of yourself as working for the firm that has the account on its books. Ask yourself 'What has happened to us as far as Anna Machin is concerned? Did we supply her with goods, or did she supply us? Did we pay her, or did she pay us? etc., etc.' You have to take a practical, down-to-earth view of each transaction. What happened here? The answers are given in an Answer Section below, but try to answer them yourself before looking at the answer section.

Anna Machin A/c   L137

19 . .			£	19 . .			£
May 1	Balance	b/d	247.94	May 10	Bank	CB5	235.54
3	Sales	SDB5	429.65	10	Discount	CB5	12.40
12	Sales	SDB7	375.60	27	Returns	SRB21	29.40
23	Sales	SDB10	596.45	31	Balance	c/d	1696.95
28	Sales	SDB12	324.65				
			£1974.29				£1974.29
19 . .			£				
June 1	Balance	b/d	1696.95				

Fig. 36.3. A debtor's Personal Account.

Questions on the Account

1. Does the opening balance on 1 May show Anna Machin to be a debtor or a creditor of our business?

2. What happened on 3 May? Where would the double entry be for this entry?

3. What happened on 10 May? Where would the double entries for these two items be?

4. On 12, 23 and 28 May we have more sales—but what happened on 27 May? Where would the double entry be for this item?

5. Do you have any comment to make on the size of the balance on 1 May and the size of the balance on 1 June? If so, what is it?

Answer Section

1. She has a debit balance, so she is a debtor for £247.94.

2. We sold her some more goods, worth £429.65. The double entry would be in Sales Account, which is the account where we collect together a record of our total sales. Sales Account is a nominal account—which means an account where the money is there in name only, for record keeping purposes. The actual goods have gone to Anna Machin, and are out of our control now.

3. Anna Machin paid for the goods outstanding on 1 May, but she took a 5% cash discount for paying promptly. The double entries for these two items would be in the Bank Account (for the cheque) and in the Discount Allowed Account. This is another nominal account, where we have recorded this loss of £12.40. Nominal accounts are always either losses or profits. When we allow someone to take a discount that is a loss we agree to suffer because we prefer to receive the rest of the money owing to us—it is an inducement to the customer to pay promptly.

4. On 27 May Anna Machin returned something which was unsatisfactory for some reason. The value was £29.40. We credit her account because she gave it back. Credit the giver. We debit our own account, Sales Returns Account, because we received it back again, so the double entry is the Sales Returns Account.

5. The comment you should make is this: we trusted Anna Machin last month with goods worth £247.94. This month we are trusting her with £1696.95, which is almost seven times as much. Was this wise? A person who pays £247.94 promptly may not be so quick to pay £1696.95. It is a common thing for a debtor to place small orders and pay promptly and then place really big orders and be unable to pay. We should have a system of credit control on our debtors to limit the amount of credit they can take. If this had been set at, say, twice the previous month's figure we should have sent the first order in May on 3 May, but would have refused to send the second order unless we had some guarantee that payment would be forthcoming. As it is we have a big debt on our books now. Let us hope she pays up!

The Personal Account of a Creditor

Here is the personal account of a creditor, Woven Textiles Plc, who supply us with materials on monthly credit terms. Once again you are asked what happened at various points on the account. The answers are again given in the Answer Section.

Woven Textiles Plc A/c   L249

19 . .			£	19 . .			£
July 4	Returns	PRB27	242.60	July 1	Balance	b/d	1585.64
24	Bank	CB27	1546.00	8	Purchases	PDB37	625.60
24	Discount	CB27	39.64	19	Purchases	PDB41	735.60
31	Balance	c/d	2004.84	19	Carriage	L25	29.50
				29	Purchases	PDB48	856.74
			£3833.08				£3833.08
				19 . .			£
				Aug. 1	Balance	b/d	2004.84

Fig. 36.4. A creditor's Personal Account.

Questions on the Account

1. On 1 July was Woven Textiles Plc a debtor or a creditor? Where is the double entry for this balance b/d (b/d means 'brought down')?

2. What happened on 4 July? Where is the double entry for this entry?

3. What happened on 19 July?

4. What happened on 24 July? Where would the double entries be for these two entries?

5. Is there anything to criticise Woven Textiles Plc about as far as their credit control system goes?

Answer Section

1. Woven Textiles Plc had a credit balance on their account on 1 July. This means they were creditors; we owe them money for goods supplied last month. The double entry for this balance is directly above it on the same page. You will see a similar balance on 31 July. The 'Balance c/d' (carried down) is carried down to the next month and becomes the credit balance b/d (brought down).

2. On 4 July we returned £242.60 of goods to Woven Textiles Plc; probably some cloth was the wrong colour, pattern, quality or was damaged in some way. The double entry for this will be in the Purchases Returns Account. (PRB27 actually refers to the Purchases Returns Book, page 27.)

3. On 19 July we purchased more goods for £735.60 from Woven Textiles Plc. They were credited with this figure (credit the giver); we owe them the money. They also charged us £29.50 for carriage. The double entry for that will be in the Carriage Inwards Account on the debit side; one of the losses of the business.

4. On 24 July we paid the amount due on 1 July, but we deducted a $2\frac{1}{2}\%$ discount from the bill. The double entries for these entries will be (a) in the Bank Account as far as the cheque for £1546 is concerned, and (b) in the Discount Received Account, on the credit side. This is one of the profits of the business.

5. No, we cannot really criticise their credit control procedures at all. Last month we purchased £1585.64 of fabrics from them, and this month we have purchased £2004.84. This is a little more, but not too much more. They think we are reliable (and we know we are).

36.7 Exercises: Personal Accounts

In each of the questions below study the account and then answer the questions below it.

1. Here is K. Hall's account in the books of Simplex Products Plc.

K. Hall A/c   L27

19..			£	19..			£
Jan 1	Balance	b/d	825.64	Jan 7	Returns	SRB21	21.65
4	Sales	SDB10	325.62	15	Bank	CB29	784.36
24	Sales	SDB14	925.66	15	Discount	CB29	41.28
				31	Balance	c/d	1229.63
			£2076.92				£2076.92
19..			£				
Feb 1	Balance	b/d	1229.63				

Questions:

(a) On 1 January was Hall a debtor or a creditor of Simplex Products Plc?

(b) What happened on 4 January?

(c) What happened on 7 January?

(d) What happened on 15 January?

(e) Would the discount on 15 January be Discount Allowed or Discount Received?

2. Here is Michael Onobanjo's account with K. Sijuwade Ltd. Copy out the account, balance it off and bring down the balance. Then answer the questions below the account.

M. Onobanjo A/c   L37

19 . .		£	19 . .		£
Dec 7	Returns	21.40	Dec 1	Balance	142.68
20	Bank	135.55	4	Purchases	364.75
20	Discount	7.13	14	Purchases	856.74
27	Motor Vehicles	1500.00	28	Purchases	112.64

Questions:

(a) Was Onobanjo a debtor or a creditor of K. Sijuwade Ltd, on 1 December 19 . .?

(b) What happened on 4, 14 and 28 of December?

(c) You are told that the entry on 27 December was the sale at its book value of a motor vehicle surplus to their requirements to Onobanjo by K. Sijuwade Ltd. Where would the double entry for this entry be?

(d) At the end of the month what was the balance on this account?

(e) Was Onobanjo a debtor or a creditor of K. Sijuwade Ltd on 31 December 19 . .?

3. Here is Kim Lee's account with Processors Plc. Copy it out, complete the 'running balance' column and then answer the questions below it.

Kim Lee A/c   L56

19 . .		Debit	Credit	Balance
Feb 1	Balance			1274.56D
4	Sales	2386.50		
7	Bank		1242.70	
7	Discount		31.86	
13	Sales	1647.56		
22	Sales	3000.00		
27	Bank		2500.00	
28	Returns		64.65	

Questions:

(a) What is the final balance on the account on 28 February?

(b) Who owes it, to whom?

(c) Explain the two entries on 7 February.

(d) You are told that Processors Plc insisted on the entry on 27 February. Why do you think they did this?

(e) The managing director of Processors Plc asks you, as credit control clerk, to fix a credit limit for Kim Lee for the month of March. What would you suggest as an appropriate figure?

36.8 Nominal Accounts

Nominal Accounts are accounts where the money is there 'in name only', as a matter of record. There is nothing real there, only a record of money spent (expenses—losses—of the business) or money received (receipts—profits—of the business). For example if we pay out for rent, rates, postage, motor fuel, etc. the money paid out is credited in the Cash Account or Bank Account (according to whether we pay in cash or by cheque). Either Cash Account or Bank Account is giving the money, and it is being spent on rent, rates, etc. These accounts are debited to record the losses incurred, and later we shall see that these losses are written off the profits at the end of the year. **All Nominal Accounts with debit balances are losses of the business.**

By contrast if we receive money for any reason, such as for the sale of goods, or the supply of services (Fees Received, for example) or for such items as Commission Received or Discount Received these are profits of the business. The actual money will go in the Cash Account or the Bank Account (on the debit side because they are receiving the money) but the record of it in Sales Account, or Fees Received Account or Commission Received Account will be on the credit side, because these accounts are giving the profit to the business—it is their contribution to the profits of the enterprise. **All Nominal Accounts with credit balances are profits and will be used to work out the profits at the end of the year.**

All we need to know about Nominal Accounts then is as follows:

(a) *Nominal Accounts with debit balances are losses of the business.*

(b) *Nominal Accounts with credit balances are profits of the business.*

36.9 Real Accounts

We have already seen a number of these accounts in Fig. 36.2. Real Accounts are accounts where we keep a record of the real things the business owns, which are known as the assets of the business. Thus, in Fig. 36.2 Premises Account, Fixtures and Fittings Account,

Motor Vehicles Accounts, etc. are Real Accounts. Assets are kept in the business for a long time, but they do gradually wear out and become less valuable. This is called 'depreciation', and the asset is written down in value (depreciated) by a fair amount each year. What is a 'fair' amount? The answer is that it varies with every asset. We may depreciate in several ways, but the commonest method is the straight-line method. For this we take the actual cost at start, the lifetime in years and the estimated value at the end. The depreciation is the cost at the start less the residual value at the end of the working life. The amount to depreciate each year is this loss in value divided by the lifetime.

Example 36.1 A motor vehicle costs £7250. It is expected to be in use for five years at the end of which time it should fetch £850 on trade in. The annual depreciation figure is calculated as follows:

$$\text{Annual Depreciation} = \frac{\text{Original Cost} - \text{Residual Value}}{\text{Lifetime in Years}}$$

$$= \frac{£7250 - £850}{5}$$

$$= \frac{£6400}{5}$$

$$= £1280 \text{ per annum}$$

36.10 Exercises: Personal, Nominal and Real Accounts

Here is a list of Accounts.

(a) Cash A/c
(b) Motor Vehicles A/c
(c) Advertising Expenditure A/c
(d) Rent A/c
(e) Mortgage A/c (National Building (Society)
(f) Commission Received A/c
(g) Land and Buildings A/c
(h) Capital A/c
(i) A. Supplier A/c
(j) A. Customer A/c

1. Write down the letters (a)–(j) to represent the accounts above. Then write against each letter whether the account concerned is a Personal Account, a Nominal Account or a Real Account.

2. Write the letters (a)–(j) down again to represent the list of accounts above. Now write against each whether it would normally have a debit balance or a credit balance.

3. A machine is purchased for £23 000 and is estimated to have a life of 15 years. At the end of that time it will have a scrap value of £500. What is the annual depreciation by the straight-line method?

4. A colour photocopier costs £3750. It is estimated to have a five year life when it will be disposed of for £250. What is the annual depreciation on the straight-line method?

37
An Introduction to the Final Accounts of a Business

37.1   What are Final Accounts?

Once a year all businesses are required to work out their profits and render the final accounts for the year to the Inland Revenue so that the Government can assess the amount of tax due, if any. We saw in Chapter 35 (see Fig. 35.1) that the Final Accounts of a business consist of a Trading Account, a Profit and Loss Account and a Balance Sheet of the business. These accounts are actually drawn up from the figures extracted from the accounts in a Trial Balance of the books. A Trial Balance is simply a list of all the accounts with debit balances, and all the accounts with credit balances. Since we always use double entry book-keeping, where every debit entry is balanced by an equal and opposite credit entry, the Trial Balance of the books must balance (and if it does not we must find the error). For a full account of this you must see a companion volume to the present one—called *Book-keeping Made Simple*.

   Besides the Inland Revenue there are other people who need to see the Final Accounts of a business, and may ask for a set of Final Accounts to be drawn up at any time to see the exact state of a business's affairs at any time. Such accounts are called '**Interim Final Accounts**', because they are made up at some time other than the end of the year. We will look at a set of Final Accounts in this chapter, in a very simple way, just to get some idea of how profits are calculated and what a Balance Sheet really is. It is simpler to look at the Trading Account (which produces the gross profit on trading) and the Profit and Loss Account (which produces the net profit—clean profit—on the whole business) separately. In real life many accountants run them on into one another and the result is called a Trading and Profit and Loss Account. Finally, we need to understand the Balance Sheet.

Since the starting point for all this is a Trial Balance we will look at a simple Trial Balance and prepare the Final Accounts from it.

A. Trader's Trial Balance as at 31 December 19 . .

Account	Dr £	Cr £
Sales		101 000.00
Sales Returns	1 500.00	
Purchases	63 355.00	
Purchases Returns		1 000.00
Opening Stock	7 295.45	
Commission Received		1 500.00
Discount Received		542.95
Enterprise Allowance		1 080.00
Rent and Rates	2 850.00	
Light and Heat	1 464.00	
Carriage and Postage	195.26	
Motor Expenses	952.05	
Cleaning Expenses	1 557.24	
Insurance	410.00	
Advertising	468.00	
Telephone Expenses	495.50	
Salaries	13 607.00	
General Expenses	1 265.00	
Depreciation (Fixtures)	480.00	
Depreciation (Motor Vehicles)	1 240.00	
Premises	43 000.00	
Fixtures	3 400.00	
Motor Vehicles	3 520.00	
Debtors and Creditors	3 200.00	2 568.00
Mortgage on Premises		17 500.00
Loan (Helpful Bank Plc)		2 500.00
Drawings	12 285.00	
Capital at 1 January		38 738.55
Cash at Bank	3 526.00	
Cash in Hand	364.00	
	£166 429.50	£166 429.50

Closing stock was found to be worth £11 214.60.

Fig. 37.1. A. Trader's Trial Balance.

37.2   The Trading Account

Very simply, a Trading Account is about trade, the buying and selling of goods. Since some businesses do not trade, but only offer services, they may not have a Trading Account, and will only have a Profit and Loss Account, while other professional people (doctors, dentists, lawyers, etc.) do not like even to talk about profits, and call their Profit and Loss Account an Income and Expenditure Account, or a Revenue Account.

In trading, the profit we make is the difference between the cost price (Purchases £63 355 on our list) and the selling price (Sales £101 000 on our list). However, we do have to take account of one or two other things, like opening and closing stocks in the year, and returns. The Trading Account from our set of figures comes out as shown below in Fig. 37.2. Study it, and the notes below it. Then try some of the exercises in Section 37.3.

Trading Account of A. Trader for year ending 31 December, 19 . .

L170

	£		£
Opening Stock	7 295.45	Sales	101 000.00
Purchases 63 355.00		*Less* Sales Returns	1 500.00
Less Returns 1 000.00			
		Net turnover	99 500.00
Net purchases	62 355.00		
Total stock available	69 650.45		
Less Closing Stock	11 214.60		
Cost of Sales	58 435.85		
Gross Profit	41 064.15		
	£99 500.00		£99 500.00

Fig. 37.2. A. Trader's Trading Account.

Notes

(i) The profit on trading is called the gross profit. Gross means 'fat' or 'swollen', because this profit has not yet had the overhead expenses deducted from it. That is done in the Profit and Loss Account.

(ii) The **net turnover** is a very important figure; it is the actual sales of the business when any returns from customers have been taken into account. It is important because one of the ways of comparing businesses is to compare their turnovers.

(iii) Follow the thinking on the debit side of the account. We want to find the profit. We know what we sold the goods for (£99 500—the net turnover) but what did we pay for them? We had an opening stock of £7 295.45 and we purchased £73 355.00 worth of goods. However, some of these were returned to our suppliers, so the net purchases were £62 355.00. When added to the stock in hand we had a total stock available in the year of £69 650.45.

However, when we count our closing stock (stock-taking) we find we still have £11 214.60 of goods in stock. Taking this from the total stock available we find there is £58 435.85 of stock missing. This is the stock we have sold (unless it has been pilfered). Either way we take this Cost of Sales from the selling price £99 500.00 and we find that the gross profit was £41 064.15.

37.3 Exercises: Preparing Trading Accounts

1. Peter Morecombe's Trial Balance as at 31 December, 19 . . includes the following figures: Opening Stock £7254; Purchases £36 520; Sales £88 654; Purchases Returns £1520; Sales Returns £1654. On taking stock he finds that the closing stock figure is £8254. Work out the Trading Account to find his gross profit.

2. Maira Shah's Trial Balance as at 31 December 19 . . includes the following figures: Opening Stock £4596; Purchases £49 275; Sales £137 250; Purchases Returns £3275; Sales Returns £5250. On taking stock he finds the closing stock figures to be £5096. Work out the Trading Account and thus find the gross profit.

3. Landscapes (Holbeach) Ltd, has the following figures on its Trial Balance at 31 December, 19 . .: Opening Stock £27 284; Purchases £173 250; Sales £328 290; Sales Returns £5115; Purchases Returns £13 250. Stocktaking reveals the Closing Stock figures to be £35 250. Prepare the Trading Account and hence find the gross profit.

4. Universal Dealers (Camloops) Plc has the following figures on its Trial Balance at 31 December, 19 . .: Opening Stock £117 281; Sales £12 358 600; Purchases £4 856 000; Sales Returns £158 600; Purchases Returns £56 000. Stocktaking reveals that Closing Stock is worth £88 281. Work out the Trading Account and hence the gross profit for the year.

37.4 Double Entries for the Trading Account

Before we go on to the Profit and Loss Account let us just make one point about the Trial Balance. As we make the entries in the Trading Account the double entry for each item clears the Nominal Account concerned and leaves it with no balance. Thus a debit in the Sales Account as the credit is made on the Trading Account

(Sales £101 000.00 in Fig. 37.2), clears the Sales Account completely and leaves it with no balance on it. It therefore disappears from the Trial Balance as shown in Fig. 37.4 below. Notice also that the Opening Stock figure of £7295.45 has been cleared from the Stock Account, but has already been replaced by the Closing Stock figure which was immediately brought on to the books. You might find the double entries on this a little hard to follow, so in Fig. 37.3 they have been explained.

Stock Account   L7

19 . .		£	19 . .		£
Jan 1 Balance	b/d	7 295.45	Dec 31 Trading A/c L170		7 295.45
Dec 31 Trading A/c L170		11 214.60	Dec 31 Balance	c/d	11 214.60
		£18 510.05			£18 510.05
19 . .		£			
Jan 1 Balance	b/d	11 214.60			

Fig. 37.3. Double entries and the Stock Account.

Notes

(a) The opening balance was £7295.45 and this is the balance that appears on the Trial Balance in Fig. 37.1.

(b) When this balance was carried to the debit side of the Trading Account the double entry on the credit side of the Stock Account left the Stock Account clear (no balance).

(c) However, we now had to bring on the Closing Stock after doing the stocktaking. This is of course an asset, so it must go on the debit side of the Stock Account as shown. The double entry is a credit entry in the Trading Account (but for the sake of a clear presentation we did not put it on the credit side of the Trading Account, **we deducted it from the debit side.** Deducting something from the debit side has the same effect as adding it to the credit side so it is a little bit of 'accountant's licence' to improve the style of the Trading Account and bring out the Cost of Sales. See Fig. 37.2.

(d) The Stock Account now has a balance (the Closing Stock) to be brought down to the new year, where it at once becomes the Opening Stock.

If we now draw up a revised Trial Balance we find that all the Trading Account items have disappeared except the Closing Stock figure. This is shown in Fig. 37.4. The other figure not previously available is of course the balance on the Trading Account—the gross profit of £41 064.15.

A. Trader's Revised Trial Balance as at 31 December 19 . .

Account	Dr £	Cr £
Closing Stock	11 214.60	
Commission Received		1 500.00
Discount Received		542.95
Enterprise Allowance		1 080.00
Rent and Rates	2 850.00	
Light and Heat	1 464.00	
Carriage and Postage	195.26	
Motor Expenses	952.05	
Cleaning Expenses	1 557.24	
Insurance	410.00	
Advertising	468.00	
Telephone Expenses	495.50	
Salaries	13 607.00	
General Expenses	1 265.00	
Depreciation (Fixtures)	480.00	
Depreciation (Motor Expenses)	1 240.00	
Premises	43 000.00	
Fixtures	3 400.00	
Motor Vehicles	3 520.00	
Debtors and Creditors	3 200.00	2 568.00
Mortgage on Premises		17 500.00
Loan (Helpful Bank Plc)		2 500.00
Drawings	12 285.00	
Capital at 1 January		38 738.55
Cash at Bank	3 526.00	
Cash in Hand	364.00	
Trading (Gross Profit)		41 064.15
	£105 493.65	£105 493.65

Fig. 37.4. A. Trader's revised Trial Balance.

37.5   The Profit and Loss Account

We are now ready to find the net profit (meaning the clean profit—from the French word nettoyer—to clean). The gross profit shows us the profit on trading but there are other bits of profit, such as the commission received and the discount received. A. Trader is also receiving an Enterprise Allowance of £40 per week—a Government allowance to encourage unemployed people to set up their own businesses. It only lasts for one year, but it is a help. These extra bits of profit can be added to the Gross Profit, but we must deduct all the overhead expenses to find the net profit. All we need is a double entry transferring these expenses to the debit side of the Profit and Loss Account, while the credit entry in the Expense Account will clear these accounts too, leaving them with no balance on them. They will therefore disappear from the Trial Balance too. The Profit and Loss Account for A. Trader is shown in Fig. 37.5.

Profit and Loss Account of A. Trader for year ending 31 December 19..

L171

19..	£	19..	£
Rent and Rates	2 850.00	Gross Profit	41 064.15
Light and Heat	1 464.00	Commission Received	1 500.00
Carriage and Postage	195.26	Discount Received	542.95
Motor Expenses	952.05	Enterprise Allowance	1 080.00
Cleaning Expenses	1 557.24		
Insurance	410.00	Total profits for year	44 187.10
Advertising	468.00		
Telephone Expenses	495.50		
Salaries	13 607.00		
General Expenses	1 265.00		
Depreciation (Fixtures)	480.00		
Depreciation (Motor Vehicles)	1 240.00		
Total expenses	24 984.05		
Net Profit (to Capital A/c)	19 203.05		
	£44 187.10		£44 187.10
		19..	£
		Net Profit	19 203.05

Fig. 37.5. Finding the Net Profit.

Notes

(a) The Profit and Loss Account starts with the gross profit brought in from the Trading Account.

(b) To this we add any other profits, commission, discount received and the enterprise allowance. These are all profits from the various nominal accounts.

(c) On the debit side we have all the expenses of the business. These are losses coming from the various nominal accounts (see Section 36.8).

(d) The difference between the total profits and the total expenses is the net profit of the business.

(e) To whom does the net profit belong? Obviously it is the proprietor's reward for his/her activities and is actually carried to the Capital Account as we shall see. However, it is possible that the proprietor has already drawn quite a lot of it out as drawings. Drawings are sums of money drawn out by the proprietor for personal use during the year. They are best described as '**drawings in expectation of profits made**'. If we look at Fig. 37.4 our Trial Balance shows that A. Trader has drawn out £12 285.00 during the year. Therefore much of the £19 203.05 has already been drawn out, and only the balance left will actually lead to an increase in the Capital Account. We shall see this in the next section.

In the meantime try the exercises in preparing Profit and Loss Accounts in Section 37.6 below.

37.6 Exercises: Profit and Loss Account Preparation

1. From the following figures prepare M. Smith's Profit and Loss Account for the half year ended 30 June 19 . .:

	£
Gross Profit	47 254
Discount Allowed	254
Discount Received	186
Bad Debts	360
Rent and Rates	1 490
Light and Heat	726
Packing and Delivery Expenses	1 380
Commission Received	3 250
Salaries	27 256

2. From the following particulars prepare R. Tyler's Profit and Loss Account for the year ended 31 December 19 . .:

	£
Gross Profit from Trading	42 715
Selling Expenses	3 874
Salaries	16 925
Discount Allowed	426
Discount Received	318
Rent, Rates and Insurance	3 924
Bad Debt Recovered	154
Telephone Expenses	764
Depreciation	1 240

3. M. Lee's Trial Balance contains the following items other than assets and liabilities. From them prepare his Profit and Loss Account for year ending 31 December 19 . .:

Gross Trading Profit	49 259
Salaries	21 274
Selling Expenses	4 985

Package Materials	254
Rent, etc.	3 812
Discount Received	426

Discount Allowed	720
Telephone	856
Commission Received	3 170

4. From the following list of balances you are required to prepare the Trading and Profit and Loss Accounts for the year ending 31 March 19 . ., of Peta Kingsley, a fashion designer.

	£
Stock, 1 April 19 . .	5 759
Purchases	25 254
Sales	82 656
Purchases Returns	1 759
Sales Returns	1 656
Carriage out	1 594
Salaries	23 205
Commission Paid	1 400
Commission Received	3 754
Motor Vehicle Expenses	1 875
Bank Interest	796
Rent and Rates	4 825
General Expenses	4 378
Bad Debts	224
Discount Allowed	1 875
Discount Received	234

Closing Stock at 31 March was found to be £6254.

37.7 The Residue of the Trial Balance

When both the Trading Account and the Profit and Loss Account of a business have been prepared the only items left on the Trial Balance are the assets and liabilities. This is because all the Nominal Accounts (the accounts where money is recorded in name only, for record-keeping purposes) have been cleared off into the Trading and Profit and Loss Account as the net profit is calculated. The residue of the Trial Balance shown earlier in Figs. 37.1 and 37.4 is given in Fig. 37.6.

Trial Balance as at 31 December 19 . .

Account	Type of item	Dr £	Cr £
Closing Stock	Asset	11 214.60	
Premises	Asset	43 000.00	
Fixtures	Asset	3 400.00	
Motor Vehicles	Asset	3 520.00	
Debtors	Asset	3 200.00	
Creditors	Liability		2 568.00
Mortgage on Premises	Liability		17 500.00
Loan (Helpful Bank Plc)	Liability		2 500.00
Drawings	Special item	12 285.00	
Capital	Liability		38 738.55
Cash at Bank	Asset	3 526.00	
Cash in Hand	Asset	364.00	
Profit & Loss (Net Profit)	Liability		19 203.05
		£80 509.60	£80 509.60

Fig. 37.6. The residue of the Trial Balance.

Notes

(a) All the assets are debit balances (remember Real Accounts always have debit balances).

(b) All the liabilities are credit balances—including Capital Account which is what the business owes to the owner of the business.

(c) The net profit is also a credit balance because we owe this profit to the owner of the business; it is his/her reward for running the business.

(d) The only Nominal Account left is the Drawings Account, which is the record of the money the owner has drawn out 'in expectation of profits made'.

If we just see what happens to the Capital Account we shall be ready to prepare the final part of the Final Accounts—the Balance Sheet of the business.

The Capital Account is shown in Fig. 37.7.

Capital A/c   L7

19 .		£	19 . .			£
Dec 31 Drawings	L95	12 285.00	Jan 1 Balance	b/d	38 738.55	
31 Balance	c/d	45 656.60	Dec 31 Profit & Loss	L171	19 203.05	
		£57 941.60			£57 941.60	
			19 . .		£	
			Jan 1 Balance	b/d	45 656.60	

Fig. 37.7. The profit and drawings transferred.

Notes

(a) The opening balance is £38 738.55, owed to the proprietor.

(b) The net profit for the year is also owed to the proprietor, and is therefore transferred in on the credit side. The double entry will be a debit in the Profit and Loss Account, clearing that account completely.

(c) The drawings which have already been enjoyed by the proprietor are cleared from the Drawings Account into the Capital Account and reduce the amount owing to the proprietor. The final balance is therefore £45 656.60.

37.8   The Balance Sheet of the Business

We are now ready to look at the Balance Sheet which is prepared from the residue of the Trial Balance shown in Fig. 37.6. We must first note the following things:

(a) A Balance Sheet is a snapshot picture of a business at a given moment in time.

(b) The usual time to draw up a Balance Sheet is the last moment of the last day of the financial year, after the profits have been worked out, but it can be drawn up at any time—for example when a business is to be sold, or the proprietor dies and the property passes to his/her heirs or successors.

(c) It would be logical to list the assets on the left-hand side and the liabilities on the right-hand side, and this is the way it is done in most countries. However, in the United Kingdom in the early nineteenth century it became the custom to reverse the sides, and for this reason most Balance Sheets in the United Kingdom are reversed, with the assets on the right and the liabilities on the left. This practice has been followed in the Balance Sheet shown in Fig. 37.8. Study this Balance Sheet and the notes below now.

Notes

(a) It is usual to display the Balance Sheet in the order of permanence, with the most permanent assets first and the most liquid assets last. However, banks (which have a great interest in liquidity, often reverse this order and present the assets and liabilities in the order of liquidity—with the most liquid item first).

(b) Fixed assets are assets which are used long term in the business, and make a long-term contribution to profitability.

(c) Current assets are assets which are either in liquid form (Cash and Cash at Bank) or have a lifetime of less than a year, by which time we hope they have been turned into cash (Debtors and Stock).

(d) Current liabilities are due for payment in less than a year.

(e) Long-term liabilities are due for payment over longer periods, and capital will only be repaid at the close of the business, either on sale to a new owner or at the retirement or death of the proprietor.

Balance Sheet of A. Trader as at 31 December, 19 . .

	£		£
Capital		*Fixed Assets*	
At start	38 738.55	Premises	43 000.00
Add Net Profit 19 203.05		Fixtures	3 400.00
Less Drawings 12 285.00		Motor Vehicles	3 520.00
	6 918.05		49 920.00
	45 656.60	*Current Assets*	
Long-term Liabilities		Closing Stock 11 214.60	
Mortgage 17 500.00		Debtors 3 200.00	
Loan 2 500.00		Cash at Bank 3 526.00	
		Cash in hand 364.00	
	20 000.00		
Current Liabilities			18 304.60
Creditors	2 568.00		
			£68 224.60
	£68 224.60		

Fig. 37.8. The Balance Sheet at the close of the financial year.

(f) It is usual to show the profits and drawings to bring out the net increase or decrease in capital during the year. The increase is the part of the profits the owner has 'ploughed back' into the business to allow it to grow. (If there was a decrease it would show the amount by which the proprietor had been living on his capital—by drawing out more than the profit earned.)

You should now try some of the exercises in 37.9 below.

37.9 Exercises: Balance Sheets

1. At the end of December 19 . ., T. Field's Trial Balance has the following figures. Draw up his Balance Sheet in good style, showing the various classes of assets and liabilities.
Assets Premises £60 000; Machinery £24 000; Closing Stock £9742; Cash at Bank £3 856; Cash in hand £244; Furniture and Fittings £8 560; Motor Vehicles £13 590; Debtors £850.
Liabilities Capital at start of year £90 252; Mortgage £13 412; Loan from Helpful Bank Plc £1768; Creditors £2546.
Other Balances The net profit for the year was £22 864 and Field had drawn out £10 000 during the year in expectation of profits made.

2. On the last day of December after doing the Trading Account and Profit and Loss Account the residue of the Trial Balance of 'Babywear' (Proprietor Sheila Warner) read as follows:

Trial Balance of 'Babywear' as at 31 December 19 . .

	Dr	Cr
Furniture and Fittings	8 255	
Motor Vehicles	3 750	
Closing Stock	17 256	
Debtors	348	
Capital at 1 January 19 . .		37 250
Drawings	8 000	
Balance on Profit and Loss A/c		9 855
Loan (Abel Finance)		2 500
Cash at Bank	12 925	
Cash in Hand	632	
Creditors		1 561
	£51 166	£51 166

Draw up the Balance Sheet in good style as at 31 December, 19 . ..

3. M. Adair's Trial Balance after completing the Trading Account and Profit and Loss Account is as shown below. Draw up the Balance Sheet in good style as at 31 December 19 . ..

M. Adair's Trial Balance as at 31 December 19 . .

	Dr	Cr
Premises	68 500	
Furniture and Fittings	12 500	
Investment portfolio (current asset)	82 560	
Debtors	13 950	
Motor Vehicles	23 250	
Capital at 1 January		158 955
Balance on Profit and Loss A/c		56 950
Mortgage		40 000
Drawings	30 000	
Creditors		3 835
Cash at Bank	27 255	
Cash in Hand	1 725	
	£259 740	£259 740

4. Prepare a Trading Account, Profit and Loss Account and Balance Sheet from the Trial Balance of B. Young below, as at 31 December 19 . .:

	Dr £	Cr £
Capital		66 000
Travellers' Salaries and Commissions	23 948	
Drawings	12 800	
Office Furniture	11 400	
Purchases	49 188	
Sales		159 208
Cash in Hand	884	
Cash at Bank	14 960	
Stock at 1 January, 19 ..	24 584	
Fees Received		38 576
Sundry Debtors and Creditors	14 788	16 792
Discount Received		572
Salaries	57 936	
Freehold Factory, 1 January 19 ..	110 000	
Mortgage		60 000
Rates	2 776	
Carriage Out	1 296	
General Expenses	26 076	
Loan		40 000
Plant and Machinery	20 600	
Office Expenses	9 912	
	£381 148	£381 148

Closing Stock was valued at £25 716.

37.10 The Balance Sheet of a Limited Company

A limited company is very similar to any other business in that it keeps its accounts and works out its Trading and Profit and Loss Account in exactly the same way, but its Balance Sheet is different and also the way in which its profits are dealt with is different. The reason is that the capital is not owned by an individual, but by a large number of shareholders. Consequently we cannot transfer profits to the Capital Account in the ordinary way, and the shareholders cannot draw 'Drawings' like sole traders or partners. Instead they get a **dividend** if the directors of the company recommend it. It is the usual policy to give a reasonable dividend, say, 10%, 15% or 20% but rarely more, since all profits not distributed as dividend are retained in the business to expand the company. This is usually desirable from everyone's point of view, but particularly from the directors' point of view.

There are two chief kinds of shareholders, ordinary shareholders and preference shareholders. Ordinary shareholders share equally in the profits made but preference shareholders have a preferential right to a fixed dividend, often 7–8%, but do not share in any further profits unless they own a special class of **participating preference shares**. These are fairly rare. The simplest way to follow what happens with companies is to look at the residue of a company's Trial Balance and draw from it an Appropriation Account (the account where profits are shared up appropriately among the various people entitled to them) and a Balance Sheet. The example shown below is reproduced from *Book-keeping Made Simple*, by courtesy of the author.

Example

After taking out the Trading and Profit and Loss Account at 31 December, 19 . ., the revised Trial Balance of Enterprise Ltd, is as follows:

	Dr £	Cr £
Cash	2 751	
Bank	29 250	
Stock at End of Year	27 500	
Balance from 1 January on Appropriation Account		3 894
Preliminary Expenses	3 000	
Net Profit for Year		126 106
Furniture and Fittings (cost £14 000)	12 500	
Patent Rights Owned (cost £2 000)	1 000	
Premium on Preference Shares		11 000
Ordinary Capital (authorised 100 000 shares of £1)		60 000
9% Preference Share Capital (authorised £40 000)		20 000
8% Debentures of £100 each		10 000
General Reserve		20 000
Land and Buildings (at cost)	48 000	
Plant and Machinery (cost £65 000)	58 000	
Quoted Investments held (market value £34 750)	33 000	
Unquoted Trade Investments (valued by directors at £22 450)	22 000	
Motor Vehicles and Spares (cost £24 500)	22 999	
Debtors and Creditors	4 700	13 700
	£264 700	£264 700

The directors have recommended the following:
  (a) A dividend of 9% on the Preference Shares is to be paid.
  (b) A dividend of 20% is recommended on the Ordinary Shares.
  (c) £10 000 is to be put to General Reserve Account.
  (d) Preliminary Expenses are to be written off completely.
  (e) £40 000 is to be appropriated as a Reserve for Corporation Tax.

The first thing to do is to transfer the profit to the Appropriation Account on the credit side (where there is already a small balance of £3 894. We then implement the directors' recommendations by debiting the Appropriation Account with the various amounts to be set aside for particular purposes.

Enterprise Ltd Appropriation Account
for year ending 31 December, 19 . .

	£		£
Reserve for Corporation		Balance at Start	3 894
Tax	40 000	Net Profit	126 106
Preliminary Expenses	3 000		
General Reserve	10 000		
Preference Dividend	1 800		
Ordinary Dividend	12 000		
Balance c/d	63 200		
	£130 000		£130 000
			£
		Balance b/d	63 200

Fig. 37.9. The Appropriation Account of Enterprise Ltd.

Notes
  (a) Each of the entries on the debit side means a credit entry in the various Reserve Accounts referred to. The dividends become current liabilities and the dividend warrants will be paid in due course.
  (b) This leaves a balance that is not to be distributed as shown in Fig. 37.9.

We can then go on and prepare the Balance Sheet. As you will notice in Fig. 37.10 the Balance Sheet, as laid down in the Companies Act 1985, has the assets on the left and the liabilities on the right, which is of course the correct way to set down a Balance Sheet. Parliament has (at long last) corrected the error made by 'British traditional style' in the Companies Act of 1856.

Balance Sheet as at 31 December, 19 . .

Fixed Assets				Ordinary Shareholders' Interest in the Co. (*capital and reserves*)		
Intangible Assets	At Cost (£)	Less Depreciation (£)	Value (£)		Authorised £	Issued £
Patent rights	2 000	1 000	1 000			
				Ordinary Shares of £1 fully paid	100 000	60 000
Tangible Assets						
Land and Buildings	48 000	—	48 000			
Plant and Machinery	65 000	7 000	58 000	Capital Reserves		
Furniture etc.	14 000	1 500	12 500	Share Premium Account		11 000
Motor Vehicles	24 500	1 501	22 999	Revenue Reserves		
				General Reserves (at start)	20 000	
	153 500	11 001	142 499	Add New Appropriation	10 000	
					30 000	
				Balance on Profit and Loss Account	63 200	
Trade Investments (valued by directors at £22 450)			22 000			
						93 200
			164 499	Ordinary Shareholders' Equity		164 200
Total Fixed Assets						
Current Assets		27 500				
Stock		4 700				
Debtors						
Investments		33 000				
(Market value £34 750)		29 250		*Preference Shareholders' Interest in the Company*		
Cash at Bank		2 751			Authorised	
Cash in Hand				9% Preference shares of £1 fully paid		
		97 201			£40 000	20 000
Less						
Current Liabilities	13 700					
Trade creditors				*Debentures*		
Dividends:	1 800			8% Debentures of £100 each		10 000
Preference	12 000			Reserve for Corporation Tax		40 000
Ordinary		27 500				
			69 701			
Net Working Capital						
			£234 200			£234 200
Net Value of Assets						

Fig. 37.10. The Balance Sheet of a limited company.

Notes

(a) Note that the fixed assets are split into two groups, the intangible assets—which are mere rights—and the tangible assets which are real assets, you can touch them (hence the name).

(b) Trade Investments are investments in subsidiary companies. They can be sold, but if we sell them we lose control of the subsidiary—so in a way they are fixed assets.

(c) The current liabilities have been deducted from the current assets. This brings out a useful figure called the net working capital (net current assets is another name). This figure £69 701, is the amount of current assets we would have left if we paid up all our immediate debts. Clearly Enterprise Ltd has plenty of spare current assets.

(d) On the liabilities side note that the Ordinary Shareholders own nearly everything. The Inland Revenue is entitled to £40 000 (Corporation Tax), the debenture holders (a debenture is a loan to a company) are entitled to £10 000 and the preference shareholders own their investment of £20 000 and the dividend of £1 800 to be paid to them any minute. Everything else, their original capital and all the reserves belong to the Ordinary Shareholders. This explains why shares can be worth much more than their par value. There are 100 000 ordinary shares of £1, and they are worth £164 200—so each share is worth just over £1.64.

The Vertical Style of Balance Sheet

The Balance Sheet of Enterprise Ltd can be rearranged in vertical style. The advantage of this method is that it is easy to print. It also gives plenty of room to display the depreciation, etc. Many companies have adopted this style (shown in Fig. 37.11), which is given as an alternative style in Schedule 4 of the Act, and the student should compare it with the more traditional style in Fig. 37.10. Despite its popularity in the United Kingdom our European partners reject a vertical Balance Sheet as a contradiction in terms. A Balance Sheet must by definition be horizontal, and the horizontal Balance Sheet is the only true Balance Sheet.

Enterprise Limited
Balance Sheet in Vertical Style
as at 31 December, 19 . .

Ordinary Shareholders' Interest in the Company

	Authorised £	Issued £
Capital and Reserves		
Ordinary Shares of £1 each, fully paid	100 000	60 000
Capital Reserves		
Share Premium Account	11 000	
Revenue Reserves		
General Reserves (at start)	20 000	
Add New Appropriation	10 000	
	30 000	
Balance on Profit and Loss Account	63 200	
	93 200	*104 200*
Ordinary Shareholders' Equity		*c/fwd* 164 200

b/fwd 164 200

Preference Shareholders' Interest in the Company

	Authorised	
9% Preference Shares of £1 each, fully paid	40 000	20 000

Debentures

8% Debentures of £100 each	10 000
Reserve for Corporation Tax	40 000
	£234 200

Represented by

Fixed Assets

	At Cost	Less Depreciation to date	
	£	£	£
Intangible Assets			
Patent Rights Owned	2 000	1 000	1 000
Tangible Assets			
Land and Buildings	48 000	—	48 000
Plant and Machinery	65 000	7 000	58 000
Furniture and Fittings	14 000	1 500	12 500
Motor Vehicles	24 500	1 501	22 999
	153 500	11 001	142 499

Trade Investments (valued by Directors at £22 450)	22 000
Total Fixed Assets	164 499

Current Assets	£	
Stock	27 500	
Other Investments (Market Value £34 750)	33 000	
Debtors	4 700	
Cash at Bank	29 250	
Cash in Hand	2 751	
	97 201	

Less Current Liabilities		
Trade creditors	13 700	
Preference dividend	1 800	
Ordinary dividend	12 000	
	27 500	

Net Working Capital	69 701
Net Value of Assets	£234 200

Fig. 37.11. A Balance Sheet in vertical style.

The Published Accounts of Companies

One final point about Company Final Accounts is this. If a company is a public company it must by law produce a set of published accounts in a style laid down in the Companies Act 1985. Such sets of accounts are a matter of public record and may be obtained from the company concerned. Should you wish to see such a set of accounts write to the public company of your choice (one whose name ends in Plc) and a copy will be provided.

37.11 Exercises: Company Balance Sheets

1. A limited liability company has an Authorised Capital of £180 000 divided into 60 000 9% Preference Shares of £1 each and 120 000 Ordinary Shares of £1 each. All the Preference Shares and 60 000 of the Ordinary Shares are issued and entitled to dividend. On 31 December, 19 . ., it was ascertained that the company had made a Net Profit of £68 500. There was a balance of £4 350 brought forward from the previous year. The directors decided to create a Reserve for Corporation Tax of £25 000. They also decided to transfer £18 500 to General Reserve and to pay the year's dividend on the Preference Shares. They proposed a dividend of 15% on the Ordinary Shares.

Show how the above information would appear on the Appropriation Account and bring down the balance to be carried forward to next year.

2. A limited liability company has an Authorised Capital of £320 000 divided into 120 000 8% Preference Shares of £1 each and 200 000 Ordinary Shares of £1 each. All the Preference Shares are issued and full paid; 100 000 Ordinary Shares are issued with £0.75 per share paid on each share.

On 31 December, 19 . ., the company's Revenue Reserves were £30 000; Current Liabilities £7500; Current Assets £62 750; Fixed Assets (at cost) £190 000 less Provisions for Depreciation on Fixed Assets £20 250.

Make a summarised Balance Sheet as at 31 December, 19 . ., to display this information. Set out the Balance Sheet in such a way as to show clearly the Net Value of Current Assets.

3. A limited company has authorised capital of 200 000 Ordinary Shares of which 100 000 shares of £1 are issued, and 50 000 9% Preference Shares of £1 of which 30 000 are issued. On 31 March, 19 . ., it was found that the Net Profit was £73 420 for the year. There was also a balance on the Appropriation Account of £4150 from the previous year. Fixed Assets were £165 500 and Current Assets were £44 570. Current Liabilities were £2500, before the following matters resolved on by the directors were dealt with:

(a) To put £20 000 to General Reserve and £10 500 to Plant Replacement Reserve.

(b) To reserve £25 000 for Corporation Tax.

(c) To pay the 9% Preference Dividend.

(d) To recommend a 15% dividend on the Ordinary Shares.

Show the Appropriation Account and the Balance Sheet, bringing out the Net Current Assets figure.

4. After taking out the Trading and Profit and Loss Accounts at 31 December, 19 . ., the revised Trial Balance of Pretty Pottery Ltd, is as follows:

	Dr £	*Cr* £
Cash	1 250	
Bank	23 750	
Stock at end of year	29 615	
Balance from 1 January on Appropriation Account		4 264
Preliminary Expenses	3 000	
Net Profit for Year		76 250
Furniture and Fittings (cost £24 000)	16 250	
Patent Rights Owned (cost £4 000)	3 000	
Machinery Reserve		15 000
Ordinary Capital (authorised 100 000 shares of £1)		80 000
9% Preference Share Capital (authorised £40 000)		40 000
8% Debentures of £100 each		15 000
General Reserve		11 351
Land and Buildings (at cost)	55 000	
Plant and Machinery (cost £65 000)	45 000	
Quoted Investments held (Market value £35 800)	30 000	
Unquoted Trade Investments (valued by directors at £24 000)	20 000	
Motor Vehicles and Spares (cost £24 500)	16 500	
Debtors and Creditors	2 500	4 000
	£245 865	£245 865

You are to show the Appropriation Account and Balance Sheet after taking into account the following decisions of the Directors:

(a) A dividend of 9% on the Preference Shares is to be paid.
(b) A dividend of 20% is to be paid on the Ordinary Shares.
(c) £20 000 is to be put away as a Reserve for Corporation Tax.
(d) £25 000 is to be put into a General Reserve Account.
(e) The Preliminary Expenses are to be written off completely.
(f) Patent Rights are to be reduced by £1 000.
(g) £5 000 is to be added to Machinery Reserve A/c.

38
An Introduction to Computers

38.1 What are computers?

Computers are electronic devices which can be programmed to do many routine activities. Since business calculations and accounting are routine activities, which are easily programmed it is probably true to say that the whole of this book is under attack from the electronic wizardry of the computer industry. Whilst this is true, it is also true to say that the computer is an industrious idiot, which will do what it is told at enormously fast speeds, but if there is the slightest difficulty in the instructions it receives it will stop dead until the problem is resolved. In the last analysis an intelligent human must get it going again. We still need to know our business calculations and accounting concepts.

Originally computers were huge machines depending upon the use of valves (a semi-conducting device which only allowed current to pass through them in one direction). Later much smaller semi-conductors called 'transistors' were developed, and later the element silicon was found to have the same property. Later whole circuits (integrated circuits) were printed on to a silicon chip and eventually microprocessors were developed which had a whole computer on a series of silicon chips the size of a child's thumbnail.

The essential components of a computer are shown in Fig. 38.1. They consist of a variety of **input devices**, which feed programs and information (data) into a **central processor**, often called the **CPU (central processing unit)**. Here the data is processed according to the **program** loaded into the CPU. The results are fed out to a variety of **output devices**. All data is passed in and out through cables called '**lines**' so that a direct line to a computer is an '**on-line**' system, but a lot of activities can be carried out '**off-line**'. Thus a computer which can process data at 1000 million operations per second does not want to be kept waiting while a printer working at only 200 characters per second prints out the results. The data is

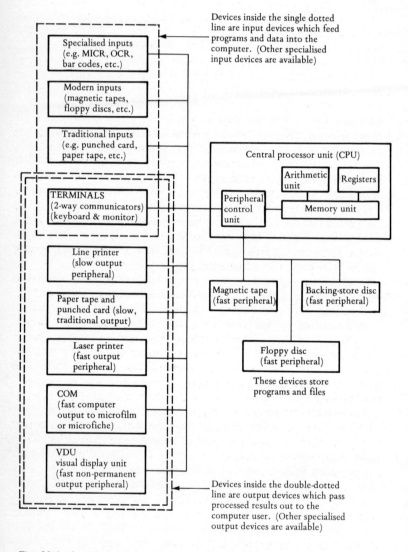

Fig. 38.1. A commercial computer configuration.

put out to a fast **peripheral** (that is a device outside the central processor) and is then **printed 'off-line'**.

38.2 Computer Hardware

Whilst a detailed knowledge of computer hardware is not necessary at this stage, it is useful to be familiar with the names of the units and the parts they play. Fig. 38.1 shows a typical commercial configuration, with alternative input and output devices.

The three essential elements in computerisation are **inputs, processing** and **outputs**. We must be able to put data and programs into the computer, which will then process the data and put out the results so that they can be understood. These three elements are provided for in the following ways.

(a) *Input devices.* The earliest input devices were punched cards and paper tape inputs. Although still in use there are faster input media today, notably magnetic tape, magnetic disc, MICR (magnetic ink character recognition), OCR and OMR (optical character recognition and optical mark recognition), bar codes and other devices. The chief method of communication with a computer by the computer user today is through a **terminal**, which consists of a keyboard and a VDU (visual display unit or monitor). The input device is the keyboard, and the VDU acts as the output device (often calling for the next instruction from the keyboard). It is an instantaneous response system from the computer which gives the user a strong sense of control over the procedures he/she is seeking to implement.

The essential point about any input device is that it turns something that is comprehensible to a human being, like a number or an arrangement of letters (a word) into something that is comprehensible to a computer. This something is a binary code. The computer can understand whether a current is positive or negative. A binary code is a code which is in the form of 1 and 0 only. One is positive and zero is negative. Every number and every letter has to be turned into a combination of 1 and 0, because only these two things are comprehensible to the machine. Most children these days learn something about binary codes, and obviously the computer programmer must be thoroughly familiar with the representation of numbers and letters in coded form. Numbers when turned into binary digits are called 'bits' for short. Letters are not so easy to turn into binary digits, and a coding system has to be developed for them.

Briefly, we may define the various input devices as follows:

Paper tape. An input device in which 8 holes punched in inch-wide tape give a unique combination for each character. The patterns are read by photo-electric cells.

Punched cards. An input device in which holes punched in a card in rows give unique character combinations for up to 80 characters. Again the patterns are read by photo-electric cells.

Terminals. These have been described above—the keyboard is the input device and the VDU acts as an output device and a buffer memory for data to be input when it has been validated (checked for accuracy).

Magnetic tape. A storage medium which stores data on magnetic oxide coatings on plastic tape. The characters are recorded in rows across the tape, with up to 6250 bits per inch. A standard tape is 2400 feet long.

Magnetic disc. It is a pack of magnetic discs on which data may be stored. Each pack has 20 recording surfaces each containing 800 tracks, capable of holding 2 500 million characters (bytes).

Floppy discs. These are single discs capable of holding about 640 K (thousand) bytes.

MICR. This is magnetic ink character recognition—widely used to read cheques. It uses characters encoded in an ink containing ferrous oxide. The cheques are encoded with the amount to be paid, alongside the account details pre-printed on the cheque.

OMR and OCR. These are input devices in which the computer is programmed to recognise optical marks and optical characters. Used in market research and similar activities the computer can 'read' the answers selected by those responding to the enquiry and takes much of the labour out of the processing of raw data. The raw scores can then be analysed and reviewed by a variety of 'number-crunching' programs.

Tags and cards. An increasing variety of magnetically marked tags, credit cards, etc. are becoming available as input devices to identify individuals, or individual items in such activities as stock-taking, EFTPOS (electronic funds transfer at the point of sale), security devices, etc.

(b) *The central processing unit (CPU).* The CPU is the main item of hardware, the computer itself, and contained within it are the **memory unit**, the **peripheral control unit or units**, the **arithmetic unit** and the **registers**.

The memory unit of the CPU determines the power of the computer, since it is here that the actual processing of data according to programmed instructions takes place.

The arithmetic unit is located in the CPU, and here the calculations such as multiplication and division are performed. The answers, and partial answers, to the calculations are stored in the registers temporarily, from where they may be transferred to the memory unit for subsequent output to tape or disc storage.

The memory unit (or main storage) holds both programs and data as required temporarily while the computer is processing part of the material, and after it has finished with it, pending more permanent storage on tape or disc. Eventually the results will be put out to an output device in readable form or to permanent storage (backing storage) in machine-readable form.

Peripheral control units are designed to deal with all the ancillary equipment used for input and output of information. Outside components are known as peripherals. The word 'periphery' means 'outside boundary' and the peripherals may be regarded as surrounding the CPU. Note that in some instances the peripheral control units are themselves peripheral to the CPU.

There are three main classes of computers in general use today, mainframe computers, minicomputers and microcomputers. A few points about each are:

Main frame computers. These have a very large capacity, and are very powerful, and very expensive. They are chiefly used by very large businesses and research establishments, and tend to be inflexible in that computer time has to be shared by a large number of users.

Minicomputers. With only medium capacity they are of greatest use to medium sized companies, though some large companies prefer several minicomputers to one mainframe, each operating in a distinct area of activity.

Microcomputers. These are quite powerful, very cheap, very small, suitable for a limited area of activity in any business but naturally of most use to the small business with more limited horizons. They are also ideal for school use, and for home use.

(c) *Output devices.* The chief method of output in the final stage is the **line printer**. This prints out the result of the processed data. It is the computer's most convenient method of communication since it can be read by the human user. Speeds vary with the type of device but an output of 1300 lines per minute, each line having a maximum of 132 characters, is representative. Other output devices such as punched cards or paper tape are less easily understood by the human user. As can be imagined, the production of output information is governed by the printer speed, which is low. To overcome this difficulty matter for printing is 'queued' on a fast medium, such as tape or disc, and then printed by a specialist program divorced from the original program. This is known as 'off-line' printing. A printer is a device which converts machine-readable binary codes into characters and figures printed on paper.

Apart from printers, the chief output devices, apart from non-readable outputs such as paper tape, punched cards and floppy discs are:

(i) COM (computer output to microfilm or microfiche) and (ii) graph plotters.

COM. This avoids vast collections of paper computer print-out by the development of microfiche output, which can be produced direct from a magnetic tape file, so that no printing is required. The computer output consists of a succession of microfilm exposures photographed from a cathode ray tube. They can be read in a microfilm reader. Their chief uses are in banking, insurance, libraries and offices such as public record offices. They are economical for archiving purposes, since they hold up to 270 A4 pages on a sheet of film 6 inches × 4 inches in size. Print-outs can be obtained of any desired document such as a customer's account.

Graph plotters. They produce diagrams by moving a pen (or several pens) across paper using a computer program to position the pen accurately.

38.3   Computer Software

Whilst each item of computer hardware is an essential element in the computerisation of any activity and has been developed to meet some need, none of them will operate without 'software' to organise their resources. Software provides the operating system and application programs to carry out the particular tasks required, such as the operation of accounting systems, payroll activities, etc.

Software in its widest sense means 'programs' or 'instructions' and can refer to a whole range of ideas and materials—in fact everything that is not hardware. Thus computer languages, documents, handbooks and 'packages' written to perform a particular function in data processing are all loosely described as software. More narrowly, software may be defined as a routine, or program, for performing a particular processing function required by a wide variety of end-users. Thus a particular program may assemble, or compile, or sort data or it may perform several such activities in succession.

Software is either supplied by the computer manufacturer as part of the basic package when purchasing a computer, or it may be supplied as an extra for a fee. Charging for software resulted in the development of 'software houses' who develop software for general use based upon the specialist work they have undertaken for individual clients.

38.4   How Computers have Changed Book-keeping

In Fig. 35.1 a chart shows how the double entry book-keeping system works. If we wish to see how computers have modified book-keeping it is useful to redraw this chart, in computerised form, and this is done in Fig. 38.2 (see pages 366–7). The chart is largely self-explanatory, but briefly we may explain the procedures as follows:

(a) When a collection of documents, such as purchases invoices, is to be put into the computer, the documents are 'batched up', coded with any necessary codes and passed to the key operator.

(b) The data is then keyed to a disc file, but in the process it will be 'edited', that is to say the computer will check it to see that it is acceptable. This is called 'validation'. Thus a coded account number would be checked to ensure that there was such an account, and if there was not the item would be rejected. A list of rejections giving the reason in each case would be produced for each batch together with a 'day-book' listing all the items accepted.

From this point on the diagram is really self-explanatory. The final result is that the batch of data can be input to the CPU which has already been loaded with a program of instructions. The individual purchases invoices will be credited to the personal account of the suppliers who have given the goods to us (credit the givers) while the total will be debited to Purchases Account which has received all these supplies.

It is not usual for computers to prepare final accounts, although they can be programmed to do so. The point here is that the cost of a program to make decisions at the final accounts level is greater than the cost of the work saved. Generally speaking the preparations of final accounts from the print-outs of the ledgers supplied by the computer is a straightforward task easily carried out manually. A study of the chart will reveal how the batched-up documents which would formerly have been entered in the day books are now recorded in the ledger accounts and on a printed list of inputs (the day book) electronically. The reader should now study the chart in Fig. 38.2.

38.5   Exercises: Computers

1. What is a computer? Why has it been called an industrious idiot?

2. Explain briefly what is meant by the following terms in the computer industry:
(a) Central processing unit;
(b) Peripheral units;

(1) Every transaction has an original document

(but now most of these documents will be produced by the computer automatically instead of manually)

Invoices from other firms, all different shapes and sizes, our Purchases

Second Copies of our own Invoices, our Sales to other firms

Credit Notes from other firms, our purchases returned

Second Copies of our own Credit Notes, sales returned to us

Invoices for Assets Bought

Bankruptcy Notices

Letters about Errors

Our Statements

Recd. with thanks

And cheques from the Debtors

Other Firms' Statements

And our cheques

Petty Cash vouchers

Other documents such as debit notes, credit notes, journal documents for journal entries are treated similarly according to their own requirements and lead to inputs, data processing and updating of all ledger accounts. The computer will thus hold the entire ledger system on its files, or as much of the system as the management decides

(2) Documents are no longer entered into Books of Original Entry. Instead groups of similar documents are coded with the necessary computer codes and 'batched-up' for preparation by the punched card operators or the key-edit operators. The resulting input media can then be fed in for processing by the computer. The sales procedure has been represented in diagrammatic form below. Other procedures have been indicated by brief notes

Purchases Invoices
(a) Coded as necessary
(b) batched up
(c) data preparation
(d) Input
(e) validation procedure
(f) print out of Input list (day book) and rejections for mis-coding etc.
(g) Creditors' ledger accounts posted
(h) Computer prepares payment list at best time to earn discount
(i) Computer prepares cheques

In computer diagrams this shape is used for any document. In this case it is our order form which customers have completed

The order comes in

The batch of orders is coded and passed to the operators for data preparation

Punched card inputs

Mag tape inputs

Computer checks the validity of inputs

List of Inputs (virtually a day book for that day)

Printout
(a) List of Inputs (virtually a day book for that day)
(b) List of rejections

Computerised Sales Procedure

(c) Computer produces invoices, dispatch notes, etc., as required

(d) Debits the personal accounts of the debtors

Credits the Sales Account

(e) Prints out statements for dispatch at the correct time

(f) Prints out the full ledger at the end of the month

(g)

(h) Answers any enquiry on difficult accounts at once

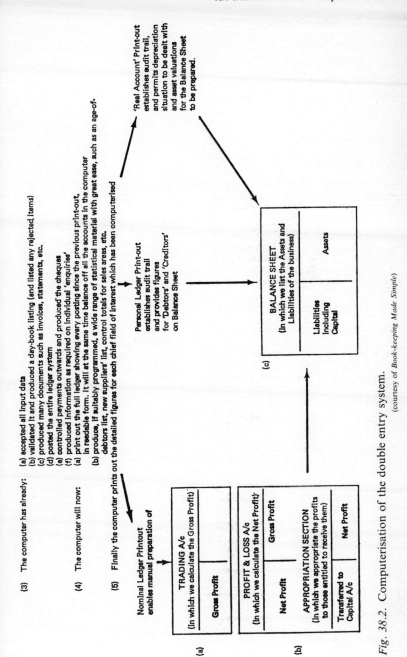

(3) The computer has already:

    (a) accepted all input data
    (b) validated it and produced a day-book listing (and listed any rejected items)
    (c) produced many documents such as invoices, statements, etc.
    (d) posted the entire ledger system
    (e) controlled payments outwards and produced the cheques
    (f) produced information as required on individual 'enquiries'

(4) The computer will now:

    (a) print out the full ledger showing every posting since the previous print-out, in readable form. It will at the same time balance off all the accounts in the computer
    (b) produce, if suitably programmed, a wide range of statistical material with great ease, such as an age-of-debtors list, new suppliers' list, control totals for sales areas, etc.

(5) Finally the computer prints out the detailed figures for each chief field of interest which has been computerised

'Real Account' Print-out establishes audit trail, and permits depreciation situation to be dealt with and asset valuations for the Balance Sheet to be prepared.

Personal Ledger Print-out establishes audit trail and provides figures for 'Debtors' and 'Creditors' on Balance Sheet

Nominal Ledger Printout enables manual preparation of

(a)

TRADING A/c
(In which we calculate the Gross Profit)

	Gross Profit
Gross Profit	

(b)

PROFIT & LOSS A/c
(In which we calculate the Net Profit)

	Gross Profit
Net Profit	

APPROPRIATION SECTION
(In which we appropriate the profits to those entitled to receive them)

	Net Profit
Transferred to Capital A/c	

(c)

BALANCE SHEET
(In which we list the Assets and Liabilities of the business)

Liabilities including Capital	Assets

Fig. 38.2. Computerisation of the double entry system.

(courtesy of *Book-keeping Made Simple*)

(c) Terminal;
(d) Batching-up;
(e) Off-line printing;
(f) Program.

3. What is meant in the computerisation of accounts by:

(a) Input validation;
(b) A day-book listing;
(c) Mag tape input;
(d) Visual display;
(e) Arithmetic unit;
(f) Disc storage.

4. List 4 types of computer input devices and explain one of them in detail.

5. List the components of a central processor and explain the functions of each.

6. List three types of computer output and explain the advantages of each.

7. Distinguish between hardware and software.

39
APR and the Consumer Credit Act

39.1 The Consumer Credit Act 1974

For about 100 years Parliament has wrestled with the problems of consumer credit, seeking to control such obvious abuses as extortionate credit (what the Americans call 'loan-sharking') and unprincipled repossession of goods purchased on credit because the unfortunate borrower has failed to pay the last instalment. After a series of measures to control various aspects of credit the whole field was comprehensively covered by the Consumer Credit Act 1974. So complex was the legislation that it took 11 years, until April 1985, to get the necessary administrative measures passed into law and every aspect of credit is now subject to close control, though the perfect closure of every legal loophole will perhaps never be achieved. Much of this legislation is inappropriate to the field of Business Calculations, but one aspect is important, the question of APR (Annual Percentage Rate).

39.2 Annual Percentage Rate (APR)

The Act requires that all those who make credit available to the public must show in their advertisements, brochures and other literature the true annual percentage rate of interest. As a matter of fact, that is not at all an easy thing to do. To illustrate the problems we will take a simple case.

Example 39.1. The Abel Motor Co. offers a new motor vehicle at £7 600 cash, or it may be purchased on payment of £760 deposit, and the balance on Hire Purchase at a flat rate of interest of 10% per annum for 3 years, repayable in 36 equal monthly instalments.
The calculation is:

	£
Cash price	7600
Less deposit	760
Amount of HP Loan	6840
Interest at 10% per annum for	
3 years = £684 × 3 =	2052
Total repayment	£8892

$$\text{Monthly repayments} = \frac{£8892}{36} = £247$$

This seems simple enough, but the flat rate of interest is not the true rate of interest, because the repayments start at once. The finance company has not loaned the customer £6840 for three years. The first £247 was only borrowed for one month (yet it paid three years interest). The second £247 was only borrowed for 2 months, yet it paid three years interest. As a matter of fact the only part of the loan that was borrowed for three years was the final £247. This is where the unfairness comes in to all credit transactions. It is convenient to talk about a flat rate of interest but the true rate of interest is much higher and the customer is to some extent deceived.

The Act requires that besides any flat rate of interest shown there must appear the true APR (annual percentage rate) which is usually more than double the flat rate of interest. Only then can the consumer really compare the different sources of credit and see which is the 'best buy' as far as the borrower is concerned. For example many banks, which are not required to calculate an APR for ordinary overdrafts, lend on overdraft at about 11–12%. To borrow on a credit card from one of the major credit card companies is usually at a rate around 23%, and for many 'store' credit cards the APR is nearer 30%.

39.3   Calculating the APR

This is by no means simple, and to save everyone a great deal of trouble the Office of Fair Trading has devised and made available a set of 15 Consumer Credit Tables. These are available from Her Majesty's Stationery Office for a few pounds for each table. The address is The Chief Bookseller, HMSO, PO Box 569, London SE1 9NH.

The range of tables is made up as follows:

Tables 1–10. These are 'charges per pound lent' tables and convert the charge per pound lent to an APR for ten different types of borrowing scheme.

Tables 11–14. These are flat rate tables, covering weekly repayments, monthly repayments and other frequency repayments and single repayment transactions. The example given above would be on a 'monthly repayment' transaction which would be covered in Table 12.

Table 15. This is a 'Period Rate Table' covering such schemes as the ordinary credit cards where 1.75% or 2% per monthly period is added to the outstanding balance.

A leaflet, *A guide to Consumer Credit Tables*, is available from The Office of Fair Trading, as is *Credit Charges*, a booklet which explains in detail how to calculate APRs.

There are three methods of calculating APRs:

(a) From the Consumer Credit Tables described above.

(b) From certain formulae which are helpful for particular types of transaction, notably single repayment transactions and period rate transactions.

(c) The present value rule. A simple outline of this is given below.

39.4 Present Values and the Present Value Rule

If you give us £247 today we have a present value of £247. If you promise to give us £247 in one month's time that is worth less to us than £247 today, because had you given it to us today, we could have invested it and obtained a month's interest on it. So the present value of £247 in one month's time is less than £247 by the amount of the interest lost. Imagining the rate of interest as 10% the interest lost in one month is:

$$
\begin{aligned}
1 &= \frac{PRN}{100} \\
&= \frac{246 \times 10 \times 1}{100 \times 12} \\
&= \frac{247}{120} \\
&= \text{£2.06}
\end{aligned}
$$

Therefore the present value of £247 one month from now is:

$$\text{£247} - \text{£2.06} = \text{£244.94}$$

Similarly £247 two months from now is:

$$£247 - £4.12 = \underline{\underline{£242.88}}$$

This basic idea of present values can be used to calculate the Annual Percentage Rate. In any transaction we know what the amount of the loan (the credit) is and we know what the total charge for credit is going to be. The true rate of interest will be that rate which makes the present values of all repayments (when added together) the same as the present value of the credit (or all the credits if funds are to be made available in more than one lump). This must be so, because what the borrower intends to do is to repay what he/she borrowed with interest.

We can see this if we take a very simple case; but first let us learn the formula for the present value of a repayment. It is:

$$\text{Present value of a repayment} = \frac{A}{\left(1 + \dfrac{r}{100}\right)^t}$$

where A is the amount of the repayment
  r is the rate per cent and
  t is the time period in years.

So, in any loan transaction the present value of all the repayments added together (calculated at a certain rate of interest) has to equal the present value of the loan made (i.e., the actual amount of the loan). For every transaction there must be a rate (the APR) where this is so.

We can see this if we take a simple case which has only one repayment made exactly one year later.

Example 1. Suppose Hardup borrows £2400 to be repaid in one year's time by a single repayment of £3000. Since only one year is involved and only one repayment (A = £3000), we can say:

$$\text{Present value of all the repayments (1 only)} = \frac{£3000}{\left(1 + \dfrac{r}{100}\right)^1}$$

The APR will be that value of r which makes the present value of repayment (shown above) equal to the amount of the loan £2400.

So,

$$\frac{£3000}{\left(1 + \dfrac{r}{100}\right)^1} = £2400$$

Transposing this simple equation:

$$\frac{£3000}{£2400} = 1 + \frac{r}{100}$$

Cancelling out the £ signs and cancelling by 600 we have

$$\frac{5}{4} = 1 + \frac{r}{100}$$

$$1\tfrac{1}{4} - 1 = \frac{r}{100}$$

$$\tfrac{1}{4} = \frac{r}{100}$$

$$\frac{r}{100} = \tfrac{1}{4}$$

$$r = \tfrac{1}{4} \times 100$$

$$= 25\%$$

Check! The APR = 25%. £2400 loaned for 1 year at 25% per annum.

$$1 = \frac{PRN}{100}$$

$$= \frac{2400 \times 25 \times 1}{100}$$

$$= 24 \times 25$$

$$= £600$$

So, £2400 loaned for 1 year at 25% per annum requires a repayment of £3000 on the due date.

Example 2. Suppose the repayment of the loan of £2400 has been made in two annual instalments of £1500.

This is a good point to define the Annual Percentage Rate with a formal definition. It reads:

APR is a rate per annum such that the sum of the present values of all the repayments made of the original loan and the total charge for credit is equal to the original loan made (or the sum of the present values of all the credits made if there were several of them) the present values being calculated at that rate.

In the case above, the present value of the first repayment is:

$$\frac{1500}{\left(1 + \frac{r}{100}\right)^1}$$

The present value of the second repayment is:

$$\frac{1500}{\left(1 + \dfrac{r}{100}\right)^2}$$

The sum of the present values of all the repayments is therefore:

$$\frac{1500}{\left(1 + \dfrac{r}{100}\right)^1} + \frac{1500}{\left(1 + \dfrac{r}{100}\right)^2}$$

Since this sum of the present values has to be equal to the original loan we have:

$$2400 = \frac{1500}{\left(1 + \dfrac{r}{100}\right)^1} + \frac{1500}{\left(1 + \dfrac{r}{100}\right)^2}$$

Since, by giving the debtor two years to pay for the same total repayment the creditor is giving the borrower a much fairer deal, the APR is in fact much lower, but we can only find out what the APR is by systematically trying various solutions. For example:

Try $r = 20\%$

$$2400 = \frac{1500}{1\frac{1}{5}} + \frac{1500}{1\frac{1}{5} \times 1\frac{1}{5}}$$

$$= \frac{7500}{6} + \frac{1500 \times 25}{36}$$

$$= 1250 + 1041.666$$

$$= 2291.666$$

This figure is too low. 2400 is not equal to 2291.$\dot{6}$.

The rate is lower than 20%: Try 18%

$$2400 = \frac{1500}{1.18} + \frac{1500}{1.18 \times 1.18}$$

$$= 1271.186 + 1077.276$$

$$= 1348.462 \quad \text{This is again too low.}$$

The actual rate is 16.25%:

$$2400 = \frac{1500}{1.1625} + \frac{1500}{1.1625 \times 1.1625}$$

$$= 1290.3225 + 1109.9548$$

$$= 2400.2773$$

This is as nearly accurate as we can be. So the APR = 16.25%.

The reader will see that these sorts of calculations are by no means elementary, and the sensible thing to do is to refer to the tables as supplied by the Office of Fair Trading. A short extract from the monthly repayments table is shown in Fig. 39.1.

Equal instalments: monthly intervals

Annual flat rate %	Number of instalments (months)								
	16	17	18	19	20	21	22	23	24
9.00	17.6	17.6	17.7	17.7	17.7	17.7	17.7	17.7	17.7
9.25	18.1	18.2	18.2	18.2	18.2	18.2	18.2	18.2	18.2
9.50	18.7	18.7	18.7	18.7	18.7	18.7	18.7	18.7	18.7
9.75	19.2	19.2	19.2	19.2	19.2	19.2	19.2	19.2	19.2
10.00	19.7	19.7	19.7	19.7	19.7	19.7	19.7	19.7	19.7
10.25	20.2	20.2	20.2	20.2	20.2	20.2	20.2	20.2	20.2
10.50	20.7	20.7	20.7	20.8	20.8	20.8	20.7	20.7	20.7
10.75	21.2	21.3	21.3	21.3	21.3	21.3	21.3	21.2	21.2
11.00	21.8	21.8	21.8	21.8	21.8	21.8	21.8	21.8	21.7
11.25	22.3	22.3	22.3	22.3	22.3	22.3	22.3	22.3	22.2
11.50	22.8	22.8	22.8	22.8	22.8	22.8	22.8	22.8	22.8
11.75	23.3	23.3	23.4	23.4	23.3	23.3	23.3	23.3	23.3

Fig. 39.1. An extract from Table 12—the 'Monthly Repayments' table.

(courtesy of the Comptroller-General, HMSO.)

39.5 Exercises: Annual Percentage Rates

1. What is the annual percentage rate if £500 is repaid with a lump sum repayment of £560 in 12 months time?

2. What is the annual percentage rate if £500 is repaid with a lump sum repayment of £300 one year later and a further £300 one year after that?

3. What is the annual percentage rate if £1000 is repaid with a lump sum of £1125 one year later?

4. What is the annual percentage rate if £1000 is repaid with a lump sum repayment of £650 one year later and a further £650 after a further year?

Answers

Chapter 2

2.3 1. 1991; 2. 5415; 3. 12 604; 4. 29 401; 5. 404 952; 6. 464 107; 7. 90 271; 8. 1 530 444; 9. 43 402; 10. 55 194.

2.5 1. 241; 2. 108; 3. 2537; 4. 3936; 5. 1468; 6. 4136; 7. 145 686; 8. 134 330; 9. 131 147; 10. 489 186.

2.6 1. 528; 2. 1266; 3. 4941; 4. 3402; 5. 5384; 6. 12 497; 7. 136 152; 8. 117 389; 9. 2 887 828; 10. 9 469 710.

2.8 1. 1806; 2. 3258; 3. 20 880; 4. 19 668; 5. 57 000; 6. 104 676; 7. 19 904; 8. 25 916; 9. 86 405; 10. 205 268.

2.9 1. 9483; 2. 35 358; 3. 190 513; 4. 349 328; 5. 113 831; 6. 289 050; 7. 2 677 095; 8. 9 208 696; 9. 20 271 024; 10. 110 043 545.

2.11 1. 118; 2. $141\frac{2}{3}$; 3. 64; 4. $104\frac{1}{4}$; 5. $79\frac{2}{3}$; 6. $104\frac{1}{4}$; 7. $260\frac{2}{3}$; 8. $432\frac{1}{4}$; 9. $1024\frac{2}{3}$; 10. $769\frac{7}{8}$; 11. $2173\frac{3}{8}$; 12. 3169; 13. $4773\frac{7}{8}$; 14. $1393\frac{3}{8}$; 15. $6893\frac{1}{4}$; 16. $7113\frac{5}{11}$; 17. $7072\frac{7}{8}$; 18. $2472\frac{9}{10}$; 19. $10\,422\frac{2}{3}$; 20. $15\,143\frac{3}{8}$.

2.13 *Note:* In checking these answers those who have used an electronic calculator will find that the fraction at the end is given as a decimal. To check this use the following procedure: (a) write down the decimal fraction found by the calculator on a scrap of paper; (b) clear the calculator; (c) enter the decimal fraction only on the calculator; (d) divide by the numerator of the fraction given in the answer, and multiply by the denominator given in the answer. The result should be 1, but it will actually come to 0.999, etc., on the calculator. If this is so your answer is correct. For example, in No. 10 below, the answer is $\frac{9}{11}$. If $\frac{9}{11}$ is divided by 9 it gives $\frac{1}{11}$ and multiplied by 11 it gives $\frac{11}{11} = 1$. Because of the continuing nature of the calculator answer it will give 0.999, etc., not 1, since you have actually left out part of the decimal fraction when you entered it on the calculator. 1. 215; 2. $254\frac{2}{15}$; 3. $292\frac{14}{17}$; 4. $365\frac{5}{16}$; 5. $1143\frac{18}{19}$; 6. $2332\frac{1}{14}$; 7. $1184\frac{3}{23}$; 8. $1274\frac{8}{29}$; 9. $2595\frac{13}{13}$; 10. $1296\frac{9}{11}$; 11. $1190\frac{1}{4}$; 12. $886\frac{40}{43}$; 13. $407\frac{50}{69}$; 14. $361\frac{69}{137}$; 15. $673\frac{45}{64}$; 16. $260\frac{22}{279}$; 17. $3188\frac{107}{256}$; 18. $3181\frac{13}{114}$; 19. $1889\frac{15}{449}$; 20. $1306\frac{26}{295}$.

Chapter 3

3.3 1. (a) 39.926; (b) 353.019; (c) 262.537 6; (d) 4648.536 3; (e) 389.084 8;

(f) 564.646; (g) 822.914 6; (h) 4 404.385 05; (i) 888.641 48; (j) 28 557.244 68
2. (a) 12.931; (b) 240.75; (c) 33.849; (d) 2212.74; (e) 190.07635; (f) 3.2895; (g) 325.864; (h) 7528.381; (i) 18.0375; (j) 95.844

3.5 1. (a) 42.75; (b) 387.5; (c) 5258.5; (d) 638.5; (e) 72 500; (f) 83 569.5; (g) 240; (h) 78 300; (i) 8695; (j) 21 000
2. (a) 2.76; (b) 32.85; (c) 1.272 5; (d) 0.018 6; (e) 4.256 5; (f) 0.072 56; (g) 21.865; (h) 0.027 985; (i) 0.008 757; (j) 0.009 695 6

3.7 1. 12.978; 2. 13.020 3; 3. 34.582 5; 4. 1372.272; 5. 166.017 75; 6. 21 137.34; 7. 48.1275; 8. 1065.333 15; 9. 9376.342 51; 10. 1825.304 75

3.9 1. 11.024; 2. 6.9; 3. 198.21; 4. 342.36; 5. 15.5; 6. 11.63; 7. 130.4; 8. 2.83; 9. 559.529; 10. 2.333

Chapter 4

4.2 1. $\frac{1}{2}$; $\frac{1}{2}$; $\frac{2}{3}$ 2. $\frac{1}{2}$; $\frac{2}{3}$; $\frac{3}{3}$ 3. $\frac{1}{4}$; $\frac{1}{2}$; $\frac{3}{4}$ 4. $\frac{1}{3}$; $\frac{2}{3}$; $\frac{1}{2}$ 5. $\frac{1}{2}$; $\frac{2}{3}$; $\frac{5}{6}$ 6. $\frac{1}{6}$; $\frac{2}{3}$; $\frac{5}{6}$ 7. $\frac{1}{4}$; $\frac{1}{2}$; $\frac{5}{6}$ 8. $\frac{1}{6}$; $\frac{1}{3}$; $\frac{7}{9}$ 9. $\frac{1}{2}$; $\frac{2}{3}$; $\frac{5}{6}$ 10. $\frac{7}{12}$; $\frac{1}{4}$; $\frac{5}{12}$.

4.3 1. $1\frac{1}{2}$; $1\frac{1}{4}$; $1\frac{1}{2}$ 2. $3\frac{1}{2}$; $4\frac{2}{3}$; $4\frac{1}{2}$ 3. $3\frac{3}{8}$; $3\frac{1}{4}$; $3\frac{1}{4}$ 4. $7\frac{1}{2}$; $2\frac{1}{6}$; $6\frac{1}{4}$ 5. $4\frac{3}{4}$; $7\frac{1}{8}$ 6. $8\frac{2}{3}$; $5\frac{1}{3}$ 7. $3\frac{1}{2}$; $7\frac{1}{4}$ 8. $9\frac{3}{10}$; $3\frac{3}{4}$ 9. $5\frac{1}{4}$; $7\frac{1}{4}$ 10. $2\frac{7}{12}$; $6\frac{2}{3}$.

4.5 1. $1\frac{17}{30}$; 2. $2\frac{1}{24}$; 3. $7\frac{3}{8}$; 4. $9\frac{5}{24}$; 5. $10\frac{5}{12}$; 6. $11\frac{11}{24}$; 7. $13\frac{14}{15}$; 8. $9\frac{23}{60}$; 9. $13\frac{7}{20}$; 10. $10\frac{43}{84}$.

4.7 1. $\frac{1}{12}$; 2. $\frac{1}{8}$; 3. $\frac{3}{20}$; 4. $\frac{1}{10}$; 5. $\frac{27}{56}$; 6. $\frac{1}{4}$; 7. $\frac{10}{12}$; 8. $\frac{1}{15}$; 9. $\frac{4}{15}$; 10. $\frac{5}{24}$; 11. $\frac{7}{12}$; 12. $\frac{17}{26}$; 13. $3\frac{11}{12}$; 14. $1\frac{11}{24}$; 15. $4\frac{1}{13}$; 16. $3\frac{9}{16}$; 17. $4\frac{28}{36}$; 18. $1\frac{32}{36}$; 19. $1\frac{7}{12}$; 20. $10\frac{19}{48}$.

4.8 1. $\frac{1}{2}$; 2. $\frac{5}{16}$; 3. $\frac{9}{20}$; 4. $\frac{1}{6}$; 5. $\frac{5}{24}$; 6. $\frac{7}{30}$; 7. $\frac{5}{64}$; 8. $\frac{7}{24}$; 9. $\frac{6}{11}$; 10. $\frac{33}{8}$; 11. $7\frac{7}{12}$; 12. $13\frac{1}{8}$; 13. 10; 14. 11; 15. $22\frac{1}{2}$; 16. 8; 17. $15\frac{3}{4}$; 18. $2\frac{7}{8}$; 19. 24; 20. 10.

4.11 1. $1\frac{1}{3}$; 2. $1\frac{1}{4}$; 3. $\frac{7}{12}$; 4. $1\frac{1}{3}$; 5. $\frac{3}{8}$; 6. $1\frac{5}{12}$; 7. $1\frac{13}{15}$; 8. $2\frac{1}{3}$; 9. $\frac{8}{15}$; 10. $\frac{9}{9}$; 11. $1\frac{1}{3}$; 12. $1\frac{19}{21}$; 13. $\frac{4}{5}$; 14. $1\frac{1}{2}$; 15. $1\frac{1}{3}$; 16. $\frac{2}{3}$; 17. $1\frac{4}{11}$; 18. 4; 19. $3\frac{1}{2}$; 20. $8\frac{4}{11}$.

4.13 1. 1; 2. $\frac{1}{2}$; 3. $7\frac{5}{36}$; 4. $5\frac{5}{12}$; 5. $\frac{1}{2}$; 6. $5\frac{7}{9}$; 7. $1\frac{1}{4}$; 8. 2; 9. $1\frac{9}{10}$; 10. 38; 11. $4\frac{1}{30}$; 12. $\frac{1}{3}$.

4.15 1. 0.375; 2. 0.8; 3. 0.7; 4. 0.533; 5. 0.778; 6. 0.857; 7. 0.417; 8. 0.917; 9. 0.273; 10. 0.938; 11. 0.95; 12. 0.575; 13. 0.212; 14. 0.308; 15. 0.975.

4.16 1. $\frac{2}{3}$; 2. $\frac{9}{16}$; 3. $\frac{2}{5}$; 4. $\frac{27}{50}$; 5. $\frac{22}{25}$; 6. $\frac{5}{8}$; 7. $\frac{99}{200}$; 8. $\frac{177}{200}$; 9. $\frac{361}{500}$; 10. $\frac{87}{250}$; 11. $\frac{201}{250}$; 12. $\frac{251}{400}$; 13. $\frac{483}{1250}$; 14. $\frac{453}{625}$; 15. $\frac{1853}{2000}$.

Chapter 5

5.3 (a) XXVII; (b) XXXIV; (c) IL; (d) LIII; (e) LXXII; (f) LXXXV; (g) CXXV; (h) CCCLXV; (i) MDCCXX; (j) MDCCCXCV.
2. (a) 17; (b) 39; (c) 61; (d) 78; (e) 95; (f) 105; (g) 362; (h) 1984; (i) 1966; (j) 2000.

5.5 1. (a) 33; (b) 110; (c) 358; (d) 870; (e) 2015; 2. (a) 6920; (b) 14 430; (c) 21 070; (d) 159 392; (e) 1 047 076.

5.6 1. 96; 2. 68; 3. 510; 4. 64; 5. 1016; 6. 116; 7. 765; 8. 8.4; 9. 15.3; 10. XXVII; 11. 64; 12. $1\frac{1}{3}$; 13. $\frac{1}{8}$; 14. $\frac{1}{3}$; 15. $\frac{7}{12}$.

Chapter 6

6.4   1. (a) £134.26; (b) £109.62; (c) £110.18; (d) £349.73; (e) £16.58; (f) £131.70; (g) £423.68; (h) £376.50; (i) £8009.52; (j) £10 615.85.
2. Junior £286 217.60; De Luxe £252 198.41.
3. Grand total £466 465.87.
4. (a) £158.04; (b) £181.72; (c) £191.31; (d) £2250.75; (e) £3221.25.
5. (a) £2.19; (b) £15.32; (c) £75.21; (d) £105.98; (e) £197.13.
6. (a) £108.86; (b) £66.96; (c) £39.77; (d) £54.82; (e) £106.83; (f) £100.23; (g) £77.69; (h) £40.93.

6.6   1. (a) £173; (b) £414; (c) £1277.50; (d) £271.04; (e) £38.25.
2. (a) £2512.50; (b) £2390.80; (c) £7228.80; (d) £1689.30; (e) £1220.00.
3. £2145.50.
4. £134 028.
5. £12 867.45.
6. £901 20.
7. £49 857.50.
8. £90 690.20.
9. £820.35.
10. £483.

6.8   1. (a) £1.72 remainder 2p; (b) £6.43 remainder 2p; (c) £3.97 remainder 6p; (d) £9.10 remainder 6p; (e) £6.08 remainder 2p; (f) £17.15; (g) £7.98 remainder 4p; (h) £13.16 remainder 3p; (i) £10.59 remainder 3p; (j) £7.05 remainder 5p.
2. (a) £21.71; (b) £45.41 remainder 4p; (c) £143.60 remainder 15p; (d) £234.03 remainder 6p; (e) £98.45 remainder 5p; (f) £238.64 remainder 13p.
3. £319.00
4. £23.25
5. £29.46

6.10   1. (a) £23.76; (b) £99; (c) £107.73; (d) £178.20; (e) £179.10.

6.11   1. 209; 2. 786; 3. 175; 4. 228; 5. £17.70; 6. £69.95; 7. £22.40; 8. 0.055; 9. 0.078; 10. $1\frac{1}{24}$; 11. $2\frac{1}{4}$; 12. $\frac{3}{14}$; 13. 1; 14. 1972; 15. IL.

Chapter 7

7.3   1. (a) 27 500 m; 27 500 000 mm; (b) 312 200 m; 312 200 000 mm; (c) 1465 m; 1 465 000 mm; (d) 2735 m; 2 735 000 mm; (e) 46 m; 46 000 mm; (f) 38.57 m; 38 570 mm; (g) 0.072 m; 72 mm; (h) 0.085 m; 85 mm; (i) 495.6 m; 495 600 mm; (j) 3872.5 m; 3 872 500 mm.
2. (a) 7500 g; 7 500 000 mg; (b) 8600 g; 8 600 000 mg; (c) 27 545 g; 27 545 000 mg; (d) 326 550 g; 326 550 000 mg; (e) 425 500 g; 425 500 000 mg; (f) 872 550 g; 872 550 000 mg; (g) 7500 kg; 7 500 000 g; (h) 18 400 kg; 18 400 000 g; (i) 250 000 kg; 250 000 000 g; (j) 149 250 kg; 149 250 000 g.
3. (a) 5700 litres; 5 700 000 ml; (b) 4300 litres; 4 300 000 ml; (c) 780 litres; 780 000 ml; (d) 490 litres; 490 000 ml; (e) 2.75 litres; 2750 ml; (f) 38.56 litres; 38 560 ml; (g) 425 litres; 425 000 ml; (h) 1755 litres; 1 755 000 ml; (i) 1 250 000 litres; 1 250 000 000 ml; (j) 875 000 litres; 875 000 000 ml.

7.5   1. £7449.30; 2. 36 620 litres left; £5945.80 takings; 3. 900 packets; 4. 24 400 packets; 5. 5100 bags; 6. 5100 ampoules; 7. 11 850 bottles; 8. 91 tonnes; 9. £36 075; 10. 1823.5 kg.

7.7   1. (a) 900; (b) 1125; (c) 2450; (d) 3150; (e) 3550; (f) 19 500

2. (a) 3375; (b) 7000; (c) 18 625; (d) 23 125; (e) 34 750; (f) 48 000
3. (a) 4250; (b) 6250; (c) 96 250; (d) 123 000; (e) 215 250; (f) 1 846 000

7.8 1. 1143; 2. XXXI; 3. 21; 4. 6.35 kg; 5. 25; 6. $1\frac{2}{3}$; 7. $\frac{3}{5}$; 8. £1.61; 9. $1\frac{1}{2}$; 10. 1000; 11. 900; 12. 1 000 000; 13. 100, 14. 6000; 15. 1939.

Chapter 8

8.8 1. 13 days; 2. 407; 3. 47 days; 4. $3\frac{3}{4}$; 5. 0.15; 6. 75 days; 7. No (an odd-numbered year is never a leap year); 8. Yes (1976 does divide by four); 9. 5.965 m; 10. 26 076; 11. No: the last year in a century is only a leap year if it divides by 400; 12. XIX; 13. Yes (2000 ÷ 400 = 5); 14. 4; 15. 3600 seconds.

Chapter 9

9.2 1. (a) 1:4; (b) 1:4; (c) 50:1; (d) 20:1; (e) 5:16; (f) 8:1; (g) 4:9; (h) 11:16; (i) 1:3; (j) 2:15.
2. (a) 1:2; (b) 1:12; (c) 1:200; (d) 1:14; (e) 1:3500; (f) 1:1.42; (g) 1:500; (h) 1:96; (i) 1:2000; (j) 1:1041.67.
3. (a) 1:0.83; (b) 1:1.72; (c) 1:2.14; (d) 1:5; (e) 1:3.5.
4. (a) (i) 1:0.52, (ii) 1:0.61; (b) (i) 1:1.67, (ii) 1:0.52; (c) (i) 1:1.43, (ii) 1:0.62; (d) 1:1.29.

9.4 1. (a) £1050, £350; (b) £1695, £1130; (c) £3675, £2205, £1470; (d) £16 160, £8080, £4040; (e) £37 500, £28 125, £9375.
2. (a) £10 000, £10 000, £7500; (b) £13 725, £13 725, £9150; (c) £8205, £8205, £5470, £2735; (d) £10 250, £8200, £6150; (e) £10 196, £10 196, £7647, £7647, £5098.
3. A takes 2800 litres.
4. £1644, £822, £274.
5. 0.42 tonnes, 0.35 tonnes and 0.28 tonnes.
6. £7500, £2500 and £5000.
7. 30 kg, 30 kg, 25 kg, 25 kg, 20 kg. Total load = 130 kg.
8. £12.48.

9.6 1. (a) 14p; (b) 9p; (c) 75p; (d) £35; (e) £30.
2. (a) £40; (b) £9; (c) £25; (d) £24; (e) £25.
3. (a) £12.96; (b) £90.80; (c) £17 712; (d) £2080; (e) £94 050; (f) £31.50; (g) £42 508.50; (h) £73 504. (i) $64\frac{3}{4}$ minutes; (j) 224 kilometres.

9.8 1. (a) 2 days; (b) $3\frac{1}{2}$ weeks; (c) 7 days; (d) 5 days; (e) 15 cartons.
2. (a) 24 days; (b) 85 bunches; (c) $7\frac{1}{2}$ weeks; (d) 54 minutes; (e) After 108 days.

9.9 1. (a) £40; (b) £227; (c) £129; (d) £300; (e) £665.

9.10 1. 722; 2. £654.01; 3. £2 700 000; 4. £345; 5. 2550 cm; 6. $1\frac{3}{4}$; 7. 147 days; 8. £75, £25; 9. 72 pence; 10. 84 pence; 11. $4\frac{1}{2}$ days; 12. 42 days; 13. 270 minutes; 14. LXXV; 15. £54.

Chapter 10

10.4 1. (a) 50%; (b) 25%; (c) $66\frac{2}{3}$%; (d) 70%; (e) 80%.
2. (a) $37\frac{1}{2}$%; (b) $87\frac{1}{2}$%; (c) $31\frac{1}{4}$%; (d) 12%; (e) $58\frac{1}{3}$%.

3. (a) $\frac{3}{4}$%; (b) $\frac{7}{20}$; (c) $\frac{3}{20}$; (d) $2\frac{1}{30}$; (e) $\frac{19}{25}$.
4. (a) $\frac{3}{8}$; (b) $\frac{7}{16}$; (c) $\frac{5}{8}$; (d) $1\frac{2}{16}$; (e) $2\frac{1}{40}$.

10.7 1. (a) 0.36; (b) 0.42; (c) 0.385; (d) 0.555; (e) 0.6$\dot{6}$.
2. (a) 0.115; (b) 0.1775; (c) 0.875; (d) 0.3$\dot{3}$; (e) 1.8.
3. (a) 24%; (b) 36%; (c) 4%; (d) 9%; (e) 37$\frac{1}{2}$%.
4. (a) 175%; (b) 132%; (c) 230%; (d) 30.25%; (e) 45.75%.

10.9 1. £980; 2. £1176; 3. 450 kg; 4. 12 120 kg; 5. 6825 hectares; 6. £16 940; 7. 32 130 electors; 8. £18 737.60; 9. 28 050 members; 10. £4426.80.

10.11 1. (a) £1.50; (b) £9.25; (c) £6.25; (d) £107.25; (e) £193.75; (f) £2; (g) £3; (h) £1.89; (i) £3.14; (j) £53.75.
2. (a) £2.50; (b) £4.60; (c) £3.12; (d) £4.79; (e) £3.34; (f) £7.16; (g) £87.82; (h) £91.24; (i) £18.16; (j) £11.62.
3. £594.40.
4. (a) £95; (b) £2875; (c) £220; (d) £109.35; (e) £12.41; (f) £242.17; (g) £1282.50; (h) £4350; (i) £691.88 (j) £2333.02.

10.13 1. 14.29%; 2. 13.33%; 3. 2.89%; 4. 6.67%; 5. 18%; 6. 1.5%; 7. 4.9%; 8. 36.67%.

10.15 1. (a) 0.03; (b) 0.12; (c) 0.35; (d) 0.072; (e) 0.15; (f) 0.064; (g) 0.000 48; (h) 0.000 15; (i) 0.004 2; (j) 0.000 18.
2. (a) 0.36; (b) 0.52; (c) 0.09; (d) 0.06; (e) 0.55; (f) 0.085 5; (g) 0.005 4; (h) 0.000 625; (i) 0.126; (j) 0.000 682.

10.16. 1. 892; 2. 1645; 3. 833; 4. 120 000; 5. £12.35; 6. £95.40; 7. $\frac{9}{40}$; 8. $\frac{1}{4}$; 9. 175 cm; 10. 28 days; 11. MCMXXV; 12. £410; 13. 23 500; 14. £1·80; 15. £11.25.

Chapter 11

11.3 1. (a) £110; (b) £132; (c) £247.50; (d) £396; (e) £1.65; (f) £2.09; (g) £0.22; (h) £0.44; (i) £935.55; (j) £413.38.
2. (a) £69; (b) £82.80; (c) £97.75; (d) £18.98; (e) £41.11; (f) £48.88; (g) £316.82; (h) £976.92; (i) £0.97; (j) £0.55.
3. £1016.40; 4. £45.62; 5. £19.78; 6. £4224.40; 7. £185.65; 8. £5638.12.

11.5 (a) $\frac{1}{11}$; (b) $\frac{1}{6}$; (c) $\frac{1}{5}$; (d) $\frac{3}{23}$; (e) $\frac{2}{27}$; (f) $\frac{3}{28}$; (g) $\frac{4}{29}$; (h) $\frac{9}{39}$; (i) $\frac{7}{57}$; (j) $\frac{31}{231}$.
2. (a) £3; (b) £60; (c) £6.30; (d) £9.60; (e) £7.83; (f) £75.65; (g) £55.37; (h) £41.80; (i) 76 pence; (j) £16.50.
3. (a) £1000; (b) £2500; (c) £3250; (d) £4060; (e) £541.34; (f) £569.43; (g) £6480.43; (h) £8580.36; (i) £7140.87; (j) £1082.25.
4. £11 940; 5. £6904; 6. £148 630.96.

11.6 1. £2.30; 2. 6558; 3. 915; 4. £237.50; 5. £172.50; 6. 48 pence; 7. 66$\frac{2}{3}$%; 8. 525 cm; 9. 1 : 3; 10. £10, £5, £5; 11. AD 2000; 12. £4140; 13. 0.25; 14. £85; 15. £134.

Chapter 12

12.4 1. (a) £40; (b) £297; (c) £102; (d) £243.75; (e) £30.80; (f) £622.20; (g) £178.50; (h) £777; (i) £286.75; (j) £992.25.
2. (a) £100; (b) £195; (c) £302.40; (d) £535.50; (e) £1081; (f) £6393.75; (g) £14 235; (h) £8174.38; (i) £15 480; (j) £39 283.12.

12.6 1. (a) £384; (b) £840; (c) £4320; (d) £15 000; (e) £6750.
2. (a) £135; (b) £269.50; (c) £815.62; (d) £496.10; (e) £1105; (f) £648;
(g) £312; (h) £16 312.50; (i) £17 600; (j) £131 250.

12.8 1. (a) £750; (b) £1200; (c) £2500; (d) £4600; (e) £1800.
2. (a) 14%; (b) $12\frac{1}{2}$%; (c) $8\frac{1}{2}$%; (d) 27%; (e) $13\frac{1}{2}$%.
3. 3. (a) $2\frac{1}{2}$ yrs; (b) $3\frac{1}{2}$ yrs; (c) 5 yrs; (d) $8\frac{1}{2}$ yrs; (e) 25 yrs.
4. £8500; 5. 11.5%; 6. $1\frac{1}{2}$ years.

12.10 1. (a) 72 days; (b) 81 days; (c) 69 days; (d) 137 days; (e) 119 days; (f) 53 days;
(g) 140 days; (h) 68 days; (i) 47 days; (j) 48 days.
2. (a) 85 days; (b) 97 days; (c) 207 days; (d) 148 days; (e) 74 days; (f) 280
days; (g) 257 days; (h) 81 days; (i) 114 days; (j) 212 days.
3. £36; 4. £170.50; 5. £56; 6. £76.50; 7. £11.70; 8. £37.40; 9. £255; 10. £21.

12.12 1. £30; 2. £360; 3. £85; 4. £160; 5. £22.50; 6. £11.25; 7. £26; 8. £540; 9. £200;
10. £900.

12.13 1. 1375; 2. 68; 3. £15.74; 4. $1\frac{3}{15}$; 5. $\frac{1}{15}$; 6. 10 000; 7. £640; 8. 36 pence;
9. 0.25; 10. 350 cm; 11. £300; 12. £22.50; 13. £400:£200:£400; 14. £500;
15. £1050.

Chapter 13

13.3 1. (a) 8; (b) 7; (c) 30; (d) 23; (e) 147; (f) 343; (g) 392.75; (h) 2373; (i) 42 m;
(j) 19 kg.
2. (a) £35.30; (b) 32 min 17 sec; (c) 4.81 litres; (d) 3881.25 kg; (e) £678;
(f) £20 013.75; (g) 323 tonnes; (h) $4365\frac{2}{3}$ tonnes; (i) 3 h $20\frac{1}{2}$ min; (j) 4 h
$55\frac{1}{2}$ min.

13.5 1. 64.2% 2. £1.65; 3. (a) £25; (b) £108.90; (c) £6; 4. (a) 28.8 tonnes; (b) 18
tonnes; 5. £5400; 6. 70.6 sec; 7. 174.2 cm; 8. £3327.50.

13.7 1. 10; 2. 15; 3. 70; 4. 31; 5. 26; 6. 103; 7. 820; 8. 10 123; 9. 20 056; 10. 75 040.

13.8 1. 1918; 2. 896; 3. £215.66; 4. $5\frac{1}{8}$; 5. 0.25; 6. 945; 7. 2500 grams; 8. 120
pamphlets; 9. 7; 10. 31 days; 11. £650; 12. £1440; 13. 50%; 14. 2 years;
15. 3017.

Chapter 14

14.2 1. (a) 90p; (b) £1.20; (c) £1.50; (d) £3; (e) £3.45; (f) £7.80; (g) £4.80; (h) £9.45;
(i) £6.75; (j) £15.75.
2. (a) £3.60; (b) £7.80; (c) £12; (d) £32.40; (e) £18.72; (f) £22.20; (g) £30.36;
(h) £58.56; (i) £600; (j) £744.
3. (a) £5.25; (b) £6.30; (c) £11.90; (d) £19.60; (e) £25.20; (f) £43.75; (g) £64.75;
(h) £84; (i) £1225; (j) £2520.

14.4 1. (a) 40p; (b) 40p; (c) 90p; (d) £1; (e) £2.16; (f) £2.75; (g) £18.90; (h) £42;
(i) £300; (j) £1200.
2. £1530; 3. £108; 4. £101.50; 5. £3150.

14.6 1. (a) £2; (b) £1.80; (c) £8; (d) £24; (e) £5; (f) 36.60.
2. (a) 45p; (b) £1.20; (c) £2.70; (d) £3; (e) £11.70; (f) £25.20.
3. (a) 50p; (b) £2; (c) £138; (d) £5.60; (e) £45.20; (f) £180; (g) £600; (h) £50;
(i) £600; (j) £1480.

4. (a) 50p; (b) £4; (c) £5; (d) £20; (e) £30; (f) £15; (g) £20; (h) £40; (i) £37.50; (j) £1.50.
5. £800; 6. £25 000; 7. £275; 8. £17 500.

14.8　1. (a) 38p; (b) 72p; (c) £2; (d) £3.01; (e) £3.80; (f) £8.96; (g) £8.60; (h) £11.25; (i) £27.20; (j) £52.
2. (a) £3.95; (b) £6.75; (c) £6; (d) £15.30; (e) £4.50; (f) £8.60; (g) £20.40; (h) £27.30; (i) £21; (j) £29.75.

14.10　1. 78p; 2. £3.56; 3. £6.15; 4. £43.80; 5. £626.50; 6. £5.64; 7. £16.02; 8. £26.95; 9. £168; 10. £9125.

14.11　1. 4706; 2. 328; 3. 39 000; 4. £15.03; 5. $\frac{1}{8}$; 6. 25; 7. $8\frac{1}{8}$; 8. 7575p; 9. £100; 10. 10; 11. £64; 12. £360; 13. 42p; 14. 103 metres; 15. £40.

Chapter 15

15.3　1. (a) £22.95; (b) £32.40; (c) £43.20; (d) £63.45; (e) £121.50; (f) £229.50.
2. (a) £144.50; (b) £1105; (c) £1041.25; (d) £3633.75; (e) £1615; (f) £3081.25.
3. (a) £2745; (b) £3820; (c) £27 453.50; (d) £39 652.80; (e) £273 607; (f) £368 546.20; (g) £1 377 204.80; (h) £2 957 215.40; (i) £7 454 646.20; (j) £7 953 627.30.

15.5　1. A = 27 pence in £1; B = 65 pence in £1; C = 74 pence in £1; D = 56 pence in £1; E = 88 pence in £1.
2. V = 31 pence in £1; W = 35 pence in £1; X = 85 pence in £1; Y = 55 pence in £1; Z = 69 pence in £1.
3. (a) 1.3 pence in £1; (b) 3.1 pence in £1; (c) 21.5 pence in £1; (d) 2.6 pence in £1; (e) 5.9 pence in £1.
4. (a) £727 800; (b) 19.5 pence in £1.
5. (a) 11.6 pence in £1; (b) 0.1 pence in £1.

15.6　1. 2512; 2. 1245; 3. 4455; 4. 1090; 5. 0.21; 6. 13; 7. $1\frac{11}{12}$; 8. £1100; 9. $\frac{3}{5}$; 10. MCMLXXX; 11. 165; 12. £120; 13. £38.75; 14. £125; 15. £4750.

Chapter 16

16.3　1. (a) £108.02; (b) £60.88; (c) £28.30; (d) £130.48; (e) £91.84.
2. (a) £82.23; (b) £111.66; (c) £83.49; (d) £99.05; (e) £85.58.
3. (a) £109.85; (b) £84.64; (c) £68.30; (d) £122.00; (e) £120.94.
4. (a) £1007.50; (b) £1350.12; (c) £1812.08; (d) £2108.30 (e) £2537.32.

16.5　1. (a) £53.92; (b) £27.96; (c) £26.56; (d) £50.24; (e) £55.41.
2. (a) £33.04; (b) £42.90; (c) £46.66; (d) £27.54; (e) £53.75.
3. (a) £1192.23; (b) £2334.41; (c) £5419.54; (d) £3108.37; (e) £4787.60.

16.7　1. (a) £60.33; (b) £39.76; (c) £73.64; (d) £428.17; (e) £113.57; (f) £215.21.
2. (a) £74.16; (b) £64.22; (c) £163.96; (d) £168.35; (e) £38.11.

16.9　1. 77°F; 2. 59°F; 3. 89.6°F; 4. 30°C; 5. 45°C; 6. 60°C.

16.10　1. 3288; 2. 1484; 3. 4 tickets; 4. 3; 5. 0.28; 6. $8\frac{1}{8}$; 7. 1 000 000; 8. $7\frac{1}{2}$ days; 9. 450 seconds; 10. £6600; 11. £53.50; 12. £18.75; 13. £16; 14. 1982; 15. £65.

Chapter 17

17.2 1. (a) £12; (b) £16.30; (c) £28.80; (d) £39.20; (e) £92.80; (f) £106.20; (g) £189.20; (h) £280.60; (i) £637.70; (j) £913.40.
2. (a) £50.44; (b) £150.26; (c) £64.17; (d) £164.24; (e) £300.94.
3. (a) £860.20; (b) £1236.24; (c) £398.78; (d) £464.20; (e) £1757.37.

17.4 1. A = £560.91; B = £720.66; C = £894.87; D = £1460.41; E = £1303.37.
2. AB Plc = £440.06; CD Plc = £521.46; EF Plc = £637.90; GH Plc = £954.87; JK Plc = £1043.79.

17.6 1. 65 000; 2. 80 000; 3. 36 000; 4. 244 000; 5. 210 000.

17.7 1. 495; 2. 73 566; 3. 2; 4. 0.115; 5. £210; 6. 54; 7. £138.45; 8. £1500; 9. £3562.50; 10. $8\frac{4}{5}$; 11. £910; 12. £4.23; 13. £6000: £6000: £4000: £2000; 14. 20°C; 15. £460.

Chapter 18

18.2 1. (a) (i) £1964, (ii) 8.2 pence per km; (b) (i) £3392, (ii) 8.1 pence per km; (c) (i) £7500, (ii) 13.4 pence per km; (d) (i) £13 960, (ii) 15.5 pence per km; (e) (i) £15 985, (ii) 15.7 pence per km.
2. Smith (i) £1620.50, (ii) 9.0 pence per km; Jones (i) £1629.50, (ii) 8.1 pence per km; Green (i) £2303.40, (ii) 9.6 pence per km; Johnson (i) £2359.80, (ii) 7.2 pence per km; Wilde (i) £3421.50, (ii) 6.3 pence per km; Mortimer (i) £3539.50 (ii) 9.8 pence per km. Mrs Wilde's vehicle gives the most economic performance.
3. (a) £2270.17; (b) 9.1 pence per km.
4. (a) £2174; (b) 9.9 pence per km.
5. (a) £6508; (b) Depreciation = 46.9%, licence = 5.0%, insurance = 4.4%, hazardous goods insurance = 7.7%, servicing = 5.8%, repairs = 10.1%, diesel = 8.3%, tyres = 6.5%, overheads = 5.4%; (c) 18.1 pence per km.

18.4 1. A = 240 km; B = 484 km; C = 449.5 km; D = 96 km/h; E = 48 km/h; F = $8\frac{1}{2}$ h; G = $4\frac{3}{4}$ h; H = 67.2 km/h; I = 4 h 15 min; J = 516 km.
2. 22 kilometres per hour.
3. (a) 376 km; (b) 53.7 kilometres per hour.
4. (a) 109.5 km; (b) 19.9 kilometres per hour.
5. (a) 4 h; (b) 76 kilometres per hour.
6. 77.6 kilometres per hour.
7. 82.5 kilometres per hour.

18.5 1. 126 km; 2. 540 km; 3. 6 h 30 min; 4. 8 h 10 min; 5. 4 h 30 min.

18.6 1. 28 944; 2. £1272.35; 3. £198.40; 4. $5\frac{13}{16}$; 5. 1.875; 6. 5500 litres; 7. £12.88; 8. £25; 9. £7.56; 10. £14; 11. £22 500; 12. £53.40; 13. £180; 14. £150; 15. 20 km/h.

Chapter 19

19.3 1. £2797.25; 2. £864.74; 3. £549.61; 4. £1518.43.

19.4 1. £69.14; 2. £117.85; 3. £270; 4. £126; 5. £123; 6. £225; 7. £286; 8. £3240.

19.5 1. 3638; 2. 2 430 000; 3. $\frac{1}{4}$; 4. 272.7; 5. 73.85 kg; 6. £110; 7. £2550; 8. 34; 9. £412.50; 10. £440; 11. 60 days; 12. £375; 13. 49; 14. 220.5 km; 15. £2820.

Chapter 20

20.3 1. (a) £87.12; (b) £78.38; (c) £52; (d) £80.25; (e) £94.95; (f) £98.18; (g) £52;
(h) £142.35; (i) £125.20; (j) £81.76.
2. (a) £73.12; (b) £81.00; (c) £69.38; (d) £101.89; (e) £74.68; (f) £107.19;
(g) £102.80; (h) £69.88; (i) £99.45; (j) £89.10.

20.6 1. (a) £725; (b) £533.55; (c) £24.25; (d) £92.50; (e) £191; (f) £495; (g) £1755;
(h) £10 000; (i) £12 100; (j) £200 000.
2. (a) £98; (b) £134; (c) £143; (d) £206; (e) £296.
3. (a) £360; (b) £355; (c) £475; (d) £745; (e) £725.
4. £64.70; 5. £441.25; 6. £893.75; 7. £1177.90.

20.9 1.

	Taxable pay to date (£)	Total deductions (£)	Net pay (£)
AB	70.65	33.18	51.12
CD	77.85	32.29	79.81
EF	52.30	27.28	50.62
GH	48.00	20.07	45.43

Total net pay: £226.98
Total tax due: £74.10
Total national insurance (employees' + employer's): £72.33
Total trade union contributions: £2.00
Total charity: £0.35
Total SAYE: £10
Total superannuation: £17.80

2.

	Taxable pay to date (£)	Total deductions (£)	Net pay (£)
R.S.	86.78	34.06	60.97
T.U.	60.31	29.47	45.64
V.W.	116.94	52.05	97.59
Y.Z.	150.96	73.84	94.42

Total net pay: £298.62
Total tax due: £123.60
Total national insurance (employees' and employer's): £104.67
Total trade union contributions: £2.60
Total charity: £0.40
Total SAYE: £25.00
Total superannuation: £30.96

20.11

	1 A.B. £	2 C.D. £	3 E.F. £	4 G.H. £
Gross pay	71.05	126.30	97.04	101.20
Gross pay for tax purposes	67.50	119.98	92.19	96.14
Gross pay to date for tax	67.50	As given	As given	As given
Taxable pay to date	41.35	646.80	604.70	1028.90
Tax	12.30	9.10 (refund)	14.50	17.20
Total deductions	17.78	9.45	21.79	24.61
Net pay	49.72	110.53	70.40	71.53
Refunds	—	9.10	—	—
Total Payable	49.72	119.63	70.40	71.53
NI Employer's	9.25	16.44	12.63	13.17
NI Contributions	14.48	25.74	19.77	20.38

20.12 1. 1491; 2. 1355; 3. 1475; 4. 81 000; 5. £52.50; 6. 36; 7. £1150; 8. £175 000; 9. 168 km; 10. £560; 11. £190; 12. 0.40; 13. 0.4; 14. £26.88; 15. £33.75.

Chapter 21

21.3 1. (a) (i) £8.10, (ii) £45.90; (b) (i) £20, (ii) £40; (c) (i) £17, (ii) £68; (d) (i) £36, (ii) £84; (e) (i) £57, (ii) £228.

2. (a) £7.67; (b) £29.32; (c) £37.50; (d) £10.18; (e) £14.58.

3. (a) £7.50; (b) £14.38; (c) £10.42; (d) £18.75; (e) £21.67; (f) £8.00; (g) £10.89; (h) £13.00; (i) £20.94; (j) £31.18.

4. (a) £1.99; (b) £2.43; (c) £4.81; (d) £6.97; (e) £8.50; (f) £4.06; (g) £4.23; (h) £5.92; (i) £7.05; (j) £9.29.

21.4 1. £16; 2. £112; 3. £1600; 4. £875; 5. £550; 6. £600; 7. £1450; 8. £1040; 9. £37.50; 10. £20.

21.5 1. 5100; 2. 70; 3. £8.50; 4. $\frac{1}{2}$; 5. £525; 6. 16.35; 7. 41 days; 8. 51; 9. £1680; 10. £12 000; 11. £78; 12. £18 000: £6000: £6000; 13. £4800; 14. £6340; 15. £3160.

Chapter 22

22.2 1. $585; 2. 2190 DM; 3. 7707 francs; 4. 223 912.5 yen; 5. 116 928 pesetas; 6. 97 968 escudos; 7. 226.2 Kuwaiti dinars; 8. 2772.9 guilders; 9. $2813.94; 10. A$ 1167.6.

22.4 1. £125; 2. £78.50; 3. £65; 4. £48.50; 5. £60; 6. £360; 7. £425; 8. £6500; 9. £7800; 10. £22 500.

22.5 1. £200; 2. 9250 pesetas; 3. 1041 Swiss francs; 4. £4000; 5. 32 500 escudos; 6. £21.50; 7. 4750 DM; 8. 3793.6 guilders; 9. £2000; 10. £300.

22.6 1, 1598; 2. £1109.96; 3. 306.4; 4. 20 metres; 5. £640; 6. 42 packets; 7. £360; 8. 2050 francs; 9. £179.50; 10. £44; 11. £12.50; 12. £4000; 13. 60 km/h; 14. $326; 15. £2000.

Chapter 23

23.3 1. (a) 25 cm²; (b) 64 cm²; (c) 7 dm² 29 cm²; (d) $2\frac{1}{4}$ m² or 2.25 m² or 2 m² 25 dm²; (e) $7\frac{9}{16}$ m² or 7.5625 m² or 7 m² 56 dm² 25 cm²; (f) 625 m² or 6 a 25 m²; (g) 1 hectare; (h) 2 ha 25 a; (i) 9 ha; (j) $6\frac{1}{4}$ km² or 6.25 km² or 6 km² 25 ha.

2. (a) 84 cm²; (b) 6 dm² 12 cm²; (c) 14 dm² 40 cm²; (d) 23 dm² 75 cm²; (e) 96 are; (f) 1 ha 50 a; (g) $4\frac{3}{8}$ m² or 4.375 m² or 4 m² 37 dm² 50 cm²; (h) $8\frac{3}{4}$ m² or 8.75 m² or 8 m² 75 dm²; (i) $2\frac{3}{4}$ km² or 2.75 km² or 2 km² 75 ha; (j) 13.34 km² or 13 km² 34 ha.

3. (a) 22 cm; (b) 24 cm; (c) 20 m; (d) 27 m; (e) 48 m; (f) 33 m.

4. (a) 12 cm; (b) 17 cm; (c) 20 m; (d) 19 m; (e) 27 m; (f) 38 m.

23.5 1. (i) 199.5 m², (ii) 32 cm², (iii) 59.5 m², (iv) 72 cm²; 2. 27.45 m²; 3. 71.875 m²; 4. (a) 211.8 m², (b) 248.82 m², (c) 153.4 m², (d) 776 m²; 5. (a) 3104 blocks; (b) £1978.20.

23.7 1 (a) (i) 20 cm, (ii) 25 cm²; (b) (i) 32 cm, (ii) 64 cm²; (c) (i) 96 cm, (ii) 576 cm²; (d) (i) 144 cm, (ii) 1296 cm²; (e) (i) 12 m, (ii) 9 m²; (f) (i) 400 m, (ii) 10 000 m² or 1 hectare.
2. (a) (i) 24 cm, (ii) 12 cm²; (b) (i) 20 cm, (ii) 24 cm²; (c) (i) 22 cm, (ii) 28 cm²; (d) (i) 30 cm, (ii) 54 cm²; (e) (i) 40 m, (ii) 96 m²; (f) (i) 56 m, (ii) 192 m²; (g) (i) 76 m, (ii) 345 m²; (h) (i) 92 m, (ii) 504 m²; (i) (i) 104 m, (ii) 640 m²; (j) (i) 132 m, (ii) 1008 m².

23.9 1. 36 m²; 2. (a) 27 m², (b) 51.25 m²; 3. 144 m²; 4. (a) 78.75 m², (b) £7; 5. (a) 168 m², (b) £16.45; 6. (a) 225 m², (b) £15.40.

23.11 1. (a) 64 cm³; (b) 343 cm³; (c) 3375 cm³; (d) 8000 cm³; (e) 3.375 m³; (f) 12.167 m³.
2. (a) 544 cm³; (b) 2024 cm³; (c) .52 m³; (d) 4.5 m³; (e) 36.792 m³; (f) 108 m³.
3. (i) 842 400 cm³; (ii) 336 000 cm³; (iii) 3.3408 m³.
4. 900 cubes; 5. 200 000 cubes.

23.13 1. 284 pence; 2. £19.20; 3. £40; 4. £65; 5. £60; 6. 1907; 7. 0.001; 8. $\frac{7}{15}$; 9. 10 000 001; 10. 0.5% or $\frac{1}{2}$%; 11. 184 m²; 12. 1.728 m³; 13. 48 cubes; 14. 16 m; 15. 1752 m.

Chapter 24

24.2 1. (a) 22 cm; (b) 66 cm; (c) 11 cm; (d) 33 cm; (e) 44 cm; (f) $37\frac{5}{7}$ cm; (g) $56\frac{4}{7}$ cm; (h) $103\frac{3}{7}$ cm; (i) 110 cm; (j) 132 cm.
2. (a) 44 cm; (b) 66 cm; (c) 88 cm; (d) 176 cm; (e) $75\frac{3}{7}$ cm; (f) $125\frac{5}{7}$ cm; (g) 220 cm; (h) 440 cm; (i) $188\frac{4}{7}$ cm; (j) $282\frac{6}{7}$ cm.
3. (a) 785 m; (b) 1 km 884 m; (c) 3 km 140 m; (d) 15 km 700 m; (e) 32 km 970 m.

24.4 1. (a) 154 cm²; (b) $38\frac{1}{2}$ cm²; (c) 616 cm²; (d) 1386 cm²; (e) 7546 cm²; (f) 1 m² 2474 cm².
2. (a) 154 cm²; (b) 616 cm²; (c) $38\frac{1}{2}$ cm²; (d) $346\frac{1}{2}$ cm²; (e) $78\frac{4}{7}$ m²; (f) $240\frac{5}{8}$ m²; (g) $176\frac{11}{14}$ m²; (h) $1964\frac{2}{7}$ m²; (i) $7857\frac{1}{7}$ m²; (j) 11 $314\frac{2}{7}$ m².
3. (a) 28.26 cm²; (b) 78.5 cm²; (c) 254.34 cm²; (d) 706.5 cm²; (e) 1256 cm²; (f) 7850 cm²; (g) 2 m² 5434 cm²; (h) 4 m² 9062 cm²; (i) 33 m² 1662 cm²; (j) 63 m² 5850 cm².

24.6 1. (a) 198 cm³; (b) 385 cm³; (c) 1100 cm³; (d) 2310 cm³; (e) 12 320 cm³.
2. (a) 62 800 cm³; (b) 942 000 cm³; (c) 2 m³ 649 375 cm³; (d) 4.71 m³; (e) 9.8125 m³.
3. 660 cm²; 4. 1508 $\frac{4}{7}$ cm²; 5. 6 m² 2800 cm².

24.7 1. 44 cm; 2. 308 cm; 3. 66 cm; 4. 110 cm; 5. $12\frac{4}{7}$ cm²; 6. $38\frac{1}{2}$ cm²; 7. $314\frac{2}{7}$ cm²; 8. $\pi r^2 h$; 9. $2\pi r^2 + 2\pi rh$; 10. 1540 cm³.

24.8 1. 909; 2. 749; 3. $5\frac{7}{20}$; 4. 0.5; 5. 55 500 escudos; 6. 56 days; 7. £60; 8. £52.50; 9. £220; 10. £4480; 11. 1851; 12. 12 764; 13. £5 950 000; 14. 22 cm; 15. 154 m².

Chapter 25

25.3 1. (a) £257.50; (b) £442.50; (c) £477.50; (d) £691.50; (e) £959; (f) £2532; (g) £461.10; (h) £289.10; (i) £275.65; (j) £151.90.

2. (a) £714; (b) £230.50; (c) £1014.67; (d) £9776.25; (e) £7147.52.
3. (a) Profit of £280; (b) Profit of £112; (c) Profit of £50; (d) Profit of £1777.50; (e) Loss of £5610.

25.5 1. (a) (i) £515, (ii) £80; (b) (i) £221.88, (ii) £112.50; (c) (i) £2850, (ii) £587.50; (d) (i) £4777.50, (ii) £812.50; (e) (i) £11 150, (ii) £987.50.
2. (a) (i) £3400, (ii) £425, (iii) 12.5%.
(b) (i) £6662.50, (ii) £796.25, (iii) 12.0%.
(c) (i) £9800, (ii) £1268.75, (iii) 12.9%.
(d) (i) £9400, (ii) £1050, (iii) 11.2%.
(e) (i) £2812.50, (ii) £312.50, (iii) 11.1%.
3. Increase in income of £71.00.
4. Fall in income of £40.
5. Increase in income £70.50.
6. Total cost = £26 975; Income = £3512.50.
7. (i) £24 500, (ii) £3985.
8. (a) Change in income is an increase of £200. Therefore recommend approval of the proposal; (b) yield = 12.2%.

25.6 1. 2100; 2. 31; 3. 12.415; 4. $\frac{1}{2}$; 5. $\frac{1}{3}$; 6. £4000: £2000: £2000; 7. 32 kg; 8. £138; 9. £56; 10. 13; 11. £129.15; 12. 10 pence; 13. £10 000; 14. £24.50; 15. 15%.

Chapter 26

26.4 1. Balance at end, £385.05; 2. Balance at end, £303.97; 3. Balance at end, £306.78; 4. Balance at end, £358.25.

26.6 1. Balance at end, £2300.20; 2. Balance at end, £4352.88; 3. Balance at end, £591.90.

26.7 1. 8042; 2. 103; 3. 380 000; 4. £133.55; 5. £68.12; 6. 1920; 7. 14; 8. $370; 9. 210 sec; 10. £300.

Chapter 27

27.3 1. Balance in hand £8.80; totals for week £56.36; imprest restored £31.20.
2. Balance in hand £2.68; totals for week £60.00; imprest restored £47.32.
3. Balance in hand £17.23; totals for week £55.65; imprest restored £32.77.
4. Balance in hand £6.65; totals for week £62.50; imprest restored £43.35.
5. Balance in hand £16.13; totals for week £57.23; imprest restored £33.87.

27.4 1. 103; 2. 784; 3. 363; 4. 216; 5. 10; 6. $1\frac{5}{8}$; 7. $4\frac{1}{12}$; 8. 0.125; 9. $33\frac{1}{3}$%; 10. 62 m; 11. £225; 12. 400 shares; 13. £12; 14. 365; 15. 47 days.

Chapter 28

28.3 1. (a) £1200; (b) £200; (c) £175; (d) £3550; (e) £3500.
2. (a) £2925 per annum; (b) The account is not shown in these answers. 3. (a) £2300; (b) £1150; (c) The account is not shown in these answers.

28.5   1. (a) Yr. 1 £875, Yr. 2 £656, Yr. 3 £492; (b) Yr. 1 £2133, Yr. 2 £1422, Yr. 3
£948; (c) Yr. 1 £960, Yr. 2 £768, Yr. 3 £614; (d) Yr. 1 £1062, Yr. 2 £797, Yr. 3
£598; (e) Yr. 1 £13 600, Yr. 2 £10 880, Yr. 3 £8704.
2. Deductions as follows: Yr. 1 £1875; Yr. 2 £1641; Yr. 3 £1436; Balance after
three years, £10 048.
3. Deductions: Yr. 1 £581; Yr. 2 £1017; Balance at end of 19–2, £3052.

28.7   1. £7.80; 2. £14.05; 3. $\frac{1}{4}$; 4. 0.125; 5. £15.13; 6. 7 500 000; 7. 2540 litres;
8. £28.80; 9. 721; 10. πr^2; 11. $\pi r^2 h$; 12. 91; 13. £12 000 : £8000 : £8000; 14. £800;
15. £1440.

Chapter 29

29.3   1. (a) £702.46; (b) £842.96; (c) £1053.70; (d) £1685.91; (e) £2107.39; (f)
£2809.86; (g) £7024.64; (h) £9132.03; (i) £10 396.47; (j) £17 983.08.
2. (a) £699.84; (b) £891.08; (c) £2007.04; (d) £3650.10; (e) £4158.59; (f)
£4470.51; (g) £5514.32; (h) £8864.73; (i) £10 411.74; (j) £13 524.00.

29.5   1. (a) £5470.52; (b) £8542.97; (c) £4296.97; (d) £17 471.44; (e) £141 152.99.
2. (a) £2680.19; (b) £8590.93; (c) £6417.37; (d) £16 653.91; (e) £45 266.37.

29.6   1. 1316; 2. 203; 3. 17.5; 4. $1\frac{1}{24}$; 5. 2; 6. £12.25; 7. £21; 8. £34; 9. 46 h; 10.
£1020.

Chapter 30

30.3   1–4. No numerical answers required.

30.5   1. 140 hundreds; 2. The correct order is D, F, G, H, C, B, I, A, J, E; 3. 52.8,
25.5, 27.3; 55.6, 27.0, 28.6; 55.9, 27.2, 28.7; 4. 7 526 000 tonnes; 5. 72 000;
6. 109 400.

30.6   1. 322; 2. 51.9; 3. $7\frac{5}{8}$; 4. 64; 5. 157 050; 6. 1 120 000; 7. 165 sec; 8. 13; 9. 45
pence; 10. £6000; 11. £125; 12. 24 cubes; 13. 27 000; 14. 0.048; 15. 1275 francs;
16. 154 cm²; 17. £154; 18. 28 million; 19. 1 m 98 cm; 20. £560.

Chapter 31

31.2   1. (a) 7, (b) 2, (c) 8, (d) 1, (e) 2; the data tells us the quality is rather erratic,
and even then tends to be biased towards a short life for the light bulbs.
2. (a) 2, (b) 3, (c) 7, (d) 11, (e) 5, (f) 2; this tells us the weights of recruits are
chiefly clustered around the 65–75 range, with a slight bias to heavier weights
than light weights.
3. The numbers in the groups are (a) 2, (b) 7, (c) 11, (d) 7, (e) 3.
4. The numbers in the groups are (a) 10, (b) 10, (c) 4, (d) 6, (e) 5, (f) 4, (g) 2,
(h) 3, (i) 6.

31.5   1. 24 329 million therms; 2. 23 637 thousand animals; 3. Grand total 232 024
thousand square metres; 4. Year 1 £15 657 m, Year 2 £26 366 m.

31.8   1. Percentages after correction are as follows: 0%; 2.0%; 2.9%; 8.9%; 18.6%;
19.6%; 25.5%; 22.5%; 0%.
2. Groups total 14, 14, 3, 3, 6 respectively. Percentages 35%; 35%; 7.5%; 7.5%;
15%.

3. Percentages = 4%; 4%; 40%; 26%; 10%; 12% and 4% respectively.
It would be incorrect to specify classes as 30–40, 40–50, etc., because uncertainty creeps in about which group certain items should be entered in, i.e. 40 might be in either of the groups named above.
4. Cumulative table reads 2, 8, 18, 25, 35, 43, 46, 50.

31.9 1. 32 256; 2. 125 735; 3. 9280; 4. 14.5; 5. 720 000 000; 6. $1\frac{19}{24}$; 7. 37; 8. £67.50; 9. £12.50; 10. £1920; 11. 30; 12. 12 750 mm; 13. 28 000; 14. 16; 15. £96; 16. 12 pence; 17. 54 cm²; 18. 16 000 000; 19. $\frac{11}{40}$; 20. £3000.

Chapter 32

32.3
32.6 }
32.8 } Numerical answers not required.
32.10 }

32.12 1. 6027; 2. 9510; 3. $1\frac{3}{8}$; 4. 7400; 5. 266 000; 6. 0.6 m³; 7. £400; 8. 19; 9. 410 francs; 10. £5110; 11. £121.50; 12. 210 sec; 13. 198 m; 14. £444; 15. 32.5%; 16. £105; 17. £48; 18. £99; 19. £4380; 20. £2800.

Chapter 33

33.4 No numerical answers required.

33.6. 1(b). £126; 2. (b) (i). £55.50, (ii) 45 hours; 3. £612.50.
Note: For the answers given above read off from the graphs a small error can be excused, and counted as correct.

33.8 No numerical answers required.

33.9 1. 1728; 2. 3387; 3. 38 475; 4. 1560; 5. 0.0016; 6. 4; 7. 2500; 8. πr^2; 9. 37; 10. £180; 11. £322.50; 12. £188; 13. 450 sec; 14. 20 pence; 15. £24 000; 16. £2.58; 17. £4800:£3200:£1600; 18. £100; 19. £2.10; 20. £2.40.

Chapter 34

34.3 1. 34 826 units; 2. 27.8 years; 3. 1120.2 books; 4. 50 981 m; 5. 288 kg.

34.5 1. 72.9 m²; 2. £770; 3. 1206 kg; 4. £2.90.

34.7 1. 236 hours; 2. 193.5 eggs; 3. £14 250; 4. £16 626.50.

34.9 1. A, 27; B, 5; C, 36.
2. A, 4; B, 2; C, 1 and 3.
3. 3-bedroomed.
4. 16 tonnes, 24 tonnes and 32 tonnes.

34.11 1. 292.237; 2. £147.77; 3. £3 500 000; 4. £1984; 5. 2400 bottles; 6. 3200; 7. 68 days; 8. 29; 9. 480; 10. £27; 11. £40.68; 12. £500; 13. 375 metres; 14. 7500 m²; 15. 75 m³; 16. £168; 17.731; 18. £287.50; 19. 154 cm²; 20. £36 000.

Chapter 35

No answers in this chapter.

Chapter 36

36.2   1. Final balance £2053.32C; 2. Final balance £16.41D; 3. Final balance £4457.23C.

36.4   1. Cash A/c is debited and Mrs K. Johnston is credited, as she is the giver.

2. Atlantic Building Society is debited (it has received back the use of its money) and Mr T. Charles is credited (he has given the Bank the money).

3. Sara Patel is credited with the two cheques she has deposited. Head Office Account is debited since it will have to arrange to debit the accounts in the two branches where A. Kadar and Wool Processors Ltd bank.

4. M. Lopez, our customer, has to be debited because he has received back the use of his money. Head Office A/c would be credited since it has to give the money to the Head Office of Midland for the Embassy of Mexico.

5. Peter Brown, our customer, has to be debited and Head Office A/c credited so that it can pass the funds on to Barclays Head Office for its Bristol branch to put in T. Marshall's Account.

6. We debit T. Smith who has received back the use of his money and credit Bolsover District Council who now have the money; Smith has paid his rates.

7. We credit M. Leighton with £856.24 and debit Head Office A/c which now has to arrange with Head Office at Lloyds to get the money from Gigantic Engineers Plc's Account at their Manchester branch.

8. We credit C. Thomas who has effectively deposited this £125.50, and debit Head Office A/c who have to obtain the funds from the Bank of Scotland in Edinburgh.

9. We credit Julie Hoyle who has effectively deposited £385.00 and debit Head Office A/c which has to obtain the funds from the Tyneside branch.

10. We credit Nirala Restaurant Ltd with its takings and debit Head Office A/c which now has to get this money from the Barclaycard authorities.

36.7   1. (a) A debtor; (b) Simplex sold more goods to Hall; (c) Hall returned some unsatisfactory goods to Simplex; (d) Hall paid the balance owing on 1 January, after taking discount; (e) It would be Discount Allowed. Simplex allowed Hall to deduct it, and therefore suffered a loss of £41.28.

2. (a) A creditor; (b) On each occasion K. Sijuwade Ltd purchased more goods from Onabanjo; (c) The double entry would be on the credit side of their Motor Vehicles Account as they cleared the vehicle from the books; (d) £187.27; (e) Onabanjo was a debtor (the account has a debit balance). It is an unusual case of a person who is usually a creditor being temporarily a debtor.

3. (a) £4469.41; (b) Kim Lee owes it to Processors Plc (it is a debit balance); (c) Kim Lee is paying the balance due on 1 February, after deducting a discount of £31.86; (d) Kim Lee has been ordering a great deal of supplies; almost three times as much. Processors Plc asked for a payment on account to reduce this higher-than-usual debt; Kim Lee seems to be able to pay on request, so perhaps he is becoming a very good customer. About £2500 or £3000 might be a safe credit limit to set.

36.10   1. (a), (b) and (g) are real accounts (assets). (c), (d) and (f) are nominal accounts (two losses and a profit). (e), (h), (i) and (j) are personal accounts (one debtor and three creditors—including the proprietor).

2. (a), (b), (c), (d), (g) and (j) are all debit balances (three assets, two losses and one debtor). The others are credit balances (one profit and three creditors, one of whom is the proprietor).

3. £1500 per year; 4. £700 per year.

Chapter 37

37.3 1. Gross profit £53 000; 2. Gross profit £86 500; 3. Gross profit £171 141; 4. Gross profit £7 371 000.

37.6 1. Net profit £19 224; 2. Net profit £16 034; 3. Net profit £20 954; 4. Gross profit £58 000; Net profit £21 816.

37.9 1. T. Field. Fixed Assets £106 150; Current Assets £14 692; total £120 842; Current Liabilities £2546; Long-term liabilities £15 180; Capital at end of year £103 116.
2. 'Babywear'. Fixed Assets £12 005; Current Assets £31 161; total £43 166; Current Liabilities £1561; Long-term Liabilities £2500; Capital at end of year £39 105.
3. M. Adair. Fixed Assets £104 250; Current Assets £125 490; total £229 740; Capital at end £185 905; Long-term Liability £40 000; Current Liability £3 835.
4. B. Young. Gross profit £111 152; Net profit £28 356; Fixed Assets £142 000; Current Assets £56 348; Capital at end £81 556; Long-term Liabilities £100 000; Current Liabilities £16 792. Balance Sheet totals £198 348.

37.11 1. Balance on Appropriation Account £14 950; total £72 850.
2. Ordinary Shareholders' Interest £105 000; Balance Sheet totals £225 000; Fixed Assets £169 750; Net Current Assets £55 250.
3. Balance on Appropriation Account £4370; Ordinary Shareholders' Interest in the Company £134 870; Preference Shareholders' Interest £30 000; Corporation Tax £25 000; Total of Balance Sheet £189 870; Current Liabilities £20 200; Net Current Assets £24 370.
4. Balance on Appropriation Account £6914; Ordinary Shareholders' Interest in the Company £143 265; Balance Sheet totals £218 265; Fixed Assets £134 750; Current Assets £107 115; Current Liabilities £23 600; Net Current Assets £83 515.

Chapter 38

No numerical answers in this chapter.

Chapter 39

39.5 1. 12%; 2. 13%; 3. 12½%; 4. 19.4%.

Index